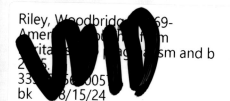

AMERICAN THOUGHT:
FROM PURITANISM TO
PRAGMATISM AND BEYOND

WOODBRIDGE RILEY, PH.D.

COSIMO CLASSICS
NEW YORK

Cosimo
P.O. Box 416
Old Chelsea Station
New York, NY 10113-0416

or visit our website at:
www.cosimobooks.com

American Thought: From Puritanism to Pragmatism and Beyond originally
published by Henry Holt & Company in 1915.

Library of Congress Cataloging-in-Publication Data
A catalog record for this book is available from the Library of Congress

Cover design by www.wiselephant.com

ISBN: 1-59605-305-4

American Thought:
From Puritanism to
Pragmatism and Beyond

TO

MY FIRST TEACHER IN PHILOSOPHY,

GEORGE TRUMBULL LADD

FOREWORD

WE, as a country, have been told that we have no philosophy, that we do but reflect the speculations of other lands. This is not wholly true. We have had philosophers, original thinkers who, though their influence may not have reached abroad, were makers of history at home. So a study of the speculative movements in America leads to a clearer understanding of our national character, for these very movements are so closely allied to our history and our literature that they may be said to form a background for both.

The colonial background I have presented in a previous volume—*American Philosophy: The Early Schools*. This described the most important forms of thought as they crossed from the Old to the New World, developed during two centuries, and slowly prepared the way for the native philosophy of Emerson. The present work condenses the previous account and continues the development of national thought until it emerges triumphantly in pragmatism—a typical American philosophy.

CONTENTS

AMERICAN THOUGHT

CHAPTER I

PURITANISM

1. PHILOSOPHY AND POLITICS, FROM ABSOLUTISM TO DEMOCRACY

THE influence of philosophy upon politics in America is easily seen in the evolution of such a familiar phrase as life, liberty, and the pursuit of happiness. This declaration of independence was derived indirectly, by way of reaction, from a declaration of dependence. The belief of the Puritans was a belief in passivity, determinism, and pessimism. They considered that man was a mere worm, a dull instrument in the hands of Deity; that his acts were predestined, Deity foreordaining whatsoever comes to pass; that his life was a vain show, and nature a vale of tears. Over against these lugubrious doctrines of the Puritans we may put those of their successors. It was the deists who believed in activity, freedom, and optimism. They held that man was a real agent; that he was free to do what he chose; that his goal was perfection itself, and they even went so far as to say that whatever is, is right. These beliefs slowly spread among the people and were gradually translated into the plain language of the day. Instead of passivity the deists believed in activity,—that is, life; instead of determinism they believed in freedom,—that is, liberty; instead of pessimism they believed in optimism,—that is, the pursuit of happiness. In short, between the Boston Platform of 1680 and the Declaration of Independence of 1776 a marked change had come about. The deistic sun had arisen, dispelling the winter of Puritan discontent. Humanity was considered perfectible and this world the best of all possible worlds.

A more striking instance of the influence of philosophy upon politics is seen in the problem of political sovereignty. Popular government in this country was gained only after a long struggle in which philosophical tenets played a large part. Developing side by side, the one influencing the other, the philosophical and political movements passed through the same changes. In the seventeenth century we find men's interest chiefly centered about God. In the eighteenth century that interest is twofold: it concerns itself with nature, as well as with God. In the nineteenth century the interest has transferred itself mainly to nature. The same transfer of thought takes place in politics. In the seventeenth century the interest centers in the king; in the eighteenth century in both king and people; in the nineteenth century the people fill the foreground.

We may go back and express this great movement in terms of metaphysics, and say that the conception of the absolute in America is, in the seventeenth century, monistic; in the eighteenth century, dualistic; in the nineteenth century, pantheistic. Under Puritanism there is a belief in one, supreme, self-sufficient being, the sole ruler and disposer of all things. Under deism there is a belief in a deity whose powers and functions are limited by a law outside himself,—the law of nature, inviolable and immutable. Under transcendentalism, the deity, becoming immanent, is submerged in nature, can scarcely be distinguished from the cosmic processes.

We have here three philosophical conceptions. It is not hard to show that they were influenced in their growth by the current theories of government. At the time of Puritanism there is a belief in absolute monarchy, when sovereignty is conceived to be given by God to the king, who thus rules by divine right. Then, at the time of deism there is a belief in limited monarchy, when sovereignty is conceived to be shared between ruler and subject, under a dual control. Finally, along with transcendentalism there arises a true conception of representative democracy, when sovereignty is conceived as vested in the people through the inalienable right of the law of nature. Between these two movements there is a striking parallel. In philosophy, the predominant interests are first: deity; then deity and nature; and lastly nature. In politics the kindred interests are: king, then king and people, and finally the people alone. That these sets of conceptions are really kindred is shown by the fact that one may be expressed in terms of the other. Under Puritanism the deity is represented as a dread monarch and sovereign ruler. This is the Calvinistic description of the immortal God. The same terms are used in reference to the temporal king. In the Articles of the Plymouth Church occurs the phrase: " The King's majesty we acknowledge for supreme governour," while the subscribers to the *Mayflower* compact sign themselves " loyal subjects of our dread sovereign Lord King James."

These two conceptions sound so much alike because they are derived from common principles. Both English monarchy and New England theocracy are based upon the underlying tenet of transcendence and determinism.

In religion this meant, briefly, that God was far off
from his world and that he foreordained all its events.
In politics, as Tom Paine bluntly expresses it in his
Common Sense, this meant that the state of a king shuts
him off from the world, yet the business of a king requires him to know it thoroughly. To carry out the
parallel. The state advocates of divine right made the
king high above his people and, at the same time, an auto-
crat who decided the smallest affairs in the utmost bounds
of his kingdom. The church advocates of divine sovereignty were of the same temper and held that the Most
High doth direct, dispose, and govern all creatures,
actions, and things from the greatest even to the least.

Here are two sets of belief similar in sense and leading
to similar results. Yet neither king nor Calvin was to
reign forever. A reaction followed which, in the case
of the state, led to political revolt, and in the affairs
of the church to a philosophical revolt. The former is
a commonplace of history, the latter has not been made
sufficiently prominent. The Puritan divinity was too
much like the Stuart dynasty to be long acceptable
to Anglo-American Independents. Special providences
exerted in behalf of the elect bore too striking a resemblance to his Majesty's partiality to a favored few.
And then, too, the doctrine of the sovereignty of God—
absolute and unchallenged in will, power, and decree—led
to the political equivalents coming under fire. Thus it
was that William Livingston treated of the political
correlatives and wrote picturesquely on " Passive Obedience and Non-Resistance ": " The tyrant used to club
with the clergy and set them a-roaring for the divine
rights of royal roguery. 'Twas a damnable sin to resist
the cutting of throats and no virtue more Christian and
refulgent than of a passive submission to butchery and

slaughter. To propagate such fustian in America argues a disposition prone to senility. And yet 'tis not above four years ago, that in this very province I heard a dapper young gentleman, attired in his canonicals, contend as strenuously for non-resistance as if he had been animated with the very soul of Sacheverell.''

Writing such as this marks the change from the Calvinistic or Puritan to the deistic or rational point of view. What has been said of this change in England holds true of the colonies. The theological conception of politics gave way before what may be termed the naturalistic. Instead of the constructive theory of the divine rights there was a transition to the theory of natural rights vested not only in the king but in the people. The latter, as propounded by Locke, was merely the former in disguise, for the doctrine of divine rights not only was transformed by imperceptible degrees into the theory of natural rights, but left behind it a legacy, in the sense that, because it is natural, government in general is divine.

This process was destined to be carried further. Under the constant appeals to an absolute law and absolute right, there was a tendency to substitute lex for legislator, the principle for the person, and thus to run from the dualistic to the pantheistic stage. Consequently, that law of nature which under Puritanism was a subordinate source of authority, and under deism a co-ordinate, under transcendentalism became in itself an ultimate source of authority—a veritable absolute. Or, put in terms of political history: That sovereignty which first appertained to the king by divine right, and was then shared by the people by natural right, was at last lodged inalienably in the democracy. With this supersession of the *vox dei* by the *vox populi,* there resulted a curious analogy between the pantheism of Emerson and the doctrine of popular sovereignty. With the belief that the universe governs itself, is sufficient to itself and is itself its own end, came the declaration that the federal government is a government of the people, by the people, and for the people.

2. THE NEW ENGLAND FATHERS

Puritanism in America enjoyed a metaphysical monopoly for almost two centuries. From the landing of the Pilgrims to the appearance of Emerson the prevalent faith of the colonists and their descendants was Calvinism. This faith has been summed up in five points; it can be even more briefly put under two. These are transcendence and determinism, or the conception of a deity who lives apart from the world, and still guides and governs that world in the smallest details. This belief in " one supreme self-sufficient Being, sole ruler and disposer of all " obtained along the Atlantic coast for even more miles than it did years. It was adhered to by the Puritans in Massachusetts and Connecticut, by the Dutch Reformed in New York and New Jersey, by the orthodox German sects in Pennsylvania, and in the South, on the seaboard by the Huguenots, and in the mountains by the Scotch-Irish Presbyterians, the so-called Puritans of the South.

Thus wide was the influence of Calvinism both as to duration of time and extent of space, for even the Church of England in America contained a large infiltration of Genevan doctrine.

With such a monopoly it is not surprising that Puritanism has been violently attacked, and that its history has suffered at the hands of the expositor who delights in presenting its sulphurous side. Thus a New England poem like the "Day of Doom" is taken as a fair example of the distressing illusions once inflicted upon themselves in the name of religion by the best of men, and its author is declared to have attributed to the Divine Being the most execrable and loathsome character to be met with in any literature, Christian or pagan. This is said to be his narrow and ferocious creed: All men are totally depraved, all of them caught from the farthest eternity in the adamantine meshes of God's decrees; the most of them also being doomed in advance by those decrees to an endless existence of ineffable torment, and the whole world, when the Judge of all the earth appears, to an universal conflagration.

In this sketch too black a pencil has been used. If there is a dark side of Puritanism there is also a bright one. Later we shall examine the mystical portrait of Jonathan Edwards with its sweetness and light. But now we may look at Calvinism as if it were a larger canvas painted in the grand manner. As such it included the belief in the divine Sovereignty which left men free from care. To the elect no final ill could fall because they were cared for by a Spirit, "infinite, eternal, and unchangeable." Theirs was a sublime trust and theirs a sublime fatalism. But this was carried to extremes. As the historian of colonial literature has described it: the belief in a present, watchful, and benign Providence turned to abject superstition,—the belief in a microscopic and picayune providence concerning every falling tower, capsized sail-boat, or lost cow. It is almost incredible that the sublime and the ridiculous could be drawn from the same source. But such is the fact. The tone of Puritanism is a matter of interpretation. At the first there was about it the lingering luster of the Elizabethan age; at the last it became mean and petty in the narrow routine of provincial life.

We turn now to the American system of high Calvinism as it was expressed in official standards, like the Boston Platform of 1680, and in the utterances of its expositors from the Mathers to Jonathan Edwards. Calvinism as a system stands four-square. It may be viewed from the philosophic standpoints of ontology, the theory of being; of cosmology, the theory of the world; of epistemology, the theory of knowledge; and finally of psychology, the theory of personality. First, as a theory of being, Calvinism teaches that the deity lives outside the framework of the universe; that he interferes as he sees fit according to an absolute and arbitrary will; that he works through inscrutable decrees; that he foreordains whatever comes to pass. Second, as a theory of the cosmos, Calvinism teaches that the world is under the curse of the divine displeasure; that it conceals rather than displays its creator; that it is created from nothing and is destined to return to nothing; that the evil in it is a permissive act of God. Third, as a theory of knowing, Calvinism teaches that true knowledge comes more through revelation than through reason, being a gift of the divine pleasure rather than a result of human endeavor; that the decretive will of God is involved in deep mystery, which is for us little better than learned ignorance; that man has only a dim revelation of a hidden God communicated from without; that the human mind has no natural capacity for understanding the divine nature. Fourth, as a theory of personality, Calvinism teaches that God is alien in essence from man; that human progress comes through arbitrary grace, man being by nature corrupt; that our liberty is not self-determined, but works only within the limitations of our foreordained nature; that the last dictate of the understanding determines the will,—and yet, that within the will are included the inclinations.

Such, in brief compass, was the system of official Calvinism. In its extreme form it obtained chiefly in New England, for like an Arctic current of thought, it grew slowly warmer and was gradually dissipated as it flowed south into the more genial regions of Anglican belief. We have now to consider some of the general causes which, in the course of time, have modified this frigid system. The first rival of Calvinism was Arminianism, which has been defined as an appeal to consciousness against a system of abstract logic. Calvinism had emphasized the God-ward side of theology and turned the divine government into an inexorable fate. Arminianism, on the contrary, emphasized the man-ward side of theology and regarded human activity as a necessary condition of moral responsibility. This contrast was rather in the way of professional theological rivalry; it remained for ordinary human nature to exhibit the full psychological revulsion: the head might believe in determinism and depravity, but the heart revolted against such dreadful doctrines.

The second rival of Calvinism was deism,—the coming system of free-thought. This questioned the arbitrary fiat of the Creator, and succeeded in bringing back liberty of human action. Between an absolute creator and an abject creation there was brought in a third factor, the law of nature in whose benefits man participated. However, in emphasizing the importance of that law, in making its bounds more and more extensive, deism tended to push the creator entirely away from his world. Hence by the time the law of nature was made universal, the deity was brought to a far remove, and while counted the maker, was no longer considered the ruler of the universe. Here was the absentee landlord theory carried to extreme; for with this banishment of the master the servant grew boldly arrogant. Man, looking within himself, was becoming a law unto himself; hence that air of moral conceit and self-sufficiency assumed in increasing measure towards the end of the eighteenth century.

We have anticipated and must therefore go back and study the more exact processes that brought about the disintegration of Calvinism. First, there was a gradual degradation or lowering of the doctrine of transcendence, through the belief in miraculous intervention; here the deity is brought into the world, not by immanence, but by interference, and general providence is turned into special providences. In place of the noble definition of "the living and true God, infinite in being and perfection, a most pure spirit, immutable, immense, eternal, incomprehensible," there comes a conception of a being who manifests himself in "remarkable sea-deliverances, remarkables about thunder and lightning, remarkable judgments upon Quakers, drunkards, and enemies of the church." There followed also a gradual integration or hardening of the doctrine of determinism; the freedom of the will which was verbally allowed in the Westminster standards being practically denied by the later consistent Calvinists. Instead of the provision whereby "no violence is offered unto the will of the creature, nor is the liberty or contingency of second causes taken away," there comes Samuel Willard's avowal that there is in man a "miserable impotency and malignity of will with respect to holy choices."

Nevertheless there was a gradual elimination or soften-
ing of the doctrine of the necessary depravity of human
nature; here the new world being perforce a better
world than the corrupt society Calvin had in view, men
began somewhat egotistically to plume themselves on
their virtues. Thus, in place of the ancient saying that
" all noisome lusts abound in the soul like snakes in an
old hedge," we find Cotton Mather rejoicing that the
Puritan by flying from the depravity of Europe to the
American strand doth improve his manners. Finally,
there came a more lenient conception of the character
of the Absolute. There was no longer a sovereign will
at an immeasurable distance from man, but a more
kindly leader, commander, and ruler of nature. In
place of the outpourings of the divine fury, there comes
the infiltration of the quality of mercy due to the essential benevolence of the deity.

In tracing the processes at work in the amelioration
of Calvinism we notice that the positive factors were
more powerful than the negative, the best minds preferring the progressive to the reactionary tenets. The
process of elevation, in short, was stronger than degradation. It therefore came about that Calvinism found
itself insensibly drifting into the deistic current,—away
from the pessimistic towards the optimistic, away from
the misanthropic towards the philanthropic. How strong
that current was may be seen fully only after we have
explored the contributing streams. These were three:
The political, which reached from a state-supported
church to perfect liberty of philosophizing; the naturalistic, which reached from the supernatural to the
scientific; the rationalistic, which reached from revelation to reason. These three streams or tendencies were
represented by three men: the political by Thomas Jef-

ferson; the scientific by Benjamin Franklin; the rationalistic by Ethan Allen.

3. The Revolt Against Puritanism: Ethan Allen

Ethan Allen of Vermont has been previously known for his military exploits, but quite ignored for his speculative ventures. In the preface to his *Oracles of Reason*, 1784, the captor of Ticonderoga confesses that he has been denominated a deist; whether he is he does not know, but this he does know, that he is no Calvinist. In a pungent letter to one who inquired concerning his philosophy, he writes that he expects that the clergy, and their devotees, will proclaim war upon him in the name of the Lord, having put on the armor of faith, the sword of the Spirit, and the artillery of hell fire. "But," he concludes, "I am a hardy Mountaineer and have been accustomed to the ravages and horrors of War and Captivity, and scorn to be intimidated by threats; if they fright me they must absolutely produce some of their tremendous fire, and give me a sensative scorching."

For Allen's roughness of manners and coarseness of speech Jared Sparks gives as mitigating circumstances the rude and uncultivated society in which the author lived. It might be added that the "Green Mountain Boy" was one of those backwoods thinkers who claim to be largely independent of outside ideas. Some rival asserted that he stole his title from Blount's *Oracles of Reason*, but the author of this "Compenduous System of Natural Religion" throws no direct light on its sources. He maintained that the Bible and the dictionary were his only authorities, but while he might have made a better use of both, it is hard to learn of what

other means of information he availed himself. He
tells how in his youth, being educated in what were
commonly called " Armenian " principles, he was much
disposed to contemplation, and at his commencement
in manhood, being in the habit of committing to manuscript such sentiments or arguments as appeared most
consonant to reason, he practiced this method of scrib-
bling for many years. So claiming to have something
of a smattering of philosophy, he recounts that while in
an English prison-ship in 1775 and meeting two clergy-
men,—" We discoursed on several parts of moral philosophy and Christianity, and they seemed to be surprised that I should be acquainted with such topics, or
that I should understand a syllogism or regular mode
of argumentation."

Whatever the impulses that affected Ethan Allen,
whatever the value of his claims as a self-made thinker,
his work furnishes a good example of the popular recoil
from Puritanism on the part of one who wished to pursue the " natural road of ratiocination." This negative
side of the *Oracles* is couched in a lively and aggressive
style, for the writer is appealing to readers who despise
the wearisome reasonings of philosophers and are pre-
possessed with principles opposed to the religion of
reason. In these parts of America, he explains, men are
most generally taught that they are born into the world
in a state of enmity to God and moral good and are
under his wrath and curse; that the way to heaven and
future blessedness is out of their power to pursue, and
that it is encumbered with mysteries which none but the
priests can unfold; that we must " be born again," have
a special kind of faith, and be regenerated.

Upon the priests and their so-called scheme of mysteries, Allen now proceeds to make his onslaught. This

is the substance of his tirade: the spiritualists, who pretend to be as familiar with the supernatural world as with their own home-lot, talk as if the creator and governor of the universe had erected a particular academy of arts and sciences in which they, the tutors, were alone intellectually qualified to carry on the business of teaching. With their special revelations they talk as if they only were rational creatures, and the rest of mankind a pack of clodhoppers, as ignorant as a stable of horses; but that is no revelation to me which is above my comprehension, or which from any natural sagacity I knew before. They may keep their alleged manuscript copy of God's eternal law, it is sufficient for me to possess the deistical Bible, reason, by which I judge that even the commandments of the Decalogue would not be binding upon any rational being unless they coincided with the law of nature.

Allen next proceeds to attack the Calvinistical system with all the homely wit of which he is master. Against the cardinal belief in magical interferences in the course of nature he argues that such intervention would turn nature into a supernatural whirligig, an inconstant and erring piece of mechanism; would reduce all nature to the level of fanaticism; would lead men to abandon the great discoveries of Newton for awful apprehensions of God's providence, whereby world would crash upon world, or the tail of the next comet would set this world on fire. But such apprehensions are unwarranted and lead to a logical fallacy; either the great architect of nature has so constructed its machinery that it never needs to be altered, or, admitting miracles, we must admit this syllogism: the laws of nature have been altered, the alteration has been for the better, therefore, the eternal establishment thereof was imperfect. In fine, to demonstrate such a scarecrow belief, one need but quote the anecdote attributed to his Most Christian Majesty, the King of France: " By command of the King, God is forbidden to work any more miracles in this place."

These are fair examples of Allen's anti-Calvinistic bias. Against other connected doctrines of the old systems he argues in a like short and easy manner, asserting, for example, that original sin had as little to do with the premised Adam as with the man in the moon; that the doctrine of imputation, or the transfer of the personal demerit of sin, is contradicted by the old proverb that every tub stands upon its own bottom; and that instead of insisting upon the gloomy doctrine of predestination, the teachers of this doctrine should spend their salaries in good wine to make the heart glad.

With this vigorous but coarse attack upon the five points of Calvinism, there is little wonder that Allen's miscalled theology should have been cordially detested by the orthodox, and that it should have been considered an evidence of the workings of a watchful providence that most of the edition was accidentally burned. Nevertheless the Vermont free-thinker had something else to do but startle the natives with his rustic wit. Besides the negative part of his work, in which he attempted to lop off the excrescences, there was the positive, in which he feels confident that he has struck the outlines of a consistent system. Briefly, in the place of the conception of a transcendent being, occasionally active in the affairs of the world, quite incomprehensible within the mere limits of reason, he would substitute the conception of an immanent power, continually active in the world, knowable in his nature from a man's own rational nature. Here, as the matter has been previously summarized, the origin of the conception of a superintending power is traced to the sense of dependence on the laws of nature; from studies of those laws reason discovers the perfections of that power; order implies an orderer, harmony a regulator, motion a mover, and benefits goodness; chaos would prove a creator, but order and beneficent design are necessary to prove providence.

Allen has now taken the first forward step in his system, and that step is optimism. As he expressed the matter in a line obviously drawn from the *Essay on Man:* of all possible systems, infinite wisdom must have eternally discerned the best. This, it is explained, implies the essential benevolence of the deity and thereby we discover the prime requisite of moral perfection. But great difficulties arise in attempting to discover God's natural attributes, especially his eternity and infinity: Because of these difficulties the writer is now forced to postulate two absolutes: God, the efficient cause, eternal and infinite, and nature the eternal and infinite effect; eternal here being defined as without end or duration, infinite as without degree or measure; hence, on the one side, is a cause uncaused and eternally self-existent who gave being and order to nature coeval with his own existence; on the other is nature coextensive and coexistent with the divine nature, eternal because of an eternal and immense fullness, infinite because infinitely complete and independent of any particular form.

With two absolutes on his hands Allen is now in dire trouble. He sees the break between creator and creation and tries to mend it by expanding his previous notions of nature as being in a constant state of flux.

He explains that all forms are indebted to creation for their existence. The dissolution of forms animate or inanimate neither adds to nor diminishes from creation; reduced to their original elements they are changed into new and diverse forms in never-ceasing rounds. The particles of matter which compose my body may have existed in more millions of different forms than I am able to enumerate, and be still liable to fluctuations equally numerous. This elementary fluxility of matter, which is mere creation, is as eternal as God, yet the particular productions, arising from natural causes, have a beginning and an end.

With this reference to the ancient doctrine of nature as a plastic principle one may leave the *Oracles of Reason*. This work the elder President Dwight of Yale called the first formal publication in the United States openly directed against the Christian religion; President Jared Sparks of Harvard described it as a crude and worthless performance, in which truth and error, reason and sophistry, knowledge and ignorance, ingenuity and presumption are mingled together in a chaos which the author denominates a system. These academic strictures were perhaps deserved from the standpoint of the orthodox, yet the author received some praise, for as his friend George Washington said: " There is an original something about Allen that commands attention."

The " original something" which Allen contributed was this: a clear recognition of the difficulties of dualism, the old theological separation between God and the world. Allen suggested but did not effect a compromise. He spoke of the immense creation that we denominate by the name nature, and of its being necessarily coextensive and coexistent with the divine nature. But how to identify creator and creation, how to make the two one, that final step he never took. Nevertheless, in this very failure to identify the two conceptions, to make creator and creation the same One and All, permanent and infinite, the Vermont philosopher did but leave a speculative task to be undertaken by a greater mind in a neighboring State, for it was Emerson who, struggling with the apparent dualism between God and nature, had the boldness to announce that the Absolute is one with the ordering and creative power of the universe.

CHAPTER II

EARLY IDEALISM

1. SAMUEL JOHNSON: DISCIPLE OF BERKELEY

IN Samuel Johnson of Connecticut we meet a colonial idealist of an unusual type, not a mystic and recluse, but a publicist and traveler. After graduation at Yale College, Johnson voyaged across the Atlantic, met such notables as Alexander Pope and the English Samuel Johnson, and visited Oxford and Cambridge Universities, from which in due course he was to receive honorary degrees.

Returning to the narrow bigotry of the British provinces, Johnson was not able to renew his larger interests until the visit of the Reverend George Berkeley, the Irish idealist, who in 1729 took up his residence in Newport, Rhode Island. It was there that Johnson became a convert to the "New Principle," against which he had been warned in college, but which now seemed to him more apt than any other to be the true philosophical support of faith, to harmonize with our individual dependence on the Supreme Mind or Will, perpetually present and perpetually active. Moreover, the new system offered a satisfactory substitute for certain old notions of matter. In place of the scholastic notion of an occult substance, and of the Cartesian notion of a dead, inert somewhat, Berkeley substituted spiritual causality. In place of a phantom world lying behind the visible and tangible universe, and in place of masses of matter moved by mechanical forces he would

put as " proper, active, efficient causes none but Spirit;
nor any action, strictly speaking, but where there is
Will."

Such is Berkeley's explanation of the universal immaterialism in reply to a question of his ardent
American disciple. The latter's first letter contained
some doubts as to the propriety of denying the absolute
existence of matter, though he strove to understand how
that meant nothing more than a denial of an incon-
ceivable substratum of sensible phenomena. From
Johnson's letter of inquiry, which lay unpublished for
over a century and three-quarters, we may now give
these extracts:

Rev.d Sr.
    The Kind Invitation you gave me in Reading those ex-
cellent Books which you was pleased to order into my Hands,
is all the Apology I shall offer for the Trouble I now presume
to give you: But nothing could encourage me to expose to
your views my low and mean way of Thinking & writing, but
my hopes of an Interest in that Candor and Tenderness which
are so conspicuous both in your writings & Conversation.
    These Books, (for which I stand humbly obliged to you)
contain Speculations the most surprisingly ingenious I have
ever met with: & I must confess that the Reading of them has
almost convinced me, That Matter as it has been commonly
defined for an unknown Quiddity is but a meer non-Entity.
That it is a strong presumption against the Existence of it, that
there never could be conceived any manner of connection between it & our Ideas: That the *esse* of Things is only their
percipi: & that the Rescuing us from the Absurdities of Abstract Ideas & the Gross Notion of Matter that have so much
obtained, deserves well of the Learned World, in that it clears
away very many difficulties & Perplexities in the Sciences. . . .
    That all the Phenomena of Nature must ultimately be re-
ferred to the Will of the Infinite Spirit, is what must be allowed; But to suppose his immediate Energy in the production
of every Effect, does not seem to impress so lively & great a

Sense of his Power & wisdom upon our Minds, as to Suppose
a Subordination of Causes & Effects among the Archtypes of
our Ideas as he that should makᵔ a watch or clock of ever so
beautiful an appearance & that should measure the Time ever
so exactly, yet if he should be obliged to stand by it & influence & direct all its motions, he would seem but very deficient
in both his ability & skill, in comparison with him who should
be able to make one that would regularly keep on its motion
and measure the time for a considerable time, without the
Intervention of any immediate force of its Author or any one
else, impressed upon it. . . .

It is after all that has been said on that Head, Still something shocking to many to think that there should be nothing
but a meer show in all the art & contrivance appearing in the
Structure, (for Instance) of a Human Body, particularly of
the Organs of Sense: The Curious Structure of the Eye, what
can it be more then meerly a fine show, if there be no con-
nexion more than you Admit of, between that & vision? It
Seems from the make of it to be designed for an Instrument
or means of conveying the Images of External Things to the
perceptive Faculty within; & if it be not so if it be really of
no use in conveying visible objects to our minds, & if our
visible Ideas are immediately created in them by the Will of
the Almighty, why should it be maᵔe to seem to be an Instrument or medium as much as if indeed it really were so? . . .

To these and similar queries Berkeley wrote a series
of letters, most of which are lost. But from those to
be found in his published works we learn that the master
went to great pains in forming the opinions of his
pupil. How ably the latter expounded the doctrines
of universal immaterialism and the divine visual language we shall see in the works of his maturity. Meanwhile Johnson had visited Berkeley at Whitehall, the
latter's country place near Newport, and within another
year Berkeley had finished his *Alciphron; or, the Minute
Philosopher,* which formed a most pleasing set of idealistic dialogues, wherein, from their many allusions and

touches of local color, Berkeley may be said to stand for Euphranor, the philosophic farmer, and Johnson for his friend Crito. So it was about this time that the neophyte expressed his conversion to the ideal theory, since, as he himself acknowledges, he found the Dean's way of thinking and explaining things utterly precluded skepticism, and left no room for endless doubts and uncertainties. His denying matter at first seemed shocking; but it was only for want of giving a thorough attention to his meaning. It was only the unintelligible scholastic notion of matter he disputed and not anything either sensible, imaginable, or intelligible; and it was attended with this vast advantage, that it not only gave new incontestable proofs of a deity, but moreover, the most striking apprehensions of his constant presence with us and inspection over us, and of our entire dependence upon him and infinite obligations to his most wise and almighty benevolence.

On quitting the American strand, Berkeley has been most vividly described as leaving behind him a metaphysical double, another self, sharing his faith, speaking his language; viewing all things from the same angle; reasoning, discussing, concluding as he himself had done or would have done. In dedicating his principal work, from the deepest sense of gratitude, to George, Lord Bishop of Cloyne, Johnson admitted the truth of this description, for he confessed that he was in a particular manner beholden to that excellent philosopher for several thoughts that occur in the following tract. This was the *Elementa Philosophica: Containing chiefly, Noetica, or Things Relating to the Mind or Understanding; and Ethica, or Things Relating to the Moral Behavior.*

From the *Elements* we may take two passages. The

first of these, like the Irish idealism, emphasizes the
vision of all things in God; the second, with a certain
colonial independence, gives to the individual some
share in the acquirement of knowledge:

The notices which the mind has, derive originally from (or
rather by means of) the two fountains of sense and consciousness. By means of the senses we receive simple ideas. These
are sorted out into a vast variety of fixed combinations or
compound ideas distinct from each other, in which the simple
ideas are always found to co-exist; of these compound ideas
consist every individual body in nature, such as we call horse,
tree, &c. These various distinct combinations, connected together in such a manner as to constitute one most beautiful
and harmonious whole, make up what we call universal nature
or the entire sensible or natural world. In the perception of
these ideas or objects of sense we find our minds are merely
passive, it not being in our power (supposing our organs
rightly disposed and situated) whether we will see light and
colours, hear sounds, &c. We are not causes to ourselves of
these perceptions nor can they be produced in our minds without a cause, or (which is the same thing) by any imagined, un-
intelligent, inert or inactive cause. Hence they must be derived from an almighty, intelligent, active cause, exhibiting
them to us, impressing our minds with them, or producing them in us. Consequently it must be by a perpetual
intercourse of our minds with the deity, the great author of
our beings, or by his perpetual influence or activity upon them,
that they are possessed of all these objects of sense and the
light by which we perceive them. No sooner does any object
strike the senses or is received in our imagination, or apprehended by our understanding, but we are immediately conscious of a kind of intellectual light within us (if I may so
call it), whereby we not only know that we perceive the object
but directly apply ourselves to the consideration of it both in
itself, its properties and powers and as it stands related to all
other things, and we find that we are enabled by this intellectual light to perceive these objects and their relations in
like manner as by sensible light we are enabled to perceive

the objects of sense and their various situations; so our minds are passive in this intellectual light as they are sensible to light and can no more withstand the evidence of it than they can withstand the evidence of sense. Thus I am under the same necessity to assent to this—that I am or have a being and that I perceive and freely exert myself, as I am of assenting to this—that I see colours or hear sounds. I am perfectly sure that $2 + 2 = 4$, or that the whole is equal to all its parts as that I feel heat or cold, or that I see the sun. I am intuitively certain of both. This intellectual light I conceive of, as if it were a medium of knowledge just as sensible light is of sight. In both these is the power of perceiving and the object perceived; and this is the medium by which I am enabled to know it. This light is also one, and common to all intelligent beings, a Chinese or Japanese, as well as an European or American. By it, all at once see things to be true or right, in all places at the same time, and alike invariably at all time, past, present and to come. . . .

Interesting as were Johnson's philosophical writings they were not entirely original. There is, however, a chapter in the *Elements* which anticipated by many years the psychological study of the development of the child mind. At a time when another New England idealist could publicly assert that children were "like little vipers," and almost an half-century before the first hints of the kindergarten had reached the country, Johnson gave this delightful presentation of the early stages of infancy:

The first notices of the mind are doubtless those of sense, but directly joined with a consciousness of its perception. Warmth and hunger, and probably some pains, are, perhaps, all the sensations the infant hath before its birth; and when it comes into the light of this world, it is directly impressed with the sense of light and colours, as well as sounds, tastes, odours, and frequent uneasy and painful sensations, all of which still more and more awaken its consciousness; and every fresh notice of sense and consciousness still goes on to excite its admiration and engage its attention. And being a perfect stranger to everything about it, it hath everything to learn; to which it diligently applies itself, as its consciousness more and more awakens upon the repetition every moment, of fresh impressions of sense, until by degrees, having a great number of feelings, tastes, odours, sounds and visible objects, frequently repeating their several impressions, its conscious memory still enlarging, it begins, by means of the intellectual light with which it finds its consciousness attended, gradually to collect and recollect the several relations and connections it observes to obtain among its various ideas. And at length, when it is in ease, it discovereth a wonderful curiosity and delight in observing these connections, as well as being impressed with new ideas. Now it hath been made very evident, both by reasoning and experiment, that, as Bishop Berkeley shows in his Theory of Vision, the objects of sight and touch are entirely different and distinct things, and that there is no necessary connection between them. It must, therefore, be a matter of great exercise of thought in an infant mind to learn this connection, and particularly, to learn the notion of the various distances and situations of things tangible, by its observations on the various degrees of strength and weakness, of vividness or faintness of the light reflected from them, in the things visible constantly connected with them. And at the same time that it hath these things to learn, which must be a laborious work, as being the same thing with learning a language, it is also learning the names of things, and the connection and use of words, which is another language. And, as if all these were not task enough, it hath all this while to be learning how to use its limbs, its hand in handling, its tongue, and other organs of speech, in making and imitating sounds, and its whole body in all its exertions, and particularly, at length, the poise of its centre of gravity and the use of its feet in walking. All these things require a great deal of application, and the exercise of much thought and exertion. So that it seems evident that these little creatures from the beginning, do consider, reflect and think a prodigious deal more than we are commonly apt to imagine.

The reason why so many little, low, weak and childish

things appear in them, which we are apt to despise and think beneath our notice, is not for want of good sense and capacity, but merely for want of experience and opportunity for intellectual improvement. Hence also it appears that we ought to think little children to be persons of much more importance than we usually apprehend them to be; and how indulgent we should be to their inquisitive curiosity, as being strangers; with how much candour, patience and care we ought to bear with them and instruct them; with how much decency, honour and integrity we ought to treat them; and how careful it concerns us to be, not to say or do anything to them or before them that savours of falsehood and deceit, or that is in any kind indecent or vicious. *Pueris maxima debetur reverentia* is a good trite old saying.

This remarkable sketch of the progress of the mind concludes the *Noetica*. This, together with the *Ethica*, made up the *Elementa Philosophica*, which was used in both King's College during Johnson's presidency and also in the philosophy school of the Academy of Philadelphia. And yet the use of this idealistic text-book was without palpable effect upon either institution, and that because of an unfavorable environment; in the one case there was such a spirit of commercialism as to stifle mere speculation, in the other such a tendency towards materialism that, as Franklin wrote to Johnson,—"Those parts of the *Elements of Philosophy* that savor of what is called Berkeleism are not well understood here."

But while Johnson was much disappointed that his work was not more generally appreciated, he received some crumbs of comfort. Benjamin Franklin generously assumed the expense of printing the American edition of the *Elements;* William Smith, provost of the College of Philadelphia, wrote a laudatory introduction to the London edition, and Cadwallader Colden, lieutenant-governor of New York, was so stimulated by the perusal of the latter, that he renewed his amicable controversy with Johnson regarding the material universe as a dynamic whole. Although there were these gratifying results for the Connecticut idealist in Pennsylvania and New York, in other provinces there was a different condition of affairs. During Berkeley's sojourn in Rhode Island, Edwards was living in Massachusetts, yet here there were no sure signs of the Irish idealism to be found. Even the college at Cambridge was so satisfied with its own speculations, so wrapped up in its peculiar ecclesiasticism, that it paid no attention to the distinguished foreign visitor of another faith. The same result obtained in New Jersey, but for somewhat different causes. Harvard was rationalistic to a degree, but Princeton was so imbued with the common sense philosophy that the Berkeleian idealism, which had somehow stolen into that abode of orthodoxy, was denominated a mere philosophical daydream.

Besides these special causes there were general causes for the American indifference to Berkeleism. It has been declared the fault of circumstances that Johnson's book fell on a time when the New World was engaged in conquests in the material rather than in the spiritual sphere. A Gallic critic finds this a polite but shrewd way of saying that Anglo-Americans of the late eighteenth century were unfit to receive or to develop a true idealism, for what was true in the British colonies was also true in the mother country. The indifference with which Johnson's work was received in England was owing to its appearance at a moment the most inopportune; the spiritualistic philosophy was then losing ground, a crass sensualism or a radical skepticism was taking its place. If Johnson could have presented his immaterialism to an entirely new age, he might have arrested general attention. The most that can now be said of his endeavors was that he was the metaphysical double, the ideal image of the good Bishop of Cloyne, but withal unsuccessful in spreading, to any great extent, that form of idealism for which the latter stood.

2. JONATHAN EDWARDS, MYSTIC

Tradition has marked Jonathan Edwards as the greatest of our Puritan divines, the relentless logician who left the print of his iron heel upon the New England conscience. It is true that Edwards delivered the dreadful Enfield sermon " Sinners in the Hands of an Angry God,'' and that he composed that rigid treatise, concerning the Freedom of the Will, which belied its title and doomed the bulk of mankind to the workings of an inexorable fate. But this is only one side of the picture. In public Edwards was the pitiless professional theologian. In private he was poet, mystic, philosopher of the feelings. As a boy he reached the thought that " this world exists nowhere but in the mind.'' As a young man he used frequently to " retire into a solitary place on the banks of the Hudson's River for contemplation on divine things.'' In maturity he wrote his treatise concerning Religious Affections in which he described the true believers' soul as receiving light from the sun of righteousness in such a manner that their nature is changed, that they become little suns partaking of the nature of the fountain of their light.

This inward and intimate side of the " saint of New England '' is that which makes him pre-eminently a mystic and seeker after the interior or hidden life. At a very early age he built himself a hut in a swamp. There he communed with his God, became enamored of nature, and reached the conclusion that the one was but the expression of the other. As he put it in one of his later writings: "We have shown that the Son of God created the world for this very end—to communicate Himself an image of His own excellency. . . . When we behold the light and brightness of the sun, the golden edges of an evening cloud, or the beauteous bow, we behold the adumbrations of His glory and goodness; and in the blue sky, of His mildness and gentleness. There are also many things wherein we may behold His awful majesty: in the sun in his strength, in comets, in thunder, with the lowering thunder-clouds, in ragged rocks and the brows of mountains."

We are then to count Edwards a mystic because of his wonderful sense of the immediateness of the divine presence and agency. But in addition to his youthful ecstasy he had a philosophical basis for his convictions. Shortly after entering Yale College at the age of twelve, he wrote a little essay which had this as its corollary,— " it follows from hence that those beings which have knowledge and Consciousness are the Only Proper and Real And substantial beings, inasmuch as the being of other things is Only by these. from hence we may see the Gross mistake of those who think material things the most substantial beings and spirits more like a shadow, whereas spirits Only Are Properly Substance." This is the famous undergraduate paper entitled *Of Being*, which has been declared as precocious as the *Thoughts* of Pascal and also remarkable as the counterpart of Berkeley's theory of the divine visual language. As to its originality there are many reasons for thinking

that the young Puritan did not borrow from the Church
of England divine. There is the negative reason that
the given corollary follows from a supposition to the
contrary. . . . Let us suppose for illustration this impossibility that all the Spirits in the Universe to be for
a time to be Deprived of their Consciousness, and Gods
Consciousness at the same time to be intermitted. I
say the Universe for that time would cease to be of it self
and not only as we speak because the almighty Could
not attend to Uphold the world but because God knew
nothing of it. . . .

There is also the positive reason that Edwards gives
a definition of the divine language of signs which has
been declared truly marvelous as emanating from a
mere boy. . . . Indeed, reasons Edwards, the secret lies
here: That, which truly is the Substance of all bodies,
is the infinitely exact, and precise, and perfectly stable
Idea, in God's mind, together with His stable Will, that
the same shall gradually be communicated to us, and
to other minds, according to certain fixed and exact
established Methods and Laws; or in somewhat different
language, the infinitely exact and precise Divine Idea,
together with an answerable, perfectly exact, precise,
and stable Will, with respect to correspondent communications to Created Minds, and effects on their
minds.

The logical side of Edwards's mind is not that which
we would dwell on. It is the poetical and the mystical
which give a truer insight into his nature. The first hint
of his quietistic experience is given in the phrase that
" nothing " is " the same that the sleeping rocks dream
of." The next is in his definition of inspiration as
an absolute sense of certainty, a knowledge in a sense
intuitive, wherein such bright ideas are raised, and such

a clear view of a perfect agreement with the excellencies of the Divine Nature, that it is known to be a communication from Him; all the Deity appears in the thing, and in everything pertaining to it.

Edwards is convinced of the verity of mystical intuition. At the same time he is wise enough to state that while this may be immediate, it does not come all at once nor arise without painful preparation. There are three stages in the process: first, comes by great and violent inward struggles the gaining of a spirit to part with all things in the world; then, a kind of vision or certain fixed ideas and images of being alone in the mountains or some solitary wilderness far from all mankind; finally, a thought of being wrapt up in God in heaven, being, as it were, swallowed up in Him forever. In these few words Edwards has summed up the mystic progression presented in the ancient manuals, those three stages in the ladder of perfection,—first, the purgative, brought about by contrition and amendment; then, the illuminative, produced by concentration of all the faculties upon God; lastly, the intuitive or unitive, wherein man beholds God face to face and is joined to Him in perfect union. In a passage of exquisite beauty, which may well be called a classic of the inner life, the saint of New England thus proceeds to unfold the record of his youthful ecstasy:—

After this my sense of divine things gradually increased, and became more and more lively, and had more of that inward sweetness. The appearance of everything was altered; there seemed to be, as it were, a calm, sweet cast, or appearance of divine glory, in almost everything. God's excellency, his wisdom, his purity and love, seemed to appear in every thing; in the sun, moon, and stars; in the clouds, and the blue sky; in the grass, flowers, trees; in the water, and all nature; which used greatly to fix my mind. I often used to sit and view the moon for continuance; and in the day, spent much time viewing the clouds and sky, to behold the sweet glory of God in these things: in the mean time, singing forth, with a low voice, my contemplations of the Creator and Redeemer. And scarce any thing, among all the works of nature was so sweet to me as thunder and lightning; formerly, nothing had been so terrible to me. Before, I used to be uncommonly terrified with thunder and to be struck with terror when I saw a thunder-storm rising; but now, on the contrary, it rejoiced me. I felt God, so to speak, at the first appearance of a thunder-storm; and used to take the opportunity, at such times, to fix myself in order to view the clouds, and see the lightnings play, and hear the majestic and awful voice of God's thunder which oftentimes was exceedingly entertaining, leading me to sweet contemplations of my sweet and glorious God. While thus engaged, it always seemed natural to me to sing, or chant forth my meditations; or, to speak my thoughts in soliloquies with a singing voice. Holiness, as I then wrote down some of my contemplations on it, appeared to me to be of a sweet, pleasant, charming, serene calm nature; which brought an inexpressible purity, brightness, peacefulness, and ravishment to the soul. In other words, that it made the soul like a field or garden of God, with all manner of pleasant flowers; all pleasant, delightful, and undisturbed; enjoying a sweet calm, and the gently vivifying beams of the sun. The soul of a true Christian, as I then wrote my meditations, appeared like such a little white flower as we see in the spring of the year; low, and humble on the ground, opening its bosom, to receive the pleasant beams of the sun's glory; rejoicing, as it were, in a calm rapture; diffusing around a sweet fragrancy; standing peacefully and lovingly, in the midst of other flowers round about; all in like manner opening their bosoms, to drink in the light of the sun. There was no part of creature-holiness, that I had so great a sense of its loveliness as humility, brokenness of heart, and poverty of spirit; and there was nothing that I so earnestly longed for. My heart panted after this,— to lie low before God, as in the dust; that I might be nothing, and that God might be ALL.

In the concluding passage of this exquisite rhapsody there appear what have been called the unmistakable marks of the mystic in every age,—the desire to be united with the divine, the longing to be absorbed into the inmost essence of the Absolute. But in Edwards's full narrative there are also to be found the marks of mysticism from the modern point of view. Let us now submit the matter to the test of the psychology of religion. William James has given the proper marks of mysticism as four in number: Ineffability,—the subject of it immediately says that it defies expression, that no adequate report of its contents can be given in words, —in this peculiarity mental states are more like states of feeling than like states of intellect. The noetic quality,—although so similar to states of feeling, mystical states seem to those who experience them to be states of knowledge; they are states of insight, illuminations, revelations, full of significance and importance, all inarticulate though they remain. Transiency,—mystical states cannot be sustained for long, their quality can be but imperfectly reproduced in memory, yet this is susceptible of continuous development in what is felt as inner richness and importance. Passivity,—the oncoming of mystical states can be facilitated by preliminary voluntary operations, yet when the characteristic sort of consciousness has once set in, the mystic feels as if his own will were in abeyance.

We may apply these tests to the records of Edwards's inner life in order to gain a further insight into his mental processes. The mark of transiency may be neglected. The brief duration, the constant intermittence, is an accident, not an essential of the mystic state. Edwards complained that his earlier affections were lively and easily moved, and that it was only after he had spent most of his time, year after year, in meditation and soliloquy that his sense of divine things seemed gradually to increase. Leaving aside, then, the mark of transiency, one reaches the more important mark of passivity. Here Edwards says in his early notes on the Mind: Our perceptions or ideas that we passively receive through our bodies are communicated to us immediately by God. There never can be any idea, thought, or action of the mind unless the mind first received some ideas from sensation, or some other way equivalent, wherein the mind is wholly passive in receiving them.

We should note, in passing, that there is here given a clew to Edwards's precocious idealism. The passive or quietistic state readily lends itself to a sense of the unreality of the external world. In Edwards's language this takes the form of a belief that corporeal things could exist no otherwise than mentally, and that other bodies have no existence of their own. In modern psychological terms the recognition of the unreal sense of things may be laid to a temporary absence of conæsthesia, a transient loss of the sense of the compact reality of the bodily organism. Furthermore, this indirect phenomenalism, this extreme subjectivism, being carried to its logical extreme, might well lead to the conclusion embodied in Edwards's first fragment, the corollary of the essay on Being, which protested against the view that material things are the most substantial, and affirmed that spirits only are properly substances.

Vivid, intense, personal impressions furnish in largest measure the substance of Edwards's idealism. But that idealism was only suppplementary, only an afterthought to his mysticism. We return therefore to that most positive mark of mysticism—the noetic quality. In his maturer essays on the Spiritual Light and the Religious Affections Edwards attempts to express the manner and means of his conviction of that " new sense of things " quite different from anything he ever expressed before. As a sign of the thoroughness of his thinking he takes pains to present the negative side. What is this divine and supernatural light immediately imparted to the soul by the Spirit of God? . . . It does not consist in any impression made upon the imagination, as when one may be entertained by a romantic description of the pleasantness of fairy-land, or be affected by what one reads in a romance, or sees acted in a stage-play. No, rather as he that beholds objects on the face of the earth, when the light of the sun is cast upon them, is under greater advantage to discern them in their true forms and natural relations, than he that sees them in a dim twilight, so God, in letting light into the soul, deals with man according to his nature and makes use of his rational faculties.

So far as Edwards was concerned, the objects of the mystical knowledge were as substantial realities as his Berkshire mountains, yet he felt obliged to bring home to others the proper rationality of that knowledge. Then, too, the treatise on the Religious Affections being called forth by the revival which had meanwhile swept over his parish, the Puritan divine was in a further difficult position, for he stood midway between the skeptics of his age and those persons who were of abnormal emotional sensibility. On the one side, he explains, are many in these days who condemn the affections which are excited in a way that seems not to be the natural consequence of the faculties and principles of human nature; on the other side are those of a weak and vapory habit of body and of brain easily susceptive of impressions; as a person asleep has dreams of which he is not the voluntary author, so may such persons, in like manner, be the subjects of involuntary impressions, when they are awake. But the true saint belongs to neither of these. In him the divine spirit may co-operate in a silent, secret, and undiscernible way, with the use of means, and his own endeavors, and yet that is not all. Spiritual light may be let into the soul in one way, when it is not in another; in a dead carnal frame, it is as impossible that it should be kept alive in its clearness and strength as it is to keep the light in the room when the candle that gives it is put out, or to maintain the bright sunshine in the air when the sun is gone down.

By this final figure of speech Edwards has expressed more than the inadequacy of reason to explain the mystery of the inner life. The figure is itself a reason which explains why Puritan mysticism failed to spread in the land. Edwards himself was the chief luminary in that system, and with his eclipse came irreparable loss. He was not only the chief of New England divines, but the chief native exponent of the scholastic of the heart, the dialectic of the feelings. But those teachings of his had now a lessening audience. In the mid-year of the century he was forced by an unhappy estrangement from his pastorship at Northampton and driven from the haunts of scholarship to the edge of the Western wilderness and into actual peril from the inroads of the savages. And so his arduous missionary labors among the Indians at Stockbridge had much to do in preventing the elaboration of his mystical doctrine.

3. MYSTICISM: FROM QUAKERISM TO CHRISTIAN SCIENCE

The spreading of Edwards's mystical beliefs was thwarted by local conditions. But there were other and more general causes at work to prevent the acceptance of such tenets. For one thing, orthodox Puritanism was opposed to the belief in a " divine and supernatural light immediately imparted to the soul." As Increase Mather declared: Here on earth we have but a dark and very imperfect knowledge of God; only in heaven do the glorified saints have the beatific vision. The reason for this restriction is not hard to find. The notion of self-illumination was abhorrent to those believers in historic revelations and oracles, who considered that they already possessed sufficient sources of inspiration in the Bible, the church, and reason. Of these three the first was counted chiefest. " The word of God as contained in the Scriptures " was the final record of the divine message to men. So, as Edward Channing has said in the case of Mistress Anne Hutchinson, the conception that any man—much less any woman—should pretend to be inspired by the Almighty was not to be held for one instant.

Orthodox Puritanism was therefore out of all sympathy with mysticism. Only contempt met the " familist," who depended upon rare revelations and forsook the revealed word. This explains not only the neglect of Edwards as mystic, but the Puritan persecution of the Quakers in Massachusetts, and Puritan hatred of the colony of Rhode Island, where all quietistic brethren were welcome. This colony was to its neighbors " the drain or sink of opinionists." To Friends it was a " true port and quiet habitat." Nevertheless Roger Williams and his adherents were enabled to make but little impression on the times, for the reason that New England was too narrow in its views. So it remained for the broader acres to the South to take in those who cared for the contemplative life. Foremost of these were William Penn and the Pennsylvania Quakers. The latter term, as is well known, is derisive not descriptive. Not Quakers, but Friends is the proper designation. As one of their own number has said: "There is a principle which is pure, placed in the human mind, which in different places and ages has had different names; it is, however, pure and proceeds from God. It is deep and inward, confined to no forms of religion, nor excluded from any, when the heart stands in perfect sincerity. In whomsoever this takes root and grows they become brethren."

This is the statement of John Woolman, the humble tailor of New Jersey. It may be supplemented by that of the royal proprietary of Pennsylvania. William Penn had sent to his friends a Key opening the Way to every Capacity. The key is to be found in personal illumination; not the light of mere reason, but something higher. This light, it is explained, is something else than the bare understanding man hath as a rational creature; since, as such, man cannot be a light to himself. . . . For we can no more be a mental or intellectual light to ourselves, than we are an external corporeal light to ourselves. What Penn expressed negatively another of the primitive Friends expressed positively: That which God hath given us the experience of, is the mystery, the hidden life, the inward spiritual appearance of our Lord.

We have reached the second stage in the search for the sources of mystic illumination. As to divine truth, the Puritans had taught that the Bible gives, the church expounds, the reason accepts. The Quakers now proceed to drop the second channel of communication. To them there is no need of other men as intermediaries, since it is Christ's light communicated to the soul that makes manifest the things that belong to the soul's peace. Such a sentiment as this makes a priesthood and even a ministry unnecessary. In their stead, then, arise the Friends' meeting-houses,—places for " silence and heavenly frames." Here the congregation awaits the moving of the Spirit, since it is held that resignation and quietness are the safest way to attain the clear discerning of the motions of truth.

The process of elimination did not stop even here. While the orthodox Friends appealed both to the Bible and reason, the unorthodox or Hicksite Friends appealed to reason, so far as possible unfettered by Scripture. They argued that if reason alone is competent to reach divine truth, revelation is superfluous. Thus Elias Hicks took the traditional Quaker inspiration for the union of self with a larger whole and tried to turn the feeling regarding " the universal divine principle " into a conclusion concerning the " fullness of God in us and in every blade of grass." An opponent called this a wandering off into the dreary wastes of pantheism. We dissent from the description except in so far as there was a real tendency towards a philosophical monism.

At this point we have apparently reached the conclusion of the whole matter. All three channels of mystical communication seem exhausted, yet the process of elimination was carried even further. That inward fellowship, received immediately from the divine fountain, was now sought by a group of mystics who cared less for the Bible, the church, and reason, than for reason transcended. It was the so-called Pennsylvania Pietists, who sought by direct intuition to get at "the world behind this world." Their quest was for "the real above all reason, beyond all thought." Such was the actual aim of Conrad Beissel, head of the monastic community at Ephrata near Philadelphia. Unfortunately these speculations in the "camp of the solitary" were hidden behind a veil of theosophic lore,—the esoteric doctrine of the Sophia or principle of wisdom. Pennsylvania Pietists, like the European brotherhood of which they were a branch, sought to be tasters of supreme experience, but their quest of the truly transcendental, of knowledge above knowledge, was only laughed at by their neighbors and contemporaries. As a writer of the day expressed it: "Cabbalists and Quietists all affect a mystical language, a dark kind of canting; they talk much of a light within them, instead of common sense,—whoever shall reconcile all these must be an Œdipus indeed."

Because of this essentially Anglo-Saxon way of regarding mysticism and nonsense as convertible terms, it is not surprising that early mysticism in America rapidly evaporated. One reason for its comparative failure has already been given: It opposed the standards set by church and by Scripture. But there were other reasons. Beside being unorthodox, it was inarticulate or without a vehicle of self-expression. There was, of course, Edwards's quietistic tractate on the Affections, but that was counteracted by the excesses of the religious revivals. Outside of this there was no native book which could serve as a mystic manual. John Woolman's Journal was only rescued from oblivion by the Quaker poet Whittier. William Penn's *No Cross, No Crown*, written in the Tower of London, went through several American editions, but it was too didactic to attract wide attention. " Think not thine own thoughts," " Wait to feel something divine,"—directions such as these lacked the poetic and imaginative touch necessary to mystic enthusiasm. So without living native sources the stream ran dry. Recourse was had to foreign parts. During the century of Quaker Quietism translations of Fénelon and even of Juan de Valdés were circulated among American Friends, but the imagery of France and of Spain was hardly in keeping with that of the New World.

Besides being inarticulate, native mysticism was inopportune. At the end of its century Quakerism should have borne the fruit of literary expression. But circumstances were against that fruition. The Revolutionary War arose and the results to mystical men of peace were disastrous, militarism being by nature opposed to mysticism; pomp, and outward show to the quiet concentration of all the inner forces of the soul upon supernatural objects. And this quest of a world beyond this world was hindered by another circumstance,—the cessation of immigration from the home country. For the Society of Friends this meant that there was no one to take the place of such men as Robert Barclay, and for the Pennsylvania Pietists of such men as Conrad Beissel. While both English and German suffered from the lack of fresh blood, new rivals arose in the coming of the Scotch-Irish. In place of the men of feeling and sentiment came the men of cold intellect and plain common sense. With Philadelphia as their chief point of entry these dogmatists spread over the very regions, West and South, into which pietists and Quakers had made their timid advances. This matter is one of the psychology of race and the survival of the fittest. As regards number and influence the soft-hearted were supplanted by the hard-headed. And the latter were also helped by their spiritual kin, the deists. It was a characteristic of the rationalist to look at "enthusiasts" with a coldly critical eye. The followers of Penn were not openly derided because their commercial standing was secure and their social position assured. But the followers of Jacob Boehme were called fantastic, and Franklin, who printed some of the "Dutch" books, had only contempt for those Quietists who removed hither from Germany.

We must now attempt to estimate the value and results of early American mysticism. It was unorthodox, it was inarticulate, it was inopportune. Was it ineffective? There are some who hold that mysticism is by nature passive and theoretical, not active and practical. They claim that the mystical life is a life of contemplation, not of ethical energy; that the individual, being lost in the excess of divine light, loses his sense of personality. To such critics we offer these facts: William Penn's treaty with the Indians, John Woolman's protest against slavery, and the continued agitation of the Society of Friends against militarism, from the time of the Revolution to this year's Mohonk Conference. To those who would scornfully say that mysticism is by nature theoretical and never practical, we point not only to this list of emancipators, abolitionists, pacificists, but to the causes which underlay their activities. That cause has been suggested by Whittier. It was that they were men who sincerely applied their minds to true virtue and found an inward support from above. Nevertheless a compromise must be made between critic and defender. Our early American mysticism was in a sense ineffective. Privately the practice of quietism engendered a state of tender sensibility and an appreciation of the higher morality. But publicly the movement did not spread because it was not a truly social movement. Quietists were in one sense separatists. Beside their matrimonial segregation they had their own meeting-houses and brotherhoods, and communities like that started by Count Zinzendorf, near Sharon, Connecticut. Such segregation put them out of joint with the times. The country needed public participation by all in the era of political reconstruction, and the subsequent era of commercial expansion. But after the adoption of the Constitution, and after the winning of the West, there arose again a felt need for private contemplation. This need was supplied in part by the transcendentalists of New England. Emerson found in nature the "dial plate of the invisible"; Upham saw in Christianity a field for the cultivation of the interior or hidden life. But this second mystical movement, like the first, was disturbed by a similar set of events,—another war, another period of reconstruction, another territorial expansion. So it was not until the present generation that there was either leisure or occasion for the cultivation of quietism.

Some have called the present phase New Thought. It should rather be called the oldest of thought in a new setting. As will be shown subsequently it is in large measure a revival of pagan mysticism and of medieval magic. The magical side we shall take up in another chapter, in treating of mental healing as it degenerated into the American form of mesmerism. The mystical side it is almost impossible to portray, except as we study by the outward comparative methods the spread of such a symptomatic movement as that called Christian Science. The sources of this system are inextricably confused. I have elsewhere pointed out that it contains a portion of the doctrine of the Yankee mesmeric " healer," Quimby of Maine; a portion of the doctrines of the Shaker prophetess, Mother Ann Lee of New Hampshire; a portion of the orphic sayings of the transcendental rhapsodist, Bronson Alcott. But such dissection does not explain the vitality of the movement. For an explanation we must have recourse to the comparison of the statistics of the sect with conditions in various parts of the country. The statistics are to be found in the last federal census; the conditions are suggested by an interesting, but as yet unpublished map designating the absolute number of Christian Scientists in the land.

A first glance at the map shows this threefold distribution of the sect: the East, the Middle West, the Far West. By States this means Massachusetts and New York; Illinois and Missouri; Colorado and California. This confirms the official statement that the influence is strong over comparatively limited areas in the United States. In this threefold distribution the pathological factor is primarily in evidence, for the centers of influence are large cities, with their concomitant nervous disorders, and the health resorts of the mountains and coast, where it is natural that groups of invalids and semi-invalids should welcome any new therapeutic agency. But besides the physical there is a mental factor at work, besides " Health," there is " Science," and for the acceptance of the proffered metaphysics there are deeper and more subtle influences to be considered. The new gospel of mental medicine is also a system of philosophy. " Hopelessly original," as Mrs. Eddy calls it, the system appeals to those who are inclined to novelties. Tired of the dry doctrines of the churches, to most beginners in speculation, unacquainted with the history of the schools, Christian

Science has all the air of discovery. Now such persons, who have, at the least, the merit of thinking for themselves, are found chiefly in cities, and the acknowledged preponderance of urban over rural adherents is explained by a third factor, that of free-thinking or a liberal attitude toward the unconventional. In the little town it is notoriously difficult to break from the dogma of local churches; it does not approve of changes in ecclesiastical caste. Free-thinking is, therefore, a second potent factor in the spread of Christian Science. The map of distribution by States discloses this. Connecticut and New Jersey, with conservative colleges like Yale and Princeton, are far below the average of their more liberal neighbors. It is not so in Massachusetts, that hotbed of heresies; nor in Illinois, with its mixture of foreign faiths; nor in Colorado, early home of woman suffrage; nor lastly in California, pervaded with esoteric Buddhism and the doctrine of Maya,—of the world of sense as shadow and illusion.

A third factor is financial. Christian Science has spread largely along the fortieth degree of latitude,— the richest pay-streak in our civilization. From their personal appearance and from the showiness of their churches the followers of "scientific mental therapeutics" are manifestly prosperous. Yet with this very physical prosperity there goes a spiritual change. As in the case of those primitive Christian Scientists, the followers of Plotinus who centered in rich cities like Alexandria and Rome, so these modern Neo-Platonists tend to revolt against over-prosperity. With a plethora of wealth they incline toward asceticism, and long for a breath of the upper airs of mysticism. In a word, too much of the material has brought a desire for the immaterial.

This introduces a fourth factor in the distribution of the sect, for Christian Science as immaterialism has had, as a prepared soil, the previous American idealisms. If a mental isothermal line could be drawn for such a phenomenon, it would begin in Massachusetts, stretch to that historic projection of New England—the Western Reserve—and continue on with the latter's prolongation into Illinois. This, it should likewise be noted, was the path of Puritanism; westward the course of Calvinism took its way, and on this same path, seeking his audiences among those of New England stock, Emerson brought to the winners of the West the message that "the spiritual principle should be suffered to demonstrate itself to the end."

Still another form of transcendentalism, not native but foreign, came into this region. The St. Louis school of German idealism, brought in by the refugees of the revolution of '48, worked its way up the Missouri and Mississippi and found a congenial soil in such Teutonized towns as Cincinnati and Chicago. Consequently, if one were to compare our given map with a philosophic map designating the areas of the early speculative movements in the country, this comparison would show that the preparation for the spreading of Christian Science was both positive and negative. Thus, where immaterialism was rife, it has followed; where materialism flourished, it has gained little ground. The former fact has already been pointed out. Christian Science has run along the old grooves of New England transcendentalism, just as the latter ran along those of the older English Puritanism. Now, that the North has been continuously idealistic we know; but we are not so familiar with the fact that the South has been the opposite in its speculative spirit. Indeed, in the generation before Emerson, there was a flourishing school of materialists down the Atlantic coast. Radiating from the Philadelphia Medical School that influence spread chiefly below Mason and Dixon's line. This would go to explain the peculiarity that Christian Science has found its line of least resistance north of that parallel and its line of greatest resistance south of it.

How far there are deeper underlying causes for this complex result it would be hard to say. Lacking as yet an adequate map of the distribution of races in our land, we cannot state, with precision, to what extent idealism and materialism follow the paths of racial distribution. But this, at least, is of significance,—that our Northern idealism has been Anglo-American, our Southern materialism Franco-American. In the North the philosophic succession has been through Emerson and Edwards back to the English Platonists like Cudworth, Norris, and More. In the South that succession has been through Jefferson and Franklin back to the Gallic materialists like the authors of the *System of Nature* and *Man a Machine*.

That these four factors are valid may be corroborated in a specific way. Take the case of the founder of the " Church of Christ, Scientist." First, as to the pathological factor. Mary Baker Glover's prime search was for health; after her first marriage in 1843 she tried in turn allopathy, homeopathy, hydropathy, electricity, spiritualism, and mesmerism. Next, free-thinking affected her; like the more prominent New England religionists she revolted against current Calvinism; " the horrible decree of predestination," she says, was approached only to be abhorred. The third factor applies in only an indirect way. The invalid was of necessity forced into painful ascetic practices. But the fourth factor, the search for an immaterial first principle, was one which has worked with especial strength on the discoverer of " divine science." The story of the inner life of Mary Baker is the story of a typical reaction to current philosophies. Negatively, there was a revolt against materialism; materia medica was rejected for " the higher attenuations of homeopathy " and these prepared the imagination for a sheer immaterialism, where mind was everything and matter nothing. Positively, there was an acceptance of contemporary idealism, for the terms, though not the exactitudes, of Emersonianism are to be found scattered through Eddyism. The faithful will, of course, deny that the penumbra of Concord, Massachusetts, reached to Concord, New Hampshire, just as they have denied that *Science and Health* is an adumbration of the doctrines of the magnetic healer Quimby. Nevertheless in both these cases the denial is not final. The author has pointed out elsewhere how the quarrel between Eddyites and Quimbyites can be settled by recourse to the solution of common sources,—the teachings of itinerant animal magnetizers who, like their master Mesmer, had inadvertently hit on the principle of suggestive therapeutics. In like manner, the affiliations between Eddyism and transcendentalism tend to throw new light on the problem of distribution. Although it is difficult to discover any personal contact between the frequenters of Brook Farm and Mrs. Eddy when at Lynn, except for a flying visit paid her by the visionary Bronson Alcott; yet the appeal to both the academic transcendentalist and the New Hampshire seeress was the same. The earlier movement has been described by Frothingham as having its data secluded in the recesses of consciousness, out of the reach of scientific investigation, remote from the gaze of vulgar skepticism; esoteric, having about them the charm of a sacred privacy, on which common sense and the critical understanding might not intrude. Its oracles proceeded from a shrine, and were delivered by a priest or priestess, who came forth from an interior holy of holies to utter them, and thus were invested with an air of authority which belongs to exclusive and privileged truths, that revealed themselves to minds of a contemplative cast. To the pure transcendentalist the soul, when awakened, utters oracles of wisdom, prophesies, discourses grandly of God and divine things, performs wonders of healing on sick bodies and wandering minds. This form of transcendentalism was decried by Emerson as the Saturnalia or excess of faith, lacking the restraining grace of common sense. In the case of Mrs. Eddy this extreme mysticism took the following form. As she wrote to one of the directors of her church: " I possess a spiritual sense. . . . I can discern in the human mind, thoughts, motives, and purpose; and neither mental arguments nor psychic power can affect this spiritual insight. . . . This mind reading is first sight; it is the gift of God. . . . It has enabled me to heal in a marvelous manner, to be just in judgment, to learn the divine Mind."

It would be interesting to hunt for the sources of these claims, for, if Eddyism be considered an afterclap of transcendentalism, a common ancestry can be traced through a series of intermediate links back to Neo-Platonism. At the least we can make a brief comparison between the old and new ways of thinking. The old made the possibility of knowledge dependent on divine communications, the new claims that " science is an emanation of eternal mind, and is alone able to interpret truth aright." The old denied sensible existence and strained for something behind reality; the new " reverses the testimony of the physical senses and by this reversal mortals arrive at the fundamental facts of Being." The old had a contempt for reason and physical science; the new " eschews what is called physical science, inasmuch as all true science proceeds from divine Intelligence." The old destroyed the distinction between sensible and intelligible, the new says, " matter is but a subjective state of what is here termed mortal mind."

This recrudescence of Neo-Platonism in the New World is not surprising. Like causes have produced like effects, materialism has been followed by immaterialism, one mood being a natural recoil from the other. One outburst of mystic idealism occurred in New England a generation ago, for as Margaret Fuller explains of her contemporaries, it is " because Americans are disgusted with the materialistic workings of rational religion that they become mystics; they quarrel with all that is, because it is not spiritual enough, since they acknowledge in the nature of man an arbiter for his deeds, a standard transcending sense and time." At the present day, after the struggles of the Civil War and after the commercial expansion of the country, the same phenomenon is recurring under the form of the so-called New Thought. It would be going too far afield to attempt to explain the significance of the latter movement,—its occultism or love of the mysterious, its gnosticism or claim to peculiar knowledge, its affiliations with previous mystical systems,—but we can at least point out that Christian Science is but a single phase of a larger interest which ranges from the teachings of William James to the allegories of Maeterlinck.

We may here examine, in conclusion, a final factor in the spread of the sect, namely the type of mind to which it appeals. In general that type is practical and yet uncritical, non-academic and yet speculative. Although the great mass of Christian Scientists consists of women who stand for the unrest of the new feminism, yet that given type is well represented by imaginative business men without a college training, such as are to be found in large cities, and such as predominate in the present directorate of the church. To carry out the analysis of the individual: in the first place such a man is practical, he wants results. When he sees benefits conferred upon his immediate circle he is led to speculate as to the cause. Here, he says to himself, is the movement, and here is the result, therefore the " demonstration " or the " absent treatment " must be the connecting link. Now, this is the non-academic way of thinking. It belongs to that class of persons who are capable of framing a syllogism, but not capable of discovering its fallacious forms. To the academic or college-bred type " demonstration," " absent treatment " are as much matters of dubiety as " mental telepathy " or " wireless mental messages." Now the veriest undergraduate is taught the distinction between mind and matter, and is taught to keep the two spheres apart. Not so the business man. To draw such distinctions is not in his line. Consequently, although he is a " practical " man, he will occasionally take a " flier " in a scheme that savors of alchemy, where secret formulæ are claimed to transmute metals, and, although a " self-made " man, he is often in fear of being overreached by some rival with more " magnetism," as if the latter possessed some sort of irresistible psychic effluence.

And thus arises the failure to perceive the fundamental fallacy of Christian Science; that, while it disclaims materialism, it still reeks with materialistic
terms. Even a recent edition of *Science and Health*,
in spite of its countless recensions from the original
Eddyite edition, contains such rubrics as "Mental
Offshoots" and "Gravitation Godward." It also
contains phrases of this sort: "Astronomical order
imitates the action of Divine Principle"; "Mind, God,
sends forth the aroma of Spirit, the atmosphere of Intelligence"; "If the individuals have passed away,
their aroma of thought is left which is mentally scented
and described. Mind has senses sharper than the body";
"Mental chemicalization, which has brought conjugal
infidelity to the surface, will assuredly throw off this
evil, and marriage will become purer when the scum is
gone."

This fatal flaw, this failure to distinguish between
mental and physical, is not recognized by the ordinary
"Scientist," hence the ease with which strange doctrines can be accepted. Christian Scientists deny the
existence of the material, yet are reinforced in their
beliefs by the latest physical discoveries. Just as Mesmerism was helped by "Franklinism," the theory of
psychic emanations by the fluid theory of electricity, so
"absent treatment" and silent "demonstration" are
bolstered up by appeals to Hertzian waves, X-rays, and
the like.

In fine, Christian Science is liable to spread wherever
fundamental distinctions fail to be made. Ignorant,
then, of the real procedure of suggestive therapeutics, a
procedure which has been confessedly neglected in our
medical profession; ignorant also of such historic approaches to *Science and Health* as have been made by

the classic mystic manuals from those of the Neo-Platonists to those of the Quakers, it is no wonder that, in the present state of American culture, Christian Science spreads where there is a " struggle for the recovery of invalids," and where there is a " yearning of the human race for spirituality."

CHAPTER III

DEISM

1. THE ENGLISH INFLUENCES

IN deism as a movement toward free-thought we have a typical example of English influence upon the American mind. It was a case of make haste slowly, for it was only by gradual degrees that British subjects emerged from the apologetic to the constructive, and from the constructive to the destructive type of free-thinking. The term free-thinker, as it first appeared in English philosophical literature, meant simply one whose thought is freed from the trammels of authority, who sought a characteristic Anglo-Saxon compromise between the Bible and the church on one side, and reason on the other. This was reflected in such works as *Christianity Not Mysterious* and *Christianity as Old as the Creation.*

Such an attitude was too vague, too apologetic. So it was succeeded by one more positive, more constructive. This attitude was reflected in a search for a natural or universal religion, a platform of belief on which all good men could unite. Such were the so-called five points common to all religions, which began with the existence of a Supreme Being and ended with future rewards and punishments. But constructive deism was, in turn, succeeded by destructive. This began when natural religion was made to supplant revealed, when prophecies were eliminated, when miracles were considered not as props

to belief but as mere myths. These three phases of
English deism were exhibited in the colonies. The
apologetic is represented by Cotton Mather in his
*Christian Philosopher, or A Collection of the Best
Discoveries in Nature With Religious Improvements.*
The moderate is represented by Benjamin Franklin,
who, with judicious vagueness, offered as his creed those
old points common to all religions. The destructive is
represented by Thomas Paine, who, in his *Age of
Reason,* argues boldly against mystery and miracle.
Deism, according to him, declares to intelligent man the
existence of one Perfect God, Creator and Preserver
of the Universe; that the laws by which he governs the
world are like himself immutable; and that violation of
these laws, or miraculous interference in the movements
of nature must be necessarily excluded from the grand
system of universal existence.

American deism began in a reaction against Puritan
determinism. The belief in a deity separate from the
world, an idle spectator, an absentee landlord, was a
logical rebound from the belief in a deity constantly
interfering with the world, a magical intervener, a
local busybody. Thomas Paine's *Age of Reason,* with
its notion of a creator whose " arm wound up the
vast machine " and then left it to run by itself, formed
a kind of counterpoise to Cotton Mather's *Magnalia
Christi Americana,* with its faithful record of many
illustrious, wonderful providences, both of mercies and
judgments, on divers persons in New England. In a
way, also, these two books marked the transition between
two different political points of view, one standing for
class favoritism, the other for the natural rights of
man. The Calvinistic doctrines of sovereign grace and
an elect people savored too much of the claims of British

supremacy to be long acceptable. Hence the five points of Calvinism became so many points of irritation. Total depravity might apply to effete monarchies, but not to the New World; absolute predestination to the land of passive obedience, but not to the land where men sought to be free.

Calvinism as a doctrine of necessity was, then, the proximate cause of deism as a doctrine of freedom. The notion of a partial and arbitrary deity prepared for the religion of humanity; the system of inscrutable decrees for a religion of reason. The change was striking. Talk about creatures infinitely sinful and abominable, wallowing like swine in the mire of their sins, brought about a reaction, and the next generation went from the extreme of Puritanic pessimism to the extreme of deistic optimism, the belief in the perfectibility of the human race. This change in sentiment is recorded in the attacks on the old divinity. When the consistent Calvinist merely filed smooth the rough edges of a cast-iron system, the forerunners of the Unitarian movement boldly threw the dead weight overboard. To speak in reproachful language of the moral virtues, comparing them to filthy rags, was held absurd; while the Calvinistic doctrine of the tendency of man's nature to sin, as implying his utter and eternal ruin and the torments of hell fire, was declared shocking to the human mind and contradictory to all the natural notions both of justice and benevolence.

These protests against determinism were characteristic of early American deism; but behind these acute personal reactions there were larger and quieter forces at work. In a word the dogmas of an unnatural religion were giving way to the principles of natural religion, and rationalism had at last a chance to assert itself.   Here deism constituted the moving cause and the colonial college the vehicle in the transaction.

2. THE COLONIAL COLLEGES AND FREE-THOUGHT

Deism, as a form of rationalism, had been hanging on the skirts of Puritanism during the last quarter of the seventeenth century, but it was not until the eighteenth that it took to an independent growth and hastened the intellectual emancipation of New England. The old Boston Platform had recognized the light of nature, but more in the way of a forlorn negation than a hopeful affirmation. It spoke of natural reason as greatly impaired, saying that man retained no more of the light of reason than would conduce to tormenting reflections. From these timid limitations there arose the desire for a change from a gloomy theology to a cheering theodicy, from the doctrine of inscrutable decrees to the belief in rational purpose and benevolent design in the universe. This change is marked by two such representative works as Mather's *Reasonable Religion* and Chauncy's *Benevolence of the Deity.*

Cotton Mather did not attain his rationalistic results without some mental perturbation. At first his attitude was that of one opposed to the use of reason. Thus he uttered the warning: "Hearken ye of Harvard and Yale College to old Eubulus, exhorting you with his counsel. In most academies of this world nothing is acquired but worldly wisdom; the philosophy taught in them is nothing but foolosophy." After such strictures as these it is rather strange that Mather can avail himself of rational arguments. But this he does in his *Christian Philosophy,* where he quotes with approval the statement of an English writer that the divine reason

runs like a golden thread through the whole leaden mine
of brutal nature. Applying this principle to whatever
he saw about him, he exclaims:

How charming the proportion and pulchritude of the leaves,
the flowers, the fruits. How peculiar the care which the great
God of nature has taken for the safety of the seed and fruit!
When the vegetable race comes abroad, what strange methods
of nature are there to guard them from inconveniences. How
nice the provision of nature for their support in standing and
growing, that they may keep their heads above ground and
administer to our intentions; some stand by their own strength,
others are of an elastic nature, that they may dodge the violence
of the winds: a visible argument that the plastic capacities of
matter are governed by an all-wise infinite agent. Oh! the
glorious goodness of our deity in all these things!

There was a note in this little book that did not die.
While its scientific arguments for design fell flat, its
aesthetic elements lived on; it anticipated by a century
the transcendentalist's love of nature for its own sake.
Mather might have said with Emerson " Come into the
azure and love the day." Belonging to the same school
of apologetic deists as Mather but of far higher rank
was Charles Chauncy. In his *Benevolence of the
Deity,* in place of a being cruel, inscrutable, acting by
particular providences, we find a being benevolent, rational, acting in harmony with wise goodness and accurate justice. The deity does not communicate being
or happiness to his creatures by an immediate act of
power, but by concurring with an established course
of nature. He makes them happy by the intervention of
second causes, operating in a stated, regular, uniform
manner.

Chauncy's work combines sound matter with a noble
style; it marked a notable advance in the progress of

rationalism. To teach that man is free and not determined; active and not passive; perfectible and not depraved, was to sum up the three great tenets of deism
gained by way of painful reaction against the harsher
doctrines of Calvinism. The way in which this reaction
came about may be traced more closely in the later
writings of the Harvard worthies, who possessed one
notable means for the public expression of their views.
This was the Dudleian lectureship founded for " the
proving, explaining, and proper use and improvement
of the principles of natural religion." The significance
of this lectureship is that it furnishes an historical cross-
section of the American mind. In it may be observed
not only the rise and progress of deism, but also its
destruction through a number of powerful solvents. The
first of the Dudleian discourses furnishes an appropriate introduction to the whole course by giving an historical summary of the problems of dualism as connected with cosmology. Here President Edward Hol-
yoke was the initial speaker:

There were three opinions as to the existence of the world.
One was that it was from Eternity, & Plato it seems, was the
Father of it, and thought it flowed from God as Raies do from
the Sun, where, by the way, we may note, That tho' they tho't
the world to be eternal, yet that it proceeded from God; his
Scholar also, Aristotle, propagated the same Notion & asserted
that the world, was not generated so as to begin to be a
world, which before was none. He supposes preexistent &
eternal Matter as a Principle and thence argu'd the world to
be eternal. . . . Another Opinion as to the Existence of the
world, was that it came into this beautiful Form, by Chance,
or a fortuitous concourse & jumble of Atoms, This is by all
known to be the Philosophy of Epicurus, & his Notion was,
that the Universe consisted of Atoms or Corpuscles of various
Forms & Weights, which having been dispers'd at Random thro'

the immense Space, fortuitously concur'd, into innumerable Systems or Worlds, which were thus formed, & afterward from time to time increased, changing & dissolving again without any certain, Cause or Design, without the Intervention of any Deity, or the intention of any Providence. And yet this Philosopher did not deny the Existence of a God, but on the Contrary asserted it, but tho't it beneath the Majesty of the Deity to concern himself with humane affairs. . . . But the most prevailing *Opinion* . . . was, *That the world had a beginning*, & was form'd by some great and excellent Being whom they called God. And this indeed is a tho't that is perfectly agreeable to Reason.

The first Dudleian lecturer granted that natural religion was not unreasonable. A certain successor twenty years after argued for what he calls a coincidence of natural and revealed religion. He presents his arguments in a sort of imaginary conversation:

Reason would say: "Surely this stupendous universe is the work of some invisible agent, beyond all comparison & conception superiour to man; for such a grand complete System so infinitely complicate, & yet so exactly adjusted in all its parts, the most minute as well as the grandest, that all kinds of symmetry and perfection concur to complete the whole, could never be the effect of chance or the product of endless essays & mutations of matter. This Agent must have an unlimited mind, to comprehend these vast innumerable works in one perfect Idea, before they were made. His *power* also must be equal to his unlimited understanding. And he is evidently as *good* as he is wise and powerful; otherwise malignity against his creatures would appear in universal discords through nature, perpetually generating all manners of evil. . . . In some such manner as this Reason in its perfect state might be supposed capable of arriving at the knowledge of the *One True God,* & deducing from thence a compleat system of natural religion. Yet it can hardly be conceived, according to our experience of the labour of searching out truth, that the human mind, in its utmost strength, could by one glance of thought discover all the essential characteristics of the Deity, or the proper acts of worship & obedience which he requires. We might as well affirm, that unimpaired reason must naturally, at the first view of the heavenly bodies, have a clear knowledge of their magnitudes, distances and revolutions: or by looking round on the earth, immediately be acquainted with the innumerable gradations of animal life, & vegetable productions & fossils of all forms & kinds. . . . Therefore it may be justly questioned whether it would not have cost the labour of Ages to demonstrate a true System of religion, as it has taken nearly six thousand years to search out the laws of the material system & bring natural philosophy to its present perfection."

The arguments just presented were delivered in the year before the Declaration of Independence. It was not until after the second war with England that the Dudleian lectures show the weakening of the old conservative scheme under the assaults of the destructive deists. But it remained for a lecturer of the year before the publication of Emerson's *Nature* to recognize the drift of a priori arguments for natural religion as leading to the self-sufficiency of nature. Abstract arguments, reasons John Brazer in 1835, are objectionable because they virtually assume the point to be proved. Thus, the axiom that every effect has a cause avails little with those who deny that the universe is an effect; the axiom that whatever begins to exist must have had a cause of its existence, will have no pertinency with those who, like the ancient and modern Epicureans, assert that the universe is eternal and the creative power, whatever it be, only plastic. Again, the statement that every contrivance must have a contriver is no argument to him who denies that there is any proof of contrivance further than the particular instance in question is concerned, as did Hume. Finally, the principle that nothing can be a cause of its own existence will conclude little against him who asserts that the world is an exception to this general rule,—it being self-existent, as Spinoza maintained.

We have here at Harvard an hypothetical approach to pantheism. In this free-thought had achieved a victory over the old dualism. Instead of a creator and creation separated by a gap which could not be bridged, instead of the old doctrine of transcendence with which the apologetic deist had begun, we have now the doctrine of immanence,—the very affirmation of Emerson that nature, comprehending all existence, may be its own cause.

The rise of deism in the second oldest of the New England colleges is much like that in the first. At Harvard deism as a movement of enlightenment developed through opposition. Cotton Mather, with his eye upon the free-thinkers, had declared that " to question the being of God would be exalted folly." Similar academic attempts to stem the tide of rationalism were early made at Yale. In spite of them the freshening currents came stealing in. At New Haven, as at New Cambridge, the heads of the college could not escape the eclectic spirit of the times. Rector Thomas Clap avowed that the great design of founding this school was to educate ministers " in our own way "; nevertheless, he based his moral philosophy on the deistic Wollaston's *Religion of Nature*. But there was another head of the Connecticut college who more clearly showed the pervasive influence of English thought combined with the mental independence of a young colonial. It was President Ezra Stiles, who nourished a hope that America might be a land of British liberty in the most complete sense. As student and tutor he had read through some thirty-odd deistic works left to the college library by Bishop Berkeley. These books did much to open the eyes of their reader; at the same time they did not lead him into the most radical skepticism. He recounts how he read Clarke's *Demonstration of the Being and Attributes of God,* but did not find entire satisfaction; how he read Shaftesbury's *Characteristics* and admired them as sublime views of nature and of the moral government of the Most High. But he could not go beyond this the Deist's Bible and accept the conclusions of the arch-skeptic Hume. Against the latter's strictures upon the evidences of Christianity he exclaims, " Shall a King be able by a Seal and other infallible Signatures to evince his Proclamations to his Subjects so that they shall have no doubt of his Majesty's Will: and shall the Great Omnipotent King of the Universe be unable to evince & ascertain his Will to such a handfull of Intelligences the small System of Man? "

Having described the moral jaundice of the leader of skepticism in old England, Stiles as Anglus-Americanus turns to the movement in New England and gives a vivid account of the agitations of local thought during the French and Indian War:

. . . As we are in the midst of the struggle of Infidelity I expect no great Reformation until that [Revelation] is demonstratively established. . . . From the Conduct of the Officers of the Army you entertain an Expectation favorable to Virtue. Far from this I imagine the American Morals & Religion were never in so much danger as from our Concern with the Europeans in the present War. They put on indeed in their public Conduct the Mark of public Virtue—and the Officers endeavor to restrain the vices of the private Soldiery while on Duty. But I take it the Religion of the Army is Infidelity & Gratification of the appetites. . . . They propagate in a genteel & insensible Manner the most corrupting and debauching Principles of Behavior. It is doubted by many Officers if in fact the Soul survives the Body—but if it does, they ridicule the notion of moral accountableness, Rewards & Punishments in another life. . . . I look upon it that our Officers are in danger of being corrupted with vicious principles, & many of them I doubt not will in the End of the War come home minute philosophers initiated in the polite Mysteries & vitiated morals of Deism. And this will have an unhappy Effect on a sudden to spread Deism or at least Scepticism thro' these Colonies. And I make no doubt, instead of the Controversies of Orthodoxy & Heresy, we shall soon be called to the defence of the Gospel itself. At Home the general grand Dispute is on the Evidences of Revelation— some few of your small Folks indeed keep warming up the old Pye, & crying Calvinism, Orthodoxy &c—these are your Whitefields, Romaines, &c that make a pother: but the greater Geniuses among the Ministers are ranging the Evidences of Revelation to the public View, expunging the Augustine Interpretations of Scripture with the other Corruptions of the Latin Chh, yet retained among protestants—and endeavoring a just & unexceptionable, rational Explication of the great Doctrines of the Gospel. The Bellamys &c of New England will stand no Chance with the Corruptions of Deism which, I take it, are spreading apace in this Co try. I prophesy your Two Witnesses will avail more towards curing the Contagion than thousands of Volumes filled with cant orthodox phrases & the unintelligible Metaphysics of Scholastic Divinity, which is a Corruption of Christianity with *arabian* philosophy.

Yet Stiles was no such reactionary as some of his correspondents thought. He did not hold that the overvaluing of reason tends to promote atheism. When he was informed that Rector Clap would not suffer a donation of certain books from the free-thinking colony of Rhode Island, he wrote to the rigid Rector and made a notable appeal for unrestrained thought:

. . . Different men indeed object from different motives, some from the Love of Orthodoxy & some from the Hatred of it, & some from the generous Sentiments of that generous & equal Liberty for which Protestants & Dissenters have made so noble a Stand. It is true with this Liberty Error may be introduced; but turn the Tables the propagation of Truth may be extinguished. Deism has got such Head in this Age of Licentious Liberty, that it would be in vain to try to stop it by hiding the Deistical Writings: and the only Way left to conquer & demolish it, is to come forth into the open Field & Dispute this matter on even Footing—the Evidences of Revelation in my opinion are nearly as demonstrative as Newton's Principia, & these are the Weapons to be used. Deism propagates itself in America very fast, & on this Foundation, strange as it may seem, is the Chh of Engld built up in polite Life. A man may be an excellent Chhman & yet a profound Deist. While public popular Delusion is kept up by Deistical Priests, sensible Laymen despise the whole, & yet, strange Contradiction! joyn it, and entice others to joyn it also.—and they say all priests are alike, we all try to deceive Mankind, there is no Trust to be put in us. *Truth* & this alone being *our* Aim in fact, open, frank & generous we shall avoid the very appearance of Evil.

The protest of Stiles was unavailing. Measures were now taken to stop the infiltration of any form of deism. By a vote of the president and fellows, students were to be established in the principles of religion according to the Assembly's Catechism, Dr. Ames's *Medulla,* and *Cases of Conscience.* Yale was now outwardly a stronghold of orthodoxy; how it came to be called a hotbed of infidelity is a matter of later times. It was not until after the Revolutionary War that the satirist could describe undergraduate skepticism, could tell how the clockwork gentleman was made " twixt the Tailor and the Player, and Hume, and Tristram and Voltaire." All this might have been expected. Action and re-action were equal. As at Harvard opposition had brought electicism, so at Yale the policy of suppression brought an explosion of free-thinking upon the advent of the Franco-American deism of Citizen Paine and President Jefferson.

Meanwhile it is in order to follow the fortunes of deism outside of New England, and to see how the other colonial colleges of the first rank were laid open to the advances of rationalism.

The first head of King's College, New York, destined to become the future Columbia University, was that Samuel Johnson who had been forced out of Yale because of his liberal tendencies, which were early shown even in the reputed land of the blue laws. The very title of his most juvenile work, *Raphael, or the Genius of English America*, was a protest against colonial conservatism. But Johnson's actions spoke louder than his words. As an undergraduate he was warned against reading Descartes, Locke, and Newton; becoming a tutor, he introduced these works into the college library. As a theological student he was cautioned against a certain new philosophy, that of Berkeley, which was attracting attention in England, being told that it would corrupt the pure religion of the country and bring in another system of divinity. The warning was ineffective, for Johnson became a clergyman in the Church of England and sought to spread that very philosophy against which he had been warned. What trials met the students in the provincial seats of learning is suggested in a recently recovered manuscript entitled: *The Travails of the Intellect in the Mycrocosm and Macrocosm*. In this juvenile work Johnson leaves the little world of Puritan thought and emerges into the larger world of constructive deism. His scheme has as its beginning benevolence, and as its end evidences of cosmic design. This scheme was conceived by the author at the age of eighteen, but, being obliged to conceal his opinions with caution, it was not for half a generation and through an English magazine that the young American was enabled fully to express his views.

To show how judicious was the rationalism of this *Introduction to Philosophy* we may explain that the purpose of this small tract, " by a gentleman educated at Yale College," was declared to be: the setting before young gentlemen a general view of the whole system of learning in miniature, as geography exhibits a general map of the whole terraqueous globe. As in the natural so in the intellectual world, young students must have a prospect of the whole compass of their business and the general end pursued through the whole.

We may here cite the case of another graduate of Yale, at King's College, whose effusions, though light like straws, showed how the wind was blowing in the deistic direction. William Livingston, in his *Remarks upon Our Intended College,* wished to have the rules free to all, offensive to no sect. Fighting the efforts of the Episcopalians to obtain control of the institution, he was charged with deism and atheism. He thereupon retorted upon his opponents with a travesty of the Thirty-Nine Articles, whose tenor may be judged by the following:

I. I believe the Scriptures of the Old and New Testaments, without any foreign comments or human explications but my own: for which I should doubtless be honoured with Martyrdom, did I not live in a government which restrains that fiery zeal, which would reduce a man's body to ashes for the illumination of his soul. . . . XXXIX. I believe that this creed is more intelligible than that of St. Athanasius and that there will be no necessity for any to write an exposition of the Thirty-Nine Articles of my faith.

The position of King's College in colonial free-thinking was significant. It was a sort of half-way house between the extreme puritanism of the North and the extreme deism of the South. The former had made God everything: the latter made man everything. Samuel Johnson was a mediator between these two views: his first book made the happiness of mankind to be God's chief end; his last made the glory of God not inconsistent with our pursuing our own happiness.

To trace the further development of deism in the colonies, we pass over the College of New Jersey, defender of the faith, opponent of rationalism, and go on to Philadelphia and Franklin.

3. PHILADELPHIA AND FRANKLIN

" I was scarce fifteen," narrates Benjamin Franklin, " when, after doubting by turns of several points, as I found them disputed in the different books I read, I began to doubt of Revelation itself. Some books against Deism fell into my hands; they were said to be the substance of sermons preached at Boyle's Lectures. It happened that they wrought an effect on me quite contrary to what was intended by them; for the arguments of the Deists, which were quoted to be refuted, appeared to me much stronger than the refutation: in short, I soon became a thorough Deist."

We have here the confession of the most precocious of the American skeptics. There is added to it an explanation which takes in, with characteristic inclusiveness, the two factors of heredity and environment. Franklin explains that he was a free-thinker because of a free-thinking ancestor, and a deist because of a youthful overdose of Calvinism. Thus he relates how his maternal grandfather had written some homespun verse in favor of liberty of conscience, and that his father's little collection of books consisted mostly of polemical works of divinity. Although Franklin considered that some of the dogmas of the Presbyterian persuasion, such as the eternal decrees of God, election, reprobation, appeared very unintelligible and others doubtful, yet he never doubted that deity exists; that he made the world and governed it by his providence; that the most acceptable service of God was the doing good to man; that our souls are immortal; and that all crimes will be punished, and virtue rewarded, either here or hereafter.

This creed was nothing but Herbert of Cherbury's five points common to all religions, the veritable creed of a moderate deist, and yet Franklin tells how he was obliged to leave Boston when his indiscreet disputations about religion began to make him pointed at with horror by good people as an infidel and atheist. He next recounts how, being employed in London, at the age of nineteen, in composing as printer for Wollaston's *Religion of Nature Delineated,* and some of the author's reasonings not appearing well founded, he wrote a little metaphysical piece entitled *A Dissertation on Liberty and Necessity, Pleasure and Pain.* The purport of this essay was to prove the doctrine of fate from the supposed attributes of God, reasoning in some such manner as this: That in erecting and governing the world, as he was infinitely wise, he knew what would be best; infinitely good he must be disposed, and infinitely powerful, he must be able to execute it; consequently all is right.

Franklin stated that the printing of this " wicked tract " of 1725 was an " erratum " in the book of his life. That confession was probably meant to disarm criticism. The deistic fatalism of this pamphlet was as nothing compared with the strange views set forth three years later in his *Articles of Belief and Acts of Religion*. Drawn up among the regulations of the Philadelphia Junto or club for mental improvement, this document formed a kind of shopkeeper's litany, or home-service for young mechanics. Among its parts were the First Principles, Adoration and Petition, of which the last begged that the petitioner might be preserved from atheism and infidelity; the second urged the reading of deistic authors like Ray, Blackmore, and the Archbishop of Cambray; while the first, as if in conscious opposition to the Anglican creed, taught the doctrine, not of one God without parts and passions, but of many gods endowed with human passions.

Here, then, follow Franklin's peculiar

FIRST PRINCIPLES

I believe there is one supreme, most perfect Being, Author and Father of the Gods themselves. For I believe that Man is not the most perfect Being but one, rather that as there are many Degrees of Beings his Inferiors, so there are many Degrees of Beings superior to him.

Also, when I stretch my imagination thro' and beyond our System of Planets, beyond the visible fixed Stars themselves, into that space that is every Way infinite, and conceive it fill'd with Suns like ours, each with a Chorus of Worlds forever moving round him, then this little Ball on which we move, seems, even in my narrow Imagination, to be almost Nothing, and myself less than nothing, and of no sort of Consequence.

When I think thus, I image it great Vanity in me to suppose, that the *Supremely Perfect* does in the least regard such an inconsiderable Nothing as Man. More especially, since it is impossible for me to have any positive clear idea of that which is infinite and incomprehensible, I cannot conceive otherwise than that he the *Infinite Father* expects or requires no Worship or Praise from us, but that he is even infinitely above it.

But, since there is in all Men something like a natural principle, which inclines them to DEVOTION, or the Worship of some unseen Power;

And since Men are endued with Reason superior to all other Animals, that we are in our World acquainted with;

Therefore I think it seems required of me, and my Duty as a Man to pay Divine Regards to SOMETHING.

I conceive then, that the INFINITE has created many beings or Gods, vastly superior to Man, who can better conceive his Perfections than we, and return him a more rational and glorious Praise.

As, among Men, the Praise of the Ignorant or of Children is not regarded by the ingenious Painter or Architect, who is rather honour'd and pleas'd with the approbation of Wise Men & Artists.

It may be that these created Gods are immortal; or it may be that after many Ages, they are changed, and others Supply their Places.

Howbeit, I conceive that each of these is exceeding wise and good, and very powerful; and that Each has made for himself one glorious Sun, attended with a beautiful and admirable System of Planets.

It is that particular Wise and good God, who is the author and owner of our system, that I propose for the object of my praise and adoration.

For I conceive that he has in himself some of those Passions he has planted in us, and that, since he has given us Reason whereby we are capable of observing his Wisdom in the Creation, he is not above caring for us, being pleas'd with our Praise, and offended when we slight Him, or neglect his Glory.

I conceive for many Reasons, that he is a *good Being;* and as I should be happy to have so wise, good, and powerful a Being my Friend, let me consider in what manner I shall make myself most acceptable to him.

Next to the Praise resulting from and due to his Wisdom, I believe he is pleas'd and delights in the Happiness of those he has created; and since without Virtue Man can have no Happiness in this World, I firmly believe he delights to see me Virtuous, because he is pleas'd when he sees Me Happy.

And since he has created many Things, which seem purely design'd for the Delight of Man, I believe he is not offended, when he sees his Children solace themselves in any manner of pleasant exercises and Innocent Delights; and I think no Pleasure innocent that is to Man hurtful.

I *love* him therefore for his Goodness, and I adore him for his Wisdom.

Let me then not fail to praise my God continually, for it is his Due; and it is all I can return for his many Favours and great Goodness to me; and let me resolve to be virtuous, that I may be happy, that I may please Him, who is delighted to see me happy. Amen!

Franklin's First Principles form an astonishing document; they teach a veritable polytheism in a land monotonously monotheistic. We may postpone for a moment the search for the precise sources of this doctrine and give a general reason for its rise. It was Franklin's penetrating gaze that saw the essential weakness of the deistic tenet of transcendence. As the God of the deist was removed farther and farther from the world he became less and less an object of worship. This removal occurred in both time and space. On the one hand the conventional date of the creation was discounted; geology lengthened Genesis, and the coming into being of the world was thrust into the dark backward and abysm of time. The same thing happened in regard to space. The deity was dogmatically placed outside the framework of the visible universe, but as that universe was enlarged its maker was necessarily put beyond the uttermost bounds. So by a double process the deity became less an object of worship than a vague first cause at an infinite remove.

Franklin's strange intermediate God was perfectly logical. More than that, his pluralism of divinities had a reputable literary source. There was the prevalent belief in a graded scale of reasoning life, as when Pope sought to discover " what varied being peoples ev'ry star." More particularly, there was the familiar scheme of Wollaston, who spoke of "the fixed stars as so many suns with their several sets of planets about them." Finally, inserted in the midst of Franklin's document, there was the " Hymn to the Creator," wherein Milton sang of " Sons of light, angels, fixed stars." But we have still more exact knowledge as to what was at the very bottom of these peculiar Articles of Belief. It is known that the original manuscript was Franklin's daily companion to the end of his life, but it seems to have escaped notice, for a full century after his birth, how far he was indebted to Plato. Nevertheless it has been shown how Franklin's writings give evidence that in his youth he fell under the spell of the ancient charmer. He tells how in his sixteenth or seventeenth year he procured the *Memorabilia*. From this he adopted the Socratic method of dispute, dropping abrupt contradiction and positive argumentation and putting on the humble inquirer and doubter. To Plato, then, we may trace the polytheism of the Philadelphian. For instance, the description, in the First Principles, of the Father of the gods themselves embodies the doctrines of the *Timæus* concerning the Father who begat the world and made the eternal gods, who formed the universe and assigned each soul to a star, who was good, and being free from jealousy, desired that all things should be as like himself as possible.

Space is lacking in which to reproduce one of Franklin's delightful dialogues in the classic style, nothing to equal which for charm and fancy had so far appeared in the colonies. Space also is lacking in which to tell about his ethical schemes: his practical pocket-book for eradicating the vices; his Society of the Free and Easy, '' a sect that should be begun and spread at first among young and single men, each one of whom should exercise himself with the thirteen weeks' examination of the thirteen virtues, and only then should the existence of the Society be made a matter of public knowledge.''

We pass, therefore, from Franklin as the virtuous Poor Richard to Franklin as the advocate of free-thought. Here we should distinguish between his private and his public views. The best portraits of Franklin present as their mark of authenticity a secretive smile playing about his lips. This is characteristic. It suggests that what he expressed outwardly did not always obtain within. After his early speculative '' errata '' he assumed a cautious attitude toward religion as a public institution. Thus he writes to an anonymous correspondent, presumably Thomas Paine, that he has read his manuscript with some attention, but that the arguments it contains against the doctrine of a particular providence strike at the foundation of all religion. He therefore gives as his opinion, that though the author's reasonings are subtle, and may prevail with some readers, yet he will not succeed so as to change the general sentiments of mankind on the subject, and the consequence of the printing of the piece will be a great deal of odium drawn upon himself, and no benefit to others. He that spits against the wind spits in his own face.

Of the same nature as this homely piece of advice was Franklin's *Information to Those Who would Re-*

move to America. Here he writes that, in the New World, religion under its various denominations is not only tolerated, but respected and practiced. Atheism is unknown there; infidelity rare and secret; so that persons may live to a great age in that country without having their piety shocked by meeting with either an atheist or an infidel. This is a jesuitical generalization, its truth being contradicted by the single fact that when Franklin made a motion for the holding of prayers in the Constitutional Convention, as a means of correcting the melancholy imperfections of the human understanding, he added in a satirical note, that the convention, except for three or four persons, held prayers to be unnecessary.

These are contradictory statements, but there was a reason why Franklin's writings and private beliefs did not hang together. The reason was his utilitarian point of view: he might consider free-thinking as a thing good in itself, but like his electric fluid, it was to be guided and conducted into safe channels. In spite of his general attitude of caution there were certain times when he took a firm stand against intellectual and religious coercion. This was shown in the aid he extended to the radical Joseph Priestley, author of the *Corruptions of Christianity;* also in his request to Cadwallader Colden to stop prosecution of the editor of the *New York Gazette,* for publishing a defense of deism; and finally in his letter to Ezra Stiles of Connecticut, wherein he reiterates the deistic creed of his youth, confesses that he believes that primitive Christianity has received corrupting changes, and concludes with the observation that he does not perceive that the Supreme takes it amiss by distinguishing the unbelievers in his government of the world with any peculiar marks of displeasure.

The result of Franklin's liberal policy was that Philadelphia in his day was in the van of intellectual progress. When John Adams sarcastically observed that the
place considered itself the pineal gland of the United
States, one might have retorted that that was true since
Franklin was the seat of its intellect. It was due to his
influence as founder that the University of Pennsylvania
became noteworthy for requiring no religious test
of its instructors, and for being so unprejudiced
as to bestow an honorary degree even upon Thomas
Paine.

Forced to be cautious at home it was in France that
Franklin came out in his true colors. On his mission to
Paris in 1776 he showed a remarkable liveliness of
spirits for a man of seventy. A kind of Socrates in small-
clothes, he preserved to the last the ancient irony, the
mastery of dialogue he had shown in his youthful essays. Upon his arrival, being publicly introduced to
Voltaire, he was hailed as the Solon embracing the
Sophocles of the age. And Condorcet made the remarkable eulogy which contains the parallel between these
two men as representatives of philosophy rescuing the
race of man from the tyrant fanaticism. What the old
diplomat was thought to believe at this time is told in
a conversation which John Adams recounts having had
with De Marbois, later secretary of the French legation
in the United States: "All religions are tolerated in
America," said M. Marbois, "and the ambassadors have
in all courts a right to a chapel in their own way; but
Mr. Franklin never had any." "No," said I, laughing,
"because Mr. Franklin had no——" I was going to
say what I did not say, and will not say here. I stopped
short and laughed. "No," said M. Marbois, "Mr.
Franklin adores only great Nature, which has interested

a great many people of both sexes in his favor."
" Yes," said I, laughing, " all the atheists, deists, and
libertines, as well as the philosophers and ladies, are in
his train,—another Voltaire, and thence——" " Yes,"
said M. Marbois, " he is celebrated as the great philosopher and the great legislator of America."

4. VIRGINIA AND JEFFERSON

As Philadelphia was intellectually dominated by Ben-
jamin Franklin, so was Virginia by Thomas Jefferson.
How firmly the latter stood for liberty of thinking is
manifest in the President's express desire to have in-
scribed on his tomb: " Author of the Declaration of
American Independence, of the Statute of Virginia for
Religious Freedom, and the Father of the University of
Virginia." As the advocate of free-thought in the Old
Dominion, Jefferson was but the embodiment of his class.
In contrast to the heresy-hunting Calvinists of the North,
he typified the fox-hunting Arminians of the South. His
earliest intellectual impressions were gained from that
local species of Anglican clergy who, from reading the
fashionable, skeptical literature of the mother country,
came to be considered as lax in thought as they were
reputed to be loose in living.

Besides the Cavalier clergy, the College of William
and Mary had marked influence on Jefferson's mind.
In addition to the liberty of philosophizing advocated
in its charter the scientific spirit prevailed in the place.
William Small, friend of Watt, the inventor of the
steam engine, and of Erasmus Darwin, the grandfather
of the evolutionist, came to the Virginia institution in
1758, and Jefferson, who attended his lectures in natural
philosophy, declared that he fixed the destinies of his

life. Adding to these liberalizing forces the elective system of studies, and the naturally volatile temper of the Southerner, it was inevitable that Jefferson should develop that receptive spirit which made him the typical progressive of his times. As he wrote in regard to the proposed University of Virginia: the Gothic idea that we are to look backwards instead of forwards for the improvement of the human mind, is not an idea which this country will endure.

These were glittering generalities in education, but Jefferson backed them up by specific details. For the education of the young there was offered a scheme of Jeffersonian simplicity,—it was to start the inquiring student with books of a harmless sort and gradually and insidiously to wean him away from orthodoxy. He might begin with Hutcheson's *Moral Philosophy* and continue with Lord Kames's *Natural Religion,* but he was to end with the *Corruptions of Christianity* by Dr. Joseph Priestley, the Anglo-American free-thinker. It was under the influence of the latter that the great deist in the White House, during the strenuous year of the Louisiana Purchase, took time to write what he called a *Syllabus of an Estimate of the Merit of the Doctrines of Jesus, compared with those of others.* In this short work the author proposed to take first a general view of the moral doctrines of the most remarkable of the ancient philosophers; next, a view of the deism of the Jews, to show in what a degraded state it was; finally, to proceed to a view of the life, character, and doctrines of Jesus, who, sensible of the incorrectness of their ideas of the deity and of morality, endeavored to bring them to the principles of a pure deism.

This *Syllabus* remained a mere sketch; knowledge of it leaked out and public charges of atheism were brought

against the President. Hence in the political agitations
of the times Jefferson declared he had had no idea of
publishing a book on religion, and that he should as
soon think of writing for the reformation of Bedlam as
the world of religious sects. So the former ambitious
project for a study of comparative religions dwindled
to a home-made harmony of the Gospels. As to the harmony, Jefferson's object was merely to take the four
Evangelists and cut out from them every text they had
recorded of the moral precepts of Jesus. There will be
found remaining, he avers, the most sublime and benevolent code of morals which has ever been offered to man.
" I have performed this operation for my own use," he
continues, " by cutting verse by verse out of the printed
book, and arranging the matter which is evidently his,
and which is as easily distinguishable as diamonds in
a dunghill. The result is an octavo of forty-six pages
of pure and unsophisticated doctrine."

This production, issued by Congress in its fourfold polyglot form—Greek, Latin, French, English—a
full century after its inception, is the so-called Jefferson
Bible. Bearing the title *The Life and Morals of Jesus
of Nazareth*, the compiler acknowledges that it was attempted too hastily, being the work of two or three
nights only at Washington, after getting through the
evening task of reading the letters and papers of the day.
To the larger undertaking Jefferson never went back,
perhaps, because he realized that the rôle of a philosophical higher critic was an impossible one, that to distinguish between primitive Christianity and later accre-
tions was a task beyond the scholar of that age. Jefferson's partial comparative studies remain as the most
formal, but not as the sole expression of his beliefs. In
addition to the *Syllabus* and the *Bible* there is a volu-

minous correspondence, from which the Virginian's somewhat motley philosophy may be reconstructed. In general, that philosophy was an eclecticism of a pronounced deistic type, since it was the very peculiarity of the deist to wear a patchwork philosopher's cloak, yet to wear it in the fashion of the day. Thus, when on different occasions Jefferson exclaimed: " I am an Epicurean," " I am a Materialist," " I am a sect by myself," there was discoverable beneath these various disguises the strut and swagger of the age of reason.

Of the different phases of thought through which Jefferson passed the most interesting was the materialistic. It was his five years' residence in France, before the outbreak of the Revolution, that gave the free-thinking Southerner an insight into the possibilities of materialism when carried to a logical outcome. As American minister Jefferson had the fortune to enjoy the society of the same lively set of spirits as did his predecessor, Franklin. Thus he could recall to Cabanis the pleasant hours he passed with him at the house of Madame Helvétius; confess that the French literati are half a dozen years ahead of the American, and yet make no effort to catch up with them.

Here Jefferson's fundamental deism held him back. Like the more moderate exponents of the Enlightenment, while disbelieving in a revealed, he was at the same time convinced of the advantages of a natural theology. So it was that " the savage from the mountains of America," living in the midst of the intellectual seductions of Paris, could still remain a believer in the Être Suprême. The system of Diderot, D'Alembert, and D'Holbach was designated by his friend, Baron Grimm, an exposition of atheism for chambermaids and barbers. Jefferson, not so witty but more wise, criticised this extreme presentation more broadly and more soberly. Remarking that the atheistic was a more numerous school in the Catholic countries, while the infidelity of the Protestant took generally the form of deism, he puts the arguments of both sides thus: When the atheist descanted on the unceasing motion and circulation of matter through the animal, vegetable, and mineral kingdoms, never resting, never annihilated, always changing form, and under all forms gifted with the power of reproduction; the theist, pointing " to the heavens above and to the earth beneath and to the waters under the earth," asked if these things did not proclaim a first cause, possessing intelligence and power.

Thus far Jefferson's view of the universe was that of a moderate deist. The same attitude is taken in his characteristic compromise between the Epicurean doctrine of the eternity of the world and the Puritanic doctrine of interference with the ordered course of nature. Calling himself a skeptical reader, he nevertheless reasons on the supposition that the earth has had a beginning. However, he does not agree with those biblical theorists who suppose that the Creator made two jobs of his creation, that he first made a chaotic lump and set it in motion and then, waiting the ages necessary to form itself, stepped in a second time to create the animals and plants which were to inhabit it.

The last phase through which the Southern thinker passed was that of natural realism, or that form of thought which emphasizes intuition and common sense. When he was young Jefferson recalls that he was fond of speculations which seemed to promise some insight into the hidden country. After his retirement from active life he rests content in the belief that there is a reality which we directly recognize in beings, and that we are guided unconsciously by the unerring hand of instinct. In defense of his final faith in the common sense of moral sense the reminiscent statesman puts this patriotic question: If our country, when pressed with wrongs at the point of the bayonet, had been governed by its heads instead of its hearts, where should we have been now? Hanging on a gallows as high as Haman's. The heads began to calculate and compare numbers; the hearts threw up a few pulsations of their warmest blood; they supplied enthusiasm against wealth and numbers; they put their existence to the hazard when the hazard seemed against us, and they saved the country.

To bring Jefferson's philosophy into bolder relief it may be compared with that of John Adams, the cautious speculator and taster of systems, who, even in the days of their political rivalry, Jefferson considered " as disinterested as the being who made him." Now, it was after their reconciliation through Benjamin Rush that the correspondence between the Whig and the Federal ex-presidents discloses two gentlemen of the old school, both omnivorous readers, both averse to Calvinism and clerical obscurantism, both interested in the rising study of comparative religion, both tinged with the current deistic thought. Of the two the Southerner was more prone to generalizations, more impatient of other men's beliefs; the Northerner more tolerant, not inclined to go beyond " New England guesses." " The Philosophical Chief of Monticello is such a heterodox and hungry fellow," so runs a doggerel couplet of the day; Adams appears equally versatile but far less ardent. Confessedly afflicted with a kind of Pyrrhonism, he numbers himself among those Protestants *qui ne croyent rien.*

Adams's ironical deprecation of his own knowledge was doubtless one reason for Jefferson's drifting away from the Gallic speculation. Adams is sensible of the services of the French philosophers to Liberty and Fraternity, yet he cannot but think that they are all destitute of common sense:

They all seemed to think that all Christendom was convinced as they were, that all religion was "visions Judaicques" and that their effulgent lights had illuminated all the world. They had not considered the force of early education on the millions of minds who had never heard of their philosophy. And what was their philosophy? The universe was matter only, and eternal; spirit was a word without a meaning. All beings and attributes were of eternal necessity; conscience, morality, were all nothing but fate. Who, and what is fate? He must be a sensible fellow. He must be a master of science. He must calculate eclipses in his head by intuition, and what is more comfortable than all the rest, he must be good natured, for this is upon the whole a good world.

In these jocular criticisms there was a sly dig at Jefferson's deism. The French fate bore a striking resemblance to his benevolent deity, trust in whom would bring the philosophic millennium. And so Adams writes again: "Let me now ask you very seriously, my friend, where are now in 1813, the perfection and the perfectibility of human nature? Where is now the progress of the human mind? Where is the amelioration of society? . . . I leave those profound philosophers to enjoy their transporting hopes, provided always that they will not engage us in French Revolutions. . . ." And so throughout the correspondence,—the impartial Novanglian meets the strenuous Virginian with whimsical advice. When as Epicurean he becomes too stoical, he urges him to eat his canvas-back duck; when as deist he becomes too dogmatical, he remarks: " It has been long, very long, a settled opinion in my mind, that there is now, never will be, and never was but one being who can understand the universe. And that it is not only vain, but wicked, for insects to pretend to comprehend it."

It was easy for Adams to write in this way; an agnostic's apology was tolerated in the case of one who would leave " metaphysics in the clouds." But with Jefferson things were different; politics complicated the situation and faction spoiled philosophy. The Federalists linked together Jeffersonianism, atheism, and the excesses of the French Revolution. They called the President a Jacobin, an infidel, and a republican villain. They spoke of a dangerous, deistical, and Utopian school of which a great personage from Virginia was a favored pupil. They said his principles relished so strongly of Paris, and were seasoned in such a profusion of French garlic, that he offended the whole nation. In these attacks the Federal clergy of New England were implicated. When Jefferson had brought over from France the arch-infidel Thomas Paine in a government ship, they spoke of him as an Ephraim who had become entangled with the heathen. Jefferson's defenders were unable to mend matters. The author of the *Hamiltoniad, or an Extinguisher of the Royal Faction of New England* dismisses the worn-out tale of the President's irreligion by retorting that " he has thrown into the lap of Morality the purest apothegms of the Apostles and Fathers; he confounds the politicians by calling them Tory bloodhounds, yelping upon the dangers that may arise from the Virginian or Southern influence." These mixed metaphors betray a political

confusion in which Jefferson found it hard to preserve a philosophic calm. He asserted that the priests,
to soothe their resentments against the act of Virginia
for establishing religious freedom, wished him to be
thought atheist, deist, or devil, who could advocate freedom from their religious dictations. Having opposed
the scheme of a state-supported church—" Christianity
for pence and power "—he pronounced Massachusetts
and Connecticut the last retreat of monkish darkness
and bigotry.

And so against the narrowness of the North and as
a bulwark against the " pious young monks of Harvard
and Yale," Jefferson proposed to erect his Southern
University. In the plan for this institution which he
proposed to the Virginia legislature, he intended to
place the entire responsibility for religious training
upon an ethical basis, where all sects could agree. As he
explained the matter: " The proofs of the being of a God,
the creator, preserver and supreme ruler of the universe, the author of all the relations of morality, and
the laws and obligations these infer, will be within the
province of the professor of Ethics; to which adding
the development of these moral obligations in which all
sects agree . . . a basis will be found common to all
sects." Because of his plan of having no professorship
of divinity and allowing independent schools of theology to be established in the neighborhood of the University, Jefferson complained that a handle had been
made to disseminate an idea that this is an institution,
not only of no religion, but against all religion. But in
spite of his opponents' fulminations " the liberality of
this State," concludes the Virginia humanist, " will
support this institution and give fair play to the cultivation of reason."

5. Thomas Paine and Popular Deism

In examining the books of the early colleges and the thoughts of their representative men, there have been found numberless signs of colonial free-thinking, of mental independency before political independence. In addition to these academic studies there must now be made a search for the more elusive traces of the spreading of infidelity, before the actual outburst of revolutionary thought. As has been already intimated, this movement, beginning as a popular reaction, was more felt than avowed, more a matter of subtle distrust than of precise knowledge. It was the faint smoke in the air, presaging the coming forest fire. It was a time when the clergy might warn against "the insidious encroachments of innovation," but when the laity preferred the Indian summer of indifference. Toleration was pervasive. It has been described as gradually diffused over the land by such fostering circumstances as colonial impatience with prescription and custom, and that original adventurous spirit which, combined with dissatisfaction with home conditions and voluntary exile, insensibly fitted the mind for the propositions of liberty.

Of these propositions, the liberty to think and feel as one liked was the most conducive to the coming of free-thought. Paine's *Age of Reason* was especially opportune because it was in agreement with that liberty of conscience granted or implied in so many of the Revolutionary documents. Among these documents we may refer to Patrick Henry's Bill of Rights, in which he held that religion can be directed only by reason. To this Madison added that all men are equally entitled to the full and free exercise of religion according to the dictates of conscience. This was followed in 1785 by Jefferson's Declaratory Act, establishing religious free-dom in Virginia, and by the Pennsylvania constitution, advocated by Franklin, which contained the clause as to the natural and inalienable right to worship according to the dictates of the understanding. In brief, twelve out of the thirteen original States allowed an increased measure of mental freedom. It was only in Massa-chusetts that a dread of liberty was expressed. There we find the question debated as to whether public offices might not be held "even among those who have no other guide to the way of virtue and heaven, than the dictates of natural religion."

The political expressions of rationalism in the Revo-lutionary period are many, the philosophical few. Be-tween the Stamp Act and the adoption of the Constitu-tion, there was but one native work worth mentioning in the deistic connection. But Ethan Allen's *Reason the Only Oracle of Man* did not arrest the popular at-tention. So it remained for a naturalized American to turn the tide of thought. It was the *Age of Reason* of Thomas Paine which marked high water in the deistic movement, for it was carried upon the wave of enthusi-asm caused by the author's Revolutionary pamphlets *Common Sense* and the *Rights of Man*. The radical writer affirms that, as his motive in his political works had been to rescue man from tyranny and false sys-tems and false principles of government, so in his re-ligious publications it was to bring man to the right reason God had given him, unshackled by fable and the fiction of books.

The *Age of Reason* is a perfect example of the popu-larizing of current deistic opinions. It has the same method of so-called mathematical proof, the same me-

chanical view of nature, the same disregard of the
problem of evil, the same aversion to mystery, the same
iridescent dream as to mankind's perfectibility, the
same delusion as to monotheism being a primitive belief,—" Adam was created a deist " says this prehistoric critic. In a word, the book is anything but original. With the exception of a phrase or two like the
" religion of humanity," there is not an idea in it which
cannot be matched in the writings of the English free-
thinkers of the Georgian era. Paine simply repeats, in
the language of the street, the arguments of Collins
against prophecy, of Woolston against miracles, of
Tindal against revelation, of Morgan against the Old
Testament, of Chubb against Christian morality.

This is the negative side of the book. More effective
is the positive. In place of the false " bases of Christianity " Paine would put what he calls a true theology.
He cannot see how man can hold to a system where
Satan is deified and given power equal to that of the
Almighty; where man is called an outcast, a beggar, a
mumper, calling himself a worm and the fertile earth a
dunghill, and all the blessings of life but the thankless
name of vanities. But there is a substitute for all
these corruptions " from Moloch to modern predesti-
narianism,"—it is eighteenth-century optimism, thus
grandiloquently set forth: If objects for gratitude and
admiration are our desire, do they not present themselves every hour to our eyes? Do we not see a fair
creation prepared to receive us the instant we are born
—a world furnished to our hands, that costs us nothing? Is it we that light up the sun; that pour down
the rain; and fill the earth with abundance? Whether
we sleep or wake, the vast machinery of the universe
still goes on.

The effect of the *Age of Reason* on the community may be easily imagined. The clergy attacked it, the colleges criticised it, but the populace read it. Dedicated to the author's fellow-citizens of the United States of America, it was sold for a few pence the copy or given away gratis. The first edition, printed in France, was spread broadcast through the free-thinking societies affiliated with the Jacobin Club of Philadelphia. Within two decades the pamphlet was to be found on the banks of the Genesee and Ohio; within two more it was circulated among the readers of Volney and Voltaire and in those places in Tennessee and Kentucky whose names still attest the French sympathies of the first settlers. It is astonishing how far the light of nature threw its beams. The president of Transylvania University was suspected of teaching an unrestrained naturalism, and a friend of Abraham Lincoln reported that in Indiana the *Age of Reason* passed from hand to hand, furnishing food for the evening's discussion in tavern and village store.

The book, moreover, met with that sincerest form of flattery—imitation. An example of this was Elihu Palmer's *Prospect, or View of the Moral World for the Year 1804*. According to the allegorical thunder and lightning frontispiece, the Book of Saints and Ten Commandments are being dashed to the ground from the Altar of Truth and Justice to be supplanted by the *Age of Reason* and the *Rights of Man*. Of an equally destructive aspect was George Houston's New York *Correspondent* of 1829, containing lectures delivered before the Free Press Association on the inconsistencies, absurdities, and contradictions of the Bible. This journal also presented the advanced views of Fanny Wright, a sort of Wilhelm Meister in petticoats, who wandered over the country

from Woodstock, Vermont, to Cincinnati, Ohio. The
opponents of popular deism now raised their heads.
The free-thinking societies, spread through New England and the Middle States, were designated the
banded Goths and Vandals of political atheism. The
author of the *Sceptic's Manual* retailed petty and ma-
licious gossip concerning the last days of Hobbes and
Hume, Voltaire and Paine. In the *Antidote to Deism*,
Ethan Allen is called an ignorant and profane deist,
Paine a drunkard, to reason with whom would be like
casting pearls before swine.

Such were the attacks of the minor clergy. In the
colleges the battle was waged more in accordance with
the rules of war. The most prolific of the writers against
deism, and the materialism which happened to be asso-
ciated with it, was President Timothy Dwight of Yale.
As one of the Hartford wits, he had composed a sort of
American Dunciad, the *Triumph of Infidelity,* which
was ironically dedicated to Voltaire. How that poem
confined the deist in the pillory of his own terms, and
flung into his teeth his own arguments, is to be seen
from these lines:

"His soul not cloath'd in attributes divine;
  But a nice watch-spring to the grand machine.

　·　　·　　·　　·　　·　　·　　·

Enough, the Bible is by wits arraigned,
Genteel men doubt it, smart men say it's feigned."

In contrast to this effusion were the earlier poems of
Dwight's salad days which showed a decided leaning to
the philosophy of the French Encyclopædists. In the
Columbia and the *Conquest of Canaan,* French
phrases are curiously wrought into a sort of biblical
epic on the New World. The sons of this " blissful Eden

bright " are urged to " teach laws to reign and save the
Rights of Man." The author subsequently explained
that these were the mock heroics of a time when the
strong sympathy towards the leaders of the French
Revolution prepared to make us the miserable dupes of
their principles and declarations. But the doctrines of
the 14th of July were not to be confused with those of
the 4th of July. As the head of Yale College, Dr.
Dwight became the leader of the forces against deism.
His *Century Discourse* gives a trenchant account of the
progress of infidelity,—its descent from the lofty philosophical discourse to the newspaper paragraph, its
spread among the masses, and the ultimate return to
more sober thought. " Infidelity," the discourse proceeds, " was first theism, or natural religion, then mere
unbelief, then animalism, then skepticism, then partial,
and finally, total atheism. The infidel writers have used
terms so abstract, and a phraseology so mysterious as to
attract readers fond of novelty, but the common people,
never honored by Voltaire with any higher title than the
rabble or the mob, have been caught by these writers,
who volunteered to vindicate their wrongs and assert
their rights. Happily it was soon discovered that the
liberty of infidels was not the liberty of New England;
that France instead of being free, merely changed
through a series of tyrannies; and that man, unrestrained by law and religion, is a mere beast of prey.
Even sober infidels began to be alarmed for their own
peace, safety, and enjoyments."

The air of gravity and severity about this passage is
explained by what men remembered of the events following the peace of 1783, the intrigues of Genet, the
terrorism incited by Freneau, when Market Street,
Philadelphia, was filled with a mob, the distrust of

Napoleon implied in President Adams's proclamation. This passage is also explained by the wild and vague expectations everywhere entertained, especially among the young, of a new order of things about to commence, in which Christianity would be laid aside as obsolete. In the exultation of political emancipation, infidel philosophers found ready listeners when they represented the restraints of religion as fetters of the conscience, and moral obligations as shackles imposed by bigotry and priestcraft.

At Harvard College, the academic attitude toward deism was somewhat complicated. Federal in politics and Unitarian in religion, it was doubly averse to the enthusiasms and raptures of Franco-American rationalism; it deplored the " foul spirit of innovation," and sought some check to the " infuriated steeds of infidelity." At Princeton the *Age of Reason* was opposed by the philosophy of common sense. Where Berkeleian idealism had been driven out, the Bridgewater Treatises came in. According to its catalogue, the library abounded in volumes like *Dick's Celestial Scenery Illustrating the Perfections of the Deity,* and Prout's *Chemistry, Meteorology and the Functions of Digestion considered with reference to Natural Theology.* The favorite text-book, as in the majority of conservative colleges, was Dugald Stewart, and Stewart's aim was declared to be to stem the inundation of the skeptical, or rather atheistical publications which were imported from Europe. But a conservative literature does not alone explain the stringent policy of Princeton; behind the books were such facts as that, after the revolutionary war when the students had been " freed from all sanctuary and Sabbath restraint," there was left only a handful of students who professed themselves Christians and that, in 1802, the trustees in their "Address to the Inhabitants of the United States," declared that their purpose was to make this institution an asylum for pious youth, in this day of general and lamentable depravity.

Popular deism was rejected by the clergy and thrust out by the colleges. It remains to be seen how the public first accepted, then grew tired of it. Chancellor Kent said that in his younger days there were very few professional men who were not infidels; Ezra Ripley, that a large portion of the learning not possessed by the clergy leaned to deism. A few specific events will illustrate how this rapid growth of the army of free-thinkers was followed by an equally rapid defection from the ranks. In 1801, James Dana of Connecticut said that infidelity appeared to be gaining ground; by 1810, it was reported that infidelity abounded to an alarming degree and in various shapes in the district west of the Military Tract in New York. In 1822 an anonymous "letter to a deist in Baltimore" stated that deism is taking root rapidly and soon will grow up surprisingly and become the only fashionable religion. In Virginia about the same time Bishop Meade asserted that in every young man he met he expected to find a skeptic, if not an avowed unbeliever.

This was the advance of the movement. A reaction followed which started in protests from the church, the state, and the professions, and ended in a series of religious revivals. In 1798, the Presbyterian General Assembly uttered a warning against the abounding infidelity which tends to atheism itself; in 1800, the President referred to the dissemination of principles subversive of the foundations of all religious, moral, and social obligations, that have produced incalculable mischiefs in other countries; in 1824, Dr. Charles Caldwell thought fit to write a *Defence of the Medical Profession against the charge of Infidelity and Irreligion*. The unpopularity of deism is likewise exhibited in the light literature of the day. Fenimore Cooper describes one of his heroines as being properly impressed with the horrors of a deist's doctrines, and another as shrinking from his company. Harriet Martineau wrote back to England how she was told of one and another with an air of mystery, like that with which one is informed of any person being insane, or intemperate or insolvent, that so and so was thought to be an unbeliever.

The results of deism in America may now be briefly summed up. Among the people the majority were drawn off by an emotional substitute for thought, the revivals that swept over the country. At bottom the deistic system was too cold and formal; it externalized deity, lacked a continuing enthusiasm, and so failed to satisfy the cravings of emotional excitement. The philosophy of a Franklin might appeal to the business, it did not appeal to the bosoms of men. In the colleges those who were not affected by revivalism were held in check by circumscribed courses presenting the similarities between natural and revealed religion. Finally, among the clergy, the great part stood for orthodoxy. As expressed by one of the numerous century sermonizers, there was no neutral ground to be taken between evangelical doctrines and infidelity.

Such were the results of the hundred years' war for free-thinking,—apparently fruitless unless judged by later events. One such event was New England transcendentalism, whose programme on its negative side was almost precisely what the deists had been denying; on its positive, an assertion of what they had been lacking. Transcendentalism denied the need of miracle, revelation, dependence on an outward standard of faith; it affirmed the need of intuition, mystic ecstasy, inward dependence upon an immanent life. As the philosopher of Concord exclaimed: " Here is now a perfect religion, which can be set in an intelligible and convincing manner before all men by their reason."

CHAPTER IV

MATERIALISM

1. The French Influences

THE story of materialism in America is the story of a struggle for existence but not of the survival of the fittest,—so at least thought its opponents. The movement was at first chiefly described by those who were hostile to its spirit and its aim. As a form of genial naturalism it was in marked contrast to the austere supernaturalism of the North. And yet it is to its Northern adversaries that we must go for our earliest accounts. One of the founders of the Harvard Medical School explains that modern philosophers say matter is inert, yet that there are certain powers which the particles of matter have of acting on one another, as gravitation, cohesion, the attraction of crystallization, of magnetism, of electricity, of chemical attraction. But none of these merit the name of vitality, nor in them is the origin of intelligent ideas to be looked for. Sensible objects may be the destined medium to awaken the dormant energies of man's understanding, yet these energies are no more contained in sense than the explosion of the cannon in the spark which gives it fire. Again Noah Webster, the lexicographer, has " some doubts " concerning Erasmus Darwin and his " laws of organic life." The author of such " laws " by merely observing the phenomena of animal motion might trace them to fibrous contractions, and fibrous contractions to irritation of external objects, to pleasure, pain, volition, or association; but at last he is compelled to inquire why and how the fibers become obedient to the impulses of stimulus. Mounting a step higher in the catenation of causes, he is compelled to create or imagine a certain something to reside in the medullary substance of the brain to which he gives the denomination of the spirit of animation. What this principle is he makes no attempt to explain; and the very existence of it is rather assumed than proved.

These opinions represent the jealous attitude of the North toward the prevalent system of the South. A fairer and indeed a mediating attitude was taken by a writer of the Middle States. Reviewing the opinions of the principal materialists of the eighteenth century Samuel Miller of Princeton shows how they resemble those of the ancients. Just as when Epicurus supposed the soul of man to be a material substance, but a very refined and attenuated kind of matter, so Dr. Priestley denies that there is any ground for making a distinction between the soul of man and the body, supposing the whole human constitution to be made up of one homogeneous substance.

In turning from the English to the French materialists such as Condillac and Helvétius, the Princetonian touches on the heart of the matter. The real agents for the naturalizing of French materialism in the South were Franklin and Jefferson. It was Franklin as a philosopher, in the eighteenth-century use of the word as a natural philosopher, who chiefly stimulated the interchange of ideas between France and the western world. Had it not been for the Philadelphian's electrical experiments, there would have been fewer points of contact between the two republics. The modern

Prometheus drew lightning from the clouds, as Turgot's famous lines expressed it; he also drew ideas from men, and despite that non-conducting medium, the Anglo-American mind, succeeded in introducing into the colonies many of the stimulating notions of his French acquaintances. Among those of a philosophic turn who had a transatlantic influence were Buffon, whose *View of Nature* fortified the American deists; Cabanis, whose materialism influenced Jefferson; Chastellux, who anticipated the philosophic travels of De Tocqueville; Condorcet, whose *Progress of the Human Mind* received an early printing in Maryland; Crèvecœur, whose letters on America fascinated and misled Europeans; du Pont de Nemours, who projected a settlement of philosophers on the Mississippi; Lavoisier, whose pneumatic theory was used to explode the phlogistic view of Priestley in Pennsylvania; Quesnay, a follower of Lafayette, whose grandson sought to found a kind of French academy in Virginia; Rochefoucauld duc d'Enville, who translated the Constitutions of the thirteen original States; Volney, whose *Ruins, or Revolutions of Empires* stirred up great popular interest.

In this impressive list of those who threw in their lot with the struggling republic there is one that stands out. When Jefferson exclaimed: "I am a materialist," it was not so much because he had read Epicurus as because he had heard Cabanis. While the Virginian was in Paris, Cabanis had delivered before the Academy the series of lectures on the relations between mind and body which contained the famous apothegms: "the brain secretes thought," "the nerves make the man." So, on hearing the lectures of the distinguished sensationalist, Jefferson asks: Why may not the mode of action called thought have been given to a material organ of

a peculiar structure, as that of magnetism is to the
needle, or of elasticity to the spring by a particular
manipulation of the steel? They observe that on igni-
tion of the needle or spring, their magnetism or elasticity ceases. So on dissolution of the material organ
by death, its action of thought may cease also, for nobody
supposes that the magnetism or elasticity retires to
hold a substantive and distinct existence.

Jefferson's sympathy with the Gallic culture was important; indeed his mission to France was a vital impulse in his life and equally vital in the life of Southern
thought. That sympathy was, of course, fostered by the
political situation. The regard felt by the French for
this country led to an intellectual *entente cordiale*. In
spite of this good feeling there were some who deplored
the presence of such effective advocates of the new naturalism as were the followers of Lafayette. These advocates were described by the elder President Dwight of
Yale as men of polished manners, improved minds, and
superior address, who knew how to insinuate the gross-
est sentiments in a delicate and inoffensive manner,
and were at the same time friends and aids of the American cause—*nos très chers et très grands Amis, et Alliés.*

As a mirror of the Gallic mind Jefferson became a tar-
get for the orthodox. Whenever he tried to introduce
French literature he was invariably criticised. When
he thought Bécourt's *Sur la Création du Monde* to be
merely an innocent attack on the Newtonian philosophy,
he was mortified to find that certain persons contemplated its censorship by the government as an offense
against religion. In these affairs, Jefferson's countrymen showed themselves in a bad light; once they had
been willing enough to receive French gold, now they
seemed to fear the Gauls even when they were bearing

gifts. What this narrow attitude led to, and how the Gallic invasion was checked has been pointed out. If French ideas had really penetrated Virginia society they would have become as dominant in the South as German ideas later became in the North; it was one of the difficult tasks in Southern educational history to dislodge French philosophy from its academic strongholds in North and South Carolina; it was done by a strong current of Scotch Presbyterianism proceeding from Princeton College southwards. And so it was that after all his endeavors to introduce the philosophical culture of France, the President's plans seem to have met with defeat.

2. JOSEPH PRIESTLEY, AND THE HOMOGENEITY OF MAN

In 1794 there came to America Joseph Priestley, metaphysician and materialist. In the words of Jefferson, he fled from the fires and mobs of Birmingham in order to gain a refuge in the land of free thought. His reputation, based on his discovery of oxygen, preceded him and insured his welcome. Also his particular praise of Franklin in his history of electricity, prejudiced Americans in his favor. In this history Franklinism was used to explain the constitution of matter. Instead of that coarse and impenetrable substance which it is generally represented to be, Priestley utilizes the conception of the American's electrical fluid as consisting of particles extremely subtle, since it can permeate common matter.

We have here Franklinism combined with a dynamism much like that of Colden's. It is interesting to know how the distinguished English chemist unites these doctrines in order to explain the relations of mind and body. His aim is to show that these apparently contradictory substances are really homogeneous. He renders them of like substance by performing a contrary process upon each. Mind he coarsens to a certain degree; matter he attenuates to a like degree. There is now a common area upon which the two substances overlap. This is human nature, for in man there is a meeting-point where the two substances are harmoniously joined. No longer is body that coarse and impenetrable substance which it is generally represented to be. No longer is mind that indefinite and aërated substance to which tradition has held. No, the two are practically consubstantial and one can be put in terms of the other. Indeed, the learned author has no objection, if his critics choose to call this matter by the name of spirit. Nor does he object if they say that he is materializing mind. His ultimate object, he contends, is to show that there is no real conflict between mind and matter, since one substance may admit of the properties of both, if that substance be characterized by active powers and impenetrability.

Such is the doctrine of anthropological materialism. It appeared so novel to most Americans that it was little appreciated and less understood. In spite of the author's friendship with Franklin and with Jefferson, and in spite of his seeking in America a refuge for free thought, this Priestleyanism, as it was called, was violently attacked. For example, these three inferences were drawn from the supposition that the whole human constitution was made up of one homogeneous substance; first, that there is no distinction between the soul of man and the body; second, that the idea of the natural immortality of the soul is wholly fallacious; and third, that the properties of sensation and thought must be extinguished by the dissolution of the organized mass in which they exist. To explain the unpopularity of Priestleyanism we need only point out how these inferences ran counter to current beliefs. The first was against the dualism of the day. The second was against the prevalent hope that the soul is by nature indestructible. The third implied a belief in pantheism. Now, of these three doctrines it is clear that the first two were opposed to the past, and the third was an anticipation of the future. For their doctrine of dualism, the men of the eighteenth century looked back to the authority of Descartes. For the doctrine of natural immortality, they relied upon the Christian tradition. These were positive factors against which Priestley had to contend. Finally, the coming native form of pantheism, the doctrine of an immanent world-soul, had not yet received clear expression. It remained for Emerson to brush away the difficulties that were offered by a world of apparently passive matter.

Priestley's system was carried from Pennsylvania into the South by his son-in-law, Thomas Cooper. In spite of his ingenuity, this companion of the great chemist had a personality which antagonized the public. He was attacked by the clergy when proposed by Jefferson as first professor of natural science and law in the University of Virginia. He was indicted in Pennsylvania for his violent writings against the Federal party. Finally he engaged in the nullification agitation in South Carolina. In short, he was a living example of his own doctrine of nervous irritability. He had, however, one advantage over Priestley in his wider knowledge of the literature of materialism from Blount to Broussais. Thereby he is able to show that Priestley's historic method was as diffused and porous as that homogeneous matter for which he contended. So, too, in his *View of the Metaphysical and Physiological Arguments in Favor of Materialism* he is able to state the arguments on both sides in a way that his older colleague could not. Thus, he shows that the prime argument for immaterialism is, that from matter and motion nothing but matter and motion can result. Hence life and the properties connected with it must have been originally impressed by that being to whom all creation is to be ascribed. But this statement, which favors creationism, Cooper cannot accept. He therefore takes up another line of reasoning in favor of his doctrine: The chief metaphysical argument is that one thing is the property of another because of the universality in which they accompany each other. Such is the necessary connection between the nervous system of animals and the properties of sensation and of perception. These properties are inseparable, for no one can explain how the immaterial soul can act on a material body, without having one property in common with it. But let the soul have no property in common with matter, then neither can act upon the other, else one might conceive of erecting the Coliseum of Rome by playing Haydn's Rondeau.

Cooper next turns from metaphysics to physiology. We need not resort, he continues, to the doctrine of some distinct and superadded being, such as the intellectual, sensitive, or vital soul of the ancients, since that would give an immortal soul to an opossum or an oyster. Nor need we resort to some being of analogous existence to the immaterial soul of the orthodox, for, if the seat of the soul be in the medullary substance, then has it all the properties of matter. On the contrary, all the mental phenomena are explicable as phenomena of the body, or attributable to the nature of the society in which we are thrown. For example, a man born and educated in Constantinople will have one set of impressions and associations, and a man with a similar arrangement of nervous apparatus, born among the Quakers of Philadelphia, will have another. All this is the result of generating causes extraneous to the system.

In this emphasis on the external or environmental, Cooper strikes a fresh note, for when he says that the intellectual faculties vary with education and with habitual difference in the stimuli applied, he is approaching the coming doctrine of plasticity. This is a valuable addition to the doctrine of homogeneity. It brings in the principle of differentiation. Granted that man is of one substance and that there is a like nature among men, how are we to account for the varieties among races? Cooper was on the verge of the new evolutionary theories. What Lamarck was doing in France, he had a chance to do in America, but it remained for another thinker of South Carolina to carry out the principles of environment to a logical conclusion. It was not Thomas Cooper but Joseph Leidy whom Charles Darwin acknowledged to have anticipated, in a measure, the principle of natural selection. That principle, as a partial resultant of materialism, we shall recur to later.

3. Benjamin Rush, and Mental Healing

In Dr. Benjamin Rush of Philadelphia we have the most notable of the American medical materialists of the eighteenth century. His reputation was due not so much to the high offices he held, such as that of physician-general of the Continental Army and professor of the institutes of medicine in the new University of Pennsylvania, as to his anticipations of modern thought. As a metaphysician he is at times weak, but as a physician he shows himself cognizant of such difficult discoveries as the cure of mental disorders by suggestion. He has been called the father of psychiatry in America. That is a true description, for his whole life was filled with speculations as to the practical application of mental medicine. These speculations began with his early work, the *Influence of Physical Causes upon the Moral Faculty*. At that time the mental faculty was considered something apart from the physical. It was a faculty which had a high office, as it never mingled with the material. Indeed, the moral sense was so sublimated that it was made almost unreal. It was an intuition, an instinct, mysterious in its movements. Rush changed all this. He showed that the moral faculty could be treated in a scientific way. It was not like a sensitive plant, acting without reflection; it was rather something subject to physical influences. This conception, of course, ran counter to current beliefs. It seemed to be a base materializing of a lofty spiritual principle. To meet this prejudice Rush attacks the problem in the form of an indirect question: Do we observe a connection between the intellectual faculties and the degrees of consistency and firmness of the brain in infancy and childhood? The same connection has been observed between the strength and the progress of the moral faculty in children. Do we observe instances of a total want of memory, imagination, and judgment, either from an original defect in the stamina of the brain, or from the influence of physical causes? The same unnatural defect has been observed, and probably from the same causes, of a moral faculty. A nervous fever may cause the loss not only of memory but of the habit of veracity. The former is called amnesia, the latter unnamed malady will compel a woman, be she even in easy circumstances, to fill her pocket secretly with bread at the table of a friend.

In this judicious parallel drawn between the physical and the psychical, we see Rush's method of approach upon the dark things of the mind. That these things were dark; that the mental operations are mysterious, the physician grants when he confesses that, in venturing on this untrodden ground, he feels like Æneas when he was about to enter the gates of Avernus, but without the Sibyl to instruct him in the mysteries before him. In order to clear up these winding subterranean ways, he throws the clear light of definition on his pages. In the case of mental derangements he begins by making a definite list of the aberrations of the mind. Thus a weakened action of the moral faculty is called micronomia, its total absence anomia. These are technical terms. They are mere names. But, beside them, Rush offers real explanations. These aberrations, he says, may be caused not only by madness and hysteria, but also by all those states of the body which are accompanied by preternatural irritability, sensibility, torpor, stupor, or mobility of the nervous system. It is vain, he continues, to attack these accompanying vices, whether of the body or of the mind, with lectures upon morality. They are only to be cured by medicine and proper treatment. Thus the young woman that lost her habit of veracity by a nervous fever, recovered this virtue as soon as her system recovered its natural tone. Furthermore, it makes no difference whether the physical causes that are to be enumerated act upon the moral faculty through the medium of the senses, the passions and memory, or the imagination. Their action is equally certain whether they act as remote, predisposing, or occasional causes. For instance, the state of the weather has an unfriendly effect upon the moral sensibility, as seen in the gloomy November fogs of England; so does extreme hunger, as in the case of the Indians of this country, who thus whet their appetite for that savage species of warfare peculiar to them. Again, the influence of association upon morals is strong. Suicide is often propagated by the newspapers and monstrous crimes by the publication of court proceedings. And as physical causes influence moral, so do they influence religious principles. Religious melancholy and madness will yield more readily to medicine than simply to polemical discourses or casuistical advice.

A treatment such as this for moral lapses must have shocked the community. Discourses upon morality had hitherto been the cure for those lapses. So it seemed to degrade these advices to say that a chief influence was that of physical causes. Rush realized that an objection would be raised from his being supposed to favor the materiality of the soul. He meets the objection by saying that he does not see that his doctrine obliges us to decide upon the question of the nature of the soul. Still he cannot help giving his own opinion as a materialist, and boldly states that matter is in its own nature as immortal as spirit.

Rush's well-known essay on the *Influence of Physical Causes upon the Moral Faculty* was followed in the last year of the century by another upon the same influences in promoting an increase of strength and activity of the intellectual faculties of man. This treatise, which was delivered as an introductory lecture to Rush's students in medicine, is a model of its kind. It is clear and intelligible; it is scientific and practical. In a happy analogy he helps out the undergraduate in grasping the mysteries of the mind. The faculties, he says, may be compared to a well-organized government: the memory and imagination to the House of Representatives, the understanding to the Senate, in which the transactions of the House of Representatives are examined, the moral faculties to the Courts of Justice, the conscience to the Court of Appeals.

At this point the Philadelphian begins his fruitful study of abnormal mentality. This study is based on the safe doctrine of the co-ordinate value of the physical and psychical. Those dreams and phantasms and supposed voices which have been superstitiously ascribed to supernatural influences, the physician now explains in a natural way. For instance, unfavorable changes discovered in diseases in the morning are often the effect occasioned by the disturbing dreams of the night before, while the pain of a surgical operation is often lessened by telling the patient that the worst part of it has been performed. A reference like the last is remarkable for that day and generation. It was the principle of suggestive anæsthesia stated some forty years before the application of material anæsthetics in America. The former principle Rush had not as yet developed, for it was now his purpose to render the general science of mind a more exact science. He disparages metaphysics as consisting only of words without ideas, of definitions of nonentities. In its place he would put the stress upon the physical science of the mind, for which he asks to be allowed to coin the word phrenology. This was another anticipation. A decade before the word was used by Europeans—the American applied it to explain dreams. For example, he stated that whatever part of the brain is affected, the dream that takes place is of that nature; different parts of the brain being allotted to the different faculties and operations of the mind. Thus, if the moral part is affected, we dream of committing crime, at the very thought of which we shudder when awake.

We shall see later how phrenology was rendered ridiculous by misuse. At this point we may only note that Rush used it in the sensible way of brain localization. His suggestions of this period were supplemented by more exact descriptions of mental derangements in some remarkable little papers on the "Different Species of Phobia and Mania." Among the former are instanced the cat-phobia, and the solo-phobia, the phobia being well defined as a fear of an imaginary evil, or an undue fear of a real one. Troubles like these may be cured, asserts the doctor. To compose and regulate the passion, there are to be found means ranging from the physical influence of music to the removal of painful associations of ideas, as when a fever, got while out gunning, was cured by removing the gun from the ill man's room. So much for the psychical side; the physical is now expanded in the statement that all operations in the mind are the effects of motions previously excited in the brain, and every idea and thought appears to depend upon a motion peculiar to itself. A statement like this might almost be counted a rough formulation of the modern theory of psycho-physical parallelism. At the least, it is a practical working hypothesis, or, as Rush puts it, a system of principles that shall lead to general success in the treatment of the diseases of the mind.

This last phrase is the title of the work which gives to Rush his chief claim to fame. In it the American alienist seeks to discover the various causes of intellectual derangements. Briefly put, these are of two classes: first, those that act directly upon the body, as malconformations and lesions of the brain; second, those that act indirectly upon the body through the medium of the mind, as intense study over the means of discovering perpetual motion, or even researches into the meaning of certain biblical prophecies. Rush next takes up the difficult subject of the derangement of the will, in which subject he is declared to have led his generation and forecasted the later work of the French school. At this time he was in touch with the Gallic speculations for the treatment of such a negative affection of the will as aboulia, or what he would call a debility or torpor, or loss of all sensibility to the stimulus of motives. This disorder may be cured in two ways: From the physical side he has been informed by his friend Brissot that animal magnetism will cure like cases; for himself he prefers the psychical remedy, what we would now call mental suggestion. In fact, he actually anticipates the modern formula of the will to believe when he states, that a palsy of the limbs has been cured by the cry of fire, and a dread of being burned. Why, he asks, should not a palsy of the will be cured in a similar manner? There is a more subtle mental disorder connected with that of the will, it is a palsy of the believing faculty. For this form of a weak mental digestion, Rush's treatment is to go back to a plain intellectual diet. If the will to believe is deficient, the remedy should consist in putting propositions of the most simple nature to the mind, and after gaining assent to them, to rise to propositions of a more difficult nature.

That the mind is capable of re-education is now seen in a negative way. Just as there are various forms of a weak will, so are there of a weak memory. There may be an oblivion of names and vocables, or of the sounds of words, but not of the letters which compose them, of the qualities or numbers of the most familiar objects, of events, time, and place. These different varieties of forgetfulness are summed up in the remarkable case of an Italian victim of yellow fever, who, in the beginning of his malady spoke only English, in the middle only French, and on the day of his death only the language of his native country. And just as there is a discontinuous memory in fevers, so there may be a continuous memory in trances. Here was a hint of the later French discoveries that by means of subconscious states it is possible to patch up the lost recollections of the normal conscience into an unbroken secondary series. To Rush the best instance of this so-called dual personality is somnambulism. Somnambulists, he asserts, recollect in each fit what they did in the preceding one. They appear to have two distinct minds, but he inquires, may this not be owing to impressions made on the other parts of the brain and excited by the same stimulus?

It is unfortunate that the Philadelphia physician did not have an opportunity to work on such interesting cases as these. He complains that such abnormal experiences are commonly considered to be supernatural and that people are averse to having them treated in a scientific way. At that time there was little field for the application of Rush's theories outside of his own private patients, with a single exception. That exception referred to what he calls his system of Christian jurisprudence, in which he tried to apply to public institutions like the Philadelphia jail the principles of a merciful mental healing. In a final passage, which anticipates by a full century the modern treatment of the criminal insane, Rush speaks thus feelingly:

It would be as absurd to inflict the punishment of death upon a fellow creature for taking away a life under a deranged state of the will, as for a surgeon to cut off an arm or a leg because in its convulsive motions it injured a toilet or overset a tea table. Now, while these morbid operations of the will may include in their consequences even theft and murder, yet they are to be considered, not as vices, but as symptoms of a disease. Therefore, for persons thus afflicted legislators should abolish the punishment of death, cropping, branding, and public whipping, and substitute for them confinement, labour, simple diet, cleanliness, and affectionate treatment. As is shown by the moral effects thus produced in the jail of Philadelphia, the reformation of criminals and the prevention of crimes can be better effected by living than by dead examples!

It is somewhat of a problem to find out why with such a good foundation for mental healing in America, the subject was not properly developed. To obtain a solution we shall have to make a drag-net of generalization. There were two schools in the country which were destined to have different opinions about the relations of mind and body. Following Rush's example, we find the Philadelphia school emphasizing the reciprocal influences of the physical and psychical. Thus, Provost Beasley of the University of Pennsylvania asserted that in every case in which there is performed an operation of the mind, there takes place, at the same time, a correspondent, correlative, and consentient operation of the body. Here was a good alliterative anticipation of the formula of psycho-physical parallelism, in which the material side of human nature is given its due. Now we can say that this just balance was owing to the influence of the English materialists Hobbes and Hartley, Darwin and Priestley, and the French materialists from Holbach to Cabanis.

Over against the Southern followers of these materialists we may put the immaterialists of New England and the North. These were the followers of Cudworth and Norris, of Berkeley and Edwards. They emphasized the principles of pure reason at the expense of the principles of physiology. They were descendants of ascetic Puritans and so attempted to live on supersensible realities. Moreover, Plato being their spiritual father, they sought to disparage the body and to cure the ills of the flesh by denying their real existence. They were so bent on cultivating the inner self, that they neglected the bodily self. Emerson himself said of this kind of transcendentalism, that it was the Saturnalia or excess of faith, wanting the restraining grace of common sense.

From this point there stretch before us two diverging lines of possible development. For reasons to be explained later, Americans did not try to strike a balance between these lines, but flew off on two tangents. One group leaned toward the materialistic side, another to the idealistic. Among the former were the mesmerists, the phrenologists, the electro-biologists. Among the latter were the spiritualists and so-called new thoughters. A rational development in the materialistic direction was blocked by an unfortunate revival of some crude theories of the olden time and the exaggerations of these theories in the form of animal magnetism. It will be recalled that old-fashioned English corporealists, like Thomas Hobbes, believed that the gap between mind and matter could be passed over by means of the animal spirits which were thought of as so many volatile gases in a retort,—subtle and invisible fluids similar to the products of the alchemist's distillation. These good old-fashioned spirits were united with the late eighteenth-century notions regarding the electric fluid, and thus was obtained a composite elastic and electric fluid. This had a twofold function. As an elastic fluid it was the medium of communication between the individual's brain and his body. As an electric fluid it could be projected beyond the limits of the individual; thus arose thought-transference, clairvoyance, and mental healing, both local and long-distance.

So far, we have merely an Anglo-American combination of Hobbism and Franklinism. This was made more potent by being rendered occult. The French came in and mesmerism aided the medical theory by means of physical affluxes and the magnetic-sympathetic system of the seventeenth and eighteenth centuries. It is strange how theories from different countries were united in the notorious movement called animal magnetism. The ball was started rolling in America by Franklin himself, although he came later to stop it. The invention of the lightning conductor stimulated the popular imagination by rendering the marvelous probable. Now there was palpable proof of the electric fluid as subtle and universally diffused and this seemed to corroborate the theory of Mesmer that there was a radiation from all things, but especially from the stars, magnets, and human bodies, of a force which could act in all things else and which was in each case directed by the indwelling spirit. This was Mesmer's theoretical postulate. His practical achievement consisted in application of these occult doctrines in the way of psycho-therapeutics. He took hold of the so-called universal radiating fluid and applied it to the sick by means of contacts and passes. When he claimed that he could effect cures irrespective of age, temperament, and sex, it can be seen how his practice became a scandal. At last Franklin had his revenge for the misuse of his scientific views. When the French king appointed royal commissioners to investigate mesmerism, the name of the American ambassador headed the list. That Franklin's common sense was outraged by the claims of the mesmerists appears from the severe language of the royal report. It concluded as follows: " The commissioners have ascertained that the animal magnetic fluid is not perceptible by any of the senses; that it has no action, either on themselves or on the patients subjected to it. They are convinced that pressure and contact effect changes which are rarely favorable to the animal system, and which injuriously affect the imagination. Finally, they have demonstrated by decisive experiments that imagination apart from magnetism produces convulsions, and that magnetism without imagination produces nothing."

The effect of these strictures upon the fate of immaterialism in America can be imagined. Franklin's name carried great weight and his countrymen so trusted him that they did not question his criticism. In a way, it is an historical calamity that in this famous report the kernel of truth was lost in the heap of rubbish. Underneath Mesmer's talk about passes and contacts and complicated apparatus of tractors there lay the true principle of suggestion, namely, that through suggestion the subject may regain his nervous stability, relieve himself of mental overtension, and so tone up the system as to hasten the process of cure.

Animal magnetism, with its good and its evil, was kept out of the country for a full generation. It came in again, not by means of legitimate practitioners, but by means of quacks and extremists. The first of these was Charles Poyen, who had been " cured mesmerically" of a nervous disorder, and in 1837 published his *Progress of Animal Magnetism in New England.* In the same year came Durant's *Exposition, or a New Theory of Animal Magnetism with a Key to the Mysteries.* In this animal magnetism is declared to be a branch of electricity, a science which gives a new life to the religious principle, creates a new method of pathological investigation, and settles therapeutics on a basis hitherto unknown to the medical world.

Finally, there came a localized form of mesmerism, Dr. Grimes's electro-biology, which started the whole tribe of Yankee magnetic healers. This is not the place to show how this exaggerated materialism was turned into a propaganda among the pious. It would lead to a long digression to explain that incredible American mixture of religion and medicine which has been noted by foreign observers. It is enough to say that we did not have the good fortune of France, where certain physicians took up the subject scientifically and developed out of the magical beliefs of Mesmer the real phenomena of hypnotism, hysteria, and suggestion. Nor have we time to more than suggest the direction of the other line of development of mental medicine. In that diverging wedge of early tendencies the immaterialistic side, the line of emphasis upon the spiritual was apparently lost. The fact was, it was only latent, for the idealistic emphasis upon the primacy of mind lay dormant in American thought. It was last seen in the works of Johnson and Edwards. It did not reappear during the course of deism, nor that of materialism. It only came to life again when the warmth of the transcendental movement reached it. In Emerson we find a constant appeal to self-reliance, to the ability of the mind to comfort itself against the adversities of life.

Self-reliance and the supremacy of the spiritual—these two tenets of Emerson suffice to explain the revival of immaterialistic mental healing in our day. Just as the earlier idealism of colonial times was thwarted in its growth by such events as the war of independence and the conquests of the English colonies, so the idealism of the nineteenth century was thwarted by another war, and a further conquest of the continent. But the longing of the native mind for the supersensible; the true mystic conviction that spirit can conquer matter—if that be considered as dull, dead, inert—that conviction never died. It has again come to life and we have an immaterialism of the present day with works which range in value from Hudson's *Laws of Psychic Phenomena* to William James's *Energies of Men* and the *Will to Believe*.

We have left the two lines of mental healing in America at their widest point of divergence. On the one hand there was the extreme materialistic view which emphasized the bodily function. On the other hand, there is the current emphasis on the psychical. At present the prevailing tendency is to appeal to supernumerary powers of the mind such as the subconscious. This is the side taken up by the laity and one in which the regular medical profession takes comparatively slight interest. For a just development of the two sides, the lines must be drawn nearer together. It is desirable that in our medical schools we should return to the practice of Dr. Rush of a century and a half ago, which means that a student should be required to study psychology in connection with physiology. This would seem to promise a correction of extravagances and to lead back to the old principle of the Philadelphia school, that there is a co-ordinate value in the study of mind and body.

CHAPTER V

REALISM

1. The Scottish Influences

NATURAL realism, according to an early American exponent, consists in the doctrine that the mind perceives not merely the ideas or images of external objects but the external objects themselves. In short, the distinguishing mark of such metaphysics is an appeal from the delusive principles of the idealism of Berkeley and the skepticism of Hume to the common sense of mankind as a tribunal paramount to all the subtleties of philosophy. This is the definition of Samuel Miller, the Princeton historian of the eighteenth century, in his exposition of the system of Reid. It may be supplemented by a defense of President McCosh, the pupil of Hamilton, two generations later. Realism, says the latter, is that system which holds that there are real things and that man can know them; that we have no need to resort to such theories as those of internal ideas or occasional causes coming between the perceiving mind and the perceived objects; but that the mind knows directly and intuitively three kinds of reality: first, matter, whether existing in the body or out of the body as external, extended, and resisting; second, the perceiving self as thinking or willing, a reality as certain and definite as matter, but perceived by self-consciousness and not the external senses; third, the objects perceived by our conscience or moral perception, the higher knowledge of voluntary acts as being morally good or evil.

Such is that natural realism which has been claimed to be *the* American philosophy. This claim is true if one considers realism's rapid growth, its wide spread, and its tenacious hold upon the popular mind. Brought in as a transatlantic offshoot of the Scotch school, it overran the country, and had an exclusive and preponderant influence well beyond the centennial of the country's independence. For this astonishing success several reasons have been given: not only was the common sense philosophy of Reid, Stewart, Brown, and Hamilton in harmony with the practical note of the country, but it was also an aid to faith, a safeguard to morality as against the skepticism of Hume and the atheism of the Voltairians.

But there are further reasons, which may be considered from two points of view: internally as intrinsic excellences; externally as adventitious aids. Looked at from within, natural realism is claimed to possess a unity not only in the circumstances that its expounders have been Scotchmen but also in its method, its doctrine, and its spirit. Its method is that of observation and induction, and not of analysis and deduction, which explains phenomena by mere assumed principles. Its doctrine is that of self-consciousness as the instrument of observation, and not the mere observation of the brain or nerves which tends to neglect our inward experience. Its spirit is that of common sense, which, by direct awareness and not by a chain of reasoning, reaches principles which are natural, original, and necessary. We shall have to consider later if these points are really excellences.

At first sight natural realism makes a false simplification like a child's picture of a man, and the adult realist's mind seems to work more easily than that of the child once portrayed by the idealist. Without looking further from within we must now consider the matter from without. Besides intrinsic excellences there were adventitious aids which contributed to the success of the movement. First, it happened to fit the needs of educational and ecclesiastical orthodoxy. It was not, as in Scotland, favored by the union of church and state, but by the peculiar American combination of church and college. Here not only was the philosophy of reality convenient, compact, and teachable, appealing to a common sense of which every youngster had some spark, but it was also an eminently safe philosophy which kept undergraduates locked in so many intellectual dormitories, safe from the dark speculations of materialism and the beguiling allurements of idealism. Or, as the details have been given by another, Hobbes, because of his atomism, was considered a guide to atheism; Hume, because of his skepticism, the arch-enemy of orthodoxy, while Berkeley was always suspected to be a leader in the same direction. Therefore, to prevent the undermining of the faith, college professors took philosophy seriously and not speculatively, and a religious bias helped to determine the hold of realism in education.

A second cause for the success of realism lay in the organizations upon which it chanced to fasten. In its propaganda it used most of the denominational colleges on the Atlantic seaboard, and was also backed by the denominations themselves. Here the churches, like well-constructed machines, turned out uniform sets of opinions all fitting the same mold of common sense; to obtain many men of one mind, the Protestant clergy of these times were practically all formed from the Scotch pattern, the text-books of Reid and Stewart, Beattie and Hamilton coming from the native press in an almost unbroken series of editions. A third cause of the success of realism was the character of the immigration into the country. Between the New Englanders and their modified Calvinism, and the Southerners with their diluted Arminianism, there came a wave of new settlers, which on touching the American shore spread itself more widely than any other. The Scotch-Irish, entering chiefly by way of the ports of the Middle States, carried along with their Presbyterian connections their philosophy of common sense. To trace this movement into the Alleghany Mountains and down the valleys of Virginia and of the Cumberland, is to trace a kind of intellectual glacier, an overwhelming mass of cold dogma which moved slowly southwards and ground out all opposition. This glacial age in American thought was of the greatest significance. Because of it deism disappeared, save in the tide-water counties where planters of English blood still remained, and materialism was wiped out, save in the Gallicized portions of the country, such as the Carolinas, and the Bourbon sections of Kentucky.

That the union of church and college was a fortuitous aid to the spread of realism is clear from the fate of its rivals. Deism lacked new blood because English pioneers of the cultured class had ceased coming to the country. Idealism languished because its special means of communication, the Anglican church, was practically a channel cut off; few scholars of Oxford and Cambridge, no ecclesiastic of the type of Berkeley came into the country after the second war with England. But it was materialism that suffered most for want of those auxili-

aries under which realism flourished. As compared with
realism the contrast is striking. Immigration did not
help it, and sparks struck out by men like Priestley and
Cooper were a mere flash in the pan. Nor were the
colleges of much avail; the University of Pennsylvania
by political mismanagement, Transylvania by its poverty
and remoteness, and the University of Virginia by political complications, were together rendered inoperative as
aids to materialism. Even if Jefferson's late conversion
from materialism to realism had been known, his political
affiliations would have damaged him in the sight of the
orthodox. Thus, by way of contrast, the elder President Dwight of Yale had more weight in the scales of
orthodox philosophy than the President of the United
States himself; the one standing for respectable federal-
ism, the other for infidel democracy. But the lack of
efficient organization was the great drawback to the
materialistic cause. Had Jefferson succeeded in founding his central society after the model of the French
Academy, had there been anything approaching the
Royal Society of England in the whole land, scientific
investigations like those of Colden and of Rush might
have received the stamp of institutional approval.

If these are mere conjectures as to what might have
happened, what did really happen was that materialism,
left to itself as a mere speculative movement, practically
disappeared from the field of thought, and that a rival
movement which was backed up by a strong organization, a rigid faith, and well-trained agents, with all its
faults, inconsistencies, contradictions, and superficiali-
ties, remained as the dominant force in the field. Such
a force was Scottish realism, which held the Atlantic
States as a private preserve and Princeton College as
its hunting lodge.

2. THE PRINCETON SCHOOL

Traditionally Princeton is committed to a realistic metaphysics as opposed to agnosticism, materialism, or idealism. This is the opinion of one of its historians at the one hundred and fiftieth anniversary of the founding of the institution. The opinion is that of one who takes pride in an air-tight system; yet it has the advantage of summing up the early history of the college as it passed through successive reactions to the current phases of speculation. First, it was opposed to the agnosticism of extreme deism, considering the age of reason as little else but the age of infidelity; next, it was opposed to materialism, whether that meant a no-soul psychology as with Buchanan, or a reduction of psychology to a psychology of the nerves as with Cooper, or an identification of body and mind as with Priestley. Lastly, it was opposed to idealism in all its forms. In place of the mediate perception of Berkeley, Hume, and Kant, the Scotch intuition puts immediate perception, a direct knowledge of real qualities in things. In brief, the Princeton system was a complete dualism: in its cosmology, between the world and deity; in its psychology, between soul and body; in its epistemology, between subject and object.

The advantage of such a dualism was the avoidance of the difficulty of trying to think things together. Now this accommodation of its teaching to the general intelligence led realists like McCosh to claim that such a natural realism as was taught at Princeton was what an American philosophy should be. The claim may be disputed, yet it has in its favor the fact that the College of New Jersey, from its very foundation, had impressed upon it a national character, inasmuch as it was not the college of an established church, nor of a single colony, nor of a people sprung from a single nationality, but had for its charter an undenominational document, for its heads graduates of Harvard and Yale, Glasgow and Edinburgh, and for its students the sons of English Friends, New England Puritans, and Presbyterians from Scotland and Ireland. But although in this connection it be granted that Princeton was the freest college in the country in its beginnings, it was hardly so in its development. A fatal polemic spirit seized hold of it, and as the institution passed through three external stages, corresponding to the three speculative movements of the age, it grew more and more restricted and unreceptive.

During the Revolutionary War Nassau Hall was a refuge for the military, but not for the intellectuals; it received Washington and his forces, but shut out the stray followers of Locke, Berkeley, Hume, Hartley, and Darwin. In a word, the college which had been a defense of the faith against the attacks of the deists became what one of the defenders of natural realism has called a bulwark of impregnable truth before which all forms of error and irreligion must give way. To explain this state of affairs a parallel may be drawn. As Princeton, situated on the highway between New York and Philadelphia, was a critical battleground between the British and the Americans, so it became a position of strategic importance between the idealists of the North and the materialists of the South. But in the latter case, the victory over the opposing forces was gained only at considerable expense, the loss of a certain spirit of liberality, due to the replacement of speculation by dogma, of philosophy by theology. Starting as a non-ecclesiastical body, formed by the broader men of the synod of New York, a Presbyterian form of belief came in with Witherspoon, increased with Stanhope Smith, until with the appearance of Ashbel Green in 1812, the theological seminary so dominated the college, that the two were persistently identified up to the very sesquicentennial of the University.

All this may serve to explain the Princetonian claim that it was the Scottish-American realism, and not New England transcendentalism, that was to be considered, in largest measure, the peculiar philosophy of the country. Nevertheless, for the settling of these alternatives, one might ask which of the two systems better fulfilled the criteria of native origin, of progressiveness, of liberality of spirit, and of toleration of other forms of thought. The question is a large one and answerable only after one has gained the proper historical data, data which are in turn furnished only by a consideration of the personal representatives of natural realism.

In its early days Nassau Hall went through a period of unthinking placidity. But with the advent of President Witherspoon in 1768, the philosophical situation became as agitated as was the political, for now English deism vanished, an American form of idealism was driven forth, and Scotch realism became the official system of the place. In short, the era of deduction and design was succeeded by the era of induction and common sense, or as the new college head phrased the matter —it is safer in our reasonings to trace facts upwards than to reason downwards.

The accounts of the personality of Witherspoon vary. A recent biographer describes him as a man of extraordinary force, versatility, and charm; eminent as a teacher, preacher, politician, law-maker, and philosopher, and with the exception of Washington, as having more

of the quality called presence than, perhaps, any other
man of his time in America. On the other hand,
Thomas Carlyle said that he was of a disagreeable
temper; Jonathan Odell satirized him as " fierce as the
fiercest, foremost of the first "; John Adams declared
him clear but a little heavy in his speech; and President
Stiles of Yale shrewdly remarked that while the doctor was of a reasoning make, his philosophical learning
was not great. In truth Witherspoon was a man of
action rather than reflection. As a further hindrance to
free speculation he had entered the country with his
mind somewhat rigidly made up, and at the age of five-
and-forty possessed ideas more conservative than those of
his predecessors. The former heads of the college,
graduates of Harvard and Yale, had been open to the
influences of the earlier optimistic deism; they had
argued in favor of this being the best possible world;
they had looked on the workings of nature with such
admiring eyes as to be well-nigh ready to grant it self-
sufficiency. But to the lineal descendant of John Knox
the external world bore a different aspect; in itself it
was far from being perfect or self-sufficient; rather it
was a created thing, a limited thing, a thing full of
defects.

Moreover, for those who have great charity for atheists and deists, Witherspoon draws up, in obvious parody
of the Anglicans, what he denominates his Athenian
Creed:

I believe in the beauty and comely proportions of Dame
Nature, and in almighty Fate, her parent and guardian. . . .
I believe that the universe is a huge machine, wound up from
everlasting by necessity, and consisting of an infinite number
of links and chains, each in a progressive motion towards the
zenith of perfection and meridian of glory; that I myself am

a little glorious piece of clockwork, a wheel within a wheel, or rather a pendulum in this grand machine swinging hither and thither by the different impulses of fate and destiny; that my soul (if I have any) is an imperceptible bundle of exceeding minute corpuscles, much smaller than the smallest Holland sand. . . . I believe that there is no ill in the universe, nor any such thing as virtue, absolutely considered; that these things, vulgarly called sins, are only errors in judgment, and foils to set off the beauty of nature, or patches to adorn her face.

Harassed by the host of enemies raised by this anonymous satire of his, Witherspoon accepted the repeated offer of the presidency of the New Jersey College, which was pressed upon him by Benjamin Rush, then a student of medicine at Edinburgh, and journeyed to America, where he was received as if he were the very prince after whom the college was named. But his duties at Princeton were not easy. In teaching alone, in addition to a course in moral philosophy, he included lectures to the juniors and seniors upon chronology and history, composition and criticism, Hebrew and French. Then, too, speculative troubles stared him in the face; on his arrival he found that the Irish idealism had obtained a footing in the locality. According to the later account of President Ashbel Green, the Berkeleian system of metaphysics was in repute in the college when Witherspoon entered. The tutors were zealous believers in it and waited for the president with some expectation of either confounding him or making him a proselyte. They had mistaken their man. He first reasoned against the system, and then ridiculed it till he drove it out of the college. The writer has heard him state that before Reid or any other author of their views had published any theory on the ideal system, he wrote against it, and suggested the same trains of thought which they adopted, and that he published his essay in a Scotch magazine. This essay has at last been discovered, yet an extract from it will show that it was but a dubious refutation of Berkeleianism. According to Witherspoon we never hear of a deceitful sound, a deceitful smell, or a deceitful taste; but only, that the objects we see are not in all respects the same as we may imagine them upon the first inspection. A square tower at a distance appears to be round; the body of the sun seems to have but two feet diameter; objects in the same line, though at different distances, appear to be contiguous; what does this imply, more than that an accurate discovery of the bulk, figure, and distance of bodies, cannot, and was never intended to be made from sight alone? It is very probable, from the manner in which children view objects at first, that they appear to them all in a plain, or rather that the image makes a sensible impression on the retina of the eye, that it is by experience they learn to place them at different distances, and by the connection of ideas that they have an immediate perception of the distance when the image strikes them. Perhaps it may be objected, that color, which is allowed to be the proper object of sight, and of sight alone, is not in the object, and yet is supposed in it. I answer, it is as much in the object as other secondary qualities are. The object hath not our sensation, but a power to produce it; and there is a real difference in the object to make it of a different color, viz., a peculiar disposition of its parts to reflect only rays of such or such a kind. Upon the whole, it is nothing else, but the very excellence of the sense of sight, or its great serviceableness to us in more respects than its immediate office, that gives occasion or any plausibility to its being charged with delusion.

All that the critic offers in support of this strange compound opinion, is an argument from analogy, that there are delusive or deceitful perceptions conveyed to us by our senses in the natural world, that the representations of objects and their qualities differ from what philosophy discovers them to be. Of this he gives one particular instance, from the objects of sight, that a surface appears smooth and uniform, whereas it is rough and uneven when examined with a microscope. He then observes in general, that it is now universally admitted, that the qualities called secondary which we by natural instinct attribute to matter, belong not to matter, nor exist really without us; that color is not in the object, etc. Now, an analogical argument cannot be more effectually destroyed than by showing the falsehood of the fact upon which it is founded. '' I affirm, therefore,'' concludes Witherspoon, '' that the observation he makes, and takes for granted, is not just; but that the ideas we receive by our senses, and the persuasions we derive immediately from them, are exactly according to truth, to real truth, which certainly ought to be the same with philosophic truth.''

We shall return to Witherspoon's fight against the American form of idealism. Meanwhile in his *Lectures on Moral Philosophy* he had the distinction of being the first college head in the country to set forth in his classroom a definite system of ethics. This system, as Lansing Collins, the editor of the recent reprint of the *Lectures*, has said, was the realism of Thomas Reid and the Scottish common-sense school, a philosophy not unknown in Princeton before Witherspoon came, and one which by the labors of the next twenty-five years he was to firmly intrench in the congenial soil of the New World. To prove the Scotch school right Witherspoon would prove that the other schools are wrong. He explains that in opposition to such infidel writers as David Hume, who sought to shake the certainty of our belief upon cause and effect, upon personal identity, and the idea of power, some writers have advanced, with great apparent reason, that there are certain first principles or dictates of common sense, which are either first principles, or principles seen with intuitive evidence. These are the foundations of all reasoning, and without them to reason is a word without a meaning. They can no more be proved than you can prove an axiom in mathematical science. These authors of Scotland have lately produced and supported this opinion, to resolve at once all the refinements and metaphysical objections of some infidel writers.

Witherspoon's method of attack sheds light on the most interesting philosophical event of his administration at the College of New Jersey. That event was his successful attack on idealism. A single tutor, Joseph Periam, had been the unhappy vehicle for the Berkeleian metaphysics, and Stanhope Smith, the president's own son-in-law and successor in office, had become infected with the taint of what was described as that impious skepticism which wholly denies the existence of matter. According to one version, Periam, soon after his graduation in 1762, embraced the bishop's theory denying the existence of the material universe, and Smith, who was intimate with him, was thereby in great danger of making shipwreck of his religious principles. Of the precise manner in which immaterialism was introduced into Nassau Hall we have no record. It is very unlikely that Samuel Johnson's Berkeleian *Elements of Philosophy* was used there, as it was in the Philadelphia Academy, for Johnson, as head of the Episcopalian King's College in New York, had called the rival Presbyterian College of New Jersey a fountain of nonsense.

Nor did the other colonial idealist leave behind him any trace of his peculiar mystical theory of knowledge. Jonathan Edwards lived too short a time as president of Princeton to affect the college directly. So we are forced to seek a roundabout way by which idealism may have filtered in. There is record of one Ebenezer Bradford, a Connecticut student and a subsequent advocate of the Northern immaterialism, who wrote to Dr. Bellamy, one of the later Edwardeans, the following ingenuous tale: " Dr. Witherspoon was a great enemy to what they call the Eastward or New Divinity, which was so much exploded by all in college that when I came here I was advised by a particular friend not to let my sentiments be known by any means, alleging it would be of great disservice to me. I found two or three, however, who dared to think for themselves, and we agreed to promote what we judged to be truth in as private and hidden manner as possible. We ventured to read some of your books with the title pages cut out, which were much admired by those who professed themselves enemies to the New Divinity."

By whatever devious path idealism worked its way into Princeton, it is tolerably clear, from this naïve account, that Witherspoon was a high conservative, preferring above all things what the narrator terms " notions which appear greatly confined." The result of this bias was practically seen in the career of Periam, who, from being a " very ingenious young man," became " a very serious man." But before this change of mind had occurred, Princeton's earliest idealist had influenced a person of much greater importance than himself.

Samuel Stanhope Smith, the son of an Irish Presbyterian divine, and in turn student, tutor, professor of moral philosophy, and president, coming to the college at the age of sixteen, before President-Elect Witherspoon had arrived from Scotland, was consigned more especially to the care of tutor Periam. Now, Periam, continues Smith's biographer, had not confined himself to the study of mathematics, but had extended his inquiries to metaphysics also, and become infected with the fanciful doctrine of Bishop Berkeley, which consists, as is generally known, in denying the existence of a material universe, and converting every object of the senses into a train of fugitive perceptions. How this professor, who had been habituated to the hardy pursuits of mathematical science and the inductive philosophy, could ever have brought himself to embrace such a visionary theory, a theory so repugnant to common sense, and rather an object of ridicule than of serious consideration, it is difficult to explain, unless it be upon the principle that, having been accustomed to require the most conclusive proof of everything before he assented to its truth, he so far misconceived the subject as to imagine that he must have arguments drawn from reason, to convince him of the existence of an exterior world, before he would admit the reality of it; and this surely is an evidence which Nature would deny him, as she rests the proof of it solely and entirely upon the simple testimony of the senses. However this may have been, Periam had address and ingenuity enough to infuse the principles of the Bishop of Cloyne into the mind of Smith, and he began seriously to doubt whether there were in the world such real existences as the sun, moon, and stars; rivers, mountains, and human beings.

In this ponderous account we catch the unsympathetic tone of realism toward idealism. To convert the pervert back to the true faith the method of vilification is now used. The account runs how, upon the arrival of Dr. Witherspoon, the poor undergraduate, captivated by the specious fallacies of the Bishop of Cloyne, held in bondage by the silken chains of a fantastic theory, was conducted out of the dark labyrinth into which he had been betrayed, and from the cloudy speculations of immaterialism brought back to the clear light of common sense.

Stanhope Smith being the first graduate of the college to become its head, Princeton was now subject to a sort of intellectual inbreeding. By this the strain of realism tended to become fixed. This is discovered in the writings of the next representative of the Princeton school. In his *Retrospect of the Eighteenth Century,* Samuel Miller informs his readers that the writers of the common-sense school have contributed the most important accessions which the philosophy of mind has received since the time of Locke. Their first service was to cease the senseless prattling about occult terms; their next in observing the skeptical conclusions which Berkeley had drawn from the old theory of perception when he contended that all the varied beauties of creation which we behold are nothing more than fancy or images impressed on the mind.

Here is a triple misinterpretation. It was not the realists but the immaterialists who earliest attacked occult terms such as material " substance." Again, Berkeley did not use the old theory of perception, but put in its place a new theory of vision. Finally, the good bishop did not draw skeptical conclusions in making what are usually called material objects " mere fancies, and not in accordance with the lawful language of signs "; rather did he teach a spiritual realism, in which the objects of sense are so many alluring words of a divine visual language.

Miller's *Retrospect* was called in irony the funeral discourse of the eighteenth century. From this it might easily be inferred what system he would next consign to the philosophic potter's field. It was materialism. Its principles he supposes many superficial thinkers have been seduced into adopting by the plausible aspect which it wears. Its object is to reduce all the energies of intellectual and animal life to the operation of an invisible fluid secreted by the brain, and existing in every part of the body. But does this fluid exist? If so, it explains nothing; the whole business of causation is as much in the dark as ever, even after all the parade of development through contractions, fibrous motions, and appetencies. Indeed, the sensorial power, as applied to explain the phenomena of mind, too much resembles the occult qualities, the phantasms, and the essential forms of the schoolmen; for when using the word idea sometimes to signify the fibrous motion and sometimes the sensorial, it signifies both the cause and the effect.

This is unjust. Most of the materialists in the land did not pretend to explain the nature of causation, but only to describe things caused. All they claimed was that nervous contractions and fibrous motions were not the efficients but merely the occasions of the accompanying mental phenomena. They only stated that the physical and the psychical occurred side by side and thus anticipated, in large measure, the modern doctrine of parallelism. But Miller cannot see the new trail which was destined to open the way for the future experimental psychology. Instead he concludes his work with the pessimistic remark that if the physical sciences have received great improvement during the century under consideration, it is feared that the same cannot with truth be said respecting the science of the human mind; in this wide field, new experiences and discoveries, in the proper sense of the word, can have no place. By such a denial the Princeton historian went far to impair the claim that realism was to be the coming philosophy of America, for such a denial ran counter to the inventive genius of his countrymen, cast reflections on such psychological experiments as were framed by Rush, and perhaps thereby prevented the rise of a school of experimentalists among such Princetonians, for example, as the electrician Joseph Henry. But fancies aside, the facts are that the spirit of common sense left little to the imagination, desired no novel inventions, but preferred to keep its adherents revolving in the treadmill of traditional thought. In fine, the policy of the New Jersey College was to turn out safe minds content to mark time in the old way.

3. THE LESSER REALISTS

With the lesser realists we foresee the breaking up of the old system. Thus Frederick Beasley recalled how in the College of Princeton the fanciful theory of Bishop Berkeley, as a kind of philosophical day-dream, was superseded by the Scottish school, but that these men had done their predecessors very great injustice. Against these misinterpreters Beasley now proceeds to raise against his adversaries what he calls the literary tomahawk. He does this with such cruel effect as to lay bare the skulls of his enemies and to discover to the world brain capacities not so large as had been presumed. The propensity of the Scots, he exclaims, is to cavil at the doctrines of preceding philosophers, especially Berkeley's new theory of vision and his theory of the visual language. Yet these two theories may be upheld by two concrete cases. There is the case of a woman in Pennsylvania who, having cataracts removed from both her eyes, declared that her sensations were indescribably delightful, but, at the same time, her newly recovered power of vision was for some time of very little use to her; she was perpetually stretching out her hands for fear of running against objects, being unable to distinguish their distances or magnitudes. Again he illustrates the justness of the observation, that in all our acquired perceptions we proceed according to the interpretation of signs, and whenever the sign of anything is presented, the mind naturally concludes that the thing signified is present. A gentleman passing along the streets of Philadelphia imagines that he perceives a steamboat in the Delaware at a distance, but upon approaching it, finds that he was deceived, for that the object he saw was a sign-post before an inn, upon which the representation of a steamboat was rudely painted.

We have here the subjective principle of interpretation brought against the Scottish common sense with its absolute and universal principles. Another instance of a similar sort is found in the doctrine of relativity, of a personal as against a public standard, as propounded by another of the lesser realists, Charles Nisbet. He explains that the old saying of Heracleitus— that a man cannot go into the same river twice—applies to the mental life. Every person may be said to have a certain relative measure of that which is peculiar to himself and suited to his own feelings, so that a lecture in philosophy may seem as long as a game of cards, though the latter be actually three times longer. Nevertheless, when we are attentive to our own thoughts we discover a sort of pomp or procession of ideas which succeed one another in our minds with a regular pace or march, and this regularity could not exist unless we had a common measure without ourselves, a means whereby mankind can agree with each other with respect to the length of determinate things.

We could multiply instances of the lesser lights who discovered breaks in the system of common sense, but such men were not wanted and remained ignored. So it is that in reviewing the triumphant course of natural realism we get the illusion of unbroken ranks of believers, from the early Princeton leaders to the later Northern representatives. Throughout there was apparent agreement, from the official heads in the colleges to the popular exponents who held that Reid had said the last safe word in philosophy and that Kant opened up the abysses of skepticism.

With the rise of New England transcendentalism there came a life and death struggle between the old and the new. We have previously raised the question which system was destined to be *the* American philosophy. We can now suggest an answer. Which of the two forms of thought best fulfilled the requisite of native origin, of progressiveness, of liberality of spirit, and of toleration of other forms of thought? In regard to natural realism, it may be said that as it was foreign in its origin, so it remained an exotic in its characteristics, lacking those qualities on which the men of the New World prided themselves. First, it was unprogressive, being rightly accused of failure to advance; thus the two principal definitions of the movement, although seventy years apart, were in substance essentially the same. Again, it was illiberal towards unrestrained inquiry; being op-

posed to the speculative ferment of Hume and the free
critical methods of Kant, it was rationalistic, but only
within the limits fixed by respectability. Lastly, it was
intolerant of other systems; as it fought the European
forms of deism, idealism, and naturalism of the eighteenth century, so it came to look askance upon the French
positivism, the German idealism, and the British evolutionary doctrines of the nineteenth. These are the
shortcomings of realism, but, inasmuch as its aim was to
be a safe and sound philosophy, they are to be considered not as fundamental deficiencies but only as the
defects of its qualities. In marked contrast, however,
to the Scottish realism was the New England transcendentalism, whose characteristics were the direct opposite of its chief rival. Instead of being a foreign
importation brought over in the original form, it was
essentially a native growth deeply rooted in its age and
surroundings. Historic forces were visible in it, but
these had been so assimilated that they appeared not so
much initial impulses as remote resultants. Hence
transcendentalism possessed the typical marks of the
receptive American mind. First it was progressive;
starting with the Platonism latent in Puritanism, it
drew nourishment in turn from the Berkeleian, Kantian,
and Hegelian idealism. Again it was liberal; instead
of opposing the spirit of free inquiry, it exhibited a
generous interest in regard to other systems, translating not merely the philosophical classics of France and
Germany but, as in the case of Emerson, seeking inspiration from the sacred books of the East. This
lenient attitude towards an unrestricted immigration of
foreign thought brought about the last and most obvious
characteristic of transcendentalism, its utter tolerance
of other systems. Thus it took from the Puritans their

individualism, from the deists their arguments for design, from the idealists their phenomenalism, from the materialists their dynamic conception of the universe, from the realists themselves their doctrine of immediate intuition. This may be considered such an extreme eclecticism as not to deserve the name of a system; it may nevertheless be said in conclusion that whether or not transcendentalism was the coming philosophy of America, it at least furnished a native epitome of American philosophy as it was developed in its early schools.

CHAPTER VI

TRANSCENDENTALISM

1. EMERSON, INTERPRETER OF NATURE

THERE is an inscription on an old wall of Revolutionary days, that, ruined by the war, it was rebuilt more strongly out of the old materials. This, in a figure, explains the beginnings of transcendentalism in America. After the dark and sterile period in our philosophy, the movement in New England suddenly gathered up the forces of the previous times. Transcendentalism summed up in itself the marks of all three centuries,—the faith of the seventeenth, the reason of the eighteenth, the feeling of the nineteenth. As we may recall, the age of unreason, or dependency on inscrutable decrees, had been succeeded by that of reason, or the power of man fully to understand nature, and that in turn by the age of sentiment,—the outpouring of the romantic spirit. It remained for one man to fuse these three factors into a system. Emerson believed in faith in self, or self-reliance; he believed in reason in nature, for nature was the present expositor of the divine mind; he believed in feeling toward his fellow-men, for he looked on man as a façade of a temple, "wherein all wisdom and all good abide."

This fusion of the spirit of three centuries brought a new note into philosophy. No longer was man alone worshiped as admirable; no longer was nature considered as self-sufficient, but the two were counted complementary. Therefore transcendentalism may be looked at from a double aspect; practically, as an assertion of the inalienable worth of man; theoretically, as an assertion of the immanence of the divinity, not only in nature, but in human nature: "There is one mind, and all the powers and privileges which lie in any lie in all."

Whence arose this more ardent interpretation? How were the old ideas transfused by emotion? How was it that the worship of nature and of human nature were thus intimately conjoined? The answer may be put in a word. These changes are due to a reaction, a revulsion against intellect as the sole source of truth. Sensibility and will now demanded their share. Men wanted to be warmed, to be inspired to do something. For these positive needs there had been a long negative preparation. That the Northern transcendentalism was such a close union of thought and feeling was due to the fact that for two centuries New England had been emotionally starved. The echoes of the Elizabethan age had long since died away. The fervor and color of a richer civilization had disappeared. In philosophy, no system between 1600 and 1800 had offered a satisfactory blending. There were three alternatives, no one of which was adequate: Calvinism had degenerated into superstition; deism, with the cold, dry light of reason, had killed enthusiasm; realism had brought all down to the common level of common sense.

At the beginning of the new century, then, there was a felt need for a larger life; the most thoughtful had been so long frozen in their feelings that they waited eagerly for warmer currents of thought. The younger generation in college had to find emotional stimulus outside of the curriculum. The change that came about was, briefly, a return to nature. The rationalism of that day was like a formal English garden with its straight walks and clipped hedges. Transcendentalism was like the American fields and forests with their broad acres and their tangled wildernesses. A new race of thinkers thus arises. The closet philosopher is succeeded by the transcendental traveler, ever in the air and face to face with the sun. He is willing to wander far in search of spiritual nourishment; he seeks for the fruits of nature by his own efforts and thereby engenders an appetite for those fruits. Thus comes the keenness of the younger spirits in the new movement. They are eager to transcend the trammels of society, to go apart by themselves, to live in the woods, in order to penetrate the secrets of nature, to learn the mind of outdoors.

Having considered the negative preparation of previous movements and the positive incitements of the country that lay about them, we may take up the fundamental beliefs of New England transcendentalists. The first of their beliefs was monism, which meant not only the unity of the world in God, but the immanence of God in the world. On the one hand, nature is the expositor of the divine mind; on the other, man is the soul of the whole, of the Eternal One. A second belief is that of the microcosm,—because of the indwelling of divinity, every part of the world, however small, is held to contain within itself all the laws and meaning of the universe:—Man is conscious of a universal soul within his individual life, he is an analogist and studies relations in all objects; placed in the center of beings, a ray of relation passes from every other being to him. A third belief is that of the macrocosm, which holds that the soul of each individual is identical with the soul of the world and contains latently all which it contains:—Man is a universal mirror; every rational creature is entitled to partake of the soul of the world by his constitution. A final belief is that of symbolism. The transcendentalist holds that nature is the embodiment of spirit in the world of sense; nature is a great picture to be appreciated, a great book to be read. As Emerson expresses it, there is radical correspondence between visible things and human thoughts. . . . What was it that nature would say? Was there no meaning in the live repose of the valley behind the mill? The leafless trees and every withered stem and stubble, rimed with frost, contributed something to the mute music. . . . This is the symbolism through which the poetic pantheist finds a higher use in the study of nature. Nature, he ever insists, is the incarnation, not only of the true and beautiful, but of the good. Through it, the individual comes in contact with the very spirit and being of God. . . . Taking the old figure, that the visible world and the relation of its parts is the dial plate of the invisible, he adds that the universe becomes transparent and the light of higher laws than its own shines through it.

It is in his love of nature and in his ability to read the meaning of its symbols that Emerson showed himself a native representative of the romantic movement. Fond of the fields and a wanderer in the woods, he had known nature in all its moods, and had learned the feeling of kinship between man and the world in which he lives. Indeed his first written confession was that in the wilderness there is something dear and connate. Words such as these furnish the prime bond of connection between native thought and that of Europe. In holding that nature and human nature are akin, Emerson is in harmony with the English romantic movement of his day. In reading Wordsworth he declares that

The Excursion awakens in every lover of nature the right feeling. We saw stars shine, we felt the awe of mountains, we heard the rustle of wind in the grass, and knew again the ineffable secret of solitude. . . . Does a declaration of this sort mean that the American was unoriginal? Such a conclusion can hardly be drawn from the passage, for Emerson speaks as one who already had experienced the feelings of a lover of nature, already known its ineffable secret. We may, therefore, hold that the early New England transcendentalists were of like spirit with Wordsworth and Coleridge, but did not use them so much for authorities, as for corroborators of their kindred beliefs. They did not borrow, they sympathized, and that because they had already been under common influences.

Of these influences the earliest had been the French. In America as in England the turmoil of the great revolution had stirred men's minds, for the mental unrest which followed was an outgrowth of the old liberty of philosophizing. Upon the ancient stock of English independency there was grafted the vigorous branch of French liberty. In New England there had been an unbroken expression of the rights of individual judgment. Those Independents who came from the eastern counties of England, once settled by the roving Danes, held that every man had a full right to his own beliefs. But more fervent expressions of these beliefs and their junction with the emotions of the heart now took a French form. The spirit of liberty was English, but warmth and ardor were brought to the cool Anglo-American by his Gallic brothers. The rights of man were no longer to be expressed merely in public documents, in measured terms, but each man was to follow his own private inclinations, to break down the trammels of society, to rely upon himself. Seldom before had individualism reached such heights. Indeed by a sort of paradox it led to a degree of detachment that was at times indifference. The transcendentalist had so freed himself from tradition that he at once broke from sectarianism.

In the case of Emerson, the break came first in religion. As an individualist, he felt a lack of interest in the dogma of his denomination. He publicly expressed his opinion, that the Christian scheme no longer interested him. In the words of an English critic, he left his church with a yawn.

The refusal to be tied by tradition may also be laid to the influence of developed deism. Non-sectarianism was an heritage of the old belief that all religions are but parts of one great religion, the religion of nature. It made no difference to the transcendentalist whence he drew his inspiration, provided there was inspiration. A marked aspect of our day, observed Bronson Alcott, is its recovery and recognition of past times and great names. The same thought was expressed by Emerson, in an early number of the *Dial*, when he asserted: We have every day occasion to remark transcendentalism's perfect identity, under whatever new phraseology or application to new facts, with the liberal thought of all men of a religious and contemplative habit in other times and countries.

The transcendentalist as a cosmopolite is a strange figure. He has been commonly represented as priding himself on being a point around which all thought revolves, and has led the scornful to infer from this, that he was a vanishing point. But his conceit was really not based upon mere egotism, but upon a broad knowledge and a remarkable range of reading. It is seldom remembered that by the time Emerson published his first volume, *Nature,* in 1836, he had traveled in Europe; had known many cities and many men, and had read widely of other days and other climes. He had been considered an eclectic philosopher; he should rather be called an ethnic philosopher. He casually puts Jesus and Socrates on the same level and then goes on to quote Coleridge and Spinoza, Plato and Plotinus, Zoroaster and the Hindoos, and ends with the quiet assertion: "All goes back to the East."

There are already sufficient factors noted to account for the philosophy of Emerson, not only in its matter, but in its form. The matter was got from his inner experience and from his own countryside, that fair apparition that shone so peacefully about him. The form was gained from much reading in the old English poets, the Cambridge philosophers, and the ancient classical writers.

We are now in a position to explain three principles at the bottom of Emerson's philosophy. They are immanence in respect to nature; benevolence in respect to God; self-reliance in respect to man. Immanence implies the unity of the intelligent principle in the world, in the creation itself. Here man calls the universal soul, reason; it is not mine or thine, or his, but we are its. And the blue sky in which the private earth is buried, the sky with its eternal calm, is the type of reason. . . . Again, immanence implies that all that exists, exists in God, and that there is no difference in substance between the universe and God. Man as a part of nature is akin to the divine spirit. . . . When I behold the sunrise . . . I seem to partake of its rapid transformations. . . . Thus does nature deify us.

In these broken words Emerson hints at that fundamental coalescence between the circles of his system. Man partakes of nature, nature partakes of deity, and, through the enshrouding universal spirit, each partakes of all. These beliefs came as a revulsion from the old Calvinistic transcendence. The doctrine of a deity separate from his world, absolute, arbitrary, inscrutable in his ways, is now supplanted by the doctrine of the deification of the world, and the rendering of it reasonable by the indwelling of an intelligent principle. There is also a revulsion from another sort of transcendence, that of deism. Instead of the mechanical separation between deity and humanity that was held almost up to Emerson's day, there comes a joining of the two by means of a mediating principle, great nature itself. Because God is in his world and man is part of that world, it comes to pass that man feels within himself the divine currents, is conscious of a universal soul within his individual life.

There is next the principle of benevolence in respect to the deity. It is a good God that has made this goodly world. With this conviction there arises the splendid optimism in the pages of the transcendentalist. After Emerson had laid down the fundamental principles of immanence, he takes up as the first use of nature that of commodity. Under this general name he ranks those advantages which our senses owe to nature. By it we may explore that steady and prodigal provision that has been made for man's support and delight on this green ball which floats him through the heaven. . . . In all this there is a close resemblance to the old deistic delight in nature as an embodiment of the divine goodness. But a glamor is put upon it by the poetic New Englander. The argument for deistic design had degenerated into such forms as the *Bridgewater Treatises*, which af-

forded a combination of special providences with the
shallow sciences of the day. Now, the purpose or the
utility, or the commodity which Emerson found in nature was not special but general; not mechanical, but
æsthetic. Hence arises his poetic apostrophe: What
angels invented these splendid ornaments, these rich
conveniences, this ocean of air above, this ocean of
water beneath, this firmament of earth between; this
zodiac of lights, this tent of dropping clouds, this striped
coat of climates, this fourfold year?

Immanence and benevolence have been combined in an
optimistic form of pantheism. This is in decided contrast to the pantheism of Europe, which had so often
tended towards the pessimistic. On this side of the
water there was no world-weariness, but a joy of living
and a true love of the soil. This was a new land for
life, liberty, and the pursuit of happiness. There was
no pressure on population, but a chance for all men to
make their way. The fact that the ardent spirit might
plant his foot on the ladder of fortune had much to do
with the bright outlook. When the younger generation
left New England, men were heartened by the reports
of their success on the frontier. Indeed, the winning
of the West was a highly exciting and vivifying process.
And, finally, while much of the pessimism of the cold
world may be laid to the gray skies of the northern
climes, here, the clear skies, the cold waves, the rapid
changes in temperature, stirred up the blood and stimulated the animal spirits. So we find Emerson an optimist, pointing to those " admirable stars of possibility
and the yet untouched continent of hope glittering with
all its mountains in the vast west." It is for these reasons also that we find not a single prophet of woe among
the transcendentalists. Alcott's optimism was carried

almost to excess; he seldom saw anything except in the fervid hue of rosy hope. Thoreau, though a Diogenes, was not a Cynic: he lived by himself, but he lived joyously; his withdrawal from society, his return to nature, were made not because he was a fatalist, but because in nature he found a field where man was free to hunt for happiness.

The optimism of this philosophic era of good feeling was extended from nature as a whole to human nature. Taking over the high deistic praises of human goodness, that complacency over man and his achievements which marked the eighteenth century, the younger generation joined this to an incipient doctrine of development. If nature is growing perfect, man as a serial part of nature is perfectible. All this explains the sudden outburst of egotistic optimism which took place in New England. In the Unitarian Manifesto of 1815, in the diaries of the radical transcendentalists, we find a revulsion against Puritanic pessimism, and a reviling of the doctrine of human depravity. In one way all these phases of thought do not obtain in Emerson's case. It was a sign of his precocity that he very early decided that this was a good world, and the men in it good; that deity was kindly disposed towards all, and that all men were open to the solicitations of the spirit. And yet Emerson's life was not without adversity. He had fought against poverty, ill health, and family losses; and it was through his own courage that, after a period of morbidity and doubt, he came out with that serenity of faith that characterized the essay on Nature and all he wrote thereafter.

To the last principle of Emerson's thought we need devote but a few words. That self-reliance on which he dwelt is to be derived from the doctrine of the perfectibility of man. It is a result of the deistic complacency, and not, as has often been held, a corollary of Calvinism. Puritans have been called self-reliant; they were, but not through the principles of their creed. Amongst the best of them, their self-reliance was naught but God-reliance. A logical Calvinist could not depend on himself, but had to lean on Providence. Amongst the weak brethren was this especially true. The Calvinist who believed in particular providences was always begging for favors from his God. We need but note Cotton Mather's agonies of soul over his impotence to save himself and the sniffling spirit with which he sought for special privileges. Neither one way nor the other can self-reliance be derived from the doctrines of Puritanism. There were other factors at work; British blood and American achievements were the real causes for the new spirit. The whining attitude, which at times possessed New England's religionists, passed rapidly away after the second war with England. With their eyes on the naval victories of that day, the commonalty became so excessively self-reliant that, in a cant phrase of the times, they could whip the universe. Yet the country was better represented by those of more quiet minds, who came to rely on themselves and not on a reputation. Descendants of the Puritans, they longed for spiritual improvement and sought it in the oneness of the individual with nature.

It is here that there arises a contradiction between the reliance on self and the reliance on the not-self. Emerson resolved this contradiction by making the two, one. Because man is a part of nature, because nature partakes of deity, there is an unbreakable bond between these elements. Man may rely on his reason because this reason is not to be distinguished from the divine essence.

This is the paradox of pantheism at which Emerson ultimately arrived. But in order that there may be no
abrupt identification between human and divine, he
brings in a third factor, the external world, which gives
to man the perpetual presence of the sublime.

The inference may still be made that if Emerson was a
pantheist, he must be a determinist and a fatalist. We
nevertheless find him reiterating his belief in the dignity of human nature and the excellence of self-reliance.
How may this be reconciled with his statement that
nature is an embodied law whose divine order is inviolable to us? In reply we may point out that this is
not the Puritanic fatalism where nature is arbitrary,
full of strange and overwhelming mischances. No,
Emerson is opposed to arbitrary decrees; to him nature
is inviolable, but never inscrutable. Provided man is
open to the solicitations of the spirit, nature is essentially comprehensible and rational.

In this Emerson shows his Americanism. His determinism is modified in a novel way. It does not resemble the European fatalism derived from a philosophy
of the unconscious, based upon a blind will working in
us, we know not how. As a true son of the soil Emerson
is willing to be ruled, but not as a puppet worked from
behind the scenes. If he obeys the law like a good citizen, he wants to know how he is ruled. As in the proper
form of the American government, from the town meeting to the administration of Washington, he expects to
find things run in an open and above-board fashion.
And thus he comes to put this political interpretation
upon nature: It is something to be scrutinized in its
actions; it also stands as a representative of the will
of man.

Nature is open to scrutiny first by symbolism; it always has a meaning; it can be interpreted. The use of natural history, says the transcendentalist, is to give us aid in supernatural history. Thus arises that radicalism in Emerson's philosophy which did so much to soften its apparent determinism. In its first aspects nature seems a discipline; its function that of a taskmaster, and a mere obedient subject to that law which is king of kings. But Emerson, as a representative of a self-ruling people, will not allow that this is a final end of nature. Law as law is not paramount. Mere scientific formulæ are not enough. He declares that we must seek for a higher end and purpose, a spiritual principle running through all phenomena. So idealism is an hypothesis to account for nature on other principles than those of carpentry and chemistry, and the spiritual principle should demonstrate itself to the end. In the mastery of nature, man has first to learn its ways. . . . By discipline is the unspeakable but intelligible and practicable meaning of the world conveyed to man, the mortal pupil in every object of sense. But, adds the idealist, man as part of the universe has an immediate and intuitive knowledge of its innermost essence, and thus may he transcend those very objects of sense. Therefore, he continues, if the reason be stimulated to more earnest vision, outlines and surfaces become transparent, and are no longer seen; causes and spirits are seen through them.

This is the turning point in the resolution of determinism. Knowledge is power and by this power man is able to pierce through the veil and to find that nature, which before this seemed all-powerful, has a secondary place. Emerson carries out his reasoning in the following remarkable passage: But whilst we acquiesce entirely in the permanence of natural laws, the question of the absolute existence of nature remains open. It is the uniform effect of culture on the human mind, not to shake our faith in the stability of particular phenomena, as of heat, water, azote; but to lead us to regard nature as a phenomenon, not a substance; to attribute necessary existence to spirit; to esteem nature as an accident and an effect. . . . With this assertion of the primacy of reason a strict determinism vanishes. The great principle is not fatality, but regularity; nature is no longer dominant over man but man learns to manipulate nature. The sensual man, continues Emerson, conforms thoughts to things; but the poet conforms things to his thoughts. The one esteems nature as rooted and fast, the other as fluid; he impresses his being thereon; to him the refractory world is ductile and flexible.

Emerson had stated that nature's divine order was inviolable to us; he now goes so far as to make that nature a mere appendix to the soul. This reversal of a former judgment needs to be explained. How may we reconcile the discrepancy as to the over-lordship of man? It is by recalling the kinship that exists between man and the world. Both are imbued with reason, in each is a common essence. The solid-seeming block of matter has been pervaded and dissolved by a thought; this feeble human being has penetrated the vast masses of nature with an informing soul, and recognized itself in their harmony, that is, seized their law.

In offering this solution Emerson has united two sides of his nature, his law-abiding disposition and his strain of Puritanism. The one side acknowledges conscious law as king of kings; the other contemns the unsubstantial shows of the world. But again, it may be asked, does not the latter belief preclude the former? If all is an illusion, is not nature's law an illusion? Emerson, with

his inherent common sense, cannot so answer. He remarks that while the devotee flouts nature, he loves it,
for the advantage of the ideal theory over the popular
faith is that it transcends the world in precisely that
view which is most desirable to the mind,—a " vast picture which God paints on the instant eternity for the
contemplation of the soul." In this theorizing some
may say there is shallowness; that it is merely the artist's
way of working; that it attempts to wipe out all nature
as an unsubstantial pageant. This is a misinterpretation. Emerson is no illusionist, but an ideal realist.
Nature is not an accident, in the sense of being a mere
chance happening, but rather in the sense of being the
manifestation of a substance most profound and real. So
he clings to this brave lodging, wherein man is harbored,
and holds that this is the use of nature, that it is faithful to the cause whence it had its origin. It always
speaks of spirit. It suggests the absolute. It is a perpetual effect. It is a great shadow pointing always to
the sun behind us.

2. The Sources of Transcendentalism

In his definitive address on the Transcendentalist
Emerson remarks that the first thing we have to say respecting what are called the *new views* here in New
England at the present time, is that they are not new,
but the very oldest thoughts cast into the mold of these
new times. Upon this disavowal there follows a definition of the movement in which the author was enmeshed.
What is properly called transcendentalism among us,
he continues, is idealism, idealism as it appears in 1842.
As such it is a protest against materialism. In place of
experience, of the data of the senses, of the force of cir-

cumstances, of the animal wants of man, it insists on consciousness, on the power of thought and of will, on inspiration, on individual culture. Again, while the materialist respects sensible masses, the idealist has another measure which is metaphysical, namely the *rank* which things themselves take in his consciousness; not at all the size or appearance. He does not respect labor, or the products of labor, namely property, otherwise than as a manifold symbol, illustrating with wonderful fidelity of details the law of being. His experience inclines him to behold the procession of facts you call the world, as flowing perpetually outward from an invisible unsounded center in himself. Finally, he believes in miracle, in the perpetual openness of the human mind to new influx of light and power; he believes in inspiration and in ecstasy.

It is obvious from this confession of philosophic faith that New England transcendentalism was, in many points, only a new name for old ways of thinking. Clearly did it re-echo the voice of the past: that of Plato in its doctrines of the scale of being and of the symbolism of nature, that of Plotinus in its insistence on emanation and on ecstasy. And as Emerson was not unmindful of his debt to antiquity, so also was he conscious of more recent influences. Many, he recalls, have been the prophets and heralds of the transcendental philosophy, for this way of thinking, falling on prelatical times, made Puritans and Quakers; and falling on Unitarian and commercial times makes the peculiar shades of idealism which we know.

Thus far Emerson has suggested many sources of his thought,—from Platonism to Puritanism, from Neo-Platonism to Unitarianism. But not until this point does he mention that name above all names which popular opinion has held to be the fount and origin of the New England transcendentalism. It is well known to most of my audience, he explains, that the idealism of the present day acquired the name of Transcendentalism from the use of that term by Immanuel Kant of Königsberg, who replied to the skeptical philosophy of Locke, which insisted that there was nothing in the intellect which was not previously in the experience of the senses, by showing that there was a very important class of ideas or imperative forms, which did not come by experience, but through which experience was acquired; that these were intuitions of the mind itself; and he denominated them *Transcendental* forms. The extraordinary profoundness and precision of that man's thinking have given vogue to his nomenclature in Europe and America, to that extent that whatever belongs to the class of intuitive thought is popularly called at the present day *transcendental*.

Emerson has suggested three sources of his philosophy —Hellenic, American, and Germanic. As the Germanic is considered the most important it may be left to the last; only after other possible alternatives have been weighed can we decide upon the alleged preponderance of the Teutonic influences. So, too, of the nearer native influences there must be taken into account the reactions from the movements current in the stream of Emerson's own life. Thus, in the way of revulsion, he developed from the Hobbite materialism a preference for the instinctive and intuitive; from the Lockean negation of innate ideas the assertion of subjective principles of reason; from the Humean skepticism the avowal of a faculty transcending the senses and the understanding. In addition, there were other forms of thought, actually naturalized in the land, containing the very elements of transcendentalism which Emerson was destined to acquire. Thus, Unitarianism furnished him with its liberality, Quakerism with its mystic spirit, and Puritanism with its individualism. This was the trinity of powers that energized his growing mind. Born eighth in a line of Puritan divines, he received as his heritage discipline without dogma; inclined by this heritage toward the interior or hidden life, he was prepared to welcome the habit of introspection and solitude. But, above all, living in the transitional era of Unitarianism, he was subject to all the varying forces of which that movement was the resultant.

The resolution of these forces has been attempted, but not from the philosophic point of view. It has been pointed out how the old Calvinistic stock split into two branches—orthodox and Unitarian, and the Unitarian again into conservative and transcendental. Such is the family tree of the New England mind in black and white. But obviously we need a greater variety of hues to give its natural appearance, to explain the transition from the mere light and shade of Calvinism to the highly colored emotionalism of radical transcendentalism. That transition forms a veritable speculative spectrum of the times. In New England men had passed through various phases: Puritanism had sought the purity of faith; in the worship of a transcendent Absolute the ascription of any feeling was deemed to stain the white radiance of eternity. Next, Calvinism was succeeded by deism, the worship of deity by the worship of humanity, and with the succession there came a change towards the warmer tones of emotion. Lastly, arose a true philosophy of feeling, for romanticism discovered a division between those Unitarians who were content with the cold light of reason and those who preferred the rosier hues of en-

thusiasm and ecstasy. Romanticism has been properly
given as the cause of the transition from coldness to
warmth, from sense to sensibility. Before this there was
little to satisfy the heart. Just as the Most High God
of the Puritans had degenerated into a mere dispenser of
special providences, so the light of reason of the deistic
rationalists had faded out into the twilight of Humean
skepticism—" the frigid and empty theism " against
which Emerson rebelled. Unitarianism had suffered
from a heart-withering philosophy. As Channing put
it, men must look to other schools for the thoughts to
thrill them, to touch the most inward springs, and disclose the depths of their own souls.

Whence were to come these new thoughts, half desired,
half feared? It was the romantic movement as it took
the several forms of French naturalism, English pantheism, and German idealism that was to furnish the
influences. Of these three forms the first had least
weight. Rousseau's return to nature came to be interpreted as a return to natural passion, and the Gallic
materialism to be confused with the excesses of the mob;
indeed the New England Federalists turned a cold
shoulder upon the rights of man as exemplified in the
French Revolution. Thus, at the age of nineteen, Emerson himself confesses his belief that nobody now regards
the maxim " all men are born equal," as anything more
than a convenient hypothesis or an extravagant declama-
tion. Of the English romantic influences it was the
poetic pantheism of the Lake School that so warmed the
heart of Emerson. The old Puritanic aloofness from the
world, the conviction that matter and spirit are essentially alien, was now giving way to a feeling of kinship
between human nature and the world of nature.

To come to the crucial point. It has been commonly

thought that the transcendentalists early partook of the
German idealism; that from across the Rhine came the
fresh breezes that drove away the " pale negations of
Boston Unitarianism." It was in 1820 that Edward
Everett, George Bancroft, and George Ticknor returned
to America from Goettingen. Yet of these men Emerson,
in this connection, mentions but one, and gives no hint
that he imported a knowledge of technical transcendentalism. Germany, Emerson recalled later, had created criticism in vain for us until Edward Everett returned from
his five years in Europe and brought to Cambridge his
rich results . . . he made us for the first time acquainted
with Wolff's theory of the Homeric writings and with
the criticism of Heine.

This is the fullest statement, before his first published
book *Nature,* that the author makes as to the influence of
Germany upon his mind. Previous to 1836 we find in
his *Journals* only these nominal references: to Kant
once; to Fichte thrice; to Schelling twice; to Hegel twice.
Indeed the American's knowledge of German metaphysics was slight and secondary. He made a few extracts in his blotter from a translation of Fichte, not
knowing as yet the tongue of the original. Later, at the
solicitation of Carlyle, he learned to read the works of
Goethe, yet even here he found but a confirmation of his
own beliefs and his sense of originality did not forsake
him. Five months before the proof-sheets of *Nature*
reached him he made this complacent note: Only last
evening I find the following sentence in Goethe, a com-
ment and consent to my speculations on the All in Each
in *Nature* this last week.

In truth it may be repeated that Emerson's knowledge
of the German schools was not only slight, but secondary, when he could declare that the love of the vast came

from Germany to America through Coleridge. How the latter became the medium through the American edition of his *Aids to Reflection* we shall consider subsequently; meanwhile we must seek for other and earlier tendencies that brought the Massachusetts leader into the transcendental drift. Of these tendencies he was more or less unconscious, for the name of transcendentalism, he asserts, was given nobody knows by whom, or when it was first applied.

Yet for us, looking back on those times, it is not impossible to point out certain definite factors that led to the Emersonian type of mind. The prime factor was British. It was an Anglo-American environment that was furnished by the Boston of that day. Here two forms of thought led to the transcendental strain: the Irish idealism of George Berkeley, the English idealism of the Cambridge and Oxford Platonists. Of the former there were few general traces, for though the good bishop had lived for three years in Rhode Island his views, as those of an Anglican churchman, were not acceptable to Massachusetts Congregationalists. And yet we have a record of the great immaterialist's power over Emerson when he said: " I know but one solution to my nature and relations, which I find in remembering the joy with which in my boyhood I caught the first hint of the Berkeleian philosophy, and which I certainly never lost sight of afterwards." To what extent Berkeley held sway over Emerson it would be hard to say, for the kindred beliefs in sense symbolism and the divine visual language the latter might have drawn from the Platonizing poets. Such were Quarles and Vaughan and especially George Herbert, from whom Emerson was so fond of quoting lines that taught the congruity between things and thoughts, between forms and mind.

Such were certain of the earlier idealistic influences upon the young New Englander. Yet more important than the Irish idealist, and the poetic symbolists, was the influence of the older English lines. That influence was of double significance, since through men like Cudworth and More, Norris and Collier, Emerson was led to manifest his spiritual affinity with both Kant and Plato. How far the Koenigsberger was anticipated by the Cambridge and Oxford Platonists has been suggested by William James and carried out by Arthur Lovejoy. For example, in Cudworth's *True Intellectual System of the Universe* are to be discovered not only a general emphasis on nativism, and preference for the innate and intuitive over the empirical and sensualistic, but also an anticipation of the Kantian a priori concepts of objects and the wisdom of pure speculative reason. It was in Cudworth that Emerson had read from time to time for years, and through him, in his college days, had obtained his first glimpse into Plato. Again it was Cudworth who prepared the way for Coleridge, and Coleridge who furnished the easiest way to Kant for English readers. That the *Aids to Reflection* should have been issued as early as 1829 in New England is not surprising, when we remember that Emerson declared that the feeling of the Infinite finds a most genial climate in the American mind. So the Cambridge Platonist opened the way back to his ancient master. Of Plato Emerson exclaims: " I hesitate to speak lest there should be no end. He contains the future, as he came out of the past." Statements like these call for a reversal of the ordinary judgment as to the inspiration of our foremost transcendentalist. In truth it was the philosopher of the Academy and not of Koenigsberg who, by his own early confession, was Emerson's master. As is shown by that

essay in *Representative Men* he was almost convinced
that " transcendental truths have a kind of filial retrospect to Plato and the Greeks."

We have examined the three suggested sources for
the Emersonian philosophy, namely the Germanic, British, and Hellenic. The first, in the prevalent opinion,
is held to be paramount, but that opinion cannot be adhered to if the two others will account for the facts. The
acquisition of the Kantian system was a well-nigh impossible task in a land where German literature was, as
yet, known only by name. For instance, the first reference to Immanuel Kant in the country was given in a
Philadelphia magazine of 1798, and that reference was
only at second hand, while the first decent exposition of
the *Critique of Pure Reason* was published by a Yale
graduate in 1842. Meanwhile in Massachusetts, in the
period half-way between these dates, there was a piti-
able dearth of literature on the subject. George Ticknor,
before he set sail for Goettingen in 1815, was obliged
to send to New Hampshire, " where he learned there was
a German dictionary." It is true that in the same year
there was for sale by a Boston bookseller a London translation of the *Elements of the Critical Philosophy,* but
it was not for some years later that the little band of
enthusiasts from Goettingen returned to Harvard. This
was the band, headed by Edward Everett, that Emerson
mentions as arousing an interest in German modes of
criticism. Now that criticism, it will be recalled, was
more literary than philosophical.

In the meantime Emerson's drift towards idealism had
been hastened more by a revulsion against the current
metaphysic than by a knowledge of the new. Shortly
before he came of age, he protested against the college
curriculum with its emphasis on " reasoning machines,"

such as Locke, and Clarke, and David Hume. In his required studies he had received such an overdose of the *Essay on Human Understanding* that he wrote that " while the inspired poets will be Platonists, the dull men will be Lockeists." It is this dislike of the sensationalistic denial of innate ideas that brought out Emerson's latent transcendentalism. Against empiricism he protested that there were truths higher than those given by experience; against sensationalism that there were intuitions higher than those given by the senses. So, from a temperamental reaction Emerson went back to the English Platonists and through them back to the ancients. Immediately after the issuance of his first work he writes: Any history of philosophy fortifies my faith by showing me that what high dogmas I had supposed were the rare and late fruit of a cumulative culture,— and only now possible to some recent Kant or Fichte,— were the prompt improvisations of the earliest inquirers.

Such confessions show how lastingly Hellenism was impressed upon the mind of Emerson. As a boy in college, through Cudworth's citations, he had come upon Plato; later he added that " it was a great day in a man's life when he first read the *Symposium*." Lastly there was the notable essay in *Representative Men* showing that Plato forms the most continuously powerful influence in Emerson's thinking. Moreover, we know from new sources that the ancients were Emerson's chief teachers in transcendentalism. The *Journals* tell us how as an undergraduate, having no faculty for mathematics, he was wont to console himself with Plutarch and Plato at night; how, again, he considered himself, and not his instructors, the true philosopher in college, because he read for " lustres " in Plato; how, finally, he sought

Coleridge in England and from him learned that the problem of philosophy, according to Plato, is for all that exists conditionally, to find a ground unconditioned and absolute.

Three years after the visit to Coleridge, Emerson utilized this opinion as his definition of idealism in his first book, entitled *Nature*. How largely that work was woven out of the shining fabric of antiquity can be seen from an analysis of its contents. The original edition has for its motto a sentence of Plotinus: " Nature is but an image or imitation of wisdom, the last thing of the soul." The same author furnishes the grounds for that baffling dualism which Emerson ever sought to resolve into its spiritual elements. Plotinus declares: " What the world ends in, therefore, is matter and reason, but that from which it arose, and by which it is good, is soul." In like manner Emerson, giving as his postulate, " philosophically considered, the universe is composed of nature and the soul," goes on to sublimate nature in those sections which begin with Commodity, pass through Symbolism, and end in the doctrine of Universal Spirit, or Over-Soul.

How kindred to his own mind was the ancient way of thinking is clearly seen in the successive sections of this little book with all its transport and radiancy of thought. Given as our task to interrogate the great apparition that shines so peacefully around us, the lover of nature is defined as he whose mind and outward senses are still truly adjusted to each other; who has retained the spirit of infancy even in the era of manhood. Here is the Platonic doctrine of reminiscence which, as originally suggested to Emerson by Wordsworth's *Ode on the Intimations of Immortality*, was carried out in his own boyish poem, " Man in the bush with God may meet."

Again in the section on Commodity we have as the first of the fourfold root of the final cause of nature, the doctrine of compensation,—that all parts of nature incessantly work into each other's hands for the profit of man. Following the lines of the Platonizing Herbert's poem on Man, this is but the expression of Emerson's youthful experience when he lay on his bed pleasing himself with the beauty of the Lord's equilibrium of the universe, instead of shuddering at the terrors of his judgments. . . . Also is a nobler want of man served by nature, namely the love of beauty; for such is the meaning of the word cosmos; as understood by the Greeks the world demands, as essential to its perfection, the presence of a higher, spiritual element. While Emerson designates this want of man as Hellenic he would add to it that æsthetic interest of his own people,—the love of the beauty of holiness. So, he adds, the problem of restoring to the world original and eternal beauty is solved by the redemption of the soul.

Now Emerson approaches a cherished belief—that of nature as a great symbol. As if following the apocalypse of loveliness unfolded by Berkeley in his divine visual language, he explicitly states that language is the third use which nature subserves to man and has a threefold degree: first, words are the signs of natural facts; again, particular natural facts are symbols of particular spiritual facts: every appearance in nature corresponds to some state of the mind, for man is conscious of a universal soul within or behind his individual life; lastly, nature is the symbol of spirit; because it is emblematic the universe becomes transparent, for the light of higher laws than its own shines through it; this is the standing problem which has exercised the wonder and study of every fine genius since the world began, from

Pythagoras and Plato to Bacon, Leibniz, and Swedenborg.

That nature is the symbol of spirit lies at the bottom of
the *Timæus*. But the next contention concerning the
ethical import of natural law, or what Emerson calls discipline, is not strictly Platonic. In other words, that the
axioms of physics apply to morals is not of the Academy but of a later school, being rather of Plotinus than
of Plato. For this confusion two reasons have been
given,—Emerson's use of Thomas Taylor's translation
of Plato which was edited from the Neo-Platonic point
of view, and Coleridge's attempt to harmonize Plato's
philosophy of the good with Lord Bacon's search of
truth. But this is going too far afield. There is a more
natural and more native source for this inversion of
Platonism. If Plato found the idea of the good giving
unity to the ideas in the intelligible world, Emerson
found the laws of the world leading up to the universal
good, and this because he was in the deistic drift. Cosmic
benevolence was a favorite theme of the Harvard worthies. Even the austere Cotton Mather, as we recall, had
composed a cheerful little book entitled, *The Christian
Philosopher. A Collection of the Best Discoveries in
Nature with Religious Improvements*. And his more
genial successor, Charles Chauncy, issued his *Benevolence of the Deity*, which was in harmony with that series
of Dudleian lectures which were a familiar feature of
college in Emerson's undergraduate days. It was the
philosophic age of optimism in his own land that left
their mild marks on Emerson's doctrine of discipline.
At the opening of his literary career, he feels noble emotions dilating him as his mind apprehends, one after another, the laws of physics. Later he found the survey

of cosmical powers a means of consolation in the dark
hours of private misfortune.

The transcendentalist here discloses himself more than
a Platonizer; he is a modernizer. Cudworth opened to
him the Platonic symbolism; " analogy-loving souls "
like Bruno and Donne, Herbert, Crashaw, and Vaughan
gave him its poetic form; he himself now attempts, as an
higher synthesis, the harmony of religion and science.
How wide was his reading in the latter subject may be
inferred from his book lists, where are to be found
mention of such masters of science as Newton, Laplace
and Hunter, Linnæus, Lamarck and Herschel, Owen,
Lyell, and Faraday. An earlier reference shows for
what end he had been gathering these stores. As he
had already declared: the religion that is afraid of science dishonors God and commits suicide; it acknowledges
that it is not equal to the whole of truth, that it legis-
lates, tyrannizes, over a village of God's empire, but it is
not the immutable, universal law. But because all things
are moral, and in their boundless changes have an unceasing reference to spiritual nature, herein is apprehended the unity of nature,—all the endless variety of
things make an identical impression.

Substantiating his belief in the essential unity of nature by a reference to Xenophanes, Emerson now passes
to that most central and vital of his doctrines. For his
first lesson in idealism he recalls when as a child he
amused himself in saying over such common words as
" black," " white," " board," twenty or thirty times
until the words lost all meaning and fixedness, and he
began to doubt which was the right name for the thing.
Now, a nobler doubt perpetually suggests itself . . . to
give a sufficient account of that Appearance we call the
World; in my utter impotence to test the authenticity

of the report of my senses, to know whether the impressions they make on me correspond with outlying
objects, what difference does it make, whether Orion is
up there in heaven, or some god paints the image in the
firmament of the soul? How is the doubt resolved?
By the end for which nature exists; whether it enjoys
a substantial existence without or is only in the apocalypse of the mind, it is alike useful and alike venerable
to me.

As the section on Discipline suggested that the ethical
character so penetrates the bone and marrow of nature
as to seem the end for which it was made, so that on
Idealism bears this notion out. Religion, in teaching
that the things that are unseen are eternal, does for
the unschooled what philosophy does for Berkeley. It
discloses the whole circle of persons and things, of actions
and events, as one vast picture which God paints on the
instant eternity for the contemplation of the soul. . . .
In this ardent exposition of the divine visual language,
the Irish idealist of the eighteenth century has found
an American disciple in the nineteenth. That westward
strand, whither Berkeley came with such high hopes, at
last brought forth a follower who could sympathetically
interpret the uses of nature. Behind nature, throughout
nature, says Emerson, spirit is present; one, and not compound, it does not act upon us from without, that is in
space and time, but spiritually, or through ourselves;
therefore, that spirit, that is, the Supreme Being, does
not build up nature around us, but puts it forth through
us, as the life of the tree puts forth new branches and
leaves through the pores of the old. . . . Nature is thus
an incarnation of God, a projection of God; its serene
order is inviolable to us; it is, therefore, to us, the present expositor of the divine mind.

With this rhapsody over spirit—the dread universal essence—Emerson concludes his great essay on Nature with a section entitled Prospects. To what end is this apparition that shines about us? A little poem by George Herbert on Man gives him the clew. When the English Platonist affirms, "nothing we see but means our good," the American, in a like strain, exclaims, "When I behold a rich landscape, it is to know why all thought of multitude is lost in a tranquil sense of unity." Here is a final note of mysticism, of the absorption of the self in the All, and with this Emerson rounds out that Platonism which was his by heritage, by temperament, and by training. By heritage he was familiar with the latent idealistic teachings of the Puritans concerning "the unsubstantial shows of the world as vanities, dreams, shadows, unrealities." Nevertheless he did not accept the Puritan's morbid and distorted use of such teachings. I have, he adds, no hostility to nature, but a child's love for it. I do not wish to fling stones at my beautiful mother. . . . If Emerson's temperament sweetened the strain of idealism handed down from Puritan days, his training strengthened it. And that training, it must be insisted, was largely self-training. It was not Plato and Berkeley, but Locke and Reid who were impressed upon the boy in college, and least of all had the Germans any effect upon his thought. As he informed a friend, in this connection, he need not consult the Germans, but if he wished at any time to know what the transcendentalists believed, he might simply omit what in his own mind he added (to his simple perception) from the tradition, and the rest would be transcendentalism.

That Emerson was not of the Germanic type, but rather a legitimate successor of the British Platonizers is further borne out by the direct testimony of Coleridge, who contends that the Concord philosopher was one of those few Americans who, in opposition to the current empiricism, which made all human knowledge derived from sensations, took up with Berkeley's idealism, which made immediate divine agency the sole cause of all the phenomena of the material world. In regard to Coleridge, Emerson had visited the sage of Highgate in 1833, but the visit he pronounced rather a spectacle than a conversation, of no use beyond the satisfaction of one's curiosity. Meanwhile in an adjoining State there had been issued an American edition of the *Aids to Reflection* with a competent introduction by President Marsh, and it was this work which did most to introduce the modified German philosophy into our country.

If Emerson has any strain of the foreign transcendentalism, it is in this modified and mediate form. He possessed no such direct knowledge of Kant as did Marsh or Murdock; in fact, his reading of the German text was begun at Carlyle's solicitation only after the publication of *Nature*, and was confined largely to Goethe, of whom he "contrived to read almost every volume." Now, although these men may have first brought Emerson into direct contact with the Germans, he expressly refutes the implication that he was more of an interpreter of Coleridge than an original thinker. And although he had gained some knowledge of the Germans, he lets it be known that it was not merely in an imitative way. While Murdock utilized Tenneman to compile his own historical narrative of the progress of speculative philosophy in modern times, Emerson exclaims that "the whole value of opinions like Tenneman's is to increase my self-trust by demonstrating what man can be and do." And, lastly, although in the crucial essay on *Nature* he had apostrophized the Germany of mystic philosophy, he now exclaims: " Leave me alone; do not teach me out of Leibniz or Schelling, and I shall find it all out myself."

Emerson's son also bears testimony of him, that in his eighteenth year he was delighted with the saying that all goes back to the ancient East, yet for modern systematic metaphysics he cared little and seldom read. That characteristic American attitude of independence (despite the initial admission that none escapes the debt to past thought), is borne out by this supplementary statement from the essay on *Quotation and Originality:* " To all that can be said of the preponderance of the Past, the single word Genius is a sufficient answer.   The Divine resides in the new; and the Divine never quotes, but is, and creates. . . . Originality is being one's self; genius is sensibility and capacity of receiving just impressions from the external world, and the power of coördinating these after the laws of thought.   If the thinker recognizes the perpetual suggestion of the Supreme Intellect, the oldest thoughts become new and fertile whilst he speaks them."

CHAPTER VII

EVOLUTIONISM

1. THE FORERUNNERS OF EVOLUTIONISM

THE three centuries of American thought present three phases of the doctrine of evolution. To summarize these phases we may conveniently use the Comtean formula of the law of the three stages. In the seventeenth century the interest was theological: evolution—if such it may be called—was an unfolding of the divine plan according to the mere good pleasure of the Most High. In the eighteenth the interest was metaphysical: the divine plan became rationalized, evidences of design were diligently sought after, man's task was to discover God's ways of working in the world. In the nineteenth the interest became positive: only after theology and teleology had been left behind was it possible to fasten attention on evolution in the stricter modern sense of epigenesis, of the origin of species, of the descent of man. In brief, the history of evolution in America, as in Europe, has been from the cosmic to the organic, has passed through the logical phases from supernatural election to natural selection.

As in other speculative movements the development of the doctrine of evolution exhibits a parallel growth with that abroad. This does not imply a slavish adherence to foreign opinion, but a common pedigree and a common logical sequence. There is a continuity of thought in one case as in the other, but that continuity, on this side of the water, has not yet been traced in its entirety.

In the beginning there is, of course, great indebtedness to former suggestors. Here the Greeks lead. Aristotle, though confounded with the Scholastics, and ranted against by such pious worthies as Cotton Mather, traced the first faint lines which subsequent speculation was to follow. Edwards and Emerson were especially influenced by the Stagirite, and the later theologians, like the earlier Christian fathers, depended upon Hellenic speculation to reconcile the Mosaic account of creation with the growing naturalistic explanations. Some time before the appearance of Darwinism men like President Hitchcock and Tayler Lewis and Arnold Guyot did much in the attempt to reconcile Genesis and geology, to show the harmony between the revealed and the rational. The outburst of controversy upon the appearance of the *Origin of Species* in 1859 was, therefore, no unexpected thing. An earlier generation had been storing the powder to be exploded in the battles of the '60s. Here the scientists were the chief sappers, and ran long galleries of anticipated objections. So when the theory of natural selection had gained its adherents, the supernaturalists were ready for them. The battle was extended and furious. Southward from Harvard to William and Mary College, westward from New York to St. Louis, there was a continuous campaign of scientific controversy which lasted even longer than the civil strife which rent the country. The echoes of that conflict still reverberate, and in the remoter fortresses of tradition like the *Presbyterian Review* and the *Bibliotheca Sacra* the garrisons have not yet pulled down the flag. In brief, from the day of Puritanism to the day of pragmatism there have been so many skirmishes, battles, and general engagements as almost to merit the name of the warfare between evolution and revelation in America.

In the history of this warfare there are two main periods. Adopting the distinction of Lord Bacon, the period before 1859 may be called that of anticipation; after that crucial date, that of interpretation. In the first men sought for evidences of design, and design was an assumed general principle, and facts were, in large measure, made to fit the theory. In the second period induction was increasingly used; facts were sought for their own sake, and theory, or the framing of an hypothesis out of the bits furnished by the sciences, was a more cautious and hesitating procedure. It is no cause for astonishment that an inevitable conflict was to be expected. Between the men of deduction and the men of induction there was a clash of temperaments which was bound to throw out sparks. The men of the first period, who followed the high a priori road, were men of imagination; they beheld visions of cosmic order and divine purpose. The men of the second period, who kept to the narrow paths of careful experimentation, were not particularly interested in absolute order and supreme purpose. They were empiricists, not transcendentalists, and gloried as much in the humility of their tasks as their opponents did in the grandeur of their speculations. The transcendentalists and supernaturalists looked with scorn upon the grubbers after detail, and charged them with not seeing the beauty of the forest for the study of the trees. The empiricists and naturalists, in turn, felt it no disparagement that they should " creep by timid steps and slow, on plain experience lay foundation low."

Let us take up the first period, that of deduction, of pure speculation, of high imagination. From Edwards

to Emerson there is a line of Platonizers who looked
at the natural through the bright lens of the supernatural; who could meet with never a fact without gloss-
ing it in the colors of eternity.   These were the
" analogy-loving souls " who saw a double meaning in
all events.   When the Puritan divine " viewed the moon
for continuance " it was the glory of the Lord shining
before him; when the Concord sage crossed " a bare
common in snow puddles at twilight under a clouded
sky " it was to enjoy a perfect exhilaration.   This poetic
spirit of interpretation impregnated the New England
mind for two hundred years.   Besides the masters we
find it in Cotton Mather's *Christian Philosopher*, in
Charles Chauncy and his *Benevolence of the Deity;*
and in the Alvord professorship at Harvard, whose
avowed purpose was to show the coincidence between
the doctrines of revelation and the dictates of reason.

Bred in the bone, this Platonizing instinct came out
in all the acts of life.   Its holders sought to hitch their
wagons to stars, to drive them according to divine design.
But their aims were so high that as men they became, at
times, unpractical, and fell an easy prey to those who
merely followed their own noses and were guided by
common sense.   It might be shown how they floundered
in the seven seas of new facts furnished by the scientists,
but this is a sight upon which it is not fair to dwell.   In
the change from a pessimistic theology to an optimistic
theodicy we can sympathize with Cotton Mather's enthusiasm over the " nice provisions of nature in the
vegetable race," based, as it was, in the plastic capacities
of nature as governed by an all-wise agent.   This belief,
in fact, furnished the way out of the maze of determinism.   Indeed it was but a step from the old Puritanic
faith in arbitrary interferences to the deistic conviction

that God does not act by interposition continually repeated, but by concurring in an established course of nature. It was this distinction between interference and concurrence that later allowed Asa Gray to meet the storm of opposition raised by the doctrine of natural selection. By utilizing the concourse of second causes he claimed that morphology and teleology—things as they were formed and things as they were foreordained —were to be harmonized, since the doctrine of specific creation was to give way to the larger principle of design.

This distinction was unfortunately forgotten. Gray complains of the absurdity of associating design only with miracle, for this association was one which did much to hinder the acceptance of Darwinism. At this point the Harvard botanist might well have appealed to those Dudleian lecturers who, in his own college, had been aiming to prove that " the structure and constitution of the world and the accurate adjustment of its various parts prove an intelligent, wise, and good Cause." But the argument for design became confused with the doctrine of special creation, and the latter was one of those presuppositions which hindered the acceptance of a naturalistic view of evolution. The confusion was worse confounded by the attempts to harmonize Genesis and geology. In this the American exegetes were not such literalists as the English. The Hutchinsonian school, which held that the Scriptures contain a complete system of natural philosophy, had little vogue in the land. Benjamin Franklin, for example, complained that such a manner of philosophizing was much out of his way. But the psycho-theological school had some followers. As early as 1811 Thomas Dobson declared that the geological discoveries, which seem to indicate a much longer duration of the earth than six thousand years, are not inconsistent with the Mosaic history because the word creation means not creating out of nothing, but putting the chaotic world with its furniture in the beautiful order in which it is arranged. Again, as late as 1852, we find in President Hitchcock's *Religion and Geology* the acceptance of the theory that the six days of creation were but six continuous pictures that were made to pass before the vision of Moses. This kinetoscopic cosmology has its absurd side, but along with the ludicrous there was a certain logical framework discoverable in the scheme. It had these three factors: special creation, permanence of species, cataclysmic destruction. In other words, that which the Almighty had been pleased to create, remained fixed, until it was again his good pleasure to destroy. As if after the analogy of man who was created perfect, then fell, and was lastly punished by death as the universal law, so each organic species is created by special dispensation of the deity, then allowed to develop up to certain limits, and finally swept away in a vast catastrophe, the " platforms of death " portrayed by Hugh Miller in his *Footsteps of the Creator*. Now this scheme of supernaturalism had, as its counterpart, the scheme of naturalism which had sprung up in the century preceding Darwin. Against special creation there was put spontaneous generation; against permanence of species, mutability; against cataclysmic destruction, degradation through disuse.

To trace the differences between these two schemes and the gradual displacement of the former by the latter, is to trace a sort of philosophic " fault," a metaphysical cleavage which occurs where the pressure is greatest. The last of these factors we may dispose of at once because it destroyed itself by its very exaggeration.

Cataclysmic destruction was a sort of a French Revolution in nature, a transfer of political disasters to the realm of the different natural kingdoms. As one of its advocates declared: earth has its tempests as well as the ocean; there are reserved without doubt in the destinies of nature fearful epochs for the ravage of human races, and there are times marked on the divine calendar for the ruin of empires and for the periodic renewal of the mundane features.

We return to the first factor, the first point of pressure in the new line of cleavage. This was spontaneous generation. That meant briefly that life is inherent in matter and under certain favorable conditions will burst forth into active being. This point was controverted by the cautious Hitchcock, who declares that not many years since the equivocal or casual production of "animalculi," without any other parentage than "law," was thought to be made out by a multitude of facts; but now the advocates of this "law" hypothesis have been fairly driven from this stronghold of their argument. This theory, he continues, was first drawn out by the French zoölogists, who endeavored to show by the inherent vitality of some parts of matter, how the first or lowest classes of animals and plants may have been produced; and how from these, by the theory of development and the force of circumstances, all the higher animals, with their instincts and intellects, may have been evolved.

The second point of pressure was mutability, or the gradual transmutation of species into one another through natural causes. This doctrine came very near being reached by an early Princetonian. In his notable *Essay on the Causes of the Variety of Complexion and Figure in the Human Species,* Stanhope Smith, as early as 1787, virtually accepted the Lamarckian principle of the origin of variations from the factors of use and disuse, food, climate, or the effort of the individual. The varieties of human nature, he contends, are to be explained by the known operations of natural causes and the necessary laws of the material world, such as climate, the state of society, and the manner of living. Particular differences are small. It is the example of the whole that surprises us by its magnitude. The combined effect of many minute varieties, like the product arising from the multiplication of many small numbers, appears great and unaccountable. . . . Human nature being much more pliant than animal, and affected by the greater variety of causes from food, clothing, lodging, and manners, is still more easily susceptible to change, according to any general standard, or idea, of the human form. To this principle, as well as to the manner of living, it may be in great part attributed that the Germans, the Swedes, and the French, in different parts of the United States, who live chiefly among themselves, and cultivate the habits and ideas of the countries from which they emigrated, retain, even in our climate, a strong resemblance to their primitive stock. Those, on the other hand, who have not confined themselves to the contracted circle of their countrymen, but have mingled freely with the Anglo-Americans, entered into their manners, and adopted their ideas, have assumed such a likeness to them, that it is not easy now to distinguish from one another people who sprung from such different origins. . . . So, in proportion as the citizens of the States approach the vicinity of the Indian tribes, similarity of situation produces also a great approximation of manners; they decline the labors of agriculture as a toil and prefer the fatigues of hunting to all other pleasures, and the charms of indolence and independence to the refinements and attractions of civil society.

In Stanhope Smith there was a certain advance over the old way of thinking: the old held that species were adapted by the Creator, the new that they were created adaptable. But while this adaptability is a step toward a naturalistic view, unfortunately for the purely scientific aspect of his acute observations the Princetonian gives a supernaturalistic turn to his arguments. The flexibility which he concedes is but fractional compared with the fixity of the species; it is only a principle of pliancy given to divinely endowed primitive man, in order that he may be capable of accommodation to every situation in the globe.

As an early American ethnologist Stanhope Smith had great opportunities, but an unfettered doctrine of mutability was impossible because of his prior belief in special creation. Hence for a full quarter of a century the doctrine of mutability lay undeveloped in native thought. But in 1813 William Charles Wells wrote a paper on the *Formation of Races,* which had the distinction of being favorably spoken of by Charles Darwin in his *Historical Sketch* of his forerunners. Referring to man's selective action regarding domesticated animals Wells gives this pregnant passage: '' But what is here done by art seems to be done with equal efficacy though more slowly by nature, in the formation of varieties of mankind fitted for the country which they inhabit.'' The paper of Wells was so little known that Morton, the Philadelphia craniologist, could declare that nothing was done in ethnology in the United States between Stanhope Smith and himself. So Morton recounts how, at the commencement of his study in 1824, he was taught that all mankind were derived from a single pair, and that diversity, now so remarkable, originated solely from the operations of climate, locality, food, and other physical agents. Yet Morton is satisfied with neither of these views—the old or the new—neither the special creation of the literalist, nor the mutability of the transformationist. The ordinary exposition of Genesis is declared impossible: that all human races are of some one species and one family is contradicted by their present variations. Again that all mankind were derived from a single pair, and that the diversities now so remarkable originated solely from physical operations, would demand indefinite periods,—those chiliads of years which Prichard came to advocate. . . . It cannot be that chance, alone, has caused all the physical disparity among men from the noblest Caucasian form to the most degraded Australian and Hottentot. Therefore one must conclude that these diversities are not acquired, but have existed *ab origine*.

In attempting to avoid the difficulties both of uniform creation and purely natural transmutation Morton takes a mediating view. He favors a doctrine of primeval diversities among men,—an original adaptation of the several races to those varied circumstances of climate and locality which, while congenial to the one, are destructive to the other. On the surface, this use of the word adaptation might lead to the inference that Morton advocates natural selection. Such is not the case. His adaptation is supernatural, not natural. It affirms that diversity among animals is a fact determined by the will of the Creator. It denies the competency of physical causes to produce the effect alleged. It is, therefore, not to be interpreted as approaching a theory of mutation. It may be pointed out how close were these views to those of Agassiz. In fact Morton's definition

of species as primordial forms, prepared the way for
the promulgation of the kindred theory of the Swiss
naturalist, as he expressed it later in his introduction to Morton's own *Types of Mankind*. Morton's
views were spread in the South through his pupil,
Knott of Mobile. They came to a curious use at the
hands of the politician, John C. Calhoun, who argues
that if all men had a common origin, whites and blacks
would be equal; but there has been a plurality of origins,
and one of these primordial varieties was the negro, who
was originally created the inferior of the Caucasian;
therefore, between whites and blacks there is no real
equality.

In contrast with such special pleading and in logical
connection with the paper of Wells, are the conjectures
of Haldeman and Leidy on the possibilities of natural
variation. It was the former who declared: Although we
may not be able artificially to produce a change beyond
a given point, it would be a hasty inference to suppose
that a physical agent, acting gradually for ages, would
not carry the variation a step or two farther, so that
instead of the original (we will say) four varieties, they
might amount to six, the sixth being sufficiently unlike
the earlier ones to induce a naturalist to consider it
distinct. This interesting conjecture was published in
Boston in 1843. One similar to it appeared in Philadelphia in 1850. Joseph Leidy, the paleontologist, asserted: The essential conditions of life are five in number, namely: a germ, nutritive matter, air, water, heat,
the four latter undoubtedly existing in the interior of
all animals. The result is that very slight modifications of these essential conditions of life are sufficient
to produce the vast variety of living beings upon the
globe.

There are none so blind as those who will not see. Here were two fruitful suggestions which lay practically forgotten until the appearance of the *Origin of Species*. This neglect was calamitous, yet the inability to grasp the significance of these naturalistic arguments was not without reason. The preformationists were in the majority and were still thinking in terms of the Platonic archetypes. There still lingered in their mind the Leibnizian conception of a great chain of being which binds together into a single system the past and present epochs of organic life. This doctrine of descent according to the analogy of the chain, precluded that of growth according to the analogy of the tree, the true tree of evolution with its many collateral branches springing from some single internal principle. And so until the appearance of Asa Gray, defender of Darwin, there was this great hindrance to the doctrine of organic evolutionism,—a preference for transcendence over immanence. Just as the Aristotelian scale of being had fallen in with the Puritanic doctrine of predestination, so now, among the descendants of Puritans, there was a difficulty in passing from the conception of special creation of species, fixed by fiat, to that of the continuous manifestation of the divine activities as shown in an orderly unfolding of the universe. In fine, tradition's rigid programme, an intellectual imposition upon matter of what should evolve from it, was opposed to nature's having any part in initiating variations, in originating novelties. In a word, the fiat of the Creator is set over against any conception of creative evolution, in the sense of the self-sufficiency of the universe, and this rendered difficult the reception of Darwinism. That reception was now rendered doubly difficult by the intrusion of a foreign force.

2. The Antagonism of Agassiz

The coming of Louis Agassiz in 1846 was hailed with
delight in the camp of the preformationists and supernaturalists, because the revival of Lamarck's naturalism
threatened the old guard with defeat. But now as at
Waterloo help came from the East, and Agassiz, like another Blücher, turned the tide of battle. The reënforce-
ment consisted in the Swiss naturalist's importation of
his master's views, for it was from Cuvier that he had
derived the fixed ideas of immutability of species,
special creation, and cataclysmic destruction. And so
because he brought in these reënforcements from the
flank Agassiz received a warm welcome at the hands of
the reactionary scientists and likewise at the hands of
the populace. It was not only because of his sanguine
personality, that, to use his own phrase, he became " the
spoilt child of the country," but because his convictions
fell in with those of an essentially conservative democracy. Evolution in the sense of physical derivation was
identified with materialism, and materialism to the
groundlings meant atheism. To all this Agassiz furnished an antidote. Believing that the order in the
cosmos depends upon intellectual coherence, not material connections, he asked if the divisions of the animal
kingdom have not been instituted by the Divine Intelligence as the categories of his mode of thinking, and, if
this be so, whether we do not find in this adaptability
of the human intellect to the facts of creation the most
conclusive proof of an affinity with the Divine Mind?

That which was put as a query became so fixed a
dogma that Agassiz could assure a committee of the
Massachusetts Legislature visiting his museum, that in
the future generations there would not be a child who

would not have the opportunity of understanding the scheme of creation as thoroughly as he understood his multiplication table. Now, the public liked such an assertion. It pointed out an easy road to learning. It also fell in with their views of a benevolent Providence, who from the very dawn of creation saw to it that this world should be arranged for the benefit of man. Thus the tenets of intelligibility and benevolence were two strings with which Agassiz worked the public. The same tenets were not without influence upon the conservative scientists. These he utilized in that famous Essay on Classification in his widely sold *Natural History of the United States*. He also utilized them in his persistent attacks on Darwin. In his review of the *Origin of Species* he repeats his favorite formula that order in the organic world consists in intellectual coherence, not material connection. Otherwise it would be impossible to show that branches in the animal kingdom are founded upon different plans of structure, patterns of form, categories of thought existing in the divine mind and, therefore, intelligently and methodically combined in all parts.

At this point it may be interesting to inquire why the arguments presented by Darwin in favor of a universal derivation from one primary form, made, as Agassiz confessed, not the slightest impression on his mind. The reason may be discovered earlier in his life than his biographers suggest. For many years back, he declared, he lost no opportunity of urging the idea that while species have no material existence, they yet exist as categories of thought in the mind of the Creator. Now what is the ultimate source of this belief? It is found in Agassiz's defense of his old teacher Oken and the physio-philosophical systems based on Schelling. So when it is recalled that in his youth Agassiz listened to Schelling and that Schelling was a Platonizer, much of the type of Emerson, one can understand the popularity of such views when they were freshly imported into America. It was not so much that Emerson knew something of the speculations of Schelling and Oken from Coleridge, but that he was a constitutional Platonizer who believed in the intelligibility of the world as due to the essential identity of the operations of the human and divine intellect. This transcendental opinion was one of the medley held by Agassiz. From it he inferred that the world is not due to the working of blind forces, but is the creation of a reflective mind establishing deliberately all the categories we recognize in nature, and combining them in that wonderful harmony which unites all things into such a perfect system. In defense of what he acknowledges to be a priori conceptions relating to nature, Agassiz falls back upon One Supreme Intelligence, Author of all things, by whose almighty fiat all animals, with all their peculiarities, were created upon the general plan of structure of the great type to which they belong. Here the Swiss zoölogist talks like a Platonizing Puritan. He goes even further in his reaction against naturalism. As to the origin of existing animals and plants he presents for consideration three theories: spontaneous generation; the action of the established laws of matter; the immediate intervention of an intelligent Creator. Of these three Agassiz boldly advocates the last because the first is not proven, and the second would stultify his postulate and preclude design. Granted that the four different plans of structure exhibited in the animal kingdom illustrate four great primordial ideas, then, unless the physical agents at work in the early days of the existence of our globe could have devised such plans, and impressed them upon the material world as the pattern upon which nature was to build forever afterwards, no such general relations as exist among all animals could ever have existed.

In his recoil from naturalism Agassiz has gone to such an extreme of supernaturalism as to have lost those very arguments for design in the constituted laws of nature, so skillfully employed by the deists. At the hands of such a reactionary the earlier arguments, therefore, fall to the ground. Intelligibility and intervention are mutually exclusive. One makes the world comprehensible, the other incomprehensible. When the rational conceptions fail, it is necessary to call in the help of the deity. The argument is again put in the form of a query: There are certain extraordinary changes which one and the same animal may undergo during different periods of its life;—does not this prove directly the immediate intervention of a power capable of controlling all these external conditions, as well as regulating the course of life of every being? To attack such a position those who would deny the intervention in nature of a creative mind must show that the cause to which they refer the origin of finite beings is by its nature a possible cause, which cannot be denied of a being endowed with the attributes which we recognize in God.

With such an outward creed Agassiz came into a country where the deists had won the day in behalf of the rationality of the constituted laws of nature. It is little wonder that, when the master repudiated his primary principles, his followers should go over to the new views. This explains why Agassiz's pupils surrendered in a body to Darwinism. In the first place, they found their leader's immutable classifications constantly changing; then they discovered that he did not understand the bearing of his own laws; and lastly they found that these laws fitted into the new scheme better than into the old. Agassiz's great idea of the identity of the three series—structural, individual, racial—really favored naturalism at the expense of supernaturalism. To neglect second causes and refer organic changes directly to a first cause—the plans of the Creator—made this triple identity unnatural, unreasonable, dependent on the mere whim of the Almighty. It was an impossible position that Agassiz took that, since species exist as thoughts, and individuals as facts, there was no material connection between the latter. To base common descent on formal grounds and at the same time to exclude a physical differentiation of the objects themselves, was merely to make a plan of a picture and never to use the actual pigments. Indeed Agassiz seemed incapable of filling in the figures, of blending the whole into a continuous canvas. He postulates his four plans of structure, but denies that they are transmutable the one into the other. In a word, his was a static, not a dynamic conception; his cosmos a prearranged programme, not a spontaneous growth. So he inveighs against natural selection as a misnomer, since selection implies design and the powers to which Darwin refers the orders of species can design nothing.

It was this insistence on the ancient form of the argument for design that enabled Asa Gray to turn some of Agassiz's own guns against him. Those natural divisions which to the latter existed only as categories of thought in the supreme intelligence, and were of an independent existence and unvarying as thought itself, Gray put into the ordering processes of the universe. In other words, that which had been a static, transcendent postulate now becomes a dynamic, immanent principle. To Gray this was not the exclusion of the supernatural, but its inclusion in the natural. No longer do species endure in a subjective and ideal sense, but they are interrelated by an objective inheritance from a common stock. In short, the adamantine chain of foreordination is replaced by the living tree of genetic descent. In this way the material, against which Agassiz inveighed, is turned inside out and shown to be interwoven with purpose. Thus Gray criticises Agassiz's review of Darwin and contends that the *Origin of Species* is not atheistic, since a material connection between the members of a series of organized beings is not inconsistent with the idea of their being intellectually connected with one another through the deity. Agassiz is theistic to excess because the Creator is put so supremely above his creation. The way out of the apparent difficulty of lack of design is, therefore, to regard the intervention of the deity " not so much as done for all time, as doing through all time."

Whether such an interpretation was a proper immanent theism, or a perilous approach to pantheism, may be judged better when we take up other of Darwin's reviewers. Meanwhile it remains to be shown how the appearance of the *Origin of Species,* instead of modifying Agassiz's beliefs, tended to fix them. A favorite disciple acknowledged that it was a special characteristic of Agassiz's mind, intensified by the teaching of his great master Cuvier, seldom to acknowledge an error, but, on the contrary, to try by all means to maintain his position. That characteristic now became prominent. At the meetings of the American Academy of Science and of the Natural History Society of Boston in 1860, he raised the sharpest objections against the acceptance of Darwin's theory, which he considered a " mania to be outlived." This was before the scientists. Before the public he again brought his views in his *Methods of Study in Natural History,* declaring that there was a repulsive poverty in this material explanation that is contradicted by the intellectual grandeur of the universe. Finally, in a posthumous article appearing in the *Atlantic Monthly,* he left a scientific last will and testament in which he reiterated the convictions which he had brought into the country. In this document there are three salient sections: First, that the law of evolution keeps types within appointed cycles of growth which revolve forever upon themselves; second, that the argument of Darwin is purely negative, resting upon the assumption that transition types have dropped out from the geological record; and lastly, that Darwinians are reluctant to grant intervention of an intellectual power in the diversity which obtains in nature, under the plea that such an admission implies distinct creative acts for every species.

In the first of these tenets Agassiz goes back to the nature-philosophy of his youth, takes evolution in the literal sense of an unrolling of an absolute, and suggests, if he does not borrow, the cyclic processes of Vico. This is historically consistent, for the doctrine of a recurring cosmic process has often been bound up with the scheme of preformation. That the argument of Darwin is negative is not so well taken. Agassiz indeed insisted on the interrelations of the three series—structural, embryonic, geologic—for the sake of the light that each sheds on the other. Now, the first of these series presumes the existence of the third, for embryonic growth was a positive suggestion that the geologic succession was not discontinuous, and this Agassiz's immediate successors discovered. In the last objection there was more weight. The young and ardent spirits of the day were reluctant to grant intervention, as it seemed to carry the doctrine of design to an extreme. Thus Agassiz's colleague, Asa Gray, reported the Lowell Lectures as being planned upon high ground and yet with a certain animus against Lamarck and the *Vestiges*. Likewise Agassiz's pupil, Joseph Le Conte, interpreted the master's writings as aimed to uphold a designed development, and yet one not by organic forces within, but according to an intelligent plan without,—an evolution not by transmutation of species, but by substitution of one species by another.

We leave Agassiz with his last will and testament,— a stumbling-block in the path of philosophical progress. We turn to his colleague and counterpart, Asa Gray, who did more than any single native writer to hasten the reception of Darwinism.

3. The Reception of Darwinism

In Asa Gray we have the New World's most efficient defender of Darwinism after the appearance of the *Origin of Species* in 1859. The Harvard botanist confesses himself a convinced theist with no prepossession in favor of naturalistic theories. Nevertheless he says that within half a generation it can be affirmed that the general doctrine of the derivation of species has prevailed over that of specific creation, and this in spite of the fact that so many of the reviewers attack the *Origin* as pantheistic, if not atheistic. In his first review of March, 1860, he writes that " this book is exciting much attention " and that already two American editions are announced. He foresees a spirited conflict among opinions of every grade,—a struggle for existence in which natural selection itself will destroy the weaker and allow the stronger to survive. Such conflicting opinions are those of Dana of Yale, whose idealistic *Thoughts upon*

Species will not readily harmonize with the naturalistic scheme, and those of Agassiz, who widely diverges from Darwinism.

Gray now draws an instructive parallel between the views of the Swiss-American and those of the Englishman in order to bring out the main features of the theory of the origination of species by means of natural selection. While Agassiz discards the idea of common descent as the real bond of union among the individuals and holds that each species originated at the same time over the whole geographical area it occupies, Darwin holds the orthodox view of the descent of all the individuals of a species not only from a local birthplace, but from a single ancestor or pair. He adds that each species has extended and established itself, through natural agencies, wherever it could; so that the actual geographical distribution of any species is by no means a primordial arrangement, but a natural result.

By the " orthodox " rule of descent, Gray evidently meant the Bible view, since the theory of a plurality of centers of origin lent itself to the common American belief in the possibility of special creation in order to repair the ravages of cataclysms. If, now, we substitute for the word orthodox the word current, we see that Agassiz had the people on his side. His theory, continues Gray, referring the phenomena both of origin and distribution directly to the divine will, both being equally primordial, equally supernatural, and also upholding that every adaptation of species to climate and of species to species, is as aboriginal and, therefore, inexplicable as are the organic forms themselves,—this theory is theistic to excess. The opposite theory is not open to this objection. The question of primordial origin may be left in abeyance, but geographical distribution is not a primordial arrangement but a natural result. Moreover, adaptation is a phenomenon according to which plants and animals are subject from their birth to physical influences, to which they have to accommodate themselves as they can. Is it not possible to harmonize these two theories, if the former makes the unity of plan only intellectual, and the latter makes inheritance material? In other words, is it not most presumable that an intellectual conception realized in nature would be realized through physical agencies? To Gray the compromise between theological views and physical causation seems not impossible. When Agassiz refers the whole to the agency of intellect as its first cause and when Darwin does not deny an intellectual connection between species —as related to a supreme intelligence—Gray dimly apprehends a probable combination of these divergent theories, and in that combination the ground for a strong stand against " mere naturalism."

In this last phrase the compromiser is really not one-sided. The proof that he does not take a stand against the natural is that he is opposed to the exclusively supernatural. Thus he adds that substantive proof of specific creation is not attainable, but that of derivation or transmutation of species may be. The propounders of the latter view are bound to do one of two things: either to assign real and adequate causes, the natural or necessary result of which must be to produce the present diversity of species and their actual relations; or, to show the general conformity of the whole body of facts to such assumption through its competency to harmonize all the facts. Lamarck mainly undertook the first line, but his doctrine of appetencies and habits of animals reacting upon their structure met with a somewhat undeserved ridicule. The shadowy author of the *Vestiges of the*

Natural History of Creation can hardly be said to have undertaken either line, in a scientific way. He would explain the whole progressive evolution of nature by virtue of an inherent tendency to develop, thus giving us an idea or a word in place of a natural cause, a restatement of the proposition instead of an explanation. Darwin attempts both lines of proof and in a strictly scientific spirit.

Nothing could have been more fortunate than this presentation of the case. It disarmed criticism of the naturalistic hypothesis by throwing the burden of proof upon the propounder. It allowed for a sufficient margin of deistic interpretation to satisfy the supernaturalists. Darwin, in proposing a theory which suggests a method that harmonizes these facts, into a system we may trust, implies that all was done wisely, in the largest sense designedly, and by an intelligent First Cause. Gray expressed trust in Darwin's deistic drift through the latter's allowing Paley's argument a further extension, and through his changing the meaning of the intervention of the Creator as done for all time, to an intervention as doing through all time.

It is possible that Gray strains a point in trying to accommodate Darwinism to the traditional Anglo-American philosophy. Yet he makes full allowance for the difficulties in the way of the acceptance of the new theory. The first difficulty is the imperfection of the geological records. Of the records of fossil lithography all but the last volume is out of print, and of its pages only local glimpses have been obtained. But for these gaps, we need not " invoke cataclysm to involve the world," for the theory of uniformity will account for all geological changes in a quiet and easy way. The second difficulty is that of the " missing link." Wide is the gap between the highest quadrumana and man; but where is there the slightest evidence of a common progenitor? In evolution the prospect of the future is encouraging; but the backward glance alarming. There may be a closer association of our ancestors of the olden time with "our poor relations" of the quadrumanous family than we like to acknowledge. But the whole argument in natural theology for a final cause, say in the structure of the hand, is just as good on the supposition of the descent of men from chimpanzees and gorillas as it would have been in the case of the first man supernaturally created. Meanwhile intermediate links between the two-handed and the four-handed are lacking altogether, so we must needs believe in the separate and special creation of man.

A third difficulty is that of sterility. Darwin labors to show that sterility is not a special endowment, to prevent the confusion of species by mingling, but an incidental acquirement. But this arrangement to keep apart those forms which have, or have acquired, a certain moderate amount of difference, looks to us as much designed for the purpose as does a ratchet to prevent reverse motion in a wheel. A fourth and a most formidable difficulty is that of the production and specialization of organs. All organic beings have been formed on two great laws: unity of type, and adaptation to the conditions of existence. The special teleologists, such as Paley, occupy themselves with the latter only, referring particular facts to special design, but leaving an overwhelming array of the widest facts inexplicable. The morphologists build on unity of type, which requires each individual "to go through a certain formality," and to accept, at least for a time, certain organs, whether they are of any use to him or not. If philosophers seek to harmonize these two views theoretically, Darwin harmonizes them naturally: adaptation is the result of natural selection; unity of type, of unity of reason.

In this summary statement Gray has given due weight to both sides of the controversy. He confessed that at first he had no prepossession in favor of naturalistic theories and that the evidence presented by Darwin had been so strong that he could not but give his studies the name of Darwiniana.

In turning from the college at Cambridge to the college at New Haven we find an illustration of the sarcastic saying that where Harvard leads Yale follows—at a distance. In James Dwight Dana, the geologist, we have a preformationist who through his uniformitarian views came to a gradual but grudging acknowledgment of Darwinism. As early as 1848 Dana writes to Gray that the view which he had favored of late was one suggested by Professor Henry of Washington, who considered the forces in animate nature chemical forces, but also that there was a directrix behind all, modifying or governing the results. He compared it to a steam engine whose forces within were directed in their operation by the engineer. Here was a sort of deistic dynamism, the raw material which Dana worked over for thirty years and left in this finished law of development: " Unity evolving multiplicity of parts, to successive individualization, proceeding from the more fundamental onwards."

The first modification of this suggested transcendent dynamism was to make it partially immanent. In his idea of species as certain amounts or kinds of concentrated force, Gray told Dana that he fell back upon the broadest and most fundamental views, and developed them with great ability and cogency. The praise is just. Dana's *Thoughts on Species* is a clearly reasoned study of the comprehensive principles that pervade the

universe, with the purpose of finding out the meaning
of permanency, and the basis of variations in species.
In this study of 1857 the author hopes to illumine a
subject as yet involved in doubts and difficulties, by
reasoning from central principles to circumferential.
From the study of the inorganic world we learn that
each element is represented by a specific amount or law
of force. The essential idea of species thus deduced is
this: a species corresponds to a specific amount or condition of force, defined in the act or law of creation. But
in organic beings, unlike the inorganic, there is a cycle
of progress involving growth and decline. The oxygen
molecule may be eternal as far as anything in its nature
goes. But the germ-cell is but an incipient stage in a
cycle of changes, and is not the same for two successive
instants. Thus an indefinite perpetuation of the germ-cell
is in fact effected; yet it is not mere endless being, but
like evolving like in an unlimited round. Hence when
individuals multiply from generation to generation, it
is but a repetition of the primordial type-idea, and the
true notion of species is not in the resulting group, but
in the idea or potential element which is at the basis
of every individual of the group.

In Dana's elaborate series of definitions we have several points of attachment with his fellow-scientists.
The cyclic conception is that of Agassiz, while the definition of the primordial type-idea is acknowledged to be
nearly the same as that of Morton, when he described a
species as a primordial organic force. But there is yet
a difference. With Dana there is greater emphasis upon
the immanent element in the evolutionary process. Each
species, he continues, has its own special mode of development as well as ultimate form or result,—its serial
unfolding, inworking, and outflowing. The precise na-

ture of the potentiality in each species is expressed by the line of historical progress from the germ to the full expansion of its power. We comprehend the type-idea only when we understand the cycle of evolution through all its laws of progress, both as regards the living structure under development within, and its successive relations to the external world.

Thus far there is much that is significant in Dana's essay. It has an air of novelty. In its reference to the influence of the external world it appears to lean toward the environmental influences of Darwin. Meanwhile the *Origin of Species* had appeared and the doctrine of variation through natural selection was rife. But as Dana wrote to Darwin in 1863, geology has not afforded facts that sustain the view that the system of life has been evolved through a method of development from species to species. Darwin, in turn, admits that his correspondent's objections are perfectly valid, but he adds this demurrer: " As my book has been lately somehow attended to, perhaps it would have been better if, when you condemned all such views, you had stated that you had not been able yet to read it. But pray do not suppose that I think for one instant that, with your strong and slowly acquired convictions and immense knowledge, you could have been converted. The utmost that I could have hoped would have been that you might possibly have been here or there staggered. Indeed, I should not much value any sudden conversion, for I remember well how many years I fought against my present belief."

The conversion of Dana to Darwinism—if such it may be called—was indeed slow. A dozen years after this letter he insists that the transition between species, in the system of progress, has not yet proved to be gradual and that man is not of nature's making, but owes his existence to the special act of the Infinite Being whose image he bears. But the tide at last turned, and, twenty years later, naturalism and supernaturalism came to a compromise in his mind. As he wrote in the last and revised edition of his *Manual of Geology,* the former speculative conclusions are not all in accord with the author's present judgment. In giving up the general principles with regard to the progress in the earth's life—such as progress from the aquatic to the terrestrial, from the simple to the complex—he states that all these principles are in accord with a theory of evolution, and, through the added facts of later years, they favor the view of evolution by natural variation. Such added facts are that Arctic America contained in tertiary time plants so much like species existing in the forests of both temperate North America and Japan, that the former have been pronounced the undoubted progenitors of the latter. Also along the Pacific Coast and Gulf Coast of Central America there are so many identical and nearly related species of aquatic animals that migration during a time of submergence of the narrow strip of land, with subsequent variation, is regarded as the only reasonable explanation.

Dana's old preformationism with its fixed types now gives place to great plasticity in organic structures under variant agencies. A telling proof here is a fossil collection of Dana's pupil, Marsh, exhibiting the descent of the horse from the primitive five-toed species to the present one-toed variety. This collection was a palpable proof to Huxley, yet Dana was never entirely won over to naturalism. The causes of variation mentioned by Darwin are acknowledged to be real causes, but they are held to act directly, after the Lamarckian method, without dependence for success upon the principle of natural selection. This theory is not essential to evolution because it is based on the assumption that variations come singly or nearly so, and that the selected are, therefore, few compared with the multitudes that disappear. The idea is derived from facts recorded of domestic or cultivated races whose structures are in a strained or artificial state and deteriorate when care ceases. But in wild nature variations are, in general, the slow and sure results of the conditions. When, therefore, a variation appears that admits of augmentation by continued inbreeding, progress should be general, and the unadaptable few should disappear, not the multitude. Man affords an example. The gradual gain of some races in lands and supremacy and the disappearance of the inferior races is one example of the survival of the fittest, or natural selection. But the superior races derived the power which led to their survival and preëminent position through favoring conditions in environments, that is, in geographical, geological, and biological conditions and resources; through the powers of endurance, and courage, and mind power, and will power, which conflict with nature and other races of men in the world is fitted to develop; and through the power of self-assurance which comes of a high moral sense. Hence victory, survival. The survival of the fittest is a fact; and the fact accounts in part for the geographical distribution of the races of men now existing and still in progress; but not for the existence of the fittest nor for the power that has determined survival.

In this half-hearted avowal of Darwinism the Yale geologist betrays a certain confusion on the subject. Asa Gray suggested such a confusion or lack of comprehension when he wrote to Dana: " Every now and then something you write makes me doubt if you quite get hold of Darwinian natural selection. . . . Suppose the term be a personification, as, no doubt, strictly it is. One so fond as you are of personification ought not to object to what seems to me a happy term."

The reception of Darwinism at Yale College was lukewarm. A similar state of affairs existed at Princeton. In President McCosh we have a treatment clear, candid, and incisive, but a method of approach ominous to scientific naturalism. The new college head tells us that he was not a week in Princeton till he let it be known to the upper classes of the college that he was in favor of evolution—properly limited and explained. This qualification is in harmony with the speaker's previous words. In his first published volume, *The Method of the Divine Government,* he sought to unfold the plan by which God governs the world. He concedes that he found it in an orderly manner—that is, by law. He is now prepared to believe that there might be a like method in the organic kingdoms and to listen to Darwin when he showed that there was a regular instrumentality in the descent of plants and animals. In place, then, of undiscriminating denunciation of evolution from so many pulpits, periodicals, and seminaries, a denunciation which assumes evolution and Christianity incompatible, the Princetonian propounds a definition to harmonize the two: Evolution is the drawing of one thing out of another; it proceeds from causation which is universal, for in the world things are so connected that every one thing proceeds from some other, and all things from God. This is the dogma. Can it be proved? Darwin is constantly making the distinction between natural selection and supernatural design, between natural law and special creation. Now, the difference between the two

opposing theories as thus put is misleading, since the
supernatural power is to be recognized in the natural
law, the Creator's power being executed by the creature's
action, the design seen in the mechanism. Chance is
obliged to vanish because we see contrivance. There
is purpose when we see a beneficent end accomplished.

So much for the preamble. Apparently the newly
imported Scottish divine is back in the eighteenth century, the age of reason, which saw in all things benevolence and design. That attitude was more fully expressed in McCosh's joint work on *Typical Forms and
Special Ends in Creation*. But he now recognizes that
the matter is not so easy of solution. It will not do to
Platonize. The types of the animal kingdom have been
fondly contemplated and admired by our profounder
minds. They have been identified with the grand ideas
which, according to Plato, have been in or before the
divine mind from all eternity. Pious minds like Cuvier
have ascribed them to God, whose thoughts are embodied
in them. On the other hand, the great rival of Cuvier,
St. Hilaire, ascribed the types to a common descent, and
used language which sounded as if the animal by its
wishes could add to its organs; could call forth fins to
swim with, and wings to fly. The controversy came to
a head when Goethe declared that it was of more
importance than the French Revolution.

There is undoubtedly a difference between the two
views; but McCosh asks if there may not be a reconciliation? It may be by descent that types are
formed, and yet all be done by a plan in the
divine wisdom which is thus manifested. The two
great Swiss-American naturalists, Agassiz and Guyot,
delighted to perceive clearly that there was a
system in the descent of animals which they were

sure was conceived in the divine mind, but doubted whether it could have been produced by natural law or material agency. But surely, in analogy with divine procedure in all other parts of nature, we may discover a divine plan, and at the same time a creature agency to carry it out, which agency makes known God's plan to us. We may see that the relations which constitute types are genetic, and as we perceive in them wisdom and beauty, we can also perceive that they are instituted by God. This view gives to classes a connection in the very nature of things, and makes species intelligible to human intelligence, which thereby rises to some comprehension of divine intelligence, in the image of which human intelligence is formed.

The ground is gone over again and the same conclusion reached,—the comfortable conclusion of benevolence, design, and the human capacity to comprehend the cosmic purposes. Anything the scientist brings forward may be clearly beheld in this bright light of optimism. When the geologist points out the series of changes in the horse tribe from the five- to the one-toed varieties, the writer holds that it is all for the best: God has provided the horse with its hard hoof for man, who to make it harder adds a shoe. "I hold that there are as clear proofs of design in the hoof as in the shoe upon it." Against this complacent supernaturalism the new doctrines make but little headway. McCosh mentions among the causes of variation the one to which Darwin has given such prominence. It is natural selection, which to McCosh seems a not very happy phrase, as it is apt to leave the impression that there is a choice on the part of nature, whereas it is all produced by the arrangements made by the Creator. This is the doctrine of final cause, a doctrine of natural religion. Nevertheless it is not opposed to the absolute mutability of species, which in its turn has become almost a religious doctrine, around which has gathered a sacred feeling which it is thought dangerous to disturb. With this opinion McCosh has little patience. It is a question for science to settle and not religion.

To science, then, the author turns to trace the geological history of the earth. His data he draws chiefly from Dana of Yale and Guyot of Princeton—both "reconcilers" of Genesis and geology. From these data he argues that that which the scientists call a system is what Platonists call an idea, and theologians design or purpose in the history of organic life. Of course in all this there is the universal law, established by a wide and uncontradicted experience that nature is uniform. This much against the anti-evolutionists. But at this point also extreme evolutionists are to be met, by showing that there are other powers which have modified evolution such as light, life, sensation, instinct, intelligence, morality!

The Princetonian has missed the chief point made by naturalism. When he claims that none of these agents are producible by the power of nature, he shows himself incapable of grasping the doctrine of immanence, the belief in a universal principle inclusive of these manifold agencies and all to be put under the name of nature. The old-fashioned dualism of this thinker is again exposed. As evolution by physical causes cannot produce life with all its variations, he infers that God does it by an immediate fiat, even as he created matter and the forces that act in matter. All that can be allowed in restating the problem is that Darwinism has modified design only to this extent: by making these high agencies an act of Providence instead of an act of creation. It is not neces-

sary to go much further in exposition of the views of Mc-
Cosh. They are more fully set forth in another book—
Development: What It Can Do, and What It Cannot Do.
But a word more is needed on the attitude of the man
toward the whole movement. He has been held to have
welcomed Darwinism, and to have set evolutionism on its
legs in a conservative community. The truth of the matter is quite the contrary. Evolution might be discussed
in the college, but in the eighteenth, not the nineteenth
century meaning of the term. Defined originally as the
drawing of one thing out of another the conclusions
drawn from it were didactic. The college head hence-
forth shall do the thinking for his pupils. Darwinism
never teaches that nature is red in tooth and claw, but
that the survival of the fittest is a beneficial law. Just as
the common soldier did not discover all the wisdom of
Napoleon, so this, McCosh concludes, should be our position in regard to God's works: we discover enough of the
arc to calculate the rest; and as we see so much wisdom in
the little that we know, we argue that there is vastly
more in the much that is beyond.

The compromising deist of the previous century speaks
in the Scottish-American divine. He fully admits that
there are results following from the laws of God which
it is not easy to reconcile with the omniscience and
benevolence of the deity, yet since " by a higher arrangement of nature, or rather, the God of nature, the organic
world is progressing. . . . There are cereals when before
there were only heaths and mosses, and man himself is
further removed from the savage state. . . . We have
thus a promise that the earth may become a perfect abode
for a perfected humanity."

McCosh has been considered by some Princetonians an
advocate of Darwinism. But as Alexander Ormond has

pointed out, he never became an evolutionist in his fundamental thought, and was never able to enter into the new theory because his age was a period of transition.

The same may be said of McCosh's learned pupil, Charles Woodruff Shields. The latter asserts, in his *Philosophia Ultima*, that his master from the first had led the creationists into alignment with the evolutionists and adds that from present signs it would seem that the tide of controversy has turned in favor of evolution, in some form and degree as logically consistent with the strictest creationalism. Shields makes this assertion, despite the fact that there are two rival schools which have arisen in the attempt to solve the great metaphysical problem, the development of absolute being. According to the former, he explains, the whole universe, both spiritual and material, has proceeded from deity, by successive acts of creation. According to the opposite school of thinkers, the totality of existence proceeds from some creative substance or principle, under physical laws of evolution, embracing all mental as well as material phenomena. This is a fair generalization. So is the next to the effect that while German thinkers attempt chiefly the problem of harmonizing the physical with the logical development of the universe as projected by science and philosophy, English and American writers deal largely with the more practical task of reconciling evolution with morality, religion, and orthodoxy.

The latter point of view is peculiarly that of Shields. The great aim of his *Final Philosophy* is to give a survey of the sciences wherein rational and revealed are ultimately brought into reconciliation. The method of reconciliation in the case of evolution is somewhat strained. It consists in giving high praise to the supernaturalists and faint praise to the naturalists. For example, in the case of the anthropological science concerning the doctrine of human evolution, " distinguished " biologists have maintained that the fœtal development of man, so far from proving his animal pedigree, merely reflects that unity of plan which has pervaded the organic world from the beginning. Likewise, " leading " ethnologists hold that there is a profound gulf without connection or passage, separating the human species from every other. On the other hand, the " so-called " archæo-geologists have also been met upon their own ground, Dawson, for instance, maintaining that the famous Neanderthal skull is simply exceptional. . . . In short, if the " notion " of transmutation be separated from that of progression, we can readily imagine the scale of civilized and savage humanity descending as well as ascending from the image of a God and the image of an ape.

The animus of Shields' voluminous work is finally laid bare by such statements as these,—that Joseph Vandyke has argued elaborately that both theism and revelation are required to explain the origin of man; and that although the Presbyterian Professor Woodrow, of South Carolina, has been deprived of his theological chair for teaching a partial evolution, yet President Patton has stated the theory as still a hopeful problem in apologetics.

Shields made a valiant attempt to be a balance-wheel between two opposite forces, but the dead weight of dogma pulled him back. Thus while he can assert that George Ticknor Curtis has " judicially " tested the theory of evolution and found it not proven, Charles Darwin remains for him a mere " speculative " naturalist. In fine, Shields, like his master McCosh, was in an age of transition and unable to grasp the significance of the new movement.

We now turn from the apologist of Princeton to another thinker in a neighboring university, who, although a transitionalist, was also a transmutationist. Edward Cope of Philadelphia has the distinction of having founded an "American school of biology" which attempted to go beyond Darwin's natural selection. Cope's evolutionary philosophy was expressed in his chief work, *The Origin of the Fittest*. This work was notable coming at the time it did. In Philadelphia the tradition of free-thought had run into a narrow channel, but it was still partially preserved in the University and in those scientific societies fathered by Franklin. But the public in general had lost that tradition of liberalism, and the town which had once been so hospitable to all comers had now closed its doors to foreign thought. Therefore, Cope expostulates, let those excellent people in whose minds there is considerable repugnance to the acceptance, or even consideration of the hypothesis of development, restrain their condemnation. They may object that the human species is certainly involved and man's ascent from the ape asserted; and also that the scheme in general seems to conflict with that presented by the Mosaic account of creation; but it now behooves those interested to explain the events and to look any consequent necessary modification of their metaphysical or theological views squarely in the face.

Of the two main consequences above portrayed, the first seemed the more distasteful. If the hypothesis here maintained be true, explains the naturalist, man is the descendant of some preëxistent generic type, the which, if it were now living, we would probably call an ape. It would be an objection of little weight could it be truly urged that there have as yet been discovered no remains of ape-like men, for we have frequently been called upon in the course of paleontological discovery to bridge greater gaps than this, and greater remain, which we expect to fill. But we *have* ape-like characters exhibited by more than one race of men yet existing. We all admit the existence of higher and lower races, the latter being those which we now find to present greater or less approximations to the apes. The peculiar structural characters that belong to the negro in his most typical form are of that kind, however great may be the distance of his remove therefrom. The flattening of the nose and prolongation of the jaws constitute such a resemblance; so do the deficiency of the calf of the leg, and the obliquity of the pelvis, which approaches more the horizontal position than it does in the Caucasian. The investigations made at Washington during the war, with reference to the physical characteristics of the soldiers, show that the arms of the negro are from one to two inches longer than those of the whites: another approximation to the ape. In fact, this race is a species of the genus Homo as distinct in character from the Caucasian as those we are accustomed to recognize in other departments of the animal kingdom; but he is not distinct by isolation, since intermediate forms between him and the other species can be abundantly found.

The second objection as to the conflict between the Mosaic account of creation and the Darwinian is to be met in the same way. '' Believe in the expert '' and the old view goes by the board. The modern theory of evolution has met with remarkably rapid acceptance by those best qualified to judge of its merits, namely, the zoölogists and botanists, while probably the majority of the public, in this region at least, profess to reject it. This inconsistency is due to two causes. In the first place, Darwin's demonstration contained in the *Origin of Species* proves little more than that the species of the same genus have had common origin, and also his theory of natural selection is incomplete as an explanation of their origin. In the second place, the unscientific world is unreasonable, little knowing the slow steps and laborious effort by which any general truth is reached. Hence they find in incompleteness ground of condemnation of the whole. Now Science is glad if she can prove that the earth stands on an elephant, and gladder if she can demonstrate that the elephant stands on a turtle; but if she cannot show the support of the turtle she is not discouraged, but labors patiently, trusting that the future of discovery will justify the experience of the past.

Cope's appeal to the higher court of the expert is not an appeal to authority, nor a mere substitute of present for past dogma. If some of the people find Darwin's argument incomplete, or in some points weak, it may be answered so do the student classes, who, nevertheless, believe it. This is largely because Darwin's facts and thoughts repeat a vast multiplicity of experiences of every student, which are of as much significance as those cited by him, and which only required a courageous officer to marshal them into line, a mighty host, conquering and to conquer. These will slowly find their way into print, some in one country and some in another.

In distinguishing between the fact of evolution and the various views of evolution, Cope effectively meets the objections of the old school against the new theory. The evidence in favor of evolution, he explains, is abundant; much less has been done in explanation of the law of evolution. Darwin and his immediate followers have brought out the law of natural selection; Spencer has endeavored to express them in terms of force; while, among Americans, Hyatt, Packard, and Cope himself advanced the law of acceleration and retardation. It is this latter group, headed by Cope, that has been called the American biological school. Out of this school we shall take up later one notable living representative, James Mark Baldwin. Meanwhile we must turn from the philosophy of the chair to that of the rostrum, and consider a popular representative of the movement.

4. COSMIC PHILOSOPHY: JOHN FISKE

As a summarizer of the controversy between special creation and derivation John Fiske has given us the clearest contemporary account. This account, as Josiah Royce has pointed out, is somewhat rancorous, because at that time Agassiz still dominated the current teaching, and the Darwinian theory was still on trial before the public. That public was given its choice. Was it to be special creation or derivation? The pedigree of the two theories has something to do with the decision. The former hypothesis, says Fiske, originated in the crude mythological conceptions of the ancient Hebrews and was uncritically accepted until the time of Lamarck and Goethe. The latter hypothesis originated in the methodical studies of the phenomenon of organic life, and has been held by a large number of biologists during the first half of the nineteenth century. Now, while the Hebrew writer presents us with a concrete picture of the creation of man, a homogeneous clay model of the human form at once transmuted into a heterogeneous combination of organs and tissues—the few naturalists who still make a show of upholding the special creation hypothesis carefully refrain from specification. When challenged they take refuge in grandiloquent phrases about " Creative Will " and " free action of an Intelligent Power,"—

very much as the cuttlefish extricates itself from a disagreeable predicament by hiding in a shower of its own ink. When translated, however, from the dialect of mythology into the dialect of science, the special creation hypothesis falls flat. It asserts that untold millions of molecules rushed together at some appointed instant from divers quarters and grouped themselves into an adult mammal. . . . Such an hypothesis, which involves such an assumption, is at once excluded from the pale of science.

The opposite hypothesis, that of derivation, has four kinds of arguments in its favor. The first of these is classification. This is not the scheme of Agassiz, who attempted to explain the four distinct types of animal structure by resuscitating from its moss-covered tomb the Platonic theory of ideas. Hardly! The scientific scheme of classification is a complex arrangement of organisms in groups within groups, resembling each other at the bottom of the scale and differing most widely at the top. Now, if each species has been separately created, no reason can be assigned for such an arrangement,—unless perchance someone can be found hardy enough to maintain that it was intended as a snare and a delusion for human intelligence. The old opponents of geology, who strove to maintain at whatever cost the scientific credit of the Mosaic myth of the creation, asserted that fossil plants and animals were created already dead and petrified, just for the fun of the thing. Manifestly those persons take a quite similar position who pretend that God created separately the horse, ass, zebra, and quagga, having previously created a beast enough like all of them to be their common grandfather. Now, the true theory of classification depends not upon special creation, but common origin, a given family being capable of arrangement in diverging groups and sub-groups, along lines which ramify like branches, branchlets, and twigs of a tree.

An equally powerful argument is furnished by the embryonic development of organisms. Why does a mammal begin to develop as if it were going to become a fish, and then, changing its course, act as if it were going to become a reptile or bird, and only after much delay assume the peculiar characteristics of mammals? On the evolutionary theory, these phenomena are explicable as due to the integration or summing-up of adaptive processes by which modifications, slowly acquired through generations of ancestral organisms, are more and more rapidly repeated in the embryo. On the hypothesis that each species of organisms was independently built up by a divine architect, how are we to explain these circuitous proceedings? Unless it were due to recapitulation, the process would be as futile as the work of an architect who could not erect a palace, except by first using his materials in the shape of a hut, and then rebuilding the hut as a cottage, and finally as a palace. Again there are the equally significant facts of morphology. Why, unless through common inheritance, should all vertebrates be constructed on the same type? It is a familiar fact that the arms of men and apes, the forelegs of quadrupeds, the wings of birds, and the breast fins of fishes are structurally identical, being developed from the same embryonal rudiments. Why is this so? But two answers are possible. We may either say, with the Mussulman, " it so pleased Allah, whose name be exalted "; or we may honestly acknowledge the scientific implication that such community of structure is strong evidence in favor of community of origin. Finally, the facts of geographical distribution and geological succession are in complete harmony with the development theory. On the hypothesis of special creations, no good reason can be given why the extinct animals found in any geographical area should resemble, both in general structure and in special modifications, the animals which now live in the same area. It has indeed been urged, by upholders of the special creation hypothesis, that these striking resemblances may be explained by supposing each species to have been created in strict adaptation to the conditions of life surrounding it. But there is no appreciable difference, for example, between the conditions of existence in the seas east and west of the Isthmus of Panama; yet, according to the assumption of the special-creationists, their marine faunas ought to be almost exactly alike, which they are not. The presumption raised at the outset against the doctrine of special creation is even superfluously confirmed by the testimony of facts. Not only is this doctrine discredited by its barbaric origin, and by the absurd or impossible assumptions which it would require us to make, but it utterly fails to explain a single one of the phenomena of the classification, embryology, morphology, and distribution of extinct and living organisms. While, on the other hand, the doctrine of derivation is not only accredited by its scientific origin, and by its appealing to none but verifiable processes and agencies, but it affords an explanation for each and all of the above-mentioned phenomena.

Such is the contrast drawn up by Fiske between what he comes to call anthropomorphism and cosmism. The latter term is a favorite with its author. He applies it to his voluminous work from which this discussion of Darwinism is taken. That work, on *Cosmic Philosophy*, is in large measure an interpretation to the American public of the system of Herbert Spencer, which, it is hardly needful to say, clashed with the old conservative view. To those who sought design and purpose in the universe the Spencerian Unknowable was like the House of Lords,—" it did nothing in particular and did it very well." Now, this Spencerian vagueness failed to satisfy even the ardent disciple, Fiske. He therefore proceeded to modify that system. He is opposed to any anthropomorphic theism, because personality and infinity are terms expressive of ideas which are mutually incompatible. Nevertheless, the phenomenal universe is the manifestation of some definite power. Here the older forms of design are unconvincing. The Infinite does not contrive, because the doctrine of evolution shows us that the universe is not a contrivance, but an organism with an indwelling principle of life. It was not made, but has grown. In a word, the teleology of nature is an all-pervading harmony.

Fiske as philosopher has at last been forced into the problem of the relation of Darwinism and design. A compromise which Asa Gray attempted, he seeks to effect. The conclusion is interesting, it is the old Stoic solution, the solution which requires an immanent principle. To this view of Fiske's, Joseph Cook, the Boston Monday lecturer, attached a name, remarkable in its anticipation of a famous modern work. Cook cites several theories of the origin of species, beginning with Cope's self-elevation by appetency, and ending with Dana's adjustment of natural forces with breaks of special intervention. But of all the views he gives fullest definition to this: Immanent action and direction of divine power, working by the purposive collocation and adjustment of natural forces, acting without breaks,—or the theory of creative evolution.

With this anticipation of the Bergsonian phrase, we pass on to a prominent living exponent of genetic evolutionism.

5. Genetic Evolutionism: James Mark Baldwin

Out of a controversy with Cope has arisen one of the most fruitful enlargements of Darwinism. We refer to the theory of James Mark Baldwin called " Organic Selection " as opening a sphere for the application of the principle of natural selection. Cope as a neo-Lamarckian had emphasized use-inheritance and growth-force. Baldwin as a neo-Darwinian claims that these are metaphysical assumptions for which there is only an artificial need. As the Darwinian principle of natural selection supplanted the special-creation theory, so will the new factor of organic selection supplant Cope's theory of accommodation by consciousness. After years of study and experiment with children the writer is convinced that organic selection is a direct substitute for Lamarckian heredity. It avoids the occultism of physical transmission and puts in its place social heredity, the acquisition of functions from the social environment. Thus as soon as animals can use their native impulses in an imitative way they begin to learn directly, by what may be called " cross cuts " to a desirable goal, the traditional habits of their species. The chick which imitates the hen in drinking does not have to wait for a happy accident, nor to make a series of experiments, to find out that water is to be drunk. All the remarkable accommodations of an imitative sort, so conspicuous in the higher animals, enable them to acquire the habits and behavior of their kind without running the risks of trial and error. Calling this store of habits of whatever kind " tradition," and calling the individual's absorption of them and his consequent education in tradition his "social heredity," we have a more or less independent determining factor in evolution.

Organic selection becomes, accordingly, a universal principle in so far as accommodation is universal. This meets the view of the Lamarckians that evolution does somehow reflect individual progress; but it meets it without adopting the principle of Lamarckian inheritance. Indeed it would seem that high intellectual and moral progress are matters of social accommodation rather than that of direct natural inheritance on the part of individuals. Galton has shown how rare a thing it is for artistic, literary, or other marked talent to maintain its strength in later generations. Instead, we find such endowments showing themselves in many individuals at about the same time, in the same communities, and under common social conditions. Groups of artists, musicians, literary men, appeared together, constituting, as it were, a social outburst.

Baldwin's view of the predominance of the social factor may throw some light even on the obscure subject of the origin of the genius. It is much more effective in the case of the normal child. In his first volume on *Mental Development* it is shown that the child's life historically is a faithful reproduction of his social condition. He is, from childhood up, excessively receptive to social suggestion; his entire learning is a process of conforming to social patterns. The essential to this, in his heredity, is very great plasticity, cerebral balance and equilibrium, a readiness to overflow into the new channels which his social environment dictates. He has to learn everything for himself, and in order to do this he must begin in a state of great plasticity and mobility. These social lessons which he learns for himself take the

place largely of the heredity of particular paternal acquisitions. The father must have been plastic to learn,
and this plasticity is, so far as the evidence goes, the
nervous condition of consciousness; thus the father
learned, through his consciousness, from his social environment. The child does the same. What he inherits
is the nervous plasticity and the consciousness. He
learns particular acts for himself; and what he learns is,
in its main lines, what his father learned. So he is just
as well off, the child of Darwinism, as if he were physical heir to the acquisitions which his father made.

By his emphasis on the social, Baldwin has raised the
problem of evolution to a higher plane. Adaptation by
intelligent selection makes the Lamarckian factor unnecessary. All the resources of " social transmission "—
the handing down of intelligent acquisitions by paternal
instruction, imitation, gregarious life, come indirectly to
take the place of the physical inheritance of such adaptations. This is the proof positive. The proof negative
lies in the fact that most of the psychologists are not
appealed to by the extreme facility and ease of the
Lamarckian solution. If experience is inherited, why
have not racial psychological experiences of the most
ancient and uniform order—such as those of space perception, time estimation, verbal speech, the rudiments of
the three " r's," drilled into every child and used with
absolute uniformity throughout life—why have not such
functions become congenital?

As with the human so with the animal race. The
variations which are not adequate at first, or are only
partially correlated, are supplemented by the accommodations which the creature makes, and so the species
has the time to perfect its inadequate congenital mechanism. Thus the swans of Lake Geneva show relatively dif-

ferent length of neck. Those with longer necks can feed under water over a greater area of the bottom. Constant stretching of the neck not only develops each swan, but may be supposed to have encouraged variations in the direction of longer neck, that is, variations coincident in direction with their active accommodative processes. So the long neck has been evolved.

Darwinism has been defended through organic selection as a substitute for use-inheritance. For example, the more trivial experiences of the individual, such as body mutilations, which it is not desirable to perpetuate, would not be taken up in the evolution of the race. Organic selection would set a premium only on the variations which were important enough to be of some material use, just as the new science of eugenics is founded upon the possibility of carrying further in a systematic way the intentional improvement of the race. In regard to the exclusive production of reflexes, as would be the case under use-inheritance, organic selection is adverse. Instead of the rigidity of inherited instincts we have the plasticity possible under the minimum of instinctive equipment. A chick, for example, is bound down by a mass of inherited reflexes. The child, though at first helpless from its lack of instinctive tendencies, has an enormous advantage in being able to pick and choose by means of intelligence. It is intelligence which secures the widest possible range of personal adjustments, and by so doing widens the sphere of organic selection, so that the creature which thinks has a general screen from the action of natural selection. The struggle for existence, depending upon the physical qualities on which the animals rely, is in some degree done away with.

Organic selection has now reached an interesting

speculative position. In protesting against rigid inheritance it brings in accommodation. In emphasizing intelligence it brings in educability. The old dualism is breaking down. By rendering the physical plastic, the physical becomes permeable to intellect. Out of this emerges a new phase of freedom. Instead of the determinism either of the old preformism or that of mere mechanical natural selection we have a case where natural selection operates to preserve creatures, because they adapt themselves to their environment. The directive factor is now largely self-directive, since the intelligence represents the highest and most specialized form of accommodation. In a word, organic selection has supplemented and enlarged the old natural selection by bringing in the doctrine of the survival of the accommodating. Organic selection, then, has this summary advantage: It opens a great sphere for the application of the principle of natural selection upon organisms, that is, selection on the basis of what they do, rather than of what they are; of the new use they make of their functions, rather than of the mere possession of certain congenital characters. A premium is set on plasticity and adaptability of function rather than on congenital fixity of structure; and this adaptability reaches its highest level in the intelligence.

With the entrance of consciousness as the vehicle of accommodation we are ready to consider the place of individual purpose in evolution. As supplemented by organic selection natural selection is now seen to be not unteleological. The charge made against Darwinism was that, with its emphasis on " chance " and on the " fortuitous," its workings were blind and capricious. This charge can be met, answers Baldwin: It has been found that biological phenomena—variations in particular—follow the definite law of probability; in short, that there is no such thing in nature as the really fortuitous or unpredictable. Natural selection, therefore, works upon variations which are themselves subject to law. If this be true, then natural selection may be the method of realizing a cosmic design, if such exists, the law of variation guaranteeing the presence of a fixed proportional number of individuals which are " fit " with reference to a preëstablished end. . . . A good illustration may be seen in the use made of vital statistics in life insurance. We pay a premium rate based on the calculation of the probability of life, and thus by observing this law realize the teleological purpose of providing for our children; and we do it more effectively, though indirectly, than if we carried our money in bags around our necks, and gradually added our savings to it. Furthermore, the insurance company is a great teleological agency, both for us and for itself; for it also secures dividends for its stockholders on the basis of charges adjusted to the " chances " of life, drawn from the mortality tables. Why is it not a reasonable view that cosmic Purpose—if we may call it so—works by similar, but more adequate, knowledge of the whole and so secures its results—whether in conformity to or in contravention of our individual striving?

In raising these questions the author disavows any attempt to carry them out into a philosophical view of reality, a theoretical doctrine of metaphysics. Nevertheless in a series of illuminating figures he does suggest a metaphysics of the most stimulating sort. Genetic science, he explains, in the presence of an exact and numerical science must make the reservation that it is a cross-section, not a longitudinal section to which the quantitative and analytical formulas apply. But keeping in mind the old Greek antithesis between being and becoming, genetic science, as a science of development and evolution, must preserve the prospective attitude. This, then, is the chief postulate of the theory of genetic modes, that that series of events only is truly genetic which cannot be constructed before it has happened, and which cannot be exhausted by reading backward after it has happened. As between the purely mechanical or mathematical sciences and that of the next ascending set of phenomena, biology, recent discussion is full of illuminating matter which might be cited in support of these principles. That the synthesis which is called life is different in some respects from that of chemistry is not only the contention of the vitalists, but also the admission of the adherents of a physico-chemical theory of life. In reply to those who think not only that living matter is a chemical compound, but also that there is nothing to add to this chemical formula—when once it is discovered—in order to attain a final explanation of life, we have only to put to them the further problem of genesis, as over and above that of analysis—that is, to ask not only for the analytic formula, the chemical formula, for protoplasm, but also for the laws of reproduction and growth, which always characterize life. The cross-section formula must be supplemented by the longitudinal-section formula. Here we discover the fact that the development is by a series of syntheses, each chemical, but each, so far as we know, producing something new—*a new genetic mode*. If this be denied, then we have to ask the chemist to reproduce the series; and if he claim that this might be done if he knew how, we ask him to *reproduce the series backwards*. What the biologists need to do is to recognize the limitations of one method, and the justification of the other in its own province. In the life processes there seems to be a real genetic series, an irreversible series. Each stage exhibits a new form of organization. After it has happened, it is quite competent to show, by the formulas of chemistry and physics, that the organization is possible and legitimate. Yet it is only by actual observation and description of the facts in the development of the organism, that the progress of the life principle can be made out. The former is quantitative and analytic science; the latter is genetic science.

We leave Baldwin's *Development and Evolution* at that informing doctrine of irreversibility which has been expressly utilized by the author of *Creative Evolution*. This utilization is significant, yet the American's work is valuable not only as furnishing a link between the English and French conceptions of evolution, but also as a refutation of the charge of the decadence of Darwinism. That refutation is carried on more fully in the subsequent book entitled *Darwin and the Humanities*. Originating as a contribution to the Darwinian celebration of the American Philosophical Association in 1909, this work traces the influence of Darwin in the science of mind, the humanities broadly defined. As the result of his labors for twenty-five years the author comes to the conclusion that natural selection is in principle the universal law of genetic organization and progress in nature. As applied to the first of the sciences of the mind, psychology, the Darwinian factors are found most effective. If, that is, a selection of processes and habits goes on within the organism—a functional selection resulting in a real molding of the individual—there may be at every stage of growth a combination of genetic characters with acquired modifications. Then, natural selection would fall in each case upon this joint or correlated result. The organisms showing the most effective combinations would survive. Put in psychological terms this means: Give the animal a little sense—a grain of the capacity to profit by experience, to imitate, to coöperate, to deceive, to remember and distinguish what is good for it from what is bad—a bit of *intelligence,* broadly understood, and he is started on the career of learning in comparison with which his earlier achievements become quite insignificant. If, in short, we are to allow that accommodative or learning processes of whatever kind do have any influence, however indirect, on the course of evolution, then that prime, that superb weapon of learning, mind, comes to its own and starts upon its splendid career. But if this be so, if mind be natural and also useful, then we are still of course within the Darwinian circle of ideas. Why are not mental faculties and functions to be considered characters which have been evolved by selection for their utility? Darwin held this in his *Descent of Man.* But instead of the desultory recognition of the place and effectiveness of mental states in a theory dealing mainly with the physical, we now see the universal principle of the relation of mental to organic evolution. Mind is correlated with plasticity, its evolution with that of brain and nerves. The history of the evolution of these organs is also that of the evolution of mind. In this we have the next great step in which biology and psychology join hands in a safe and accomplished generalization: that of the correlation of nervous plasticity with mind, of " educability " with " sense."

The force of this, for our present purpose, is this: plasticity is a real character, a character the opposite of fixity. It is opposed even to the potential sort of

fixity assumed by preformism—the theory that all subsequent adjustments are already present potentially in
the germ. It leaves to the organism genuine alternatives; genuine novelties of adjustment are possible. And
consciousness, intelligence, is also a real character, correlated with plasticity. Both are present together, however we may account for it; and both have been advanced
for their utility, as Darwin's hypothesis requires. This
is especially seen in the " new " logic, where the theory
of truth becomes either one of extreme " Pragmatism "
or one merely of " Instrumentalism." Instrumentalism
holds that all truth is tentatively arrived at and experimentally verified. The method of knowledge is the now
familiar Darwinian procedure of " trial and error."
The thinker, whether working in the laboratory with
things or among the products of his own imaginative
thought, *tries out hypotheses;* and only by trying out
hypotheses does he establish truth. The knowledge already possessed is used " instrumentally " in the form
of a hypothesis or conjecture, for the discovery of further facts or truths. This reinstates in the sphere of
thinking the method of Darwinian selection.

It is in his application to philosophy that Baldwin
brings out some of the most telling results of Darwinism.
He illustrates this in that summary chapter which begins with psychology and ends with religion. Psychology, he tells us, has always been the vestibule, as it were,
to philosophy, and advance in the latter never gets far
beyond that of the former. So when psychology adopted
seriously a naturalistic and positivistic method—the
method, that is, of the positive sciences of nature—
philosophy had also to recognize the generality of these
points of view. Philosophical truth, like all other truth,
must be looked upon as truth about nature—the nature

of the world and the nature of man—and its progress is secured through reflection exercised under the control of the positive instruments and methods employed in those subjects. Purely deductive, speculative and personal systems of philosophy may be useful as gymnastics and profitable as sources of individual fame; but the genuine progress of philosophy is to be looked for only through those methods of confirmation and proof which control the imagination and permanently satisfy the logical and other demands of common reflection. There may be different philosophies, but, like rival scientific hypotheses, each must show the array of facts, aims, motives, values, that it can explain better than any other. Philosophy is not an exercise of preference, but an exercise of reason!

In these directions, continues the author, Darwin has strongly influenced modern philosophical thought; so strongly that the historical issues of philosophy have taken on new forms, which, in the new names now in vogue to describe them, are unfamiliar to the old-school philosophers. Instead of the problem of "design," we now have the discussions of "teleology"; instead of the doctrine of "chance," we now have the "theory of probabilities"; instead of "fatalism" and "freedom," we now have "determininism" and "indeterminism," variously qualified; instead of "God," we hear of "absolute experience"; instead of "Providence," of "order" and "law"; instead of "mind and body," of "dualism or monism." Not that all this shifting of emphasis and change of terms are due to Darwin; but that they are incidents of the newer antitheses current since the mind has been considered as subject to "natural law," and the world, including God and man, as common material for science to investigate. Scientific naturalism and positivism are methods of unlimited scope; and the question of philosophy is, what does the whole system of things, of external facts and of human values alike—when thus investigated— really turn out to mean? So design may be illustrated by considering more fully a central problem—one common to biology and psychology alike, and one whose answer colors the whole of one's philosophy. It is the old problem of " design," giving rise in biology to theories of " special creation " and " chance," and now discussed, alike in biology and psychology, in the form of questions of " vitalism " and " teleology." In what sense, if any, is the world—and in it, life and mind— an ordered, progressive, and intelligible whole? And if it is such in any sense, how did it become so? Is it due to intelligence?—and if so, whose intelligence? The most violent controversies aroused by the publication of the *Origin of Species* were let loose about this question. To Darwin's opponents " chance," " fortuitous or spontaneous variation," was to take the place of intelligent creation, Providence, God. If there be no rule of selection and survival save that of utility, and no source of the useful save the overproduction of chance cases, where is the Guiding Hand? Does not Natural Selection dispense with a ruling Intelligence altogether?

We have only to understand the present-day statement of this problem, explains Baldwin, to see the enormous concession to naturalism which the theory of Darwin has forced. Instead of " chance " in the sense of uncaused accident, we now have the notion of " probability," a mathematically exact interpretation of what is only to superficial observation fortuitous and capricious; instead of an interfering Providence, we have universal order born of natural law. And it is within such conceptions as these, *now taken as common ground of argument,* that the discussion of teleology is conducted. The world is no longer thought of as a piece of mosaic work put together by a skillful artificer—as the old design theory looked upon it—but as a whole, a cosmos, of law-abiding and progressive change. A philosopher who knows his calling to-day seeks to interpret natural law, not to discover violations of it. The violations, if they came, would reduce the world to caprice, chance, and chaos, instead of providing a relief from these things.

So Darwin's view, argues the author, while administering a *coup de grâce* to theories of chance and special creation, both equally desultory, capricious, and lawless, replaced them once for all with law. It indicated the method of operation by which the progressive forms of nature are evolved in stages more and more ordered and fit. The operation of such a law is no less and no more " rational," no less and no more " fatalistic," no less and no more " atheistic," than is that of any other law, physical or mental. What law—meaning simply what regular method of change—is operative in nature? and what is its range, as compared with other such laws? —these are questions entirely of fact, to be determined by scientific investigation. And how far the method or law called by Darwin " natural selection " goes, what its range really is, we are now beginning to see in its varied applications in the sciences of life and mind. It seems to be—unless future investigations set positive limits to its application—a universal principle; for the intelligence itself, in its procedure of tentative experimentation, or " trial and error," appears to operate in accordance with it.

CHAPTER VIII

MODERN IDEALISM

1. The German Influences

It is hard to measure the intangible and to weigh the immaterial, yet it may safely be said that the German influences on American thought have been the most significant and the most weighty of all the foreign forces. In the words of one of our German-American lecturers this state of affairs is due, in large measure, to the after-effect of that great epoch of German humanism signalized by the names of Goethe and Kant, Schiller and Fichte. The very substance of the life-work of these men and their compeers consisted in this, that they replaced the ecclesiastical doctrine of atonement by the belief in the saving quality of restless striving. Never in the whole history of the world has there been held up to man an ideal of life more exalted, more inspiring, freer from unworthy or belittling motives than their teachings. They trusted in the essential goodness of all life; they conceived of the universe as a great spiritual being, engaged in constant self-revelation and in a constant struggle toward higher forms of existence. They believed that man, as a part of this spiritual universe, was in immediate and instinctive communication with its innermost essence; and they saw the great office of man in helping the spirit toward its fullest self-realization.

The German humanism, as thus described by Kuno

Francke, has indeed had great influence upon our ways of thinking. The proof of that lies in the very familiarity of its doctrines. But that influence and that familiarity were not matters of an instant. It took many years and many men to accomplish the result. There were in the way great difficulties, due to race, social conditions, and language. The first flight of Teutonic immigrants began with the wretched refugees of the Thirty Years' War, and ended about the time of the adoption of our Constitution. Previous to 1789 it was predominantly the peasant classes that came into the country. But among such farmers as were represented by the Pennsylvania " Dutch " one could not hope to find regular philosophers. There were indeed mystics like Conrad Beissel and his Ephrata community, but their theosophy had slight influence and remained as little appreciated as did the architecture of the brotherhood buildings and the music of its inmates.

Except for a slight infiltration of Protestant sectaries like the Lutherans, with one or two scholars of local note, the next flight of immigrants was delayed for over half a century. But with the refugees of '48 there came in both blood and brains. Men like Hecker and Koerner, Schurz and Sigel, fleeing from the reactionary militarism of the Fatherland, sought to found a new Germany in the new West. This group, and others of Germanic origin, made possible the St. Louis school and furnished the nucleus of those audiences which listened to the diluted transcendentalism of Emerson and Alcott.

That transcendentalism was indeed diluted, for it was a very much modified German philosophy which first excited attention in the country. James Murdock of Yale College, the neglected historian of the movement, explains how Coleridge, being a poet more than a philosopher, obscured, if he did not pervert understanding of the genuine tenets of Kant. The *Aids to Reflection* were indeed republished in New England as early as 1829, but they were an aid to the rhapsodists rather than to the cautious thinkers. Now, most Americans at this time were of the latter conservative type. While they belonged to the empirical school and were " slow, cautious, dubitating, and modest," the Germans belonged to the metaphysical and were " daring, bold, and self-confident." Besides these temperamental differences there were other difficulties. Such was the novelty of the principles of Kant and so strange was the terminology that another writer speaks of the absurdity of offering for the edification of sober, matter-of-fact Anglo-Saxons the unintelligible idealism of Kant, Fichte, and Schelling.

To the hostile mental attitude there were added material difficulties. George Ticknor, wishing to prepare himself for his trip to Goettingen, had to send to New Hampshire for a German dictionary, while a German grammar was hard to find in all New England. But perhaps the greatest obstruction to the free importation of foreign ideas was the servile deference to English judgment and the consequent embargo upon the intellectual goods of other nations. Intellectually New England was as yet a colony of Old England, and the pernicious interdiction of metaphysical trade with other countries still obtained. This can be illustrated by the early native accounts of the Kantian philosophy. Disregarding some hack-writer's version in the first American reprint of that Noah's Ark of all knowledge—the *Encyclopædia Britannica*—we turn to the notice given by Samuel Miller in his *Retrospect of the Eighteenth Century*. This is not so much a notice as a slander, and yet the author is hardly liable, since he obtained his information at third hand. Miller quotes from a London reviewer of an English translation of a German criticism of the critical philosophy. With no direct knowledge of the original he repeats the stale strictures upon the great thinker of Koenigsberg: Kant is guilty of indefinite evasions because his system is neither deism nor materialism, libertinism nor fatalism; he has studied to envelop his system in an enigmatic language because that system tends to undermine all religion and morals;—in short, the famous Prussian's theoretical jargon, instead of being calculated to advance science, or to forward human improvements, has rather a tendency to delude, to bewilder, and to shed a baneful influence on the true interests of man.

This so-called first notice of the Kantian philosophy in America has been styled by the Germans a piece of comical naïveté. Nevertheless that naïveté can be understood. Miller in his *Retrospect* was merely a watch-dog of orthodoxy. When other dogs barked he joined in the cry of alarm. To him, as a follower of the Scotch philosophy, realism was the most rational, idealism the most absurd of schemes. A more sympathetic attitude towards the Continental system is found in Philadelphia and among certain Pennsylvanians of German origin. In the Philadelphia *Monthly Magazine* of 1798 we find the earliest discovered notice of Kant on this side of the water. Taken largely from Lange it has some sensible and sympathetic remarks on the new philosophy. As this philosophy has considerably excited the curiosity of the learned in Europe, the compiler hopes that his sketch will prove acceptable to his readers. The gist of this sketch is as follows: It forms the chief business of the *Criterion of Pure Reason,* by measuring and ascertaining the limits of our different faculties, to exhibit a complete and distinct system of all our means of acquiring knowledge. Now, since it is only by apprehension in this our pure form, that anything becomes an object of science, knowledge thus acquired is the only kind of knowledge which can properly be called *objective;* while knowledge of every other kind is called *subjective.* To show the value of the former is the aim of the *Criterion of Pure Reason.* Kant, as has been said, distinguishes between *pure* and *practical Self.* That part of our idea which does not proceed from the thing observed, but from accidental association subsisting in our mind, is referred to the *practical Self;* and it is precisely this part of our idea which is *subjective.* When we have once learnt what portion of the idea is objective, it requires only to separate that with accuracy, and whatever remains is subjective. In this way we get clear of that portion of our subjective knowledge which is occasioned by incorrect observations and conclusions. It is true, that inasmuch as the nature of the affection of the mind depends upon the constitution of our organs of perception, it is practical or subjective appearance which we cannot separate, but this will not deceive such as understand the rules of philosophizing.

The tolerant tone of this article is remarkable. More remarkable is the conclusion added by the compiler. Though the account was taken from a mere note which Lange appended to his German translation of Stewart's *Elements,* the American editor catches the drift of the critical philosophy. This much at least, he adds, will appear from this account, that Kant's great doctrine is, that a knowledge of the human mind is not to be obtained by imagining changes in the mind itself, but by studying the various phenomena which it exhibits. The author himself compares his discovery to that of *Copernicus,* by which he showed that the phenomena of the heavenly bodies did not entitle us to attribute to them the various cyclar and epicyclar motions of the *Ptolemaic* system; that in truth we could be assured of nothing more than the existence of those bodies; and that the different changes in their appearance might as well be explained by supposing a change in our situation as by supposing any alteration in theirs.

It is a decided surprise to discover the famous Copernican comparison noticed amongst us only a few years after the appearance of the *Critique of Pure Reason.* It is, however, unfortunate that it appeared in an ephemeral journal, in a place about to lose its intellectual supremacy, and at a time when men were not yet ready to shift their philosophical point of view,—to consider themselves not as satellites but as suns, from whom might come considerable rays of wisdom. It was left for the New England transcendentalists of a generation later to do this, for Pennsylvanians of German origin were not in a position to effect the Copernican revolution in thought. In our republic of letters the Pennsylvania '' Dutch '' were little affected by the literature of the storm and stress period and remained remote, unfriended, melancholy, slow. Moreover, the scholars of German origin had their limitations. Men like Schmucker, professor in a Gettysburg college, and Rauch, president of Marshall College, were not much known outside of their local **Reformed** circles. And so when the literary leadership was shifted from Philadelphia and the South to Boston and the North, that frigid air of condescension characteristic of New England nipped the growth of the foreign plants. The head of Yale College referred to Kantianism as subversive of morality; and Harvard, although accepting a present of books from Goethe himself, feared the Germans even bearing gifts.

There was, however, one voice crying in this wilderness of exclusiveness. We refer again to James Murdock and his *Sketches of Modern Philosophy, especially among the Germans.* Here he claims that the confounding of reason with understanding, and of ideas with conceptions by Locke and by most of the English, Scotch, and American writers since (though it was a natural consequence of supposing all human knowledge to be derived from sensations and reflections on them) has spread much obscurity and confusion—and contributed not a little to render the English language unfit for clear and conclusive reasoning on metaphysical subjects. This is one great reason why so many among us cannot understand and appreciate the writings of the German philosophers. Their clear, precise, and definite thoughts, the moment they are translated into English, become obscure, indefinite, and vague; because the language into which they are translated is so. It is true that the Germans have introduced a multitude of new technical terms into philosophy which sound very strange in our ears; and Kant in particular has been censured, even by his own countrymen, for his excessive coinage: but if our language had appropriate terms for expressing the more necessary distinctions of thought, we might contrive some way to avoid the use of German technics, and yet convey to English minds the real views of the German writers.

A notorious instance of the confusion of technical philosophic terms in the English language is given by Murdock in his description of the New England movement. He says that that species of German philosophy which has sprung up among the Unitarian clergy of Massachusetts, and which is advocated especially in a recent periodical called the *Dial,* is known by the appellation Transcendentalism. The propriety, however, of the appellation may be questioned. Kant would certainly not apply it to this or to any similar system. He would denominate it transcendent, not transcendental. The difference according to his views is immense. Both terms indeed denote the surpassing or transcending of certain limits; but the limits surpassed are entirely different. That is called transcendental which surpasses the limits of sensible or empirical knowledge and expatiates in the region of pure thought or absolute science. It is, therefore, truly scientific; and it serves to explain empirical truths, so far as they are explicable. On the other hand, that is called transcendent which not only goes beyond empiricism, but surpasses the boundaries of human knowledge. It expatiates in the shadowy region of imaginary truth. It is, therefore, falsely called science; it is the opposite of true philosophy. A balloon sent up by a besieging army to overlook the ramparts of a fortification, if moored by cables whereby its elevation, its movements, and its safe return into camp are secured, is a transcendental thing; but if cut loose from its moorings and left to the mercy of the winds, it is transcendent; it has no connection with anything stable, no regulator; it rises or descends, moves this way or that way at haphazard, and it will land no one knows where or when. Now, according to the critical philosophy, all speculations in physical science that attempt to go beyond phenomena, and all speculations on supersensible things which attempt to explain their essential nature, are transcendent; that is, they overleap the boundaries of human knowledge. In violation of these cautions, Fichte, Schelling, and Hegel plunged headlong into such speculations, and yet called them transcendental; and the new German philosophers of Massachusetts follow their example.

We bring forward these criticisms for a purpose. It is to show that the current confusion of technical terms displayed an ignorance of German philosophy at first hand. In other words, the influence of that philosophy had so far been indirect rather than direct, literary rather than historical. From abroad, Coleridge and Cousin had brought in the romantic stimulus, but it was couched in anything but exact terms. At home, members of the Transcendentalist Club and the Brook Farmers cared more for free thinking than for precise thinking. Even Ripley's *Specimens of Foreign Standard Literature* were utilized more for the ferment of reform than for accurate information. As Ripley himself declared: We need a philosophy like this to purify and enlighten our politics, to consecrate our industry, to cheer and elevate society.

We now come to the question of the time of transition from the indirect to the direct study of Kant and his followers. Some have held that the direct study began with the return of the young American scholars from Goettingen in the '20s. We believe that the change came much later. It was prepared for by the various addresses, translations, and anthologies of the third decade of the century; but that decade did not emancipate the New England mind, nor open it to the freedom of foreign thought. Indeed the year 1839 put a black mark in the history of Harvard. In that year came Emerson's Divinity School Address, which was denounced by Andrews Norton, " the pope of Unitarianism," as " the last form of infidelity." But worse followed. In reprobation of the views expressed in this address Emerson himself was exiled from his own college for fully a generation.

Now, that generation was one of preparation, not of full understanding. In the '40s, for example, a translation of Fichte's *Vocation of the Scholar* was reprinted in Boston, but this, as Frothingham ironically observed, excited an interest among people who had neither sympathy with his philosophy nor intelligence to comprehend it. For such a lack of sympathy and of intelligence we have not far to seek. It was due in a great measure to what Santayana so aptly calls the genteel tradition, a tradition due to the union of church and college, to the belief that the teacher must come to the defense of the faith. Armstrong has pointed out the peculiar function of philosophy in the " old American college ": After the student had been trained in the time-honored classics and mathematics, after he had learned his modicum of rhetoric and history and natural science, there remained the " higher branches," which were held not only to train him in scholarship but to fit him for practical life. Political science would make him a good citizen; the evidences of Christianity would ground his religious faith. Now, these evidences were bolstered up by correlated courses in natural theology, in mental and moral philosophy, and only occasionally in the history of philosophy. . . . Moreover, these courses were always prescribed and generally given by the clerical heads of the colleges.

But the era of dogmatic soundness was at last succeeded by the day of the impartial discussion of metaphysics. Then came the transition from the old order to the new. The centennial of our political independence marked the beginnings of our academic independence.

By that time philosophy began to be studied as an elective and for its own sake. Several causes were contributory,—the general advance in higher education, the empirical conclusions poured in upon us by the scientists, and especially the influence of the progress of psychological science. With us that science was distinctly an importation from Germany, and with the founding of our first psychological laboratory in 1876 there comes a definite date for direct German influence—in the East, at least.

We make this qualification because of a forgotten factor in our intellectual history. Two decades before German philosophy, diluted with dogma, was being taught at Harvard by Bowen, at Yale by Porter, at Princeton by McCosh, and at the University of Pennsylvania by Krauth,—long before this, the pure doctrines of Kant and his followers were being made familiar in the West. This is one of the characteristic surprises in the history of our culture, that out of the new land comes the new knowledge. It was in St. Louis that there came into being the first Kant class in America, the first native translations of Fichte and Schelling, the first systematic study of Hegel. Indeed at the very period when the Massachusetts transcendentalists were largely outside of the pale of the church, largely out of sympathy with the colleges, there was being trained in Missouri a group of idealists who, by their freedom of thinking and philosophic knowledge, made the Concord school of philosophy possible. In fine, that later idealism, whose origin has been usually attributed to New England, had its impetus elsewhere. It was a paradoxical phenomenon. It was like one of our storms which, blowing from the northeast, has its real beginning in the southwest. To that quarter of the compass we now turn.

2. The St. Louis School: William T. Harris

It has been declared a remarkable fact that in a booming Western city—almost on the borders of civilization—apparently almost wholly occupied with material things, there should have arisen one of the leading schools of idealism in America. This was the St. Louis school, which initiated our first systematic study of German thought, and led to the publication of our first metaphysical journal, *The Journal of Speculative Philosophy*. The movement can best be studied through the men who made it. These were three: Brockmeyer the oracle, Harris the interpreter, and Snider the historian of the movement.

Of this triumvirate Brockmeyer is the most picturesque figure. Born in Germany, coming to this country at the age of sixteen, he was expelled from a freshwater Western college because of his free-thinking, and left for the East, where he became imbued with the New England teachings. But the fixed social order not suiting him he determined to become another Thoreau, to leave society and seek solitude. In this plan, he tells us, he had taken to heart the advice of Parmenides to the young Socrates: "Be sure to educate and practice yourself in the so-called useless metaphysical hair-splitting while you are still young, lest the truth should escape you." So Brockmeyer went West to the old hunting-ground of Daniel Boone, there built himself a log cabin, and with his dog as his sole companion, lived for several years supporting himself by hunting. He did this because with his gun he could procure in an hour enough food for the day, and have the rest of the time for working out the thoughts in his head. This Utopian scheme could not last. Therefore, resolving to provide himself with

a competency for his old age, he came to St. Louis. It
was there in the year 1858 that he accidentally met
Harris, who describes this unconventional backwoods
philosopher as even at that time a thinker of the
same order of mind as Hegel, for even before reading
much of the great idealist he had divined his chief
ideas and the position of his system. On my first acquaintance with him, continues Harris, he informed me
that Hegel was the great man among modern philosophers and that his larger *Logic* was the work to get. I
sent immediately to Germany for it, and it arrived late
in the year. Mr. Brockmeyer's deep insights and his
poetic power of setting them forth with symbols and
imagery furnished me and my friends of those early
years all of our outside stimulus in the study of German philosophy. He impressed us with the practicality
of philosophy, inasmuch as he could flash into the questions of the day, and even into the questions of the moment, the highest insight of philosophy and solve their
problems. Even the hunting of wild turkeys or squirrels
was the occasion for the use of philosophy. Philosophy
came to mean with us, therefore, the most practical of
all species of knowledge. . . . We studied the dialectic
of politics and political parties and understood how
measures and men might be combined by this light.
But our chief application of philosophy was to literature
and art.

To turn to Harris, the second of the triumvirate.
Brockmeyer recounts how he met his foremost disciple
at a chance meeting where those present were discussing
Oriental theosophy, spiritualism, or something of that
sort. The secretary of that meeting, he narrates, was a
young man named Harris, who seemed to me to be the
one sane person of the gathering. After the meeting I

accosted him and began to question him as we walked along. He seemed surprised that such a common working-man, as I appeared to be, should talk in this way, and we got into a discussion. He made some quotation from Cousin, and I remarked that Cousin contradicted himself on every page. On his challenging this statement I ·accompanied him to his room to prove it from Cousin's works. This was the beginning of our friendship, and the nucleus of the group of students that soon gathered together.

Here was the beginning of the first systematic study of Hegel in the country. Brockmeyer tells how Harris and two other enthusiastic young men wished him to cease working in the foundry and give his time to instructing them and to translating the great works of German thought. But the commencement of the Civil War, of which the first storm center was Missouri, interfered with this arrangement and broke up the little band of philosophers. Six months after Appomattox the philosophers met again. It was then that the third of the triumvirate appears upon the scene and gives his impressions of the other two: There was Brockmeyer, dishevelled and ragged in his working clothes, the undoubted oracle of the meeting, who would forcibly deliver his response as one having authority and could even re-create Hegel by poetizing the latter's dry, colorless abstractions. There was Harris, the active worker of the philosophic set, the eager propagandist, who with his sharp face, and rather pointed nose, could prick keenly and deeply into things. The two men were in themselves an illustration of the Hegelian dialectic, a contrast and at the same time complementary to each other,—one the man of genius, but rather indolent; the other the man of talent and very industrious.

The man of talent may now speak for himself. In one of our best philosophic autobiographies, Harris, the editor of Hegel's *Logic*, sees in himself an illustration of that logic. In the unfolding of his life there were three " moments "; the first a phase of positivism; next, a conversion to transcendentalism; and lastly, a transcending of that transcendentalism. While a student at Yale College, Harris had taken up with phrenology and the eclecticism of Cousin. This was what he called his " saurian " period, when he was mixed up with that vast swarm of *isms* which had broken loose in New England, and, as Snider says, descended upon the West in countless flights like Kansas grasshoppers. But just as Harris rebelled against the formalism of the college so did he rebel against this " nibbling at the little end of things." " The long-haired men and short-haired women " who wished to reform the world offhand were not to his taste. He wished for a guide out of the maze. He found it in idealism. He declares that he obtained his first insight into the new philosophy in studying Kant's *Critique of Pure Reason*. Seeing the necessity of the logical inference that the unity of time and space presupposes one absolute Reason,—God, freedom, and immortality seemed to him to be demonstrable ever since that December evening in 1858 when he obtained his first insight into the true inference from the transcendental æsthetic.

This conversion to transcendentalism took place in the very year in which Harris met Brockmeyer. The latter now began to declare to his followers that they must go beyond transcendentalism; that there was a greater than Kant; and that it was Hegel who was the culmination of the German philosophical movement. The practical Yankee took Brockmeyer at his word; sent to Germany for the *Logic* and, with Brockmeyer as oracle and expounder, made a definite beginning of the St. Louis movement. The city furnished good soil for the teachings of the great encyclopædist. At least in the eyes of the local thinkers it was an illustration of the Hegelian philosophy of history. First, the time was propitious. After the civil strife between North and South the reconstruction period offered an example of the harmonizing of opposing forces. Next, the place was likewise propitious. It was counted cosmopolitan and seemed altogether different from any other city of the land,—more foreign, more un-American in its conception of freedom. In it were descendants of the early French families that had settled there under Spanish and French rule, still retaining strong traces of the ancestral character. By the side of these was the very strong element of the Southerners, who possessed wealth, culture, and polish of manner, perhaps the most aristocratic element of the city. . . . The third class came from New England and the Middle States, and had brought with them culture, energy, perseverance, and indomitable will-power. Many of them were professional and business men who had come westward to better themselves financially. Finally, political trouble in the various German states had sent tens of thousands into the Mississippi Valley, and St. Louis received her full quota of them, making her, concludes the historian of the movement, a Teutonic city of the radical type.

In spite of these favoring circumstances, the movement as a whole, continues the same author, led to disappointing results. The Philosophical Society was intended by Brockmeyer as a means for publishing his translation of Hegel's larger *Logic*. But politics drew him aside and it was only long after his death that the task was completed by others. The same society was intended by

Harris as a means for working up his *Journal of Speculative Philosophy*. In this periodical Brockmeyer's writings proved a disappointment. The manuscript of the log-cabin thinker required a vast deal of correction; that which seemed the utterance of genius to his followers suffered from a kind of evaporation in print. The *Letters on Faust* which sought to philosophize literature were neither philosophy nor literature. Brockmeyer could never get himself nor his writings into shape. Yet the oracle of the school had a mission in inspiring the mind of the school,—Harris. How that mind developed is told by one of our Hegelians of the right wing in true Teutonic fashion. Harris's philosophical study in St. Louis from 1858 to 1867, says Sterrett, might be styled his *Lehrjahre* or Genesis; his editing the *Journal of Speculative Philosophy* and his work in the Concord school of philosophy for the second period, his *Wanderjahre* or Exodus, though his work in both of these spheres ran well into the period of his mastership, which culminated in his critical exposition of his great master's greatest work, the *Logic* of Hegel. Of this first stage mention has been made. It began with the study of philosophy on the low level of phrenology, and ended with the emergence from the toils of materialism and agnosticism in Harris's criticism of Herbert Spencer. This criticism was sent to the *North American Review* and rejected as unreadable. The rejection had results. It led Harris to found his own *Journal* and to strive, and with no little success, to make his exposition of Hegel readable.

With the founding of the *Journal* we have an emergence into an intense idealism, together with an attempt to Americanize that idealism. The *Journal's* motto, taken from Novalis, was this: '' Philosophy can bake no bread; but she can procure for us God, Freedom, and Immortality." The *Journal's* preface was a call to found a true " American " type of speculative philosophy. We, as a people, declared the editor, buy immense editions of John Stuart Mill, Herbert Spencer, Comte, Hamilton, Cousin, and others; one can trace the appropriation and digestion of their thoughts in all the leading articles of our reviews, magazines, and books of a thoughtful character. If this is American philosophy, the editor thinks it may be very much elevated by absorbing and digesting more refined aliment. It is said that of Herbert Spencer's works nearly twenty thousand have been sold in this country, while in England scarcely the first edition has been bought. This is encouraging for the American thinker: what lofty spiritual culture may not become broadly and firmly rooted here where thoughtful minds are so numerous! Let this spirit of inquiry once extend to thinkers like Plato and Aristotle, Schelling and Hegel—let these be digested and organically reproduced—and what a phalanx of American thinkers we may have to boast of! For, after all, it is not " American *thought* " so much as American *thinkers* that we want. To *think,* in the highest sense, is to transcend all *natural* limits—such, for example, as national peculiarities, defects in culture, distinctions in race, habits, and modes of living—to be *universal,* so that one can dissolve away the external hull and seize the substance itself. The peculiarities stand in the way; were it not for these, we should find in Greek or German philosophy just the forms we ourselves need. Our province as *Americans* is to rise to purer forms than have hitherto been attained, and thus speak a " solvent word " of more potency than those already uttered. If this be the goal we aim at, it is evident that we can find no other means so well adapted to rid us of our own idiosyncrasies as the study of the greatest thinkers of all ages and all times. May this *Journal* aid such a consummation!

This declaration has a trace of the flamboyancy of the Middle West. It led, however, to certain valuable results. The *Journal* served as a medium for the first appearance in English of a large number of German productions, from Fichte's *Science of History* and Hegel's *Philosophy of Art*, to original contributions from Von Hartmann and Michelet. It also served as a forcing-bed for native philosophers, from idealists like Howison and Royce, to Peirce, the father of pragmatism, and James its chief expositor. But the main function of the early numbers of the *Journal* was as a vehicle of Harris's own speculations. These are embodied in his *Introduction to Philosophy*, wherein he has answered, in the Hegelian way, the question asked by the reader of the *Journal*: "What is this speculative knowledge of which you speak?" And he has done more; he has re-defined the objects of the St. Louis Society and laid out the programme for the *Journal*'s contributors. The Society, he explains, was not founded for the especial purpose of studying German philosophy from Kant to Hegel, but to encourage the study and development of speculative philosophy, to foster an application of its results to art, science, and religion, and to establish a philosophical basis for the professions of law, medicine, divinity, politics, education, and literature. . . . This is a large programme. It reads like the inflated catalogue of one of our Western "universities." Yet in this very inflation there lay concealed one cardinal virtue—catholicity. Harris himself was an apostle of this spirit. Caught from the encyclopædic Hegel, he applied it to American

conditions and thereby became one of the clearest interpreters of our national consciousness.

This was the time when men's souls were tried. It
was a period of reconstruction, not only in the state
but also in the church. How then should the philosopher
handle these paramount issues of politics and religion?
Harris does it in the Hegelian way, by considering both
sides, recognizing the opposing phases and aiming at
totality. The national consciousness, he explains, has
moved forward on to a new platform during the last
few years. The idea underlying our form of government
had hitherto developed only one of its essential phases—
that of brittle individualism—in which national unity
seemed an external mechanism, soon to be entirely dis-
pensed with, and the enterprise of the private man or of
the corporation substituted for it. Now we have arrived
at the consciousness of the other essential phase, and
each individual recognizes his substantial side to be
the state as such. The freedom of the citizen does not
consist in the mere arbitrary, but in the realization of
the rational conviction which finds expression in established law. That this new phase of national life demands
to be digested and comprehended, is a further occasion
for the cultivation of the speculative.

So much for politics. In regard to religion Harris
sees an immense movement going on in this country. The
tendency to break with the traditional, and to accept
only what bears for the soul its own justification, is
widely active, and can end only in the demand that reason shall find and establish a philosophical basis for
all those great ideas which are taught as religious
dogmas. Thus it is that side by side with the naturalism
of such men as Renan, a school of mystics is beginning
to spring up who prefer to ignore utterly all historical

wrappages, and cleave only to the speculative kernel itself. The vortex between the traditional faith and the intellectual conviction cannot be closed by renouncing the latter, but only by deepening it to speculative insight.

The speculative insight for which Harris longed was given, in fullest measure, by that traveling priest of Neo-Platonic transcendentalism—Bronson Alcott, who was now invited to St. Louis, his farthest limit west. Alcott's influence in philosophy, declares Harris, was great, and his presence a powerful influence to stir into activity whatever philosophical thought there might be in a place. All people entering upon the stage of the " clearing up," or the intellectual declaration of independence, felt something congenial in the atmosphere of such a " conversation " as he conducted. The idea of Neo-Platonism is so negative to our civilization that Mr. Alcott could hospitably entertain the thoughts of any come-outer, and offer him, in return, very surprising views, that flowed naturally enough from the theory of " lapse," but were found altogether " occult " by the modern sense that holds to the doctrines of evolution and progress. It was perhaps difficult for those who attended the conversations to name any one valuable idea or insight which they had gained there, but they felt harmoniously attracted to free-thinking, and there was a feeling that great stores of insight lay beyond what they had already attained. That a person has within him the power of growth in insight, is the most valuable conviction that he can acquire. Certainly this was the fruit of Mr. Alcott's labors in the West. Ordinarily a person looks upon his own wit as a fixed quantity, and does not try a second time to understand anything found too difficult on the first trial. Alcott set people to reading Emerson and Thoreau. He familiarized them with the names of Plato and Pythagoras as great thinkers whose ideas are valid now and to remain valid throughout the ages. The shallowness of the American is due to the hard-and-fast hold he has upon his knowledge of material or physical ways and means. He is engaged primarily in the conquest of nature for the uses of civilization, and his intellectual energies are so fully occupied with this business that he has not explored the width and depth of the civilization for which he is producing the wealth. Thus it happens that American thought has for other nations a flavor of Philistinism. It is narrow and shallow. The spiritual heavens are shrunk to the dimensions of a single horizon. There is no intimation that the American Philistine ever heard of any other point of view than his own. He has heard of different manners and customs, but all these are for him utterly irrational and without adequate motives. He believes that his form of democracy is the only form of government fitted for all mankind, and he wonders that all people do not at once adopt it, just as he has done. . . . Failing to understand contemporary peoples, as the average American consciousness does, it is not surprising that there is a still worse defect in regard to the views of the world formed by the Greeks and Romans, the Persians and the Brahmins. It has been, therefore, a thing needed that we should have reproduced among us, after a hothouse mode, the ideas of other times and peoples that have performed their part in the long march of civilization. We have to learn the embryology of our civilization, and see the necessity for those stages which have been outworn, and comprehend what was of value, and what is still of value in them. The East Indian literature, the Chinese, the Persian, and especially the Egyptian, all shall be brought near to us, and our minds endlessly enriched by their lessons. Instead of our little barred window, which lets in a glimmer of light at the top of our cell, we shall then go forth into the free air, and contemplate the entire sky and all its light. We shall then for the first time see the real significance of our own work as founders of a new nation in a new world.

We have given this remarkable passage at length for two reasons. In the first place, it illustrates Harris's skillful use of the Hegelian necessity of negativity. In his *Orphic Sayings* Alcott presented, as we have seen, the Neo-Platonic view of the world, and thus gave to his contemporaries the shock they needed. This is evident by the uproar of ridicule and indignation which ensued. American common-sense and Fourth-of-July democracy had never considered the possibility of any other view of the world than its own. In the next place, the passage illustrates Harris's understanding of what he calls the morphology of our civilization and the significance of the embryology of the transcendental movement. While the most of the men of our time, he continues, despise the " embryons " which had developed into their present life, to one man—the wisest of his generation—this was an opportunity not to be neglected. That man was Emerson. He could find much sympathy with any and all idealistic views—whether European or Asiatic. Even the unrelenting theory of the Brahmins, which makes all existence an illusion, had its poetic uses for him. . . . Emerson kept this stalwart form of idealism as a sort of medicine which he could produce on occasions when confronted with the Gorgon of materialism in any new shape: What do I care, he exclaims, for the iron mills, or the slums of cities, or the cholera, or the Fugitive Slave Law, or some traveling crank, when I can see that all in time and space is only *maya*, or illusion?

From these passages we are justified in putting a high estimate upon the head of the St. Louis school. As Emerson was the interpreter of nature, so may we claim for Harris the title of the interpreter of the thought of his country, whether East or West. At this point we return to a previous suggestion regarding that confluence of currents which resulted in the Concord school. In that school Harris was a notable figure. To it he brought two things, enthusiasm and executive ability. The " philosophic fury " of his youth had not yet died down; in addition he possessed what he liked to consider a marked characteristic of the American—" directive force." Through these two factors there was now brought together a notable gathering of native philosophers. The dean of the school was the fiery-eyed Alcott, through whom had come the day of some really radical thinking. The secretary of the school was Sanborn, who was to give us our first brief glimpse of the history of speculation in America. This included the Puritanic philosophy of Edwards, the philanthropic philosophy of Franklin, the negation of philosophy (the period of deadening realistic dogmatism), and the ideal or vital philosophy of Emerson. Now, Emerson, though still living, was practically canonized as the Sage of Concord. Men really looked upon him as the great representative of our early national period, when, as Sanborn says, philosophy indicated the guide of life, the exponent and directress of national existence, rather than a certain metaphysical insight, fruitful of speculation, even when barren of results.

But the times had changed. After the Civil War there arrived a speculative stage. The interest in abolition

was supplanted by an interest in the Absolute. Under
the German influences there arose the aim of thought for
thought's sake; the new generation was enamored of
metaphysical subtlety and cultivated an air of detachment. The change was one both of method and of spirit
and the programme of the Concord school is an index of
that change. For example, Harris offers four lectures
on Elementary Insights in Philosophy and four more on
Space and Time; Causality and Self-Cause; Faith and
Freedom; and Categories of Being. Nevertheless an audience from the land of practicality could not give itself
entirely up to such abstract speculations, nor make an unconditional surrender to the unconditioned. So alongside
of Harris's special subjects, such as The Absolute as a
Personal Reason, and The World as Revelation of the
Divine First Cause, we find those of another complexion.
If Harris aimed toward monism, Howison represented the
other wing of Kantian idealism; while James's lectures
on psychology contained certain pluralistic germs which
were bound to upset any system boasting of its stability.
Indeed it would appear that idealism already contained
in its body certain anti-bodies, by-products leading to a
kind of auto-intoxication which intense transcendentalism seems ever destined to develop. But full development had not yet come. It is a fact that, in the very
year of the founding of the Concord school, Charles
Peirce suggested "certain incapacities of human
thought" which led to the disintegrating skepticism of
pragmatism. In the meanwhile, before that disintegrating skepticism could be reached, there arose two forms of
involved monism which we shall have to consider. These
are what we shall call Royce's system of romantic idealism and Ladd's system of science and idealism. To these
two masters, at Harvard and at Yale, we now turn.

3. Romantic Idealism: Josiah Royce

Josiah Royce represents the romantic side of our modern thinking. He is the Ulysses of an idealistic epic,—'' many are the men whose towns he has seen and whose minds he has learnt.'' By birth he stands for the adventurous spirit of the California pioneer; by training, for the learning of the Eastern seaboard as it was brought from Europe. A student in Baltimore, his early articles appeared in the St. Louis *Journal;* a teacher for many years at Harvard, he has been called to lecture at Aberdeen and at Oxford. From the variety and amplitude of his studies in metaphysics and mathematics, in psychology and religion, he is peculiarly qualified to interpret '' the spirit of modern philosophy.'' That spirit may be summed up in one word,—romanticism. This has as its chief activities the cultivation of the inner life; an enlargement of the powers of personality; and a cosmic imagination which strives to express all phenomena in terms of the Infinite, the Absolute. By the first activity, man learns to free his spirit from the limitations of the body; to discover that the true world is not made up of sense impressions. By the next activity, he expands his mind until well-nigh the whole world is at his feet, even time and space. By the final activity, he finds that the finite world is a voluntary limitation on the part of his infinite ego and that only what is linked with the Infinite has meaning and value. Such, briefly, is romanticism as interpreted by Novalis and Fichte and Schlegel. Of like mind is Royce, who puts the matter in a less vague and more satisfactory form because of the wealth of learning at his disposal. He begins by showing that there are two aspects of idealism. The first is an analysis which consists in pointing out that the world of your knowledge is through and through such stuff as ideas are made of. The other aspect is the one which gives us our notion of the absolute Self. To it the first is only preparatory, for this world which we interpret in terms of our ideas exists in and for a standard, an universal mind whose system of ideas constitutes the world. Now, all this may be mere speculative boasting. I may believe that the infinite conscious Self is alone sure, but I have to give a reason for this faith. Berkeley has made the method familiar when he reasons that " this whole choir of heaven and furniture of earth is nothing but a system of ideas." . . . But I must state it in my own way, although one in vain seeks novelty in illustrating so frequently described a view.

Here, then, is our so real world of the senses, full of light and warmth and sound. If anything could be solid and external, surely, one at first will say, it is this world. Hard facts, not mere ideas, meet us on every hand. Ideas anyone can mold as he wishes. Not so facts. In idea socialists can dream out Utopias, disappointed lovers can imagine themselves successful, beggars can ride horses, wanderers can enjoy the fireside at home. In the realm of facts, society organizes itself as it must, rejected lovers stand for the time defeated, beggars are alone with their wishes, oceans roll drearily between home and the wanderer.

Matter and mind may be similar in being stubborn, but does this make them essentially alike? We raise this question because idealists before this have been apt to slip into the fallacy of putting a part for the whole, or more precisely of confusing quality with totality. Royce guards against all this. Much of the outer world, he explains, is ideal: the coin or the jewel or the bank-note or the bond has its value not alone in its physical presence, but in the idea that it symbolizes to the beholder's mind, or to the relatively universal thought of the commercial world. So part of the properties of the objects yonder in this bright sense-world of ours is ideal, for odors and tastes and temperatures do not exist in those objects in just the way in which they exist in us. Thus for temperatures, a well-known experiment will show how the same water may seem cold to one hand and warm to the other. So for colors, they are not in the things, since they change with the light, vanish in the dark, and differ for different eyes. And as for sounds they exist in nature only as voiceless sound-waves trembling through the air.

These are familiar arguments and easy to accept. But can we follow the idealist in his supposition that part of the being of these properties is ideal, if not all of it; or, at the best, that such being is the embodiment of the thought or purpose of some world-mind? There are here two forward steps, one of which appears doubtful, the other dogmatic, unless the very dogma serve as a vindication of this train of reasoning. To explain: If we suppose that the place of all sense qualities is in the world-mind, then we have, as Royce suggests, a standard thought of which ours is only the copy. If this be not so, we are faced with this dilemma: Either your real world yonder is through and through a world of ideas, an outer world that you are more or less comprehending through your experience, *or else,* in so far as it is real and outer it is unknowable, an inscrutable x, an absolute mystery. There is no third alternative. Either a mind yonder, or else the unknowable; that is your choice.

We confess that this dogma relieves the dilemma, but

does it give one " the sensation of being an idealist "?
The author himself raises such a question as this: Is
not this result very disheartening? My world is thus
a world of ideas, but alas! how do I then ever reach those
ideas of the minds beyond me? This question is one
that has been called by one of the new realists the ego-
centric predicament. It may be put in this way: I may
grant that knowledge is made up of ideas, but are they
not my ideas and, therefore, am I not shut up in the
magic circle of my own mind? Royce faces the predicament and seeks to solve it in this wise: The answer is
simple, but in one sense a very problematic one. You,
in one sense, never do or can get beyond your own ideas,
nor ought you to wish to do so, because in truth all those
other minds that constitute your outer and real world
are in essence one with your own self. This whole
world of ideas is essentially *one* world, is essentially the
world of one self and *That art Thou.*

The answer here suggested is made by means of a transition from the solipsistic to the social. Yet by what
right have we thus to pass from the individual to the
common consciousness? Ordinary judgment makes the
social or common consciousness merely the aggregate of
individual minds; just as the " population " of a country is merely the sum-total got by counting heads. The
statistician no more thinks that the adding together of
little minds makes one great mind, than the strict constructionist thinks that the addition of political states
makes an extra entity called " The Union." But the
idealist reasons differently. He is neither statistician
nor strict constructionist. To get out of the little circle
of the single self he is wont to call on a larger self,—
the social consciousness, the spirit of the times, the
World-Mind,—whatever may be the name given to this

mysterious One who "relieves us from dilemmas, and saves us from predicaments."

We confess that we find it hard to follow this line of argument, for it involves a kind of cosmic conceit, a conviction that in the evolution of the Absolute, the unfolding of the Spirit, we mortals play a major part. Yet Royce goes on to declare that such participation exists in the very act of belief, for to believe anything is to stand in a real relation to truth, a relation which transcends wholly my present, momentary self; and this real relation is of such a curious nature that only a larger inclusive self which consciously reflected upon my meaning and consciously possessed the object which I mean, could know or grasp the reality of the relation.

If we were to defend this idealistic analysis, we might say that the act of knowing, being a relating process between the individual and the object, requires some connecting medium. As no wireless message can be conveyed between two points without the intangible ether, so must the knower and the known be bathed in a circumambient Absolute. This, in a figure, is what the author may mean when he refers to "that larger Self that includes you and your object." William James has disposed of this assumption in the matter-of-fact statement that a third party is not needed; that a cat may look at a king directly, and without the intervention of anything or anybody. But for the idealist this is too flat and unprofitable. It may be possible to live along on the easy path of simple awareness; but for a speculative system we require a more complicated scheme. Between the self and objects no help may be needed for a relating power from on high; but between self and other selves there is a more mysterious relation. The kinship of mind is due to a common origin and a common essence. Such may well be Royce's " one Self, organically, reflectively, consciously inclusive of all the selves,—the divine Logos which is absolutely the only sure thing from the first about this world."

To Royce, as to Schelling, man is a member of two worlds; but unlike the German idealist, who sought to preserve a perfect balance between the two, the American apparently thinks that by depreciating the world of description he thereby appreciates, or adds in value to, the world of appreciation. Without the facts of appreciation, he claims, there are no laws of description. Destroy the organic and appreciable unity of the world of appreciative beings, and the describable objects all vanish,—atoms, brains, suns, and milky ways are naught. . . . Is this Roycean paradox an apparent reversal of judgment? At first it was stated that the universe of appreciative feelings was isolated; that feelings and emotions were strictly private and, therefore, non-transferable. Now it is stated that objects in space and time are isolated, but that spiritual states are enmeshed in a common net of spiritual relationship.

Here is a return to the notion of a social consciousness, the world of appreciation being, as the writer expresses it, one of a sort of reflective publicity and interconnectedness. What is the value of this world? As minds are above molecules, so, it is argued, the world of appreciation is the deeper reality, its rival, the world of description, being a result of an essentially human and finite outlook. At this juncture there appears a defect in the system,—it is that of being a one-sided scheme. The admirable balance preserved by Schelling between the two worlds here gives way to the preponderance of the one over the other. This being so, Royce is forced to acknowledge that " the unity of the Logos is an appreciable, but not a describable unity." Certain uncomfortable consequences arise from this distinction: If the unity applies to but one world, it is not a total unity; it may apply to the higher part, but that is not the whole. There remains the world of description, a mass of intractable matter, and the final result is a dualism. Man is a member of two worlds, but between the two worlds there is no organic connection. The idealist acknowledges as much in calling his scheme an application of the double-aspect theory. Unlike other forms of that theory which declares that there is a curious kind of substance in the world, a substance mysterious and essentially inscrutable that has two aspects, the mental and the physical, this theory, contends the author, undertakes to know what this substance is. It is the conscious life of the Logos, whereof my friend is a finite instance. What I see is the physical, phenomenal aspect of his inner and appreciative life.

In using the word phenomenal Royce appears half an agnostic. The body, he claims, is merely a very imperfect translation of the mind; its laws belonging not to the inner nature as such, but to the external show of this nature; these laws being but symbols of deeper truth. If the problem rested here we might contend that the idealist has laid himself open to the inroads of skepticism, the possibility of erroneous judgment in the search for truth. His show might be considered a vain show, his translation a mistranslation. For all that the finite intelligence knows, the double aspect might be a duplex aspect, or rather an aspect of duplicity. In other words, if the two worlds are not in balance, because not coördinate, if the material and spiritual are not of an equivalence, there might ensue a colossal equivocation. The outward and visible signs might be misread, the symbols variously distorted according to the personal equation of the observer. This, we hold, is the danger run by the phenomenalist; but to the metaphysical idealist, who strives to think things through, there is a further refuge from doubt. The finite intelligence must be wholly of an agnostic cast unless the individual constructs something higher than himself. This is the infinite intelligence.

Royce had once avowed that the idealist welcomed the fullest agnosticism. We can now see the reason for this. Agnosticism is a spur to knowledge. Like a traveler in a strange land, the idealist in this material world is forced to learn the language of the country, to interpret the gestures which nature makes to him. Behind the signs, the symbols, the movements, there must be a meaning. It is this confidence in the rationality of the universe that constitutes the refuge of the high idealist. Royce has perhaps seemed to beg the question in using the term Logos, Reason. Now comes his vindication of the use of that term: You have your choice of three things. There is blank agnosticism, which makes the universe irredeemably irrational, a mere bedlam of nervous jerks, of meaningless motions. There is also a partial agnosticism, where the scientific observer is never sure that his reading of signs is not a misreading, his translation of facts not a mistranslation. There is finally a choice of a reasoned gnosticism,—not the universe of the know-it-all, but the universe of the All-Knower. The last is the choice of Royce. He allows that the world of description may be a world of partial doubt, that there may be a misreading of the mind of nature similar to a misreading of the mind of a friend. For all that he insists that the personal equation may be corrected, and, by a process of trial and error, the errors largely eliminated. But this correction, this elimination, cannot come of ourselves alone. The individual needs not only the social consciousness but the world consciousness. The problem, then, concerns a certain kind of truth, of which there are three kinds. Having recognized ourselves as finite beings, we become aware of our private world of inner truth as distinguishable from the truth as experienced by other men, and from the universal truth of the all-knowing world-consciousness. A new question then arises: How much of this private truth of ours is a revelation to us in our finitude of what other finite selves can also know? Finally comes the answer: So much as can be *described* to these other finite selves, and then, in their experience, appreciatively *verified*, may be regarded as not our private content, but as universal.

We have at last reached a true transcendentalism; a scale of truth which implies a scale of being, that is, a series of spheres in which the ardent soul may make real progress. By this means the transcendentalist breaks out of the magic circle of the self into the social consciousness, and then from the social consciousness into the higher consciousness of the " true World-Will." Such is the process of development in the realm of knowledge. There yet remains the problem of the relation of the organic world to our human consciousness. Here the author is, in a measure, obliged to modify his previous declarations. In his literal appreciation, or increasing the value, of the world of appreciation he had tended to depreciate the world of description. That world he must now bring into his total scheme, and thereby raise to a higher power. When, he explains, I think of the stars and of matter, of space and of the energy that appears forever to be dissipating itself therein, I think of something real, or else of merely a private experience of mine. If, now, the common experience of humanity is our sufficient warrant for assuming some universal reality as actually embodied in these hot stars and cold interspaces, of what sort must this reality be? In and for itself, we now answer: It must be an appreciable reality, the expression of what, in Schopenhauer's sense of the word, may be called a World-Will; as well as of what, in Hegel's sense, may be called an Universal Self-Conscious Thought.

Given these two worlds, and there is suggested an answer to the last and most difficult problem,—that of personal freedom. The transcendentalist may have his feet in the mire of matter, but his head is in the free air of the spirit. Such, in a figure, is Royce's answer, and the answer, he admits, seems paradoxical. Granted that the cause that relates to the world of description is one of temporal sequences, and that the only cause that you can seek in the world of appreciation is in a very different sense a cause, namely, a justification for this or that act,—does this relieve the situation? The double aspect theory has seemingly degenerated into an aspect of duplicity, if not of equivocation. A word means one thing here and another there. Moreover it makes man apparently a creature of caprice, constant to one thing never; one foot on the land of fixed necessity, the other on the shifting sea of freedom. How shall the idealist escape such criticism? He does it as have other romanticists, by practically denying one kind of personal volition. He concedes that what the physical organism itself will do, is physiologically determined by the whole order of nature and by the whole of past time, and that the will moves no atom of this mechanism aside from its predestined force. How explain such a paradox?

The answer is the expected answer. Royce, as a strict dualist, is a strict parallelist, and therefore allows no interaction between mind and body in the world of description.

In like manner, in the world of appreciation, he allows no interaction, in the way of control, between the individual mind and other minds. As my will cannot move the body below it, so a higher will cannot move my will, unless I choose to follow, by an act of appreciation, some thought emanating from that higher Self. We conceive the answer to the problem of freedom should stop here, with what is practically a revival of the Platonic doctrine of participation. This doctrine teaches that the lesser partakes ideally of the greater, the ectype being of the same nature as the archetype. Now, in attempting to bring our thoughts into conformity with that of the supreme Self, we may be in an ideal relation, which at any time we are at liberty to break. Yet we are hardly, as Royce contends, conscious bits of that Self, nor is our conscious volition a fragment of the freedom of the World-Will. We raise the objection that to identify an act of the individual with that of the Absolute, is to make the individual lose his personal identity. It is like an inventor working for a corporation and thereby losing all patent rights to his invention. Royce acknowledges as much in a final rhetorical question: What then, though we are bound in the temporal world, may we not indeed be free,— yes, and in a non-temporal and transcendent sense effective, too, in the eternal world? May we not in fact, as parts of an eternal order, be choosing not indeed this or that thing in time, *but helping to choose out and out what world this fatal temporal world shall eternally be and have been?*

With what he modestly calls a " dim suggestion "
Royce concludes the constructive part of this " first
sketch " of his system. The suggestion harks back to
the German romanticists as poets, makers, world-builders.
It also points forward to the current doctrine of creative
evolution, where the universe is still in the making, and
man a junior partner in the business. Or, to use a less
commercial figure, this final suggestion preserves the
Roycean system from the fate of absolutism. As in the
case of philosophy and politics, where absolute sovereignty was forced to give way to personal sovereignty,
so in this case. The seemingly insidious inroad on the
liberties of the individual is prevented by the doctrine
of voluntary participation of the free agent. Just as
there may be a political union which conserves the reserved rights of the state, so may there be organic
spiritual relations whereby " all the spirits are together
in one Spirit."

4. IDEALISM AND SCIENCE: GEORGE TRUMBULL LADD

The system of Royce is like a lofty palace with cloud-
capped pinnacles and lofty towers, but withal built upon
an insubstantial footing. The system of Ladd is a structure of a different sort. While Royce " a stately pleasure dome decrees," Ladd prosaically sets to work to
dig deep foundations. On the one hand is the romanti-
cist with high poetic imagination; on the other is the
engineer of metaphysics, who will erect no edifice until
he has carefully examined the ground, who will make no
promises until he has calculated the stresses and strains.
The foundations of philosophy, according to Ladd, are
wide and deep. They cover all the sciences and go down
as far as investigation has gone. It is, therefore, pre-

sumptuous to call philosophy the science of the sciences; it should rather be considered a summation of the sciences. Just as an immense modern business structure calls in the geologist, the engineer, the architect, and a host of allied agents, so that skyscraper called metaphysics is impossible without the aid of all knowing men. Unless it avail itself of their services and reach the rock bottom of reality, it will be not only uninhabitable, but will collapse of its own weight. Such, in a figure, is the impression conveyed by Ladd's latest work, *Knowledge, Life, and Reality*. The work is compact and well built, but like the modern business structure the first glimpse of it is not particularly alluring. Thus we are told that philosophy should be taken seriously, and that reflective thinking is a duty. With this we beg to differ. It is opposed to the very meaning of the word in question. When the author points out that philosopher means a lover of knowledge, that also means that he is a lover of pleasure,—the pleasure of knowing. The compelling curiosity of which Aristotle spoke is the real motive behind speculation. The Greeks were right. Philosophy is not so much a duty as a pleasure, and a philosopher not so much an agonizing contestant, as a spectator at the games. There is, of course, a serious side to this. One's favorite may fail and the race be lost, but this does not keep one away from the next Olympiad. We, therefore, beg to maintain that men do not enter into metaphysics " discreetly and soberly," but with curiosity and excitement. A prolegomenon to metaphysics is like a prologue to a play,—it is a spur to expectancy. A stranger in the land of speculation is as one who enters by night into a foreign city and wonders how it will look by daylight.

Although differing as to the spirit with which philosophy should be approached, we can agree as to the author's general conception of the subject. His first point is a disavowal of dogma. The philosopher who knows his business, knows that the attempt to deduce the facts and laws of the positive sciences from some form of a theory of the Idea, or of the Absolute, must be forever abandoned. He also knows that philosophy must take the world as science finds it, for it is the *real world*, and not any merely conjectured world, which philosophy desires to help science more profoundly to interpret. The philosopher is, accordingly, not a dominator but an adjudicator. He does not aspire to be the president of a syndicate which shall have bought or grabbed up all the separate mining claims. He tries to straighten out the confusion in respect to these claims. This is difficult because the confusion is cosmic. The universe being a whole, of which each science presents a part, every particular science finds itself confronted with problems which belong to the domain of some other science. Physics and chemistry cannot be kept wholly apart; chemistry is part of biology; biology is complicated with psychology, and so on.

Into this Wild West of conflicting claims enters the philosopher. He himself has staked no claims and represents no company, but like a government expert he is there to straighten out the tangle. He cannot satisfy everybody, yet he can send back a fairly clear report to headquarters. The report is accompanied by a map, and this map of metaphysics is now presented to us. There are in the field two rival companies. One is realism, the other idealism. How shall they be reconciled? By the simple expedient of a hyphen are the rivals amalgamated. Like a British-American mining company, we have, therefore, two parties—one furnishing the capital, the other the brains. Now, if this were a wild-cat company, we might have one party absconding with the capital and the other left with—the experience! But the company is legitimate and tries to do a legitimate business. It may ultimately attempt to be absolute— in that rosy future when it shall have absorbed all rivals. At present it sticks to its territory and tries to dig ore. In other words, the sources of philosophy are not chiefly subjective. A synthesis of facts, not a printing of prospectuses, is the task of the present-day philosopher, since there lies before the thinker of modern type a whole new world of discoveries.

In both methods and materials philosophy should then be empirical. Conversely, the sciences should be theoretical. Just as the sciences interpenetrate one another, so philosophy should interpenetrate the sciences. Otherwise we fall into the strange illusions of which Haeckel complains, the illusion held by the physicists that they can construct the edifice of natural science from *facts* without a *philosophical connection* of the same. Ladd, as is his wont, substantiates his opinions by German thought. It might be supplemented by French views, views such as those of Poincaré, that science and hypothesis go hand in hand, that the one cannot advance without the instrumentality of the other. And yet the American author might have reached his conclusion without any foreign aid, for his premises lead to the logical conclusion that specialization should be corrected by synthesis, that the breaking up of the larger domain into small allotments should not go on forever. " Divide and rule " is held to be an excellent maxim for the sake of concentration. Yet beside the intensive cultivation possible within the fenced lines of specialization there is an extensive cultivation of which science itself gives the hint every time it speaks of a Universe, or of a World, which is in any manner or measure One.

With these distinctions in mind we may inquire to what school we should assign the author. He wishes it to be understood that he belongs to none, and yet to all. He sees that variety in philosophy is a sign of life, just as variety in crops is a sign of fertility. In these conclusions the cosmopolite speaks. Having taught in Japan and India, as well as in different parts of America, Ladd informs us that he has learned much from his own pupils, both Oriental and Occidental. But he is satisfied neither with the mystical cry of the East, nor with the scientific formulas of the West. The dissatisfaction being profound, the crisis becomes acute. This crisis is emphasized and with a purpose, namely, that the alleviation may be the greater. It is by compromise, as a sort of adhesive plaster, that the torn wound is at last brought together. If neither a purely idealistic nor a purely realistic system of philosophy can be maintained, yet a combination of the two may hold. The combination is found in what might be entitled a vitalizing of the problem. In the body-mind controversy we have in theory two conflicting elements; but in the living self we find the two united. Likewise in the larger controversy respecting matter and spirit: Why should not man interpret the universe as a totality, in terms of reality as experienced by himself, that is to say, in terms of an experience of the life of a self? In the knowledge of life we have a suggested solution of reality. We are now enabled to go a step further. In vitalizing the given elements we look from without upon a given whole —bodies and minds brought together. In psychologizing those elements we go deeper and look from within— upon a rational whole. In a word, the principle of knowledge is personalism. As one knows his body and mind united in a single self, so may one know the body of nature as infused with one immanent mind.

This is going too fast. Before we can approach the philosophy of nature we must work out a philosophy of human nature. In this field the first problem is what kind of knowledge I have of myself. Is it illusory and transitory, or actual and dependable? Ladd gives the old realistic answer: I look within and find myself possessed of a self which is immediate and indubitable. Such knowledge has this further advantage: it makes me sure of myself. And so, for one thing, I am no stream of consciousness, since, even as a figurative watcher on the banks, I really do not separate myself from that stream. Such are the arguments of the idealist of Yale College. For the sake of the contrast let us turn for a moment to representatives of the rival institution against which these contentions are evidently directed. Against self-knowledge as immediate and indubitable we can put the statements of Royce as to the relativity and insecurity of such knowledge. To a pathological case how futile would be the advice " To thine own self be true "! Moreover, against the substantial identity of the self we can put the doctrine of James, which substitutes for a self a so-called " stream of consciousness." A favorite phrase of Ladd's is that " states of consciousness do not constitute consciousness of states." But suppose we add "—unless that consciousness of states is one of the states of consciousness." The problem is puzzling, but Royce in turn has given a subtle answer to that very question of how the true mind may find itself. It is by making its way through a medley of parasitical " minds," abnormal states of consciousness, which are to the normal self what noxious germs are to their host. And James in his doctrine of the specious moment—that snapshot glimpse of the stream of consciousness—has shown with what baffling speed the mind, so to speak, always keeps ahead of itself.

There is much food for thought in this controversy regarding the self as aberrant and evanescent, over against the self as indubitable and immediate. If the distinctions are too sharply drawn the issue becomes a false one. There may be multiple states of consciousness, yet out of these we may pick a single state and call it the principle of self-identity, and even grant that it is unique. Just as for practical purposes many political states may constitute a federal union, so that peculiar state called self-recognition, may be the bond of psychological union. This does not preclude the times and seasons in normal life when one is not " sure " of one's self, nor the abnormal cases of almost complete self-abnegation or forgetfulness. As there may be " sick " moments in a healthy mind. so may there be a healthy mind back of the sick moments. That at least is the hope upon which the pathologist, as physician of souls, carries on his work. He is not bothered with figures of speech about streams of consciousness or the futile flow of sensations; he asks only for a single sane moment of self-recognition upon which to crystallize his cure.

We wish the author had sought to reach reality through such a study of unreality. Ladd's interesting studies in hypnotism might profitably have been carried further to illuminate this problem. We may, however. suggest one way of escape out of the maze of mentality. Suppose the patient has lost the consciousness of self, or the sense of personality has temporarily disappeared. Suppose, again, that hypnotic suggestion is applied to the subconscious or subliminal realm. Now, until the submerged self has somehow been made to rise to the surface of consciousness, it cannot be dogmatically asserted that the true self is lost or non-existent. We may hold with the author that there is ever in man a rational principle, whether latent or patent, but does it follow from this that there is one immanent mind in nature? In examining the pathological doubt of self we have, as it were, been fighting for our souls, but that is far from a warfare in behalf of the world-soul. The individual may wish to remain master of this little world of self. But to turn that microcosm into a macrocosm, to undertake to run the universe after the analogy of the self, is highly presumptuous, if nothing else.

The realist, at this point, turns into the idealist. He reads in the sky " huge cloudy symbols of a high romance." We follow him with difficulty. It is one thing to say that we are sure of ourselves because we are directly aware of our states of consciousness. It is another thing to imagine ourselves identical with even the smallest part of that great soul which informs the mighty mass. The mystic claims to do it by means of his inner light; the æsthete by his supposition of " empathy," of a feeling one's self *into* an object of art. But we confess that these very claims conflict with a true individuality. Individuality means that, being myself, I am separate from other objects; that I am neither a mere spark of the divine fire, nor an imaginary state of mind of some graven image. These are some of the difficulties that we face as we enter upon Ladd's philosophy of nature. It is easy to say that as there is a mind in my body, so there is one immanent mind in the body of nature,—but it is hard to grasp this "sense sublime of something far more deeply interfused."

To obtain this high knowledge three avenues of approach are suggested: through the beliefs of the primitive man; through the beliefs of the scientist; through the beliefs of the philosopher. The primitive man believes in invisible spiritual agencies,—he has a simple, childlike way of attributing souls to certain things. The scientist believes in laws as modes of the behavior of things,—he treats regular phenomena as if they were regular habits. The philosopher believes in a system, and a system implies central control and a realization of ideal ends. Let us examine these three beliefs. Do the savage and the scientist really support the philosopher? At the most the scientist has little use for the savage, except as a sort of interesting mental scandal. As Fiske puts it: In the primitive hypothesis the forces of nature must have been likened to human volition because there was nothing else with which to compare them. Again the scientist, of the positive type, objects to being turned into a savage in having his "laws" personified. There is human behavior and cosmic behavior, but the two are by no means one.

The idealist is in a fix. Mythology will not help monism because it is too animistic. Mechanism will not help monism because it refuses to be anthropomorphic,— its god is not made in the image of man. What then? Let us confine the savage in a mental reservation of ignorance, but keep the scientist and reëxamine his beliefs. Is mechanism tenable? Can science "purify the causal concept of the elements contributed by emotion and will"? No! responds Ladd, or else science reduces explanation to a lifeless body of abstractions and empty formulas which give no real account of anything. The solution has already been suggested. It is personalism. Metaphysics, continues the idealist, interprets mechanism in terms of personal experience. There are here two grounds of reinterpretation. In general, causality is no invisible bond which seizes hold upon things from without and forces them into a semblance of unity. Causal connection, when analyzed, appears not so much like the external and merely visible connections of a machine, but rather like the felt connections of a conscious self. In particular, the student of nature sees, what the ordinary observer cannot see; he sees amœbas, and bacteria, and white-blood corpuscles, and ova, and cilia, and single cells or groups of cells, in all forms of living tissue, behaving in a more or less self-like way. Nor can he arrest his suspicions of something immanent in the reality which, in some faint measure at least, corresponds to his own conscious life, when he minutely observes the behavior of the different beings belonging to the world of plants. For, in the first place, at the lower limits of the two so-called kingdoms, it is difficult or impossible for him to tell to which of the two certain species should be assigned. And, second, many of those species, about the plant-like nature of which there is no doubt, show clearer evidences of a soulful existence than do many forms, and these by no means the lowest, of animal life.

Ladd is here approaching firmer ground. It is the ground of neo-vitalism. In place of the older mechanism, the Cartesian and Newtonian explanation of the world as made up of masses and forces, there has arisen the new biology. This grants, for example, to the ovum a nature rich and wonderful, a capacity not only to make itself behave as a being-in-itself, but also to make other beings which behave like itself. There is also the new astronomy which holds that all the planets in the solar system behave " as though they knew " how they ought to behave under all the circumstances, and taking into account their actual relations to all other things. There is finally the new physics which takes the forces of gravity as implying between the atoms literal affinities, or forces that have preferences, and thereby imports a self into mere mechanism.

There now looms up another parting of the ways. Some scientists would go on with the idealists, others would not. To many mechanism seems sufficient, and any attempt to personalize the phenomena of nature, whether organic or inorganic, appears mere poetic license. Men of this stripe refuse to accompany the idealist on the high a priori road. When he says that the measurableness of material things implies mentality, that concrete realities obey rational principles, that the category of force is the outgrowth of personal experience, they raise stout objections. For example, both those neo-realists and pragmatists, who are radical empiricists, demand that the tables be turned. They reason just the other way, arguing that mentality is derived from measurableness; that rational principles grow out of concrete realities; that personal experience is the outgrowth of the feeling of force in obstructing objects.

Is there any way in which to reconcile these divergent views? We believe there is, for the reason that the two schools have been looking at the same object from opposite sides. That object is nature. The side the empiricists look at is the outside, the environment. The stone wall of hard facts against which I run,—that is what gives me the rational principles I call empirical. Contrariwise, the side the idealist takes is the inside; he looks at nature from within; he considers himself already over the wall, already in possession of the key to the fortress of fact. And we ask again: Can these two points of view be in the possession of the same person? Ladd's fellow-idealist Royce gives an amusing illustration to show that the achievement is possible. He alleges that as selves we have the paradoxical power of being both subjects and objects: I may be meditating in my study, yet I can run out of the house and look in at the window and see myself still sitting inside. Or we might cite the case of an optical illusion, of a spherical figure which appears at one moment convex, at the next concave. To the eye that figure goes through alternating changes, yet common sense tells us that the figure itself does not change. In other words, just as the so-called specious moment of introspection may be explained by a shifting of the point of view, so may the idealist's world be looked at from two points of view. As an object by itself the world may be mechanical; but as known to man all things are self-like, since the nature of anything is internal. This is Ladd's solution of the paradox, a solution in close agreement with Royce's two worlds,—the scientific world of description, the metaphysical of appreciation. But the Yale thinker has perhaps gone a step further. To put a line of Emerson in positive form, the World-Ground might be held to say not only " I am the doubter and the doubt," but also " I am the knower and the known." Thus the absolute whole divides itself into two parts, not separate and distinct halves of a total sphere, but two aspects of the same totality; on the one side a system of things already formed, on the other a universal life, a force formative and progressive according to ideas.

With Ladd we have reached the climax of the later

idealism. Now, idealism has been called the most persistent form of philosophizing in the course of American
thought. From Johnson and Edwards to Royce and
Ladd the current, whether above or below ground, has
had an unbroken flow. It had its sources in the Platonizing Puritans, gained impetus by the deistic evidences
of design, was swollen by the spring freshet of German
romanticism, and yet has ever been kept in bounds by
the " genteel tradition " of theism. But there are signs
that this stream is fatally diverging, if not drying up.
Other interests are becoming paramount. Pragmatism,
the new radical empiricism, abandons the absolute for
the relative, cares less for cosmic purpose than for individual achievement, and owes allegiance not so much
to the reign of law as to the reign of results. But before taking up with the paramount pragmatism let us
briefly consider certain reasons for its present vogue.
One cause lies in the contrast between the amateur and
the professional philosopher. The ordinary thinker is
content to study the three problems of man, nature,
God,—as they run along side by side. The metaphysician, on the other hand, is a monopolist who seeks to
make a merger of the parallel lines. Like a railroad
magnate, to his mind all should be under a single man-
agement. But this merger may be held by many to be
logically illegal, a kind of conspiracy in restraint of
thought. Suppose the Absolute controls each and all,
where is there room for the liberty of the individual?
In this case, if liberty be granted, is it not specious,
because a mere manifestation of the divine activity?
Does not the same follow in respect to nature as the
present expositor of the divine mind? If nature be
granted an independent existence, is it not illusory, a
vain show, a phantasm of reality? Questions like these

are asked of the absolutist on the part of one who desires independency. The monist is unable to substantiate an Absolute, and the critic exclaims in desperation: Let us leave good enough alone. Let us be pluralists, believers in the existence of separate beings which follow their own particular paths. Instead of an ordered universe and an Absolute as " a seeing force which runs things," let us have before us this rich medley of facts, this world of buzzing confusion. Now, such a philosophy of pluralism, at the present moment, seems the typical American philosophy. The day of monopoly is passing. In its stead we have the age of independence, individualism, and competition,—the three marks of " triumphant " democracy.

CHAPTER IX

PRAGMATISM

1. PRAGMATISM: THE PHILOSOPHY OF PRACTICALITY

" THE Western Goth, so fiercely practical, so keen of
eye " has at last gotten himself a philosophy. It is
pragmatism, the philosophy of practicality, the gospel
of energy, whose prime criterion is success. It has been
called a business philosophy which demands results; a
bread-and-butter view of life which aims at consequences.
In short, pragmatism furnishes a sort of speculative
clearing-house which says that a philosophic theory must
have cash value and be true if it works, and false if
it fails. Pragmatism is not a metaphysical system, but
a method of testing systems. Each one applies the test
for himself and chooses that which best suits his own
particular case.

At the first glance and from a superficial view pragmatism seems a philosophy typical of the land of the
dollar. But it is more than that. Besides the material
factor it brings in the personal. As a doctrine of personalism it is aggressive; it emphasizes self-sufficingness
as against self-surrender; pragmatists are literally poets,
makers, they contribute to truth, enlarge metaphysical reality. This is the doctrine of dynamism which
lies at the bottom of the movement and explains the constant recurrence to the temperamental test, the formula
of feeling. Pragmatic truth is truth with a thrill to it;
if we can feel that our theories work, we can have the

most intense of satisfactions,—that of personal assertion.

Personalism plus dynamism is the formula of aggressive pragmatism. As such it can almost be called Americanism. It expresses the national worship of the practical inventor, the pushing man of affairs. But here the doctrine broadens into wider aspects. Besides the confidence in the application of science to the conquering of nature, the winning of the West by Yankee inventions, there is the ideal of democracy as a reënforcing factor. As we have a share in the making of our government, so we have a share in the making of truth, and, provided the principle of representation be given proper scope, there arises the irresistible might of united personalities, all having their say. And besides this sublimated nationalism there is a still wider horizon. Pragmatism becomes humanism. In his collective capacity man now finds that his fate is not wholly made for him either by mechanical forces or by supreme powers. In the high confidence that the strong will win, that nothing is impossible to the powerful, he comes to the conclusion not that he must adapt himself to environment, but that environment must adapt itself to him. In a word, finding the world so plastic, he comes to believe himself no longer man, but super man.

As personal, dynamic, human and superhuman, pragmatism has well-nigh broken bounds. Let us, therefore, turn back and trace its rise in the land of its birth. Hailed as a typical American philosophy, pragmatism has had three phases in its native growth,—the primitive of Charles Peirce, the developed of John Dewey, and the radical of William James. In this triumvirate of pragmatism Peirce taught that it was logical,—a method to make our ideas clear; Dewey taught that it was instrumental,—a useful tool for action; James taught that it was temperamental,—a way to reach personal satisfaction. Finally, these three varieties of pragmatism had different applications. The first tended to be solipsistic, to confine itself to the individual and his doubts; the second to be social, to pass over the barriers of self; the third to be transcendental, to leap beyond human barriers, to reach a pluralistic universe of higher powers, earth-angels, world-souls, with which man may have intercourse. In order of time pragmatism is primitive, or developed, or radical. In its point of view it is logical, or instrumental, or temperamental. In its application it is solipsistic, or social, or transcendental. Of these three varieties let us now take up the first.

Primitive pragmatism was started in 1878 by Charles Peirce as a logical method teaching us how to make our ideas clear. Taking, for example, the rival theories of fatalism and free-will, he gave this as a maxim to clear up metaphysics: " Consider what effects, that might conceivably have practical bearings, we conceive the object of our conceptions to have. Then, our conception of these effects is the whole of the conception of the object." Such is the mild doctrine which sought to induce reasonableness, as shown in becoming governed by laws, becoming instinct with general ideas. This doctrine lay neglected for twenty years, when it was revived by William James in his notable California Address of 1898. In this James added a personal note in remarking: " I should prefer to express Peirce's principle by saying that the effective meaning of any philosophic proposition can always be brought down to some particular consequence in our future practical experience."

The pragmatic seed planted by Peirce and watered by James grew rapidly in a congenial soil. The result was the Chicago school, whereby Dewey and his followers carried the doctrine into the wide fields of biological and social adaptation. The primitive formula was discovered to be a fundamental law of growth, the vital principle of evolution itself. The rule of logical method, inter-preted as having practical bearings, was now enlarged into a law of social success. The principle of Peirce in the thirty years of its growth had gotten out of hand. Such growth was not without reason. Transplanted from the East, the principle flourished because of a new atmosphere, the adventurous atmosphere of the West. The seed and the soil were in perfect accord. The new principle, interpreted as present and practical, ap-pealed to the pioneer who sought instant success. Here is a maxim which is made to mean simply that reason-ableness or truth is due to practical adjustment, to the choice of relations which work.

Besides practicality and workability a new quality is to be added. It is that of risk. For the sake of suc-cess one is willing to take chances, provided he is left to his own free choice. The old way was that of tradition. The new is that of adventure. No dogma is accepted, no teaching received at second hand. We must find out the truth for ourselves. What will work for me, here and now?—that is the question for me to decide. This is the spirit of the pioneer who has the excitement of exploring a land as yet uncharted, and it is this spirit which brings out the difference between the old and new philosophies. To the absolutist the world is like a well-planned city, bound to develop according to preconceived ideas. To the pragmatist the world is a world in the making; it is not the city of Washington, but the wilderness itself. So the pragmatist leaves the dull task of going over ground mapped out by another, and seeks the pleasures of the unexplored. His is the thrill of discovery. When he turns his canoe into the unknown lake, will he find his way out by a cataract or a carry? He does not want to know beforehand. He prefers to test his skill and his strength as occasion may arise. It is this spirit of the unexpected that gives point to the pragmatic formula. An idea, a thing may or may not succeed. It may be true, or it may be false. I may be able to carry my canoe to the next water, or the cataract may upset me. My plan of going out this way may work, or it may not. However, I am paddling my own canoe; I am not being guided by another. No all-knower is leading me by the blazed trail of preëstablished harmony.

Such a defense is all very well, replies the anti-pragmatic critic, but is the novice apt to succeed? Is there not woodcraft and forest lore to be learned from the guides? Can the pragmatist be a solipsist, a lone traveler in the wilderness? Does he not need the knowledge of others? . . . Questions like these led from primitive to developed pragmatism, from the solipsistic to the social stage. Peirce talked like a pioneer, some Daniel Boone of metaphysics. But Dewey, and James after him, acknowledged that the successful thinker cannot exist alone and unaided in his speculations. There is a treasure of past experience,—the accumulated wisdom of his ancestors. Such are the axioms which are accepted as true because they have been ever found to work. Our primitive predecessors did the first exploring in the unmapped maze of knowledge; they found that certain human ways of thinking succeeded, and nature, preservative of all successful achievements, handed these down as

habits of action. These are not dogmatic first principles, clear-cut innate ideas, but general tendencies,
natural promptings, instinctive leadings. Here the
hereditary transmissive factor of human knowledge appears. The solipsistic empiricist has developed into the
social inheritor of funded knowledge.

It is because of this sinking fund of the past that
Dewey, the evolutionist, gives a real cash value to instrumental truths. They pass current, not merely because of their face value, but because of their intrinsic
worth. The primitive pragmatist, like the early pioneer,
issued wild-cat currency; but with the developed pragmatist a mere personal promissory note was not enough.
The collateral of continuity was demanded and this was
supplied by the evolutionist with his doctrine of inherited
tendencies. In a word the Bank of Truth was founded
long ago.

2. PRIMITIVE PRAGMATISM: CHARLES PEIRCE

In the very first of his essays called " Illustrations of
the Logic of Science," Peirce makes a statement which
contains implicitly the three phases in the history of pragmatism,—the logical, the instrumental, the temperamental. Discussing the logic of science he says: Logicality
in regard to practical matters is the most useful quality
an animal can possess. . . . It is certainly best for us
that our beliefs should be such as may truly guide our
actions so as to satisfy our desires.

While this statement might have a threefold meaning,
might furnish grounds for all the later developments
of the movement, such is not its intent. The method of
science, continues Peirce, should be strictly logical, otherwise we run off into false methods. The first of these

is the a priori method, to think as one is inclined to think. The second is the method of tenacity where, as soon as a firm belief is reached, we are entirely satisfied, whether the belief be true or false. The third is the method of authority where one does not think as one is inclined, but because the state or some institution so wills.

But there is a method above all these,—it is that of science. It is not the method of the individual for the sake of comfortable conclusions. It is not the method of tenacity held to by society. It is not the method of authority, governing the mass of mankind and leading to the path of peace. No, there is a method above all these—above the individual, or society, or mankind itself. It is the method of science and its aim is the growth of reasonableness, shown in becoming governed by laws, becoming instinct with general ideas. . . . The test of whether I am truly following the method is not an immediate appeal to my feelings and purposes, but, on the contrary, itself involves the application of that method, which is to have a clear logical conscience.

How is the latter obtained? The answer is given in the second and best known of Peirce's papers, entitled "How to Make our Ideas Clear." Before we attain to the cardinal pragmatic principle, already quoted, there are certain preliminary steps. The first of these is to emerge from conceptions that are obscure to those that are clear, by means of belief. And what, then. is belief? It is something that appeases the irritation of doubt and involves the establishment in our nature of the rule of action, or habit. Now, since the essence of a belief is the establishment of a habit. different beliefs are distinguished by the different modes of action to which they give rise. For example, the question of free-will and fate in its simplest form is this: I have done something of which I am ashamed; could I, by an effort of the will, have resisted the temptation and done otherwise? The answer is that, if I had willed to do otherwise than I did, I should have done otherwise, and that contradictory results would follow from a contrary hypothesis. Thus we come to the clearing up of our ideas by saying that our idea of anything *is* our idea of its sensible effect, and thus, finally, we reach the rule for attaining the final grade of clearness and apprehension, namely, " Consider what effects, that might conceivably have practical bearing, we conceive the object of our conception to have. Then, our conception of these effects is the whole of our conception of the object."

Again we have the famous principle of Peirce around which so much controversy has raged. It is rightly interpreted to mean a maxim for clearing up metaphysics. It is wrongly interpreted to mean a mere rule of action. Against this misinterpretation of the principle its originator protested. He held that the principle had been carried too far when it was changed from one of methodology to one of practicality. In criticism of James, who asserted that beliefs are nothing but rules of action, Peirce contended that such doctrine assumes that the end of man is action. He added that this stoical axiom did not recommend itself so forcibly to him at the age of sixty as it did at thirty. If it be admitted, on the contrary, that action wants an end, and that that end must be something of a general description, then the spirit of the maxim itself, which is that we must look to the upshot of our concept in order rightly to apprehend them, would direct us towards something different from practical facts, namely, to general ideas, as the true interpreters of our thought. . . . This maxim leads to clearness of thought, furthers the development of concrete reasonableness so that the meaning of a concept does not lie in any individual reactions at all, but in the manner in which those reactions contribute to that development.

Few interpreters of primitive pragmatism have gone back to these sources and shown the real doctrine of Peirce. It was more general than is ordinarily thought, and also far less selfish. The doctrine is one called by its author pragmaticism. It is more than immediate empiricism; it is a game of consequences and those consequences the most remote. In a word, the pragmatist is willing to take risks in order to attain truth. All this is brought out in the third of Peirce's essays, " The Doctrine of Chances." In this it is held that a man cannot be logical so long as he is concerned only with his own fate, for the chances are against him in a short series of probabilities. Therefore, only that man who should care equally for what was to happen in all possible cases could act logically,—sure succcess comes only in the long run. It may seem strange, concludes Peirce, that I should put forward three sentiments, namely, interest in an indefinite community, recognition of the possibility of this interest being made supreme, and hope in the unlimited continuance of intellectual activity, as indispensable requirements of logic. Yet, when we consider that logic depends on a mere struggle to escape doubt, which, as it terminates in action, must begin in emotion, and that, furthermore. the only cause of our planting ourselves on reason is that other methods of escaping doubt fail on account of the social impulse, why should we wonder to find social sentiment presupposed in reasoning?

Such is primitive pragmatism, quite different from what has been generally thought. Its aim is less selfish than social, its spirit less practical than general. For this interpretation we have the word of Peirce when he further insists that his maxim is a clarifying maxim; and that even reasonableness is not a good in itself but only an aid in the evolutionary process. But the primitive principle, as the author complains, has become "transmogrified." Reality, according to present pragmatism, is to be tested by immediacy; truth to be found in the exigencies of practical life. The search, then, is for what is needed and useful. In a word the test of truth is success.

For this interpretation James and Dewey are jointly responsible. The former enlarges his modification of Peirce's principle when he says: In methodology it is certain that to trace and compare their respective consequences is an admirable way of establishing the differing meanings of different conceptions. . . . The meaning of a conception expresses itself in practical consequences, either in the shape of conduct to be recommended, or in that of experience to be expected. In like manner Dewey enlarges the primitive principle. At first his problem is how to make our ideas clear to ourselves and how to get out of them their cash value; at the last he socializes the problem and turns from commercialism to humanism. So we have next to show how this broadening of the initial principle was left to the Chicago school, and how that fine air of adventure was applied to social ethics,—to the search for practical principles destined to bring the greatest good to the greatest number.

3. THE CHICAGO SCHOOL: JOHN DEWEY

In the beginning of his first essay on " Thought and its Subject-Matter " Dewey follows in the footsteps of Peirce. The latter had advocated that sort of logic which would appease the irritation of doubt and clear up our ideas. So Dewey holds that reflective thought has as the measure of its success the degree in which the thinking disposes of the difficulty. This is applied logic. Against it the advocates of pure logic bring the charge that it deals merely with hindrances, and with the devices for overcoming them. Now, the absolutists disparage such considerations of utility, because they prefer " universal forms and principles of thought which hold good everywhere irrespective of any difference in the objects." By such disparagement the reader will readily see the absolutists cut out the entire procedure of practical deliberation and of concrete scientific research. And in their preference for abstractions, without possible reference or bearing, they expose the weakness of mere metaphysics in the sense of a metaphysics which makes a gulf between itself and science. The pragmatic method is different. What we have to reckon with is not the problem of, How can I think at large? but, How shall I think right here and now? The various modes of conceding, judging, and inferring are to be treated, not as qualifications of thought at large, but of thought engaged in its specific, most economic, effective response to its own particular occasion.

We have here reached the instrumental type of thinking. It has two advantages. Negatively, it wipes out the distinction between thought and fact, the hypothetical chasm between pure and applied logic which a false metaphysics created. Positively, it falls in line with the evolutionary process, wherein biology and social history disclose the fact that every distinct organ, structure, or formation, every grouping of cells or elements, has to be treated as an instrument of adaptation to a particular environing situation.

Dewey thus boldly lays down the platform of instrumentalism. In pointing out its negative and positive sides we may suggest that it is finally to be judged by the rule of Leibniz, that philosophers are not so much true in what they deny, as in what they affirm. This explains why the absolutists have been up in arms against Dewey's denials. They do not relish his bald dilemma, namely, that we have no choice, save either to conceive of thinking as a response to a specific stimulus, or else to regard it as something "in itself." But are we left to this bare dilemma between Cæsar or nobody? When Dewey protests against the diremption between thought and things, he is protesting against a false transcendentalism which would put a line of cleavage between the world of fancy and the world of fact. His own solution actually approaches a true transcendentalism, being a species of immanence, a marrying of thought to things. Thus he explains: As we submit each characteristic situation of experience to our gaze we find it has a dual aspect. In the course of changing experience we keep our balance, because, wherever there is thinking, there is material in question. Now the old-style logician sets the agent over against the externality of the fact, but the new does not keep "thought in itself" apart from the limits of the special work it has to do. This leads to the value of the logic of experience. Philosophy, defined as such a logic, makes no pretense to be an account of a closed and finished universe; its business is not to secure or guarantee any particular reality or value. On the contrary, it gets the significance of a method. The right relationship, the adjustment of the various typical phases of experience to one another, is a problem felt in every department of life. Intellectual control of these adjustments cannot fail to reflect itself in an added clearness and security on the practical side. . . . The value of research for social progress; the bearing of psychology upon educational procedure; the mutual relations of fine and industrial art; the question of the extent and nature of specialization in science in comparison with the claims of applied science; the adjustment of religious aspirations to scientific statements—such are a few of the many social questions whose *final* answer depends upon the possession and use of a general logic of experience as a method of inquiry and of interpretation.

Of all these suggested reforms Dewey has carried out most successfully a combination of the first two, namely, social progress and educational procedure. Through his work in connection with the Laboratory School, existing in Chicago between 1896 and 1903, his ideas attained such concreteness as comes from embodiment and testing in practice. The problem is considered to be one of instrumental logic, the application of thought to things. The usual school has been so set apart, he explains, so isolated from the ordinary conditions and motives of life, that the place where children are sent for discipline is the one place in the world where it is most difficult to get such experience. Contrast with this the old days when the household was practically the center in which were carried on all the typical forms of industrial occupation. The clothing worn was not only made in the house, but the members of the household were generally familiar with the shearing of the sheep, the carding and spinning of the wool, and the plying of the loom. In short, the entire industrial process stood revealed, from the production on the farm of the raw materials, till the finished article was actually put into use. Not only this, but practically every member of the household had his own share in the work. The children, as they gained in strength and capacity, were gradually initiated into the mysteries of the several processes. It was a matter of immediate and personal concern even to the point of actual participation. Such was the old household system which furnished an intimate acquaintance with nature at first hand, with real things and materials, with the actual processes of their manipulation, and the knowledge of their social necessities and uses.

In contrast with this, consider the school of the present day, which appeals for the most part simply to the intellectual aspect of our natures, our desire to learn, to accumulate information, and to get control of the symbols of learning; not to our impulses and tendencies to make, to do, to create, to produce, whether in the form of utility or of art. Against this conventional modern conception, which is merely a survival of a false medievalism, the age revolts. One of the most striking tendencies at present is toward the introduction of so-called manual " training," shop-work, and the household arts—sewing and cooking. This has not been done " on purpose," with a full consciousness that the school must now supply that factor of training formerly taken care of in the home, but rather by instinct, by experimenting and finding that such work takes a vital hold of pupils and gives them something which was not to be got in any other way. Consciousness of its real import is still so weak that the work is often done in a half-hearted, confused, and unrelated way. The reasons assigned to justify it are painfully inadequate or sometimes even positively wrong.

Can we give actual reasons for what roughly may be termed the " new " education? It is useless to bemoan the departure of the good old days of children's modesty, reverence, and implicit obedience, if we expect merely by bemoaning and by exhortation to bring them back. It is radical conditions which have changed, and only an equally radical change in education suffices. In the century of changes between the household and factory systems one can hardly believe there has been a revolution in all history so rapid, so extensive, so complete. Through it the face of the earth is making over, even as to its physical forms; political boundaries are wiped out and moved about, as if they were indeed only lines on a paper map; population is hurriedly gathered into cities from the ends of the earth; habits of living are altered with startling abruptness and thoroughness; the search for the truths of nature is infinitely stimulated and facilitated and their application to life made not only practicable, but commercially necessary.

Such conditions, continues Dewey, mean much to the city-bred child of to-day. For example, the new geography is not merely the study of metes and bounds, but the earth as the great field, the great mine, the great source of the energies of heat, light, and electricity; the great scene of ocean, stream, mountain, and plain, of which all our agricultural and mining and lumbering, all our manufacturing and distributing agencies, too, are but the partial elements and factors. So, too, the new manual training is not merely utilitarian like sewing on buttons or making patches. Looked at from the proper genetic point of view, we find that this work gives the point of departure from which the child can begin to follow the progress of mankind in history, getting an insight also into the materials he is using and the mechanical principles involved. In connection with these occupations, the historic development of man is recapitulated. For example, the children are first given the raw material—the flax, the cotton plant, the wool as it comes from the back of the sheep. . . . Then a study is made of these materials from the standpoint of their adaptation to the uses to which they may be put. For instance, a comparison of the cotton fiber with wool fiber is made. I did not know until the children told me, that the reason for the late development of the cotton industry as compared with the woolen is, that the cotton fiber is so very difficult to free by hand from the seeds. The children in one group worked thirty minutes freeing cotton fibers from the boll and the seeds and succeeded in getting out less than one ounce. They could easily believe that one person could only gin one pound a day by hand, and could understand why their ancestors wore woolen instead of cotton clothing. . . . They then followed the processes necessary for working the fibers up into cloth. They re-invented the first frame for carding the wool—a couple of boards with sharp pins in them for scratching it out. They redevised the simplest process for spinning the wool—a pierced stone or some other weight through which the wool is passed, and which as it is twirled draws out the fiber, next the top, which was spun on the floor, while the children kept the wool in their hands until it was gradually drawn out and wound upon it. Then the children are introduced to the invention next in historic order, working it out experimentally, thus seeing its necessity, and tracing its effects, not only upon that particular industry, but upon modes of social life—in this way passing in review the entire process up to the present complete loom, and all that goes with the application of science in the use of our present available powers. I need not speak of the science involved in this—the study of the fibers, of geographical features, the conditions under which raw materials are grown, the great centers of manufacture and distribution, the physics involved in the machinery of production; nor, again, of the historical side—the influence which these inventions have had upon humanity. . . . Now, what is true of this one instance of fibers used in fabrics, is true in its measure of every material used in every occupation, and of the processes employed. The occupation supplies the child with a genuine motive; it gives him experience at first hand; it brings him into contact with realities. It does all this, but in addition it is liberalized throughout by translation into its historic values and scientific equivalences. It ceases with the growth of the child's mind in power and knowledge to be a pleasant occupation merely, and becomes more and more a medium, an instrument, an organ—and is thereby transformed.

From the accomplishments of Dewey's Laboratory School we may deduce the platform of the Chicago group. Like a literal platform it may be looked at from four sides. First, it is genetic: it does not recognize " an object of thought in itself," but only a series of values, which vary with the varying functions to which they belong. Next, it is instrumental: it looks upon the notion of thought as an immanent tool, as a scaffolding which is an integral part to the very operation of building. Again, it is social: it seeks for a clear and comprehensive consensus of public conviction, and a consequent concentrated and economical direction of effort. Finally, it is empirical: there is no pure thought as such, nothing real which is not a direct matter of experience.

Let us see what these four points are worth. As usual the positive are strongest. First, as genetic, pragmatism allies itself with evolutionism and has behind it all the force of that movement; its cardinal doctrine is adaptation to environment, for knowing is a function in the process of adjustment. Next, as instrumental, it allies itself with the new methods of science, it adapts tool to material, reconstructs conflicting experiences. The thinker, like the carpenter, is at once stimulated and checked in every stage of his procedure by the particular situation which confronts him; materials, price of labor, credit at the bank—all are varying factors demanding constant readjustment. This instrumental adaptability seems the stronger of the positive points. As scientific it passes over from the pure to the applied, by showing the relation of the two. As James interprets it: In instrumentalism a fact and a theory have not different natures, as is usually supposed, the one being objective, the other subjective; they are both made of the same material, experience-material namely, and their difference relates to their way of functioning solely; it is " fact " when it functions steadily; it is " theory " when we hesitate.

Again, as social, pragmatism allies itself with the broader movement known as humanism: The individual and immediate are marks of ordinary human endeavor; whereas the general and remote are marks of abstract speculators dwelling apart from the mass of mankind. . . . These statements are rather vague and indefinite; so is the social programme of the pragmatist. Indeed Dewey has overloaded his platform and has practically carried out only the first of his proposals,—the application of genetic psychology to educational procedure. But if this side of the platform remains unfinished, the last does not. As immediately empirical, pragmatism puts a strong barrier against absolutism. Upon this barrier Dewey has lavished his greatest labor: Pragmatism, empiricism, humanism, functionalism, call it what you will, needs no unknowable, no absolute, behind it or around the finite world; no absolute, either, in the sense of anything eternally constant, for no term is static, but everything in process and change. In like spirit Dewey has carried out the controversy in his more recent essays. The reason, he explains, that pragmatism has no use for a perfect, absolute, complete, finished thought is that the facts of life are crude, raw, unorganized, brute.

We take this to be the crux of the matter. Truth does not consist in conformity or correspondence with an externally fixed archetype or model, but is in process of formation like all other things. In a word, " Truth " is not something in the heavens, apart from man, mysterious and incomprehensible save to the inspired; but rather an empirical reality given to every man. Such, at least, seems to be the import of the cryptic saying, " Anything, everything, are what they are experienced as." This is the postulate of mere empiricism as expanded in the first of the essays after the Chicago studies. The empiricist, continues the author, when he talks of experience does not mean some grandiose, remote affair that is cast like a net around a succession of fleeting experiences; he does not mean an indefinite, total, comprehensive experience which somehow engirdles an endless flux; he means that *things* are what they are experienced to be, and that every experience is *some* thing. . . . From this postulate of empiricism, as a general concept, nothing can be deduced, not a single philosophic proposition. But the real significance of the principle is that of a method of philosophical analysis—a method identical in kind (but differing in problem and hence in operation) with that of the scientists. If you wish to find out what subjective, objective, physical, mental, cosmic, psychic—any philosophic term, in short—means, go to experience and see what the thing is experienced *as*. Such a method is not spectacular; it permits of no offhand demonstrations of God, freedom, immortality, nor of the exclusive reality of matter, or ideas, or consciousness. But it supplies a way of telling what all these terms mean. It may seem insignificant, or chillingly disappointing, but only to one who will not try it. Philosophic concepts have outlived their usefulness considered as stimulants to emotion, or as a species of sanctions; and a larger, more fruitful, and more valuable career awaits them considered as specifically experienced meanings.

We notice at this juncture how Dewey has outdone Peirce; how the principle of cool reasonableness has developed into the cultivation of cold reason. But in adding that all existence is direct and vital, we may ask if the author has not carried the matter to extremes. Philosophic principles, especially the great triad of God, freedom, and immortality, are wont to be experienced *as* emotional and thus we find them interpreted by William James. It is the mystic strain in the temperamental pragmatist of Cambridge that makes him follow the old saying that the heart has reasons that the reason knows not of. It would be a more generous view of life to utilize the sanctions of sentiment. But for such sanctions the Chicago pragmatist has little use. He is an iconoclast of beliefs that transcend his method. The contrast is clear. James is the promoter of the will to believe, Dewey of the reason to believe. He holds that knowledge as science is the outcome of systematically directed inquiry, not submissive acceptance of "reality" as ready-made, fixed, and of finished form.

This was the position taken in 1905 when the war was carried into the enemy's country. In Emerson Hall itself, in the very building dedicated to the chief of our absolutists, Dewey, as President of the American Philosophical Association, delivered his Cambridge address on "Beliefs and Existences." In general the address was an attack on conventionalism, and an assertion of personalism. There was about it a Western air of independence and the whole was bathed in the atmosphere of the adventurous. The modern age, it explained, is marked by a refusal to be satisfied with the postponement of the exercise and function of reason to another and supernatural sphere, and by a resolve to practice itself upon its present object, nature, with all its joys. Instead of taking an oath of allegiance to Reality, objective, universal, complete, it prefers home rule, the gallantry of adventure, the genuineness of the incomplete. Instead of the prevalent academic philosophy of passionless imperturbability, absolute detachment, it prefers need, uncertainty, choice, novelty, strife. Now beliefs are personal affairs and personal affairs are adventures; for the world has meaning as somebody's, somebody's at a juncture taken for better or worse, and you shall not have completed your metaphysics till you have told whose world is meant and how and what for—in what bias and to what effect.

It is strange how this call to independency, this challenge to originality resembles the first address of Emerson, in this very spot, a generation before. "Why should not we also enjoy an original relation to the universe?" asks the transcendentalist. "Why should not we have a philosophy of insight and not of tradition? Why should we grope among the dry bones of the past when nature's floods of life stream around and through us?" Here is one of those curious points of resemblance at the beginnings of important movements of thought. Emerson was addressing the younger generation, protesting against the dominance of the dogmatic realism of the Scotch school with its short cut of common sense. And so, in turn, the pragmatist protests against the continuance of that ancient tradition which lasted on like the Greek influence upon our local architecture. Thus is the classic spirit again met with the romantic, the conventions and unities with unconventional pluralism; universals, axioms, and a priori truths with the trials and errors of struggling human beings.

While the old conflict is repeated, the effective forces are new. Modern biology, psychology, and the social sciences, continues Dewey, proffer an imposing body of concrete facts that point to the interpretation of knowledge as a human and practical outgrowth of personal belief. The testimony of biology is that the organic instrument of the whole intellectual life, the sense organs and brain and their connections, have been developed on a definitely practical basis and for practical aims, for the purpose of such control over conditions as will sustain and vary the meanings of life. The testimony of psychology is that sensation and perception, have a motor, not a static meaning. The testimony of the historic sciences is that knowledge as a system of information and instruction is a coöperative social achievement, and that logical thinking is a reweaving through individual activity of the social fabric at such points as are indicated by prevailing need and aims.

In this, his Presidential Address, Dewey gives us the clearest statement of his creed; at the same time he leaves us with an unanswered problem which James previously designated as the gap in the Chicago system. There is no cosmology. Granted that logical thinking is a reweaving through individual activity of the social fabric, can the same be said of the cosmic fabric? In social advancement, such as the making of a state constitution or the improving of a city, we may acknowledge that the web is woven as we go. But does this hold good of the ampler life, especially of that shining apparition we call nature? If thought, as Dewey elsewhere says, is a reorganizing power because it is a vital function,—of what, we may ask, is it a function? We may dismiss the account of the static absolutist that there is some eternal pattern after which the daily pattern is woven. But does this mean that the only process is one of a stitch at a time, and that the resulting fabric has often to be unraveled because faulty and imperfect? At times the pragmatist seems content with such a narrow empiricism. He appeals to " plain, ordinary, everyday empirical reflections, operating as centers of inquiry, of suggestion, of experimentation." At other times he seems inclined towards the wider sweep of rationalism; not the wholly *at large* view of the absolutist, but " regulation " in an " auspicious " direction, tested ideas which perform a " recurrent " function. These admissions appear to furnish what James calls the real safeguard against the caprice of statement and indetermination of belief, that " grain " in things against which we cannot practically go. It is doubtful if Dewey acknowledges this grain, for in a further essay on " Experience and Objective Idealism '' he distinctly favors subjective experience. Of human arrangements and institutionalizations he claims that their value is experimental, not fixedly ontological; law and order are good things, but not when they become rigidity and create mechanical uniformity or routine.

In these passages there is raised the old controversy between the doctrines of being and becoming, of fate and free-will, of fixity and chance. The controversy is difficult, yet in its discussion it is clear that there are two positions which Dewey does not take. He is opposed to the Humean skepticism which regards experience as a chance association, by merely psychic connections, of individualistic states of consciousness. He is also opposed to that objective idealism which gives the semblance of order, system, connection, mutual reference, to sensory data that without its assistance are mere subjective flux. He stands, then, between two extremes,—solipsism, or that form of individualism which makes one man's meat another man's poison; and absolutism, which cramps humanity into the procrustean bed of preconceived ideas. No, Dewey leaves humanity to make its own bed, and if it is uncomfortable, to make it over again.

But if life is not a mere kaleidoscope of shifting events, how far can we count on any teleological element, any plan or purpose in it? To this question Dewey gives a twofold answer. As to immediate empiricism he asserts that it is not solipsistic, because that would put all error in the individual consciousness; nor is it absolutistic, because that would put all truth in the supreme consciousness; but it *is* humanistic because it puts both error and truth in human knowledge. This answer is safe and sane, but is it satisfactory? Not to the metaphysician who would go beyond human consciousness for a deeper answer to the problem. Pragmatism claims to be naturalistic. So it is, provided the word nature be confined to human nature. But what of that immensely wider environment in which man is set? Is there a " grain " in things against which we cannot go, a " system " in the cosmic game of chance against which we cannot win? Of the two main meanings of chance Dewey avoids the one, but does not grapple with the other. There is the popular sense in which chance means a capricious and incomprehensible contingency. There is another sense; namely, that of a hidden but discoverable thread of connection. To the Greek it is the thread which the Fates spin; to the gambler it is the " system " by which he tries to break the bank; to the scientist it is the mathematical, predictable element in the flux of events, that function which appears as a constant, provided the series be sufficiently prolonged. Blind chance, the scientist hates it; like Galileo he exclaims: " Vanish, ye dark vaults of heaven! "

Even here there is a distressing dilemma. Shall we say that there is a plan, but it passes man's understanding; or that there is no plan, but the nature of things is a purposeless flux? As to the former view the pragmatist demurs. Like a good Yankee he " wants to know." As to the latter view there is some uncertainty. Primitive pragmatism has been interpreted by Bakewell and others as a latter-day flowing philosophy, a revival of the ancient doctrine of Heracleitus, that man cannot dip into the same river twice. Such interpreters also give us the choice between Protagoras and Plato; between man as the measure of all things, and man as the interpreter of nature in the sense of read-

ing its secrets. Of the latter school is Emerson, while
Royce continues the tale in the *World and the Individual.*

What is the broader relation of these two views? We
fail to see that Dewey has grappled with the problem.
Given functional empiricism and thought as the vital
function, what is the immanent principle at work? Is
it humanistic or cosmic? Is it confined to civic communities, or can a Greater Chicago school take in the
cosmos as a suburb? The answer is not yet given. In a
strictly up-to-date simile Dewey, as upholder of the volitional, disparages Absolute Reason. Did purpose ride
in a cosmic automobile toward a predestined goal, he
exclaims, it would not cease to be physical and mechanical because labeled Divine Idea, or Perfect Reason.
However, we may query whether human reason is the
immanent motor or whether it is merely the speed indi-
cator in the great machine.

Let us point out plainly what Dewey has accomplished
and what remains to be done. In place of the old-
fashioned objective idealism which has grown somewhat
stiff in the joints, he has put a volitional, experimental
spirit which is willing to take risks, ready to adapt itself
to new environments. For such a volitional, experimental teleology he claims a higher ideality than is possessed by idealism itself. Values, he insists, cannot be
both ideal and given, and their " given " character is
emphasized, not transformed when they are called eternal and absolute. But natural values become ideal the
moment their maintenance is dependent upon the intentional activities of an empirical agent.

To uphold this view of his Dewey has final recourse to
Darwinism. In laying hands upon the sacred ark of
absolute permanency, in treating the forms that had

been regarded as types of fixity and perfection as originating and passing away, the *Origin of Species,* he tells us, introduced a mode of thinking that in the end was bound to transform the logic of knowledge and hence the treatment of morals, politics, and religion.   Here the touchstone was the old problem of design versus chance, mind versus matter, as the causal explanation, first or final, of things.   The classic notion was that within natural sensible events there is contained a spiritual causal force which as spiritual escapes perception, but is apprehended by an enlightened reason.   The Darwinian principle of natural selection cuts straight under this philosophy.   If all organic adaptations are due simply to constant variation and elimination of those variations harmful in that struggle for existence that is brought about by excessive reproduction, there is no call for a prior intelligent causal force to plan and preordain them.

We have here the familiar antithetical treatment of the problem of purpose. Darwinism and design are looked at as if they were oil and water, and would not mix. Hence Dewey undervalues any attempts at reconciliation or mediation. He mentions Asa Gray as favoring the Darwinian principle and, at the same time, attempting to reconcile it with design. He calls Gray's view '' design on the installment plan '': if we conceive the '' stream of variations '' to be itself independent, we may suppose that each successive variation was designed from the first to be selected. Now, this view of Gray's was based on Darwin's assertion that it was '' impossible to conceive this immense and wonderful universe, including man with his capacity of looking far backwards and far into futurity, as the result of blind chance or necessity.'' Yet Dewey in turn claims Darwin's refusal to be

offset by the great evolutionist's conviction that, since
variations are in useless as well as in useful directions,
and since the latter are sifted out simply by the stress
of the conditions for the struggle for existence, the
design argument as applied to living beings is unjusti-
fiable, and its lack of support there deprives it of scientific value.

Dewey concludes that the impossibility of assigning
the world to chance as a whole, and to design in its parts,
indicates the insolubility of the question. For this insolubility he offers two reasons: one is that the problem
is too high for intelligence; the other is that the question, in its very asking, makes assumptions that render
the question meaningless. Once admit that the sole
verifiable or fruitful object of knowledge is the particular set of changes that generate the object of study, together with the consequences that then flow from it, and
no intelligible question can be asked about what, by assumption, lies outside.

Here is a maze of objections which needs to be explored. We make bold to suggest that the problem is
not fairly stated. Possibly the maze does not end in a
blind alley. There may be a way out. If the cause of
the evolutionary flux lies outside, of course the problem is insoluble, or, what amounts to the same thing, the
problem is too high for intelligence. But suppose we
go back to the classic notion so excellently restated by the
writer. By assuming a spiritual causal force and making it immanent, we may have a suggestion of a solution.
The prime cause in this case might be an internal perfecting principle, a force that here and now is coming to
fruition. This is Aristotle's entelechy, enlarged to cosmic dimensions. As rational it may, after all, be apprehended by an enlightened reason. If we insist on the

distinction that it may be apprehended, not comprehended, we escape, on the one hand, absolute agnosticism,
and, on the other, an absolute all-knower. Granted, then,
an immanent spiritual principle, working itself out day
by day, we have that clew which Asa Gray used so
effectively. It is not design " on the installment plan,"
as if some designer were hard put in his payments.
What Gray sought was that internal, immanent, rational principle which made natural selection select,
which sifted out the useless, and which, in the long run,
has brought a gradual complexity, and, at the same time,
a gradual improvement.

If this suggested sketch of ours may be called absolutism, it is not the kind that Dewey disparages; it does
not pretend to know it all; it does not assume some far-off
divine event toward which the whole creation moves.
For all his strictures upon " inclusive first causes " and
" exhaustive final goals " we believe that Dewey is not
without sympathy with this interpretation, which is that
of the " mild-tempered rationalist." At any rate, he
concludes that the influence of Darwinism upon philosophy was to force upon it modesty and responsibility, for
it has shifted its interest from an intelligence that shaped
things once for all, to the particular intelligences which
things are even now shaping; from an ultimate goal of
good to the direct increments of justice and happiness
that intelligent administration of existent conditions
may beget.

This is the creed of the Chicago school. Beginning
with the principle of Peirce as a method to clear up our
ideas, to settle metaphysical puzzles, it develops into instrumentalism, or the view that all our theories are mental modes of adaptation to reality. This instrumentalism,
in turn, approaches humanism, yet not so as to make the

human or personal an ultimate, but only a tool in genetic development, a function in social improvement. This is Dewey's estimate of his own position and, at the same time, a forecast of what his successor was to do. The moment the complicity of the personal factor in our philosophic valuation is recognized fully, frankly, and generally, he concludes, that moment a new era in philosophy will begin.

4. THE CAMBRIDGE SCHOOL: WILLIAM JAMES

The new era predicted by Dewey was inaugurated by William James of Harvard. Pragmatism, he tells us in his Lowell Lectures of 1906, has rather suddenly precipitated itself out of the air, because in the history of philosophy we are beginning to recognize the clash of human temperaments.

Thus begins the third phase in the pragmatic movement,—the temperamental. The change is significant. It is a change from the logical to the psychological, a process which reduces the cognition of truth to the satisfaction of felt needs, to the emotional thrill. Now, while Dewey has warned us against the surrender to the emotional, James accepts it as a prime criterion whereby first to judge past philosophy, then to form the philosophy of the future.

The professional philosopher, he observes, has hitherto urged impersonal reasons for his conclusion. Yet all the time he has been following that view of the universe which best suits his temperament; *that* he trusts, *that* is the potentest of all his premises. If distinctive temperaments have been recognized in other branches of activity, why not in philosophy? In government there has been authoritarian and anarchist; in literature purists and realists; in art classics and romantics. So in philosophy we have a very similar contrast expressed in the pair of terms " rationalists " and " empiricists; "— " empiricist " meaning your lover of facts in all their crude variety, " rationalist " your devotee to abstract and eternal principles. In fine, the two types of mental make-up may have their characteristics written down in two columns. On the one side is the rationalist, who is idealistic, optimistic, religious, free-willist, monistic, dogmatical. On the other side is the empiricist, who is materialistic, pessimistic, irreligious, fatalistic, pluralistic, skeptical.

At the first glance the drawing up of this table of contrast between the " tough-minded " empiricist and the " tender-minded " rationalist seems to commit the same fault as that with which the absolutists were charged. It postulates theses, assumes their antitheses or logical opposites, and concludes that man must belong either to one set or the other. It is the same sort of artificial depiction of character that was committed by Macaulay in his contrasted portraits of Cavalier and Roundhead. But the deadly parallel column is one thing, live people another. In fact, James confesses that most of us have a hankering for the good things on both sides of the line. Let us, therefore, adopt a sort of pluralistic monism (for both facts and principles are good). Let us combine practical pessimism with metaphysical optimism (for though the evil of the parts is undeniable, the whole cannot be evil). Finally, let our scientific spirit be devout, otherwise we will find an empirical philosophy which is not religious enough, and a religious philosophy that is not empirical enough. . . . Thus may pragmatism be a mediation between tough-mindedness and tender-mindedness, thus may tenderfoot Bostonians mingle with Rocky Mountain toughs.

This is the Cambridge solution of "the present dilemma in philosophy." It is the opposite of that of the Chicago school. It is not a logical rejection of alternatives, but a psychological adaptation of one to the other. It offers a true humanism, for humanity in its choices uses its heart as well as its head. Now, all this seems quite illogical unless it be granted that there is a logic of the emotions, based upon grounds of personal preference. Such grounds James brings forward in his lecture on "Some Metaphysical Problems Pragmatically Considered." In this he assumes his rôle as a mediator. This was made possible by his personality, combining as it did a genial hospitality to all forms of thought with a marked boldness in undertaking difficult tasks. His pragmatism becomes to philosophy, then, what a court of arbitration is to capital and labor,—an organ of mediation between arrogant rationalism and complacent common sense. The new system, like its author, is essentially independent; it follows neither the professional philosopher on his high a priori road, nor the man in the street with his cocksure notions of truth. Rather does it strive to tread a path between the two, a *via media* from which may be obtained the ideal outlook of the one and the concrete practicality of the other. In this rôle of mediation pragmatism exhibits its adaptability to modern demands. Finding the world sick of abstractions and, at the same time, uninspired by the current beliefs, it offers itself as a tonic for tired minds, a pungent compound which will restore the jaded appetite for the speculative life.

Such a mediating part James had once hoped the Chicago school would undertake. That school, however, left the impression of being hostile to the abstract, the a priori. Coming from a new part of the country it was typically averse to the old culture. It is not so with the Eastern philosopher, who offers pragmatism as a means of satisfying both kinds of demand, remaining religious like the rationalisms, but, like the empiricisms, preserving the richest intimacy with facts. This is again a recourse to the pragmatic method as primarily one of settling metaphysical disputes that otherwise might be interminable. Is the world one or many?—fated or free?—material or spiritual? Disputes over such notions are unending, unless we try to interpret each notion by tracing its respective consequences.

Thus does James ingeniously escape the dilemma of Dewey. Instead of a process of mutual cancellation between different alternatives, he holds that alternatives with no practical consequences are not really differences. Thus science and metaphysics come together, for theories being instruments, not answers to enigmas, pragmatism unstiffens all our theories, limbers them up and sets each one at work. . . . Here is temperamental philosophy of the highest kind. James calls it democratic, but we should prefer to call it urbane. It does not accentuate local differences, but accepts cues from all quarters. Such pragmatism, as its author explains, is willing to take anything, to follow either logic or the senses and to count as proof the humblest and most personal experiences; she is completely genial; she will entertain any hypothesis; she will consider any evidence.

James shows in this the enthusiastic urbanity of a man of wide and varied activities. The artist in him comes out in the contrasted portraits of rationalist and empiricist, where he strives to give an impression by constant minute touches, and thus to let us see the masterpiece in the making. The physiologist is evident in the emphasis on the bodily, realistic side of life, where he shows his preference for warm vitality and thus allows us to catch the essential personal flavor. The psychologist we see in the stress on the emotions, in the emphasis on the conative side of life. Here James asks us: How does the world feel to you? What are the thoughts that thrill you? Finally, the religionist appears in the use of the Absolute as a source of spiritual comfort. As the author of the *Varieties of Religious Experience* James draws on his immense stores of knowledge,—from the strange cases of psychic-research, to the mysticism of William Penn, landed proprietor, and of John Bunyan, tinker.

An enthusiastic urbanity, a many-sided personality furnish the equipment of James, the mediator in metaphysics. So equipped he turns to some metaphysical problems which are to be pragmatically considered. Here pragmatism means not the bare presentation of abstract outlines, but a helpful method of tracing specific consequences of any given hypothesis. Assuming the empiricist attitude, it turns toward concreteness and adequacy, toward fact, toward action, and toward power. How is one to choose, say, between optimism and pessimism? By its effects on practical living, responds the pragmatist; one naturally accepts the former doctrine because it gives a happier view of the world. Or, again, what practical difference does it make now that the world should be thought to be run by spirit or by matter? In the one case there would be the hypothesis of an eternal perfect edition of the universe coexisting with our finite experience, in the other the hypothesis of blind physical forces, bits of brute matter unconsciously following their particular laws. Between theism and materialism, thus presented, it is impossible to choose hypothetically, but apply the principle of practical results and there is vital difference. The one hypothesis is pessimistic, its sun sets in a sea of disappointment; the other is melioristic and means the preservation of our ultimate hopes, since it is not blind force, but a seeing force, which runs this universe. So likewise with the controversy between determinism and free-will; pragmatism rids one of Puritanism, drives away the vapors of a bilious conscience, and puts man, if not on the road to perfectibility, at least into the fresh fields of independent action.

Thus briefly does James settle metaphysical problems by the pragmatic method. Using the test of temperamental likings he has been accused of confusing the true with the pleasant and of making the ground of preference merely personal. The first charge is that of hedonism, the second that of solipsism. Neither charge is wholly warranted. Pragmatism takes account of evil and will accept a God who " lives in the very dirt of private fact.'' Again pragmatism is not a narrow individualism. It holds that truth is made by society, and is only a collective name for verification. Being a social product it may, therefore, be called a species of higher hedonism. Thereby is it relieved of the accusation of keeping its eyes bent on the immediate practical foreground, for it dwells just as much upon the world's remotest perspectives. In this defense James, the mediator and smoother-over of transitions, gains a certain likeness to the absolutist, for he adds that the absolute things, the last things, the overlapping things, are the truly philosophic concerns. But we should interpret this as due not so much to the absolutistic as to the æsthetic motive, the artist's interest in vanishing points and disappearing lines. And along with it we must put the pragmatic check. James speaks of the vast drifting of the cosmic weather, yet he does not imply that there is such a thing as a meteorology of metaphysics. He argues that we cannot by any possibility comprehend the character of a cosmic mind whose purposes are fully revealed by the strange mixture of goods and evils that we find in this world's particulars. Apparently an æsthetic union obtains among things; they tell a story; their parts hang together so as to work out a climax. But absolute æsthetic union is another barely abstract idea; until we can affirm one sovereign purpose, system, story, the world appears as something more epic than dramatic.

The Cambridge pragmatist now reaches another of his mediations. It is in epistemology, the problem of knowledge, and concerns the choice between absolutism and agnosticism. When he affirms that in this world there are as many disjunctions as conjunctions, and hence there can be no one knower, no all-enveloping, noetic unity, we are forced into that modern form of skepticism regarding a universal substance. If there be such a cosmic connective tissue, the human observer has not yet learned to stain it—such seems to be his conclusion. In the same way we may interpret the allied problem of cosmology, the ancient puzzle of "the one and the many." Accepting design, free-will, the absolute mind, spirit instead of matter, because they have for their sole meaning a better promise as to this world's outcome, pragmatism suddenly abandons this monistic point of view and takes up with a pluralistic. This at first appears unnatural; it is as if an American of the strict constructionist type should suddenly give up the idea of the paramountcy of the federal government and become a violent advocate of States' rights. And yet this apparent reversal of judgment has its reasons; namely, the temperamental preferences of the author for that rich medley of facts called the world, rather than for that risky dogma of an absolutely perfect universe. Here the monist might be compared to the protectionist, who argues that if one break be allowed in the sacrosanct tariff system the whole will fall to the ground. To this philosophic stand-patter comes pragmatism unstiffening his theories, showing that this is no more the best of all possible worlds than that the present is the best of all possible administrations, and that pluralism, like States' rights, is necessary to the free play of parts so conducive to life, liberty, and the pursuit of happiness. Pragmatism, then, it is said, pending the final empirical ascertainment of just what the balance of union and disunion among things may be, must obviously range itself upon the pluralistic side and sincerely entertain the hypothesis of a world imperfectly unified still. Hence the actual world, instead of being complete " eternally," as the monists assure us, may be eternally incomplete and at all times subject to addition or liable to loss.

The adoption of the temperamental test has led to pluralism. Its later application to religion is made in a startling form of polytheism. Meanwhile James takes up the discussion of truth, first in its relations to common sense, and then in its higher scientific and social aspects. The former discussion is one of the least satisfactory in the book. It defends noetic pluralism on the ground that we can know the parts and some of their combinations, but not the whole. It defends this view by a figure of speech, holding that the universe is not a final *de luxe* edition, but a volume in the making,—it might well have been said a loose-leaf ledger. It finally gives, as a basis of common sense, Herbert Spencer's

shallow hypothesis that our fundamental ways of thinking about things are discoveries of exceedingly remote
ancestors, which have been able to preserve themselves
throughout the experience of all subsequent time. These
are the funded truths squeezed from the past, which appear natural to us because they were once so fruitful.

We may grant that such common-sense principles are
survivals of the fittest, but that does not answer the question why they are fit. This problem of the agreement of
truth and reality, whether there exist principles of
verity in the very constitution of the cosmos, is left
to the most crucial and the most difficult chapter of this
work. In regard to the " Notion of Truth " pragmatists
and intellectualists are both said to accept the dictionary
definition of truth as agreement of ideas with reality.
They begin to quarrel only after the question is raised as
to what may precisely be meant by the term " agreement," and what by the term " reality," when reality
is taken as something for our ideas to agree with. On
the one hand, the idealists seem to say that our ideas are
true whenever they are what God means that we ought
to think about that object; whenever they approach to
being copies of the Absolute's eternal way of thinking.
This is the great assumption of the intellectualists that
truth means essentially an inert static relation. Pragmatism, on the other hand, asks its usual question.
" Grant an idea or belief to be true, what concrete difference will its being true make in anyone's actual belief? How will the truth be realized? What experiences will be different from those which would obtain if
the belief were false? What, in short, is the truth's
cash-value in the experiential terms? "

At this hypothetical question the defense is up in
arms. Practical differences! Cash-values! Such phrases

pervert the principle of Peirce into a transaction of the Chicago clearing-house. Here one critic, adopting a sort of slang which pragmatism does not disdain to use, has defined truth as " Any old thing that works! "

That pragmatism as a gospel of success is utilitarian James frankly grants. The true, he continues, is only the expedient in the way of our thinking, just as the right is only the expedient in the way of our behaving. The first meaning of truth is, therefore, that of a method. Primarily it means a leading that is worth while. The discovery of a working hypothesis is used by the pragmatist in just the way a path is followed by a wanderer, because it looks as if it might lead out of the woods. Besides being a method of utility, pragmatic truth is a theory of reality. You can say of it, then, either that " it is useful because it is true," or that " it is true because it is useful."

In this statement we charge the author with making a false conversion of a proposition, in other words of implying that it is a poor rule that does not work both ways. It is easy to concede the last half of the proposition, for that is only saying that true thoughts are invaluable instruments of action. But in changing the proposition " it is true because it works " into " it works because it is true " we change from an object, a successful result, to a notion of some standard upon which the workability, the success, depends. Now, this notion of a standard would imply some fixed reality like Platonic archetypes, which exist eternally and outside human minds. But this is making truth static and dehumanizing it, therefore such a view is condemned, because pragmatism is dynamic and humanistic. Truth is not a fixed standard but a flying goal, and the world we know is determined by the human faculties.

Platonism and pragmatism are thus at opposite poles. The former says our ideas are true if they are ectypes of archetypes, shadows or copies of the absolute and eternal forms of thought. Pragmatism says, truths are not copies but consistencies; truths emerge from facts; they are not once and forever true but always in the making, humanity being the constant creator of working hypotheses, of tentative theories. By these it adapts itself to changing circumstances as does a marching army to the rise and fall of the road. This sharp contrast between the static and the absolute, between the dynamic and relative, is easy to draw because of the current revival of the ancient Greek conception of cosmic fluxility, of a plastic principle in nature. Conventional monism, with its insistence on eternal principles and fixed archetypes, will be hard pressed to explain away that mutability in nature, that changing pageantry in earth and sky, from which writers like Emerson and Whitman drew their philosophies. This being the day of the " rushing metamorphosis," the notion of a finished world is as hard to grasp as the notion of a finished waterfall; or, to carry out the figure, instead of being immutable, a frozen river of reality, truth is ever in mutation, ever carried forward on the flowing stream of consciousness.

This conclusion strikes many as nihilistic. According to James the pragmatic theory of reality holds that behind the bare phenomenal facts there is—nothing. Is not this an exaggeration? Though the flowing stream of consciousness has no bottom, it has banks and these we take to be the human factors, the guiding principles furnished by men's minds. For, as James concedes, instead of reality as such, ready-made from all eternity, we have a man-made reality. " It is *we* who create true principles, in *us* reality is in the making and *our* descriptions are metaphysical additions to facts." Again instead of the abstract worship of timeless reality, a pretense that the eternal is unrolling, we prefer a loose universe, truth growing up inside of all the finite experiences, " we men adding our fiats to the fiat of the Creator."

This is the Cambridge theory of reality. It is a bold doctrine. It is not merely humanism, but the worship of humanity. James recognizes this, and in his last chapter, " Pragmatism and Religion," reaches his final view of truth. Truth is not only a method to gain successful results, or a theory of reality as fluxility, but a temper of mind, an emotional belief which gives personal satisfaction. This satisfaction may be so intense as to be justly called a religion, not in the monistic, mystical way of pure cosmic emotion, but in the humanistic way,—a universe with such as us contributing to create its truth, a world delivered to our opportunities and our private judgments, where God is viewed as but one helper, in the midst of all the shapers of the world's fate.

At this turn in the road, we have come back to that temperamental test with which the book began, namely: The whole function of philosophy ought to be to find out what definite difference it will make to you and me, at definite instants of our life, if this world-formula or that world-formula be the true one. The formula which James reaches is that of feeling, of instinct, of intuition, for in the end he concludes: " It is our faith and not our logic that decides such questions,—the human imagination which lives in a moralistic and epic kind of universe, and avoids the two extremes of crude naturalism on the one hand, and transcendental absolutism on the other."

Here ends the pragmatism of James,—carried further, but not essentially changed, in his subsequent works, *A Pluralistic Universe* and *The Meaning of Truth*. But without recourse to these other volumes of delight let us summarize the system as James has left it; go back to its sources or affiliations, and, finally, attempt to give its probable place in the history of American thought.

5. THE SOURCES OF PRAGMATISM

To call the Cambridge pragmatism a system is apparently a misnomer. At the outset, protests James, it stands for no particular results; it has no doctrine save its methods. As the young Italian pragmatist, Papini, has well said, it lies in the midst of our theories, like a corridor in a hotel. Let us grant that pragmatism is this corridor, and not a metaphysical roof to cover all; it still furnishes a scheme, if not a system. In the case of James this scheme is determined by temperamental tests, by personal preferences. As a mediator, a man of pacific disposition, he is primarily opposed to dogmas. Against the *must* be of the intellectualist he puts the *may* be of the empiricist. Thus the philosophical trinity of the absolute idealist would be interpreted as follows: God,— a good working hypothesis; immortality, a vague confidence in the future; freedom,—a melioristic doctrine whereby improvement at least is possible. To absolutists this may seem like giving up strong meat for modified milk, but the Cambridge scheme is not entirely negative, does not wholly agree with another dictum of Papini's that "pragmatism is really less a philosophy than a method of doing without one." The American species is not invertebrate, it has an historic backbone. James says that it agrees with nominalism in appealing to particulars; with utilitarianism in emphasizing practical aspects; with positivism in its disdain for metaphysical abstractions. In these confessed resemblances the author is but carrying out the full title of his book—*Pragmatism, a New Name for Some Old Ways of Thinking*.

We may go further. Recalling the title of a quaint deistic work—*Christianity as Old as the Creation*—we may speak of "Pragmatism as Old as Speculation." From the Greeks to modern days the pragmatic stream has flowed unbroken. Dewey may disparage the past, but the continuity of kindred thought is a fact. We take the long leap backward and begin with Heracleitus. His doctrine we have already noticed. That all flows, that reality is fluxility, that there is no finality in truth—is the very soul of the latter-day flowing philosophy. Next, the sophistic doctrine, that man is the measure of all things, is revived in the modern individualism, where there are many men of many minds, and as many kinds of reality as there are pragmatists. Schiller of Oxford has defended this ancient sophistic doctrine as explaining the bewildering variety of human customs and beliefs, and enabling men to conceive objective "truth," not as an initial gift of the gods, but as a practical and social problem. The choice then favors Protagoras rather than Plato, for the latter's ideal theory explained nothing, just because, by being elevated above the flux, it had lost all touch with humanity.

So much for the agreement with Hellenic thought. For the medieval, James has this single word—that pragmatism agrees with nominalism in its appeal to particulars. This means that a name is nothing but a summation of experiences, a short cut to reality, not a reality itself. This is diametrically opposed to that form of Platonism revived in scholastic realism which held that back of every name there is a reality, a supersensible essence existing independent of particulars.

As pragmatism agrees with empiricism and is opposed to transcendentalism ancient and medieval, so does it stand in relation to modern empiricism and transcendentalism. In these connections we may take the Western nations briefly one by one. Among the English we find Lord Bacon,—the father of empiricism,—with his saying that knowledge is power; John Locke with his habit of testing abstract ideas, like substance, in terms of experience; David Hume with his attack on intellectualism and his advice to throw metaphysics to the flames. As to Hume the resemblance between the arch-skeptic and the modern sophist is strong. Just as James uses theories as short-cuts to reality and advises us to act *as if* this and that were true, so Hume uses belief to bridge over difficulties and asks us to invent such a notion as causality as a sort of fictitious glue to bind the cosmos together.

These are the earlier English empiricists. Among the later stand forth Darwin and Mill. The parallels with the former are obvious: the familiar phrases—adaptation to environment, struggle for existence, survival of the fittest—are the very watchwords of the modern practicalism. And so is it with John Stuart Mill, to whom James dedicates his volume as the one " From whom I first learned the pragmatic openness of mind and whom my fancy likes to picture as our leader were he alive to-day."

So much for the British empiricists. The affinities are so strong that pragmatism might almost be called Anglo-Americanism. As for the Germans there are few affinities acknowledged by the pragmatists themselves. With a practical working treaty between the two English-speaking countries it might be expected that the Germans should be left out. It is worse than that. Against the whole tribe of Teutonic idealists there is a chorus of objections, strictures, taunts, and vilifications. Thus Dewey holds that Kant never emerges from his fallacies, and James holds up to derision the " hollow god " of Hegel. But in spite of James's protestations that he has never received a single clear idea from Kant, there are marked resemblances between the philosopher of Koenigsberg and that of Cambridge. Kant's doctrine of postulates has a family likeness to James's *Will to Believe*. " I will that there be a God, in order to the living of my moral life " sounds much like James's exhortations to act *as if* there were a seeing force that runs things. Further resemblances have been brought out by Arthur McGiffert. In addition to this faith in God as an heroic deed, not a passive acquiescence, there is the doctrine of meliorism—" that the world as a whole is always improving." And besides the primacy of the will, the recognition of its activity in forming the truth, there is the doctrine of humanism,—that man is a factor in the making of reality, that there is a plastic world to which he gives meaning and value.

All this sounds, and is very pragmatic. The unpragmatic part arises in the monism of Post-Kantian idealism, that transcendentalizing of his teachings against which the master warned his disciples. In this regard Hegel was the chief offender, for he did turn theology into theosophy, the postulate of deity as an " idea made by ourselves with a practical purpose " into an assumption that by mere thinking man can find out God. Against such a perversion the pragmatists have grounds for protest. They especially dread that Frankenstein deity,— an absolute being derived by the dialectical process of the unfolding of the Idea. We do not pretend to solve the secret of Hegel, but we can understand how such formulæ would drive James mad. This rigid doctrine of " becoming " according to preconceived plans would irritate an independent American much as might the rules and regulations of a bureaucratic police.

There remains a third German idealist to be reckoned with. Schopenhauer's *World as Will* might appear akin to the Chicago civic motto " I Will " and all the implications of the strenuous life. In a measure the transcendental energism does seem like the transatlantic restlessness. But with the apparent likeness there is a fundamental difference. The German's will is a cosmic principle, a hidden fatal force which carries mankind irresistibly onward. The American's will is individual, each man is the architect of his own fortune. Now, while the false identification of the two schools of energism cannot be attributed to Dewey, it might be to James. Some take his appeal to the subliminal to be an appeal to the transcendental. This is a misinterpretation. The energies of men which he bids us use are not beyond experience, but only beneath the threshold of consciousness. Furthermore, there is a confusion of temperaments. To put James among the pessimists is an absurdity to one familiar with his personality. The will to believe, as his compatriots take it, is a will to believe in the better, and upon this temperamental quality is based the doctrine of meliorism. The Cambridge thinker would be the last to say that there is a final futility in the will, and an ultimate necessity for self-denial and self-annihilation.

It is easy to see that the resemblances between the Teutonic and transatlantic philosophers are less than the differences. The same cannot be said of the French.

Pragmatism has been charged with being a revamped positivism. The resemblances are striking. Both make much of science, and in place of absolute causes put relative laws. Both emphasize nature and prefer the observation of phenomena to metaphysical abstractions. Both are enamored of humanity and consider man's needs the ultimate aim of knowledge. In short, both are scientific, naturalistic, humanistic, and also—somewhat skeptical. They do not care for supersensible realities, like first grounds and ultimate principles, but are satisfied with the horizon of level experience. They do not seek for intellectual unification of all sciences, but are content to employ the same method in all cases.

Is pragmatism, then, a revival of positivism, the Cambridge scholar a reincarnation of the Parisian? James objected to this implication. Through his early education in France he had come into intimate relations with the positive point of view, but his return to America brought him under different influences. A French critic, Abel Rey, has exposed the difference between positivists and pragmatists. The former, he explains, are guilty of the dogmatism of the idea; pure thought, the correct formula is deemed entirely sufficient. The latter are guilty of the dogmatism of the act; cognition follows the necessities of action. There is no scientific truth, but only truths, valuable not in themselves, but only as instruments.

We may make the line of cleavage even sharper. With Comte there is a worship of reason, and the immutability of natural law is fundamental. With James the formula of feeling supplements logic, and the neglected emotions are given their proper functions of motive forces. James's pragmatism, then, has two focal points different from positivism: it is opposed to immutability; it is in

favor of emotionality. While the latter of these points
is to be sought in James's native environment, yet the
former is still French. When James spoke of all our
scientific laws being only approximations, our theories
only conceptual shorthand reports of nature, he was re-
flecting the views of Poincaré. The method of science,
says that mathematician, is that a theory is only a trial
and error scheme; there are thousands of theories, but
only a few of them fit the facts. The meaning of hypothesis is then only a working hypothesis, a tool which
serves to-day, but to-morrow will be thrown on the
scrap-heap. Such a view is congruous to both the schools
of Chicago and of Cambridge. It is evolutionary. It is
another instance of the prodigality of nature. The
theories thrown out by the human mind are like the
wasted spawn of which only a fraction comes to maturity.
This view also fits the latter-day flowing philosophy. It
tends to fluidity of thought rather than to finality of
truth. There is nothing absolutely true; not even this
statement.

All this upholds the contention of James that pragmatism is not a revival of the outworn positivism of
Comte, Renan, and Taine. Positivism is unpragmatic
in its insistency on the supremacy of reason, and its
founder maintained that the human spirit should pro
ceed to theoretical researches, completely abstracting itself from every practical consideration. On the other
hand, pragmatism is non-positive in that second point we
noticed,—emotionality. But positivism is opposed to
feeling, especially religious feeling. No Comtean would
put on the same level the experiences of science, of metaphysics, and of religion. But this is what the pragmatists
do; they reverse the positive formula of development—
the necessary successive phases; theological; metaphysi-

cal; positive—when they assert that pragmatism can utilize all experiences, from the clearest to the most obscure, from the clarities of science to the mysteries of the subconscious.

We have gone through the forerunners of pragmatism, ancient, medieval, and modern, and have discovered that the pragmatists, although contemners of the past, have had numerous predecessors. With the sophistic doctrine the affinities are more than superficial, with the nominalistic more than nominal. But with the modern the perspective is closer and distinctions loom into differences. Although pragmatism is so largely Anglo-American, the American movement is not entirely a revival of British empiricism. To Bacon's knowledge is power, James adds, knowledge is also satisfaction. To Locke's two inlets of knowledge, sensation and reflection, he adds volition. Against Hume's conception of religion as an outworn superstition, an invention of priests, he puts religious experience as an outcome of the passional needs of humanity. James is the brother of the British empiricists; he is likewise their older brother,—older in time and with a wider outlook. As Dickinson Miller has pointed out, they asked—whence it came; he asks—whither it goes; they asked—what were the originals of the conception; he asks—what is to be the effect upon future practical experience.

Pragmatism is not merely an Anglo-Saxon plant, nor does it grow solely from Continental roots. The alleged affinities disappear on closer scrutiny. The pragmatic principle cannot be identified with Kant's practical postulate in either of its two senses. It is not constitutive, like a constitution which determines the very growth of the body politic. It is not regulative, like the governor of an engine which controls the safety-valve. It is merely heuristic,—a means of finding one's way out of a maze of difficulties. Again the pragmatic principle is an individual rule, which can be made and remade to suit changing demands. Hence it is opposed to Hegel's dialectic. His scheme of evolution is like the unwinding of a ball of string, previously wound up by a machine—the machine in this case being formal logic. Finally, there is opposition to the spirit of Schopenhauer. To the pessimist the world as will comes to consciousness, only to discover the futility of that will. To the pragmatist there is no cosmic consciousness, but only a social consciousness, driving the more powerful on to become lords of this earth. If there were an essential affinity between the pragmatists and the Germans it would be through Nietzsche. Those overlords of the American business world, whose motto is " success at all hazards," are first-cousins to the Teutonic superman, who works in a realm " beyond good and evil."

So the rise of pragmatism is not to be sought in the Fatherland either through the Anglo-Hegelians or through the St. Louis school, except in the way of a recoil against their transcendentalism. Fichte, indeed, taught in his *Vocation of Man* that things in themselves are as we make them. But the few Fichtean individualists in the Middle West were swallowed up by the Hegelian absolutists. If we may say that the impulse to pragmatism did not come from Germany, the case is not so clear as to France. The unpracticality of positivism is a forgotten phase of that Gallic cult which, at one time, had such a vogue in America. So is the mysticism of Comte's later days. Unpracticality is, of course, unpragmatic, but mysticism is not, unless the scheme of James be counted a form of perverted pragmatism. Consequently there is a curious resemblance between the French and American thinkers. We find Comte's love of humanity taking a mystic turn, only after he had exhausted the possibilities of the sciences. Facts were one thing, feelings another. Hence positivism had as its supplement that religion which worships humanity itself as *le grand être*. Of this worship Comte considered himself the high priest, as shown in his *Positive Catechism, or Summary Exposition of the Universal Religion*. But such documents came forth a generation before they could have directly influenced William James. For the latter's mysticism we must therefore seek, not a foreign, but a native and more intimate source. Henry James, Sr., was the leader of American Swedenborgianism, and to this fact we may trace the son's inherited interest in a cult which taught the primacy of the emotional imagination. This reversion to a youthful form of thought goes far to explain the motives that turned James the scientist into James the religionist. Among the *Varieties of Religious Experience* we find many cases like those of the seer of Stockholm. In the *Will to Believe* there is also advocated the " right to believe " in the celestial world. Finally in the *Pluralistic Universe* there is presented that hierarchy of superhuman beings, which have a family likeness to the Swedenborgian conception of the world as a progressive spiral of perfectibility. To read the chapter " Concerning Fechner," with its earth-soul and its multi-verses, is like reading the *Earths in the Universe* and the *Heavenly Arcana*.

All this has been called the logic of irrationalism. It should rather be called a reversion to a type of transcendentalism. The " faith ventures " and " over-beliefs " which James advocated, were much like the supersensible faculties and Over-Soul to which Emerson appealed. In short, the philosophers of Concord and of Cambridge both utilized the celestial. One said "Hitch your wagon to a star"; the other—"Hitch your star to a wagon," that is, accept, for the time being, any sort of a creed, provided it will furnish you with motive power.

In this very emotional resemblance there nevertheless lurks a deeper difference. With transcendentalism the notion of truth is unconditional, it is a copy of a higher reality. With pragmatism truth is not a copy but a consistency; there is nothing in your mind to condition it except certain racial inclinations. According to transcendentalism, truth is received from on high. According to pragmatism, truth happens to an idea; it becomes true, is made true by events. In fine, pragmatism as radical empiricism means simply truth as you go along.

This casual view of truth may be called the hall-mark of pragmatism. It is that which differentiates it from previous movements native and foreign. It is that which puts it in the stream of present tendencies, the rapid current of modernism, which washes away the banks of tradition. As with "new" art, or "new" music, pragmatism is a movement opposed to the dogmatic, the absolute. As soon as a notion is fixed, a scheme systematized, it moves restlessly on. The spur of dissatisfaction of Peirce leads on to the test of satisfaction of Dewey, and this in turn to the fresh emotional responses of James. To picture pragmatism is to picture a rapid stream, eating away the fixed landmarks of custom and convention. A radical upholder of pragmatism has gone so far as to compare it to an evolutionary Niagara, whose being is doing, whose end is action.

To judge of the movement by one's emotional response, it gives one first a feeling of ease, of floating with that current of modernism which is no longer confined by the canons of art, or literature, or religion. It next gives one a feeling of being lost, of being carried on in a waste of waters, not only without bottom but without banks. This is a mixed feeling and it leads to a mixed conclusion, and that is that pragmatism is not a conclusive philosophy, but only a transitional era in thought. With Peirce it is a mere method; with Dewey a useful tool; while with James it leads not to a system but a scheme, which may contain such inconsistencies as a pluralistic monism, and free-willist determinism.

6. THE CRITICS OF PRAGMATISM

Whether pragmatism is merely a transitional era, a transformation phase, a form of Protagoreanism which presages another Plato—is hard for an American to decide. The swimmer in the flood is apt to lose his bearings. This being the case, let us turn to foreign opinions for a decision. We have the picture of pragmatism; let us hang it in the international gallery and obtain the verdict of an impartial jury. From this jury we must exclude the English pragmatists, because they are too much of a single philosophic family, although we should particularly like to accept the opinion of Schiller of Oxford when he calls William James "the last great emancipator of the human spirit."

The Germans we must exclude for the opposite reason. They have been violent detractors of pragmatism, possibly because they have for once been caught napping in the speculative race. Even the urbane James cannot stand their strictures, and accuses them of being misinterpreters of the movement. With the other Continental critics it is different. It is the Latins who are especially fitted to interpret our ways of thinking—the French for their clarity of style and luminous vision, the Italians for their penetrating practicality and social instincts. We begin with the Gauls because they, in a sort of literary revenge for the material partition of their country, have become adepts in the intellectual delimitation of other realms. Many of these critical Cæsars are known for their commentaries, but not all. We are familiar with the conquerors and classifiers of the dark continent of Kant, but not with those of the land of James. Here is a new race, they exclaim; no one has understood it; let us, therefore, undertake the task of setting in order these transatlantic barbarians. When, says Marcel Hébert, I first heard the word pragmatism, I fancied it was a sort of American slang—a useful practical formula to put truth at the service of men of affairs and men of action, men not particular as to the point of view of logic and criticism. But the interest with which their books have been welcomed in Latin countries has undeceived me. It appears that there are so many excellences and also so many paradoxes in the system that it would be useful to explain them in their broad outline.

In the same manner J. Bourdeau refers to pragmatism as a system to be expected of Yankees, because it is a philosophy of results, a philosophy of action, a philosophy of profits. It is in harmony with the American attitude towards science, which puts Edison and Morse in the first rank, Ampère and Fresnel in the second. Nevertheless, for all its insistence on the practical, it has its good points. One may expect from a semi-barbarous race only a philosophy of engineers, merchants, brokers; yet that philosophy is an excellent antidote to an aristocratic intellectualism, disdainful of consequences. In France the prestige of ideas has been abused, the people have become soft, the classes over-civilized. Hence the value of the pragmatist as an apostle of energy, a philosopher who proves his ideas not by dreaming them, but by acting them. In short, pragmatism is a practical matter, obvious to men of affairs, "business men," plutocrats by economic power and the conquest of material comfort. Now, while there is to be recognized in pragmatism the Anglo-Saxon instinct with its skepticism of pure ideas and its disregard of general notions, its love of empiricism and its aversion to complexity of thought, yet there are in France men not without affinities with James and Peirce. Thus Bergson attacks the so-called general truths of science, and traces the hypothesis to a personal source. So, too, Maurice Blondel advocates a method which would confront the various systems of intellectualism, from Descartes to Taine, from the point of view of practical consequences.

This attitude of gleaning the practical factors from rationalistic systems is what Abel Rey designates as the new tone in philosophy. It is not an eclectic positivism, for positivism lays too much stress on pure science, and tends to disregard the emotional and passional side of life. Nor is it the French neo-criticism which piously hands down the traditions of absolutism from Descartes to Hegel. The latter group of thinkers is a mere survival of the past; somewhat fossilized, it has not taken account of the anti-intellectual and mystical current, which starts with Schelling and Schopenhauer in their re-habilitation of the indeterminate, the unconscious, the irrational. Hence it is that recourse should be had to the aspirations of the heart, to the obscurer instincts of humanity. True knowledge is, in fine, to be sought not from positivistic science, not from proud intellectualism, but in the intuitions of sentiment, in moral ideas, in religious beliefs. . . . Of all these pragmatism is the synthesis.

From the French critics thus far cited it is evident that the western Goth is, after all, not so barbarous, but well in the vanguard of progress. At the last International Congress of Philosophy Émile Boutroux showed how, of the two dominant groups of thought, the pragmatists have assumed the most advanced position. On the one hand are the intellectualists who, completely satisfied with science, believe that there is little knowledge outside its boundaries. On the other are the anti-intellectualists, who, going beyond the present limits of science, honor certain irrational powers of the human soul, such as instinct, intuition, the sense of action. Berthelot stands for the former group; inheritor of the doctrines of the eighteenth century, successor of the Encyclopædists, he makes a religion of science and believes that it is the sole irrefragable foundation for the morality of races as well as of individuals. Up to 1890, continues André Chaumeix, such a rôle was held by science in philosophy, sociology, and morality. But in 1893 Émile Boutroux maintained against the mechanism and materialism of the scientists the notions of liberty and spirituality. Next, Ferdinand Brunetière followed with his attack on the fallacies of science, and showed that phenomena are always in formation and that opinions must be modified by new experiences. Finally, Henri Poincaré, criticising the values of the sciences, showed that, in place of the fixity of general ideas, we must hold to the relativity of hypotheses, that the simplicity of nature is but a convenient convention, and that scientific formulæ are but approximate accommodations to reality.

Such are the Franco-American affiliations, the points

of sympathy which have brought about a philosophic *entente cordiale* between the two republics, and have led to the visits to our shores of two such distinguished thinkers as Émile Boutroux, head of the Fondation Thiers, and Henri Bergson, author of *Creative Evolution.* These are the affiliations; naturally there are accompanying differences. Briefly there are two,—one of them respecting learning, the other religion. The contempt for culture strikes all the French observers as an earmark of the Anglo-American movement. Bourdeau shows how the hostility to rationalism makes a *tabula rasa* of all that is not English or American. Descartes, Leibniz, and Kant do not exist for the pragmatist; with him, as with Herbert Spencer and Lord Bacon, there is manifest a positive disdain for past thought. Chaumeix has noticed the same thing; Rey devotes a chapter to the pragmatic disregard for the traditional solutions of the problems of truth; while Hébert neatly turns the tables by asking if these contemners of the past have not, in fact, had numerous predecessors. The latter's search for sources is perhaps carried to excess; he has made too many of the historic figures pragmatists unconscious of their pragmatism. But the historical comparison is the only way to get the correct perspective, the relative point of view so often forgotten by transitionalists.

The second point of difference concerns religion. In this there are two opinions, one of recoil, the other of ridicule. Hébert estimates American pragmatism from the cautious Catholic point of view. In regard to the theistic conception he agrees with James that, as an over-belief, it is true because it is so useful; but he recoils from the representation of the relation between man and the higher spirits as that of dogs and cats towards their masters. This sort of Pickwickian humor, which has

attracted other Gallic writers, does not appeal to one who
holds that the deity is an object of worship, not merely
because he is *primus inter pares,* but because he is the
possessor of infinite perfections. To this modern scholastic, then, God is to be estimated not solely *ex conse-
quentiis,* but rather as an objective reality raised far
above the level of probability. In fine, since human nature is capable of seeing for the sake of seeing, of
knowing for the sake of knowing, it is necessary, over
and above such an utilitarian pragmatism, to affirm the
excellence of pure disinterestedness.

In regard to mysticism it seems to Bourdeau a paradox that a Yankee philosophy should lead to such a result.
While the French critic refers this to a reaction against
scientific snobbism, tracing it through the pragmatic appeal from the intellect to the emotions, in the case of
James an American might prefer to trace the latter's
mystic leanings to a directly inherited interest in
Swedenborgianism. But, whatever the source, it is a
veritable paradox that Occidental thought is approxi-
mating Oriental. The American mind-cure has no historic connections, as Bourdeau would hold, with the
spiritual exercises of Ignatius de Loyola. Except for
the Quakers, mystic manuals have had little vogue among
the cultivated classes in our land. Rather should this
so-called auto-imperialism, this revived Yoga system, be
traced to the Platonic element in New England Puritanism, and more especially to Emerson's interest in the
sacred books of the East. It is, therefore, not untrue to
say that the most ingenious of the modern remedies
against the evils which assail us was discovered in
America in the mind-cure, the gospel of relaxation, the
" don't worry " movement. And an American, cognizant of this degraded form of New England transcen-

dentalism, this perversion of the Emersonian doctrines of self-reliance and compensation, can agree with the witty Gaul when he compares the mind-cure to the grinding of the soul, like a hand-organ, for the sake of those optimistic previsions: "Fata viam inveniant; tout s'arrangera, parbleu! parfait! bravo!"

In pointing out the deficiency of the current pragmatism from the point of view of theology the French criticism has reached its highest point. We may, therefore, turn to the Italian attitude towards this subject. It is Alessandro Chiappelli who has most successfully exposed the insufficiency of opportunism for the deeper problems of thought and life. To him the recent renaissance of philosophy in America and France has shown a veritable originality of the speculative spirit, a new restlessness against the older forms of thought. The very revolt against the great dogmatic systems has included a revolt against science itself. Pragmatism is a proof of this. Its very discontent with intellectualism betokens a wider vision. In giving play to the emotional and the passional, in emphasizing the primacy of will, it tends towards an idealism transcending mere utilitarianism.

Chiappelli here brings to notice the latent idealism in the American nature with which the primitive pragmatist, the Yankee exponent of mere success, is bound to reckon. The principle of Peirce, which resolves our choice of speculative systems into a game of pitching pennies, cannot hold indefinitely in a land which has known Emerson and harbored Berkeley. The latter's subjective idealism Chiappelli considers to be revived in James's humanism. Whether such idealism can be rendered objective, and therefore serve as a check to the radical pragmatic empiricism, is problematic.

Italian modernism as a partial reflection of the new humanism furnishes a suggestive hint as to the theologic fate of American pragmatism. The Italian clergy at first eagerly grasped a doctrine which would rehabilitate a waning faith. The first work in James's trilogy gave to religious beliefs a new vogue. But the second of these works burned the fingers of the orthodox. The Fechnerian hierarchy of world-souls advocated in *A Pluralistic Universe* could scarcely be understood, much less accepted, outside of Swedenborgian and possibly Mormon circles! The Italian critic is, therefore, right in presaging little success amongst us for this revival of animism and polytheism. If he had known the rigors of monotheism in America, he might justly have called James a sort of Yankee Julian the Apostate. In all this an essential weakness of pragmatism is implied. As a cosmology it is an historic retrogression. As Chiappelli observes, the religious conscience has reached the highest point of its evolution in monotheism. So while a pluralistic conception may be just, as a natural protest against a too abstract absolutism, yet ultimately that pluralism is nothing but an empirical and provisional view, an atomistic form like that of the cell in a monadology.

How, then, can pragmatism and rationalism be reconciled? In the modern renaissance of spiritual values, in the attempts to complete science, justify religion, and ennoble life, there is, as Chiappelli declares, something really solemn. In the rise of American pragmatism there is, therefore, more than a grandiose manifestation of energy brought out in a young civilization greedy of imperialism. Rather is it a new philosophy of faith and feeling necessary to establish the human equilibrium after the negations of agnosticism and the limitations of criticism. For these words from a foreign observer an American may be grateful. But is it possible to bring about that suggested reconciliation between pragmatism and rationalism? Hébert had expressed a pious wish for that result, in his hope that the twentieth century would see a closer union of positive science and speculative philosophy. And while Chiappelli believes that the contrast between the new radical empiricism of the pragmatists and the rationalism of the idealists is not an irreducible antinomy, yet he confesses that their approximation may be indefinitely prolonged. He aspires to a coöperation between natural science and metaphysics, but that is as far as he gets. The difficulties of the coöperation are too great. These difficulties are brought out by one of our compatriots, to whom we may return as a final critic of the meaning of this movement. In his article on the "Emancipation of Intelligence," Wendell Bush holds that the idea that pragmatism was an apology for theism has seriously interfered with the profitable discussion of pragmatism itself. The aim of pragmatism has been to show that much of the current subject-matter in philosophy is thoroughly artificial. This does not mean that guiding philosophy has ceased to exist, but only that it has changed its name and fled into other departments of our universities, where chairs are not maintained for either saving the supernatural, or threshing the husks of idealism. Under the present pragmatic conditions, then, what a catalogue of problems disappears! There is that whole list of animistic survivals—such as God, the soul, and the universe—concerning which idealism has given certain assurances. But these are merely imaginary problems, bound to disappear just as other imaginary problems have disappeared. The work of the past generation is now bearing fruit. Darwin's *Origin of Species*, Tyler's *Primitive Culture*, Frazer's *Golden Bough* have brought about a condition of affairs similar to that at the beginnings of modern philosophy. Pragmatism is indeed but a new name for some old ways of thinking. . . . The thing has happened before. Just as the orthodox metaphysicians must have thought that Descartes ignored most of the important problems, and just as the Cartesians had to break away from the metaphysics of the Roman Catholic institution, so we have to cut loose from the metaphysics of Protestant speculation and from whatever is simply incidental to it!

CHAPTER X

MODERN REALISM

1. New Realism

In going from the old to the new realism we leave the slow, conservative caravan and forge ahead into the twentieth century. It is a leap of nearly two generations to catch up with this, the most modern of movements. In this long interval much has taken place. In the eyes of the present generation transcendentalism with its gorgeous coloring has come and gone like autumnal foliage. Absolute idealism with its cloud-capped pinnacles has likewise faded away. In their stead has arisen prosaic pragmatism, the philosophy of practicality, the creed of the man in the street, a working hypothesis which makes truth to be that which succeeds.

It is out of this atmosphere of the actual that the new plant had sprung; that will be plain later. Now, we must turn back in order to effect a junction between the two allied forces. It is safe to say that the new realism is a movement purged of the faults of the old and invigorated by the struggle with its rivals. Because of its undisputed sway, the old grew dogmatic, then weak and senile, but the new has been strengthened by a struggle with powerful rivals. Between the old and the new realism lay the tortuous road of various idealisms; by traveling along this road and grappling with these giants the youngest of the philosophies has gained its vigor.

The story of the rise of neo-realism is interesting. Its prophet was Frederick Woodbridge, who in his presidential address before the Western Philosophical Associa-

341

tion suggested some of the lessons to be learned from the historical method of handling the problem of metaphysics. Such was the futility of the distinction between appearance and reality; the necessity of an independent metaphysics; the need of a logic of definition. . . . This was in 1903. Six years later, at the New Haven meeting of the American Philosophical Association, six of the younger members happened to find themselves in agreement on certain points raised in the daily discussion. Five of them represented the old colonial foundations, from Harvard southward to Princeton. They were familiar with the former traditions of the Atlantic seaboard, but with these traditions they found they were out of sympathy. The abstract, the a priori, from Kant to Lotze, had been dinned into their ears until they longed for a change in the tune. They decided to change it for themselves. The first task was to get rid of the everlasting epistemology, the constant resolving of all problems into the problem of knowledge. How do I know? What do I know? Do I really know?—such questions had resulted in sterile quibbles, and yet all this time the scientists, whether sociologists, psychologists, or biologists, were digging up rich raw material with nobody to turn it into the finished philosophical product.

The richness of reality, direct awareness of the world —these are the prime marks of the new philosophy. Instead of thin abstraction, our eyes—if we will only look —may see a thick crust of facts, constantly growing thicker. Science, law, politics, religion—these are the rivers which are bringing down the rich alluvial deposits. The absolutists, the high idealists, directed our gaze to the mountain peaks; but those arid regions of pure abstraction are to us, they say, not half so worthwhile as the lower levels of concrete reality. Here are valleys of decision where problems must be solved, problems of actual life. Let us, therefore, cut up this land, pick out our patches, and cultivate our own gardens.

As is natural with any fresh movement, the new realism declares itself against tradition. Like the very transcendentalism against which it is a protest, it starts with a polemic. But the protest and the polemic are not expressed in a tone of irritation. A marked excellence of the school is its very knowledge of the schools. It has now reached a class-consciousness and seeks to relate itself to other forms of thought. The relation of the new realism to Kant is best seen in its attitude towards the philosophers after Kant. With them it abandons the thing-in-itself. But there the agreement stops. Let us put the matter in this way. There are certain castles on the Rhine which the Hegelians built and from which they looked down as overlords over the valley of reality. With the legislative powers conferred by Kant some of them went so far as to view consciousness as the source not only of the a priori forms of relations, but of all relations whatsoever. This overlordship was carried even further. The little lords were swallowed up in a supreme lord. The result was that our various empirical selves and the objects of their experience were all regarded as the manifestations or fragments of a single, perfect, all-inclusive, and eternal self.

Idealistic absolutism! The successors of the cautious philosopher of Koenigsberg talk at times as if they had come into possession of a Holy Roman Empire. But the road which leads to Rome splits into two. From absolutism there arises the dilemma of dualism, a new dualism of the finite and absolute. Either the experience of the fragment embraces the experience of the absolute or it does not. If the former, then the absolute becomes knowable only at the cost of losing its absoluteness and being reduced to a mere " state " of the alleged fragment. The existence of the absolute will then be known by its own fragments and each fragmentary self will have to assume that its own experience constitutes the entire universe. This is solipsism or subjectivism. If the other horn of the dilemma be chosen and the independent reality of the absolute be insisted upon, then it is at the cost of making the absolute unknowable. This is agnosticism or phenomenalism.

The road has ended, but only in two blind alleys—solipsism and agnosticism. And now enter upon this troubled scene the new realists, offering ways of escape. The escape from solipsism is to go back to that primordial common sense which believes in a world that exists independently of the knowing of it. The escape from agnosticism is to believe that that same independent world can be directly presented in consciousness and not merely represented or copied by " ideas."

The impression gained from this general confession of the realistic faith is one of healthy objectivism. The younger realists look upon the world with no jaundiced eye of solipsism. To them the world is no eject of the subject, no piece of human imagery, but its texture is made of other stuff than mere thought. It is this that leads to a new proclamation of emancipation. The emancipation of metaphysics from epistemology is necessary because of the latter's dogmatic claims. The a priori philosopher who made metaphysics to be the science of the possibility of knowledge has considered that he alone can spy out the promised land. The truth of the matter is that there are things not dreamt of in his philosophy—all the startling discoveries and inventions of the modern age from wireless telegraphy to X-ray photography. Indeed there is no discipline that can lay down for all time to come the main outlines of the world as the possible object of scientific research. Even logical propositions do not come into being or get created by the student that first learns that they are true. They are discovered and not made, as truly as was the American continent discovered and not made by the explorers of the fifteenth and sixteenth centuries. Furthermore, by its very claims to certainty epistemology has betrayed its limitations. It has sought a kind of metaphysical trust which maps out the territory and will brook no rivals.

Now, under the new régime, continues Marvin, the a priori must give way to the a posteriori, preconception to conception, as the ultimate crucial test. Indeed it is asserted that not only is the theory of knowledge subsequent to logic, but it is subsequent also to some of the special sciences, such as physics and biology. As to what knowledge is possible man has never succeeded in getting trustworthy information except empirically. In case after case man has been able to discover what scholars in another age pronounced unknowable. We have been able to study the chemistry and temperature of the stars, we can weigh the planets, we can tell with complete accuracy the area of curved figures whose sides stretch out to infinity. The place, then, of the science of knowledge among the other sciences is humble. It is not the head of the hierarchy, inasmuch as it does not give, but presupposes, the theory of knowledge. The weakness of that discipline is that in claiming to be both the beginning and the end of the various forms of knowledge it works in a vicious circle. Instead of being fundamental it is in many cases superficial, being saturated with the scientific prejudices of the day and generation of its author. Thus there is good reason to believe that the great Kant himself could not escape the Newtonian conception in drawing many of his conclusions. In short, it is impossible for the a priori philosopher to jump out of his environment and vain for him to write prolegomena to any future metaphysic.

The author here compares the old epistemology to a " salted " mine in which the most valued ore has been put not by nature, but by human hands. But such a hardened " promoter " will continue to promote intellectual distrust so long as he tries to tease out a world hypothesis by dialectic rather than to devote himself to a modest, open-minded, and industrious study of the cognitive facts. So the old-fashioned rationalist must give way to the neo-realist, for no careful philosopher would offer mankind to-day the amount of a priori information Kant claimed to derive by means of his transcendentalism. And yet we are learning much from the sciences to-day regarding subjects that were once merely presumptive knowledge—the nature of the heavenly world, the nature of matter, the nature of life, and the nature of mind.

We can put this in another way. Appeal to the pragmatic test, the verdict of history, and ask to what discoveries or doctrines of the past two hundred years is our present-day metaphysics especially indebted, to epistemology or to the progress of the natural sciences? We can go even further, take one of the oldest of the metaphysical problems, the nature of matter. In the last few years we seem to be learning more concerning the make-up of matter than man succeeded in discovering in the preceding two thousand years. Even such a hoary conviction as that mass is an absolute constant is now contradicted. What could be more startling than to be told that electricity is an all but fundamental concept in the new philosophy of nature? A thousand years of transcendentalism or of any other theory as to what matter must be, in order to be a possible experience, could not have revealed to us such truths. For these reasons we claim that metaphysics should be emancipated from epistemology, for the growth of science can again revolutionize metaphysical sciences as it did in the days of Galileo.

Marvin's emancipation of metaphysics from epistemology is a negative or rather a privative aspect of the new realist. A positive defense is offered in Perry's theory of independence. In emphasizing their emancipation the new thinkers declare themselves freed from their previous condition of servitude to the old idealism. Moreover, in making a declaration of independence they draw up a bill of particulars against that despot, the Absolute. No longer do they look to an all-knower, an universal consciousness in order to learn what to do. They do not even make an humble remonstrance, but boldly declare that both the absolute consciousness and the individual consciousness are unnecessary for the fact of existence. Things are independent of being known. Whether as a matter of fact they are known or unknown, the relation of awareness is merely accidental; it is not essential.

Spaulding next takes up analysis as the discovery in a whole of elements or parts which exist independently of the analysis and discovery. This is not the pragmatic analysis which is simply an intellectual instrument, a mode of adaptation, with an emphasis on the humanistic interpretation and its tendency towards subjective idealism. Nor is it the analysis of the type of Bergson, who arrives at the position that everything is change, flux, evolution, with such an interpenetration of parts that there are no lines of separation, but only one great viscous or mobile fluid, the whole being a continuous, flowing, trembling jelly. Such a view, with its tendency toward monism, serves to make analysis identical with falsification, for such analysis would make the finding, or inventing, or constructing of the parts to be in contradiction of the whole. For Bergson anything short of one all-inclusive, interpenetrated, evolving whole is contradictory and so false and not real. The creative evolutionist has proceeded on the view that analysis is destructive, that to articulate the skeleton is to kill the animal. But the neo-realist holds that such is not necessarily the case, since the actual world of physical, chemical, and physiological facts is discontinuous at certain points. It may be that one kind of experience finds, in a given situation, that the body, the time, and the positions, are fused and interpenetrated so as to form *one* whole. But this kinetoscopic view of reality which makes every entity analyzed to be continuous, is not the only view. There is the whole atomic world in which analysis reveals many separate existential facts. Yet this division into parts does not mean a wild discreteness. Certain substances combine in more than one proportion, and these proportions are rational. Furthermore, at the present stage in the development of science, molecules, atoms, electrons, and the relations between them, must be accepted as existing in quite the same sense as do the entities which they explain.

As Perry's theory of independence led to Spaulding's defense and analysis, so the two combined fit into Montague's relational theory of consciousness, a theory worked out several years prior to its appearance here. Objects as independent need no consciousness for their existence. Yet objects as analyzed disclose a network of

relationships between objects and the subject considering them. This suggests an hypothesis which avoids the
crudities of naïve realism and escapes the difficulties
of subjective idealism. The fact of error is the crucial
test in all these theories. The old realism was weak
because it could not account for such vagaries as the
events of a dream. The common-sense theory held to
a world of objects and consciousness like a searchlight
playing upon those objects; not creating them, but simply revealing them. But dreams demolished this theory,
for it could give no account of events outside of a world
of beings interacting in space and time. So the pendulum swung to the other extreme of subjectivism according to which the world in which we live is conceived
as a product, fashioned by consciousness from the raw
materials of its own states. The searchlight becomes
a projecting camera, consciousness being a creative
cause of that which it beholds or is pleased to
behold.

At this point arises the need of a corrective and supplementary hypothesis. The old realism emphasized objective truths and suppressed subjective errors. The
old idealism found it hard to distinguish between truth
and error. The world of the romantic idealist, for all
his fine words, remains but a world of shadow pictures
on the screen of consciousness. The true and the false,
what are they? To the neo-realist they are respectively
the real and the unreal considered as objects of a possible belief or judgment. There is, that is to say, the
same difference between what is real and what is true,
as between George Washington and President George
Washington. President George Washington refers to
Washington in a certain relation to our government.
George Washington denotes precisely the same indi-

vidual without calling attention to the presidential relation.

This is the first example given in the relational theory of consciousness. It does not concern itself with mere objects or mere subjects, but with what are usually called existential propositions. To it the real universe consists of the space-time system of existents, together with all that is presupposed by that system. Examples of such relations and propositions are such as these: Cæsar lived before Napoleon; orange resembles yellow more than green. All this may seem commonplace and obvious. But a distinction is to be made, a distinction which will clear up the confusion between truth and falsity. Truth and falsity never attach to judgments as acts, but to propositions as objects. There would be no sense in calling an act of belief as such either true or false. If we wished to know whether certain beliefs that we held about the properties of triangles were true or false, whom should we consult? The psychologist? Certainly not. We should go to the mathematician. But why? The psychologist is supposed to be an expert on mental processes, and if the adjectives true and false were to apply to beliefs as mental processes, he would be the one to settle our difficulties. We should go to the mathematician, however, because our desire to know whether our beliefs about triangles were true or false could be satisfied only by one who knew about triangles. So with all cases of doubt as to truth and falsity, we go to the person who knows about the things believed rather than to him who knows about the processes or acts of believing.

In connection with the subject of error and as the result of his varied psychological experiments, Edwin Holt seeks to find the place of illusion in a realistic

world. Illusion, hallucination, and erroneous experience
in general, we are told, can have no place in a universe
where everything is non-mental or real; and they cannot
be satisfactorily accounted for by a realistic philosophy.
This is the challenge throughout from the idealist to the
realist camp. It has to be met not by a general denial,
but by specific analysis. First come errors of space.
For example, the person squinting his eyes sees double,
that is, what is not there; hence, reasons the idealist, the
illusory object is essentially mental and subjective.
Nothing of the sort, responds the realist, it is only a case
of mechanical manipulation of the eyes. The stereo-
scopic camera also sees double. So with the case of
errors of time. The idealists' hallowed illustration of
seeing some distant star some millions of years behind
time, or millions of years after it may be said to exist,
does not make the image merely mental. The camera
does the same thing; every image there lags in strikingly
the same way behind its real physical prototype. The
case of seeing the known existing sun does not raise the
issue between reality and unreality, or between the
material and the mental, nor does the case of secondary
qualities. The colors of the landscape may change, yet
the chemical properties of the hill and wood that one
looks out upon, are practically invariable in their chemical properties. Luminous properties may change, but
this is due to the incident illumination which brings
the perpetual variety of light, shade, and hue. The
orthochromatic moving film will record this diurnal
flux in an entirely parallel way. In short, we may
overthrow the idealist's contention as to a remarkable
creative function inherent in mental processes, by
pointing out parallel phenomena in the material world.

The last of the chapters of the composite work on new

realism is remarkable in disclosing a sort of civil war, an internecine struggle between the scientists themselves. The strongest influences against realism to-day, says Pitkin, emanate from the biological sciences. Only a few years ago it was physics and mathematics which made the natural world-view seem untenable; and before them it was logic and psychology. But from a new quarter there rises a host of adversaries, declaring that the unanswerable disproof of realism is found in simple life processes. Driesch is the modern leader of this movement in his systematic attempt to establish idealistic vitalism on biological evidences. So, too, Bergson proceeds from psychology to biology. The immediate data of consciousness afford a new basis for interpreting life processes, for the latter reveal a cosmos not composed of distinct characters, but a flux wherein everything interpenetrates everything else. All distinctions are products of a " vital force " and serve only for organic controls. Driesch concludes that the entire content of experience is created by the ego, in the same manner as Kant held; Bergson that there is an objective flux that constitutes the environment of the vital force.

Against the vitalism of the German and the creative evolution of the Frenchman, Pitkin holds that reconstruction must begin. Both systems contain the old, discredited categories of idealistic psychology. The former reverts to the ancient Aristotelian entelechy, or internal perfecting principle; the latter maintains that knowledge can never give us the " real thing," inasmuch as it gives us only a few of its selected characters. Hence there is need of a formal analysis of the biological situation, an analysis free of the faults of hunting for an unknown something behind the organism, or of making the environment a hazy entity. Therefore naturally in-specting animals and their circumstances of life we find:—that they exist in a world larger than themselves; that this world sets for them certain difficulties; that some individuals overcome these difficulties; that those which signally overcome the difficulties differ, in some observable respects, from those which do not.

We have here the two familiar evolutionary factors— organism and environment. Shall we call one subjective, the other objective, and draw a line of division between the two? The realist replies—No! The reaction of the organism and the stimulus of environment are simply two phases of one unitary process, as are the two poles of a magnet. Just as the positive pole does not take something from nor add something to the negative pole, so the reaction does not consist in selecting something from the stimulus or adding to it. Each gets its character from its relation to the other. Both the structure and function of an organ vary with some variations in the external stimulus, but this variation should not be called a qualitative transformation. There is merely a change from behavior of one character to behavior of another character. For instance, a dog is frequently docile when at large and vicious only when tethered. Would anybody say, though, that in turning the dog loose *we* change his quality? Hardly: for the new circumstances bring the dog into new relations; and it is in response to the latter that it now behaves differently. Now, are these new relations real, in the objective sense, or merely creations of the mind? Are we to dig a colossal chasm between phenomenal and noumenal, between things as thought and things in themselves, to explain such behavior? The task is unnecessary. When animals, including man, adjust themselves to their environments, it is because there are resistances and positions of which they must take account. Every living creature finds itself in a world full of things distant from it and from one another in space and in time. Some of these things it seeks, others it shuns; and the precise relation of particular things to its body in space and in time is a life-or-death matter. We conclude, therefore, that geometrical, mathematical, and other relations are genuine stimuli in the very sense that material complexes are. They are not products of the cognitive reaction but the producers of it.

Such is radical realism, a system hardly held before save by Aristotle and the materialists. Pitkin confesses that he is quite aware that in asserting planes, angles, numbers, ratios, to be stimuli in precisely the same sense that the ether waves are, he is exposing himself to ridicule. But suppose we take an alternative hypothesis and, with nearly everybody except the new realists, describe the mathematical-geometrical relations as " intellectual abstractions," " constructs," " shorthand expressions," what does that lead to? To the old idealism which, starting with space and time as creations of the mind, subjective principles, led on to paradoxes which can be solved only by pronouncing the whole situation " unreal." Of course there are certain advantages in this parallelistic hypothesis which puts a phenomenal world alongside a noumenal. It avoids the ego-centric predicament which holds that a tree may seem to be unmodified by being perceived; but that is only because I know not all that is happening to it. Contrariwise it accepts certain processes as not being constituted by the cognitive process but as merely running alongside that process. Take the adaptation of the flat-fish to the sea bottom. We would be setting up a one-to-one correspondence between the phenomenal and noumenal orders if we were to declare that each discernible peculiarity in the fish's adaptive reaction resulted from some peculiarity in its noumenal environment. That is, when the flatfish, having a certain blue-gray checker pattern on its back as a consequence of resting upon a blue-gray checker sea bottom, shifts to a gray-brown sea bottom of irregular design and there soon develops on its back a gray-brown pattern of irregular design, the difference between the former and the latter noumenal situation is of the same type as that between the blue-gray checker and the irregular gray-brown pattern of the sea bottom. Nevertheless, the noumenal difference is not a difference between colors and space forms, for these are only phenomenal. Now, according to the idealistic biology, you may take any case of reaction and describe it in this manner. With Driesch you may say that space is phenomenal, that is, a form of experience, and not a form of the physical world independent of experience. With Bergson you may say that mathematical-geometrical characters are static artifacts created by the vital force. The scheme is plausible but it has its difficulties. Chief of these is the identity of indiscernibles. If there be a one-to-one correspondence there is no means of distinguishing the noumenal order from the phenomenal. The old epistemology made two systems. The new biology of animal behavior cannot distinguish the two systems. On the contrary it identifies the pair, reduces it to a single system. In fine, the supposition that there is a system beyond that which we perceive is gratuitous. There are no phenomena and no noumena, but only things, events, conditions, circumstances—all in a universe which no mind has split into two realms.

From this reduction of the old dualism there arises a

sense of relief. The uncomfortable sense of a double-dealing world is made to disappear. No longer have we one leg on the noumenal and the other on the prenomenal, but both are planted in reality. No longer is the knower a twofold being,—in one aspect transcendental, in another empirical. The advantage of this view to epistemology is patent. For example, in accepting the full reality of space, it does away with the supposed paradoxes of distance from Zeno to Bergson. It also does away with the difficulties of considering space as either an idea or a mere form of apprehension. But besides seeking the facts of geometry in the world order the author might have gone further and applied his reasonings to ethics. There stands that irritating neo-Hegelian doctrine of conduct. To say, as do Royce and Münsterberg, that we are bound in the sphere of the phenomenal, but free in the noumenal, is to make us neither bond nor free, but morally paralyzed because pulled in two directions at once. Now by doing away with these two worlds the sense of freedom is restored and this is a second advantage of the new realism.

A third advantage is the possibility of making modern philosophy less anthropocentric. It appears that a new Galileo is needed formally to analyze the broader features of the world in which the individual organism exists. Now, according to the new realism and in decided contrast to the old realism, introspection is not fundamental. Outward reality is far richer than inward meditation. All that consciousness does is to pick out one strand of the complex cosmic net. In a word, thought is not creative but selective, and at times even negative in its results. As Pitkin summarizes it, thought is only one phase in the much more comprehensive organic process, and presumably bears pretty much the same relation to this latter that the cross-sectional motions in some one plane of chemism bear to the total chemism. Suppose one might peer into a constellation of corpuscles with a microscope of transcendent power. One would there see, from any one given point of view, a vast tangle of motions, and yet discover nothing that would betray the peculiar character of the chemism; for all the motions that were significant might occur in planes parallel to the observer's line of vision, and their bearings might furthermore lie wholly beyond the microscopic field.

A sense of relief, a feeling of freedom, an impression of reserve,—these are three valuable qualities of the new realism. With them go corresponding difficulties. It is easy to demolish the high towers of the ambitious idealist, in so far as they are projections of the pure intellect. It is not so easy to bring that intellect down to the level of mere experience. Cognition may not be creative, yet is it only one of the bodily activities? Can we reduce its activities to the same order as the extra-cognitive conditions, such as blood temperature, conduction currents, colloids, and all the host of material factors which never figure discretely in the natural operations of cognizing the environment and reacting to it? In raising these questions the writer appears to favor an affirmative answer. He goes further and says that the organism in " mental activity " throws selected objects upon the cognitive field no less physically than it throws them upon the retinas. Moreover, " attending " is defined as a stretching out toward something; not a feeling nor a knowing nor a thinking, but a going to meet or to find some environmental character. Indeed, the author adds, it would conduce to clarity both in biology and psychology, if attention were admitted to be a general organic attitude and not a specialized function like cognizing. We might then speak of the phagocytes as attending to bacteria without our falling into grotesque panpsychism or idealism.

Pitkin further supposes that what a man does is not determined primarily by something which philosophers call vital force, psychoid, or ego, but that behaviors and attitudes may be assumed by the blood, or by some group of cortical cells. Now, if the realistic biologist has escaped idealism by this supposition, has he not fallen into materialism? He admits his wish to escape the suspicion of subjectivism, but has he not committed the equal crime of rank objectivism—reduced the psychic to the merely physical? The question is hypothetical and so is the answer. If we agree to define the physical world as the spatio-temporal system exclusively, then consciousness is not physical, for the projection field, or the field of consciousness, is, in the strict logical sense of the adjective, transverse to the objects projected upon it. But though consciousness be not physical this does not imply that the objects of consciousness are not physical. Nor does it even imply that cognitive relations are not relations between physical things.

This conclusion seems commonplace, a return to the old-fashioned realism where common sense saw in the world merely minds and bodies and the relations between those bodies. And yet this is not a complete statement of the content of the new realism. Since the day of Reid and Beattie there has been an immense enrichment of the world both on the subjective and objective sides. Consciousness, contends the biologist, as soon as it is investigated, appears as a feature of a '' big situation.'' This situation involves not only feeling and thinking, but also the organism,—blood and sinew and nerves and impulses and appetites,—and finally physical things,—electricity, light, matter. This is the final word of the last of the new realists. It is indeed a " big situation," containing a host of entities which are, at present, projectively indiscernible, because we do not possess all the possible angles of vision. How many such projective constants there are nobody knows, but geometry, physics, and psychology bring forward facts indicating that the variety of types is exceedingly great.

Since the publication of the *New Realism* in 1912 several of the original writers have enlarged and restated their views. While these are no longer coöperative they are, nevertheless, more or less congruous. Thus, for the historical significance of the movement we can have recourse to Marvin for the clearest summary, to Perry for the widest application of the relational theory of consciousness, to Spaulding and to Holt for what is called the most peculiar characteristic of American realism—the doctrine of the immanence of consciousness. Out of the original roster Montague and Pitkin remain to be heard from, except for occasional articles which disclose them as reconnoitering on the flank, skirmishing sharply with those critics who from time to time strive to break up the column. The line of march is again headed by Marvin, an admirable leader for the clarity of his vision and his ability in informing us of the terrain. Looking over the field of philosophy he tells us that most thoughtful men are Cartesian dualists belonging to some one of these three groups: first, those who with Descartes believe that science can infer the nature of the physical; second, the agnostic phenomenalists who believe it cannot; and, lastly, the idealists, whether subjective or objective. But besides these three groups there is a still smaller group of thinkers who believe we must go back beyond Descartes and beyond the Greeks and study again the whole problem of the mental and of the relation of the knowing mind to its object. These thinkers are called neo-realists. In their protest against the traditional way of conceiving the mental they follow two lines of argument: they claim that Cartesian dualism has been thought through during the past three hundred years, and has been shown to end in the absurdities either of agnosticism or of parallelism—the mental and non-mental being separated by an impassable gulf. Again they reason that this older dualism and its conception of the mental has come to the modern thinker from the ancient world and is not based upon an open-minded study of the facts in the light of modern science. This conception of the mental presupposes the notions of substance and cause as these notions were used in Greek thought. But modern science, since Galilei, has been outgrowing the notion of cause and has been substituting for it the mathematical notion of function. Now the ancient and even prehistoric notion of cause was probably due to our kinæsthetic feelings, whereas causes are now considered merely geometrical entities, merely mathematical relations. If, then, in solving the problem of the interaction of mind and body, we no longer conceive them to be connected as two substances causing changes of state in one another, we have but to seek the functional relation holding between the two systems. A similar objection can be made against the notion of substance. Here the stuff of which a thing is composed is not needed to explain its behavior or its so-called properties; it is not strong because it is steel, nor does it burn because it is wood. For science things are what they are, do what they do, have the properties they possess, because of their structure, structure here meaning relations of parts, or organization. And this means that science has abandoned or is abandoning the notion of substance and the search for the substance of things.

What, then, does the realist offer instead of the traditional Cartesian dualism? He urges that the belief in two sorts of stuff, the mental and the physical, be discarded, and that we learn to think of both in terms of relations, structures, or organizations having many members in common. For example, the physical chair and the chair I perceive are in part one and the same entity. In other words, one and the same entity can be both physical and mental. It is physical in those relations studied by the physical sciences, and it is mental as part of the situation to which we as behaving organisms are responding. Thus, the difference between the physical and the mental is the difference solely of relations and not a difference of stuff or of entity. In all this the neo-realists are but adopting in psychology the general positivism to be seen in mathematical physics, and more and more extensively throughout the field of modern science. They claim that by doing so the mental can be sharply distinguished from the physical, the objective from the subjective. Finally, they maintain that the paradoxes of phenomenalism, idealism, and parallelism can be eliminated and the nature of knowing stated in terms which make knowing, what it undoubtedly is, a proper object of science and experimental research.

With this conception the second of our historical surveyors agrees. Perry declares that the realist assumes that philosophy is a kind of knowledge and neither a song, nor a prayer, nor a dream. He proposes, therefore, to rely less on inspiration and more on observation and analysis. He conceives his function to be in the last analysis the same as that of the scientists. This is the independence of the fact, the thesis that the object of knowledge is always some fact that stands there independently of the knowing of it. This thesis, as a sort of common ground, forms the broad basis of a pyramid on which all realists take their stand. But the pyramid is narrowed, or the company of adherents is successively reduced, as we pass on to Platonic realism and the theory of the externality of relations, until we reach the summit composed of the relatively small group of survivors who accept the doctrine aforesaid and add to these the distinguishing conception of the immanence of consciousness. This is the conception that consciousness is homogeneous and interactive with its environment.

This puzzling doctrine which peculiarly distinguishes the limited group of American realists will now engage our especial attention. Thus, Spaulding in his work, *The New Rationalism*, boldly grapples with the problem from a pluralistic rather than an old-fashioned dualistic point of view. He contends that consciousness is not a substance, energy, medium or menstruum, for there are loci for both truths and errors in other than a substance-like consciousness. What these loci are it is for empirical investigation to find out. They may be spatial, temporal, or logical. The idealist may flatter himself that his solutions belong to the monistic Hall of Fame; the modern rationalists are willing to find their place in the Rogues' Gallery of pluralism. Besides truths and errors there are also proofs and refutations, agreements and disagreements; and besides these, emotions, instincts, behaviors, satisfactions, illusions, electrons, atoms, forces, energies, directions, laws.

Spaulding's account is more than a catalogue of ships. It reads like the selling list of a mail-order house where anything may be ordered from automobiles to tombstones. Hence, to reduce this world, so full of a number of things, to some single monistic substance is futile. For the realist there is no one underlying entity. Rather for him there are kinds that are irreducibly different, and there is an irreducible plurality of these kinds.

In this process of refinement the neo-rationalist has reached the realm of an ancient rationalist, Plato's empyrean, the locus of all archetypes. Indeed, in his final discussion as to the realistic doctrine of values, Spaulding goes so far as to say that ideals are real, justice and goodness and truth being eternal, not because they persist through all time, but because " in a heaven by themselves " they partake neither of the nature of " things " that are in space and time, nor indeed of the nature of time and space themselves. Historically all this is significant. What Spaulding said of a modern, corrected positivism is true of his new rationalism: it is " a very interesting, but a very unusual philosophy." Contrasted with the old realists, the conservative Scotch school, timid to a degree, accustomed to blink such entities of the universe as " illusory and hallucinatory snakes of delirium tremens," the new realists, especially in this neo-rationalistic wing, are bold and adventurous. In fact, however extensive the map of metaphysics, they attempt to master it. They have drifted far from the common-sense school. It might even be said that they have something of the Celtic temperament, they venture to explore " Forests and enchantments drear, Where more is found than meets the ear."

But to return to the common world; it is here that the real conflict lies. Leaving the eternal verities, let us descend to tables and books. Can the cosmological problem be solved by the bold expedient of making consciousness extended? Granting the dualism between subject and object, is not " immanence " to flimsy a structure to bridge the gap? At first sight the hypothesis of consciousness extended is as unconvincing as the aura of the occultists; and, if consciousness be correlated with the cortex, its extension or protrusion appears like the kindred theosophical doctrine of the astral body. But such doubts are unjustified. They assume that which the new rationalist expressly disclaims. Recent discussions are strongly opposed to the view that consciousness is in any way a substance. Of the various hypotheses that it must be either a dimension, a relation, a disembodied quality, or an event, Spaulding accepts the first. But if consciousness be a " new " dimension, it must conform to that definition of a dimension which receives at least fairly general acceptance in scientific circles. This definition comports with that frequent usage of the term dimension to characterize space as continuous, or dense, or possibly discontinuous.

What can we make of this final defense? A nonspatial dimension is a paradox, unless one accepts the previous identification of dimensionality with an implied linear series, as in the serial order of moral values. But this identification seems inadequate; based on a mere analogy it would never account for an actual space relation such as that between a given cortex and a distant star. And, finally, that other qualification that consciousness is extended, because it is a variable, hardly carries conviction. We may grant that the whole may be different from the parts, as water is different from hydrogen and oxygen. We may even grant that out of different kinds of elements, as organized elements, a specific sensation, as belonging to the class of awareness, may arise. But Herbert Spencer to the contrary, we cannot agree that the mere fact of these elements '' being together '' is awareness. Behaviorists are weak in asserting that the mere description of any specific kind of consciousness does away with the whole. And if they do not go far enough, does not Spaulding go too far in creating a ship of Theseus out of casual parts, a thing in itself out of a chance combination of elements? This impresses us as the very fallacy of the Hegelian whole, a hypostatizing of a mere synthesis. It is akin to the fond delusion of a certain antiquated type of American political thinker who believes that the fact of the American states being united creates a conscious entity the '' Union,'' a thing in itself, which may be apostrophized from the stump.

So this particular contention of the new rationalist does not strike us as leading in the direction of philosophical progress. Nevertheless it has a negative use. The new school has effectively disposed of the conventional account of consciousness as a substance, by putting it—as a dimensional variant—into the class of nonexistent subsistents, neither spatial nor temporal. The substantialists are done for; but have the new actualists proved their case? To identify consciousness with awareness is not so bad, but to derive awareness from '' togetherness '' is dubious. Now awareness is finally defined as '' the common property of that which, by its presence, is one class of dimensions within the universe.'' According to this definition a group consciousness might be implied in the lowest scale of being, such as in any fortuitous combination of protozoa. In short, the neo-rationalist would fall back into that very pitfall of pan-psychism against which he inveighs and his solution of the cosmological problem would be like that of Emped-ocles, when he announced how coming together, by chance, the members of the body gained a footing on the shore of life.

We confess that there is an air of distressing un-reality about this whole subject; it reminds one of some cabalistic picture by Picasso, some example of " creative form " made up of a welter of lines and curves which give strange satisfaction to the post-impressionist. As a masterpiece in this kind of a metaphysical exhibition we present Holt's elaborate study, *The Concept of Consciousness.* Directed against ornate and splendid systems of philosophy " like marble temples shining on a hill," this work aims not to construct a system but to trace the structure inherent in all being. This struc-ture is to be attributed to the renaissance of logic, the new mathematical logic, whose subject matter is " sys-tems of being " or " universes of discourse." These systems or universes are coherent because they arise from a certain " given," consisting of terms and propo-sitions which generate of their own motion all further terms and propositions. Now if these fundamental terms possess being in the system and also in the explor-ing mind of the individual we have a structure, true both of the material and mathematical realms, whereby entities are ordered in a series of graded complexities, a true hierarchy of being that may well suggest Plato's realm of ideas.

After his initial strictures against the high pontiffs of philosophy building their massive systems, the author appears to have succumbed to the same temptation of erecting a philosophic structure. For this, in a way, he is not responsible. Two impelling forces struggle within him, that of his teacher Royce to whom, he says, he owes his notions of the conceptual nature of the universe, and that of James whose radical empiricism influences his definition of consciousness. When we know that James was wont in his facetious way to " damn the absolute " of Royce, we have in their common pupil a mental complex strange to contemplate. On the one hand there appears Royce's romantic idealism, an ascending world of minds containing self-generating ideas; on the other James's counterpart to his pragmatism, his " pluralistic tychism," a doctrine of chance, or contingency, which rejects all doctrines of the absolute, and represents order as being gradually won and always in the making. These are the two diverging tendencies coming from Holt's masters, the one monistic, the other pluralistic. Does the pupil draw a median line between them? By no means. He does not attempt to harmonize his two teachers, so close in friendship, so wide apart in thought; he does not settle in the kingdom of either, but moves off into another territory, a sort of no man's land—" the neutral intermediate realm between mind and matter, subject and object."

Granted, then, that Holt has staked out his own claim, what does he get out of his " neutral mosaic " ? Considering him a prospector, investors in his new mine of thought have a right to ask some questions. If mental entities are inflexible, how can we extend consciousness which is active? The same difficulty occurred with Berkeley's attempt to apprehend passive ideas. Again, if the algebra in our mind also exists in nature, how does this make the subjective and objective overlap? A common quality does not imply a common locality. If matter and mind are of the same neutral stuff, how did the differentiation arise out of the supposed homo-geneity? And if this neutral mosaic is " pure being," does the heterogeneity arise by the intrinsic activity of propositions? If we take neutral and conceptual to be synonymous, does that get us out of the difficulty of a dualism between subject and object?

These are ontological puzzles. There are similar puz-zles in epistemology. Holt claims that the advantage of the interpretations of the universe as a purely neu-tral mosaic is that it involves no theory of reality or of knowledge. We doubt this. The neutral mosaic of pure being is not all pure gold. As soon as the lode is worked recalcitrant substances are found; the meta-physician may abstract the ore, but the logical stamping-mill is needed to separate the metal. So the acid test is here a definition of consciousness, so framed as to make it extended in both space and time. Conscious-ness, then, is defined as " that cross-section of the in-finite realm of being to which the organism specifically responds." Now this environmental cross-section may also be called a psychic cross-section, and even mind or soul. Furthermore, this cross-section may be called sen-sations, perceptions, ideas, just as one calls the units of a physical manifold atoms. But this substance remains always neutral, for it takes the entire cross-section to constitute a mind, and its individual components are no more made of mental substance than they are of cross-section substance, or no more than physical objects are made of physical substance. This definition has two advantages; it avoids the whole rigmarole about the " projection of subjective sensations into outer or real space "; also it avoids making the laws of nature " con-venient constructions " devised by man.

This definition with its corollaries forms the original

bank deposit from which Spaulding and others drew the sums which they re-invested in such different fields. It remains to strike a trial balance of the total account. We may say that Holt and Company have disposed of the substantialists; those who dealt in soul substance have now gone into bankruptcy. But has not the new firm, which deals with an extended consciousness, certain liabilities to meet? In other words is the original deposit something earned, or a loan borrowed from the past? The answer is to be found by a recourse to the mental career of James. The original sources of his thought are found more or less underground in his studies of the subliminal self, and these springs break forth into a metaphysical scheme in his presidential address of 1894 before the American Psychological Association. In this now famous essay on " The Knowing of Things Together " is put in clear and simple language what later became in the hands of others so obscure and pedantic. Here the nature of the synthetic unity of consciousness is declared one of those great underlying problems that divide the psychological schools. This division is to be overcome by agreeing that in representative knowledge there is no special inner mystery, but only an outer change of physical or mental intermediaries connecting thought and things. Now take the case of immediate or intuitive acquaintance with an object, and let the object be the white paper before our eyes. The thought-stuff and the thing-stuff are here indistinguishably the same in nature—the paper seen and the seeing of it are only two names for one indivisible fact which, properly named, is the datum, the phenomenon, or the experience. The paper is in the mind, and the mind around the paper, because paper and mind are only two names that are given later to one experience. . . . To know immediately, then, or intuitively, is for mental content and object to be identical.

This explanation, which suggests the later neutral mosaic of the neo-realist, was as yet not used in the metaphysical sense. It had no pretensions to any possible solutions; it was simply set forth to avoid mysterious notions of self-transcendency and presence in absence. But beside disposing of the associationist theory of the unity of knowledge, this theory claimed a further advantage of disposing of that scholastic entity, the soul, for which James confesses that he had a decided antipathy, arising from an ancient hardness of heart. And such a theory has the final advantage of eliminating from psychology " considered as a natural science " the whole business of ascertaining how we come to know things together or to know them at all.

Did James, the psychologist, eschew metaphysics? By no means. Twenty years later his deeper philosophical interests, engendered by all his psychological studies, carried him over into that unexplored country, that tract which is neither material nor mental. Radical empiricism and not pragmatism now becomes his favorite philosophy, or rather his pragmatism is a method which furnishes the most efficient entrenching tools to connect up his new lines. Now it is this realignment which gives fresh courage to the fighter. In his presidential address he had dug himself in; by avoiding metaphysics he had avoided trouble. But in his *Essays in Radical Empiricism* he attacks the problem formerly avoided. Along with the anti-associationists he is vitally interested in accounting for the form of unity, that union in consciousness which must be made by something. Neither attention, reminiscence, synergy, the individual soul, the world-soul—none of these will do; they are all barren verbal principles. Something new and actual is needed. What is it? A suggestion of an answer was given in the first of these Essays, "Does Consciousness Exist?" This was the bombshell thrown into the complacent camp of the neo-Kantians. What happened to this camp has been already described, but what happened to the bombshell has not. Its fragments were gathered up by the neo-realists, not merely as souvenirs, but as pieces of metal worth analyzing. Looking back we can now appreciate how thorough their analysis was. They discovered certain valuable constituents and used them effectively. Thus, the "pure experience" of James became the "neutral mosaic" of Holt; his "non-perceptual relations" became "the subsistents" of Spaulding, and so on. But it was the mere propounding of the question that awoke the philosophic camp from its dogmatic slumber. It led Montague to ask, "Has Psychology lost its Soul?" and to thank Heaven that it had. But the great advantage was that the no-soul psychology gets rid of certain distressing objections made from the dualistic standpoint.

With the neo-Kantians, continues James, there ever lies the vicious disjunction between thought and its objects. But suppose that consciousness is but the name of a non-entity, that those who still cling to it are clinging to a mere echo, the faint rumor left behind by the disappearing "soul" upon the air of philosophy. In this, consciousness the entity becomes consciousness the function, one aspect of pure experience, in which the mental operation is called thought, the physical operation thing.

This declaration was made in 1904. Coöperation immediately followed. The Chicago school under Dewey lent its powerful aid. But our interest here lies not so much with the logical instrumentalism from the west as with the younger school of eastern realists—" the six little realists " whose first programme we have previously described. These were the young contractors who in large measure took up the unfinished work of James. That which was a sketch, a blue print, now becomes a building; not a marble temple, but a comfortable country house. Being built on the unit plan innumerable additions can be made to the original block. But the first unit and the last unit, as we take it, bear the impress of the mind of James. This is no disparagement of the work of James's coöperators, for analysis will show that in this metaphysical joint-stock company the common fund consists not only of the original deposit, but also of separate individual accounts, whose growth and increase are due to the efforts of the junior members of the firm. James would be the last to say that he furnished the preferred stock, his pupils the common; his principle was coöperation, his company a trust company. So an expert accountant might audit the books and show how the later investors have increased the original sum. Thus, James's primal stuff, " pure experience," has become Holt's " neutral mosaic," and his " consciousness arising at the intersection of thought and things " has become Holt's " consciousness, the environmental cross-section." And when James says that subjectivity is not aboriginal, but a center of function, Holt says the criterion of consciousness is not introspection, but specific response. By this kind of double entry bookkeeping one might evaluate the respective contributions of James's pupils, of Perry who " early went over the border " with his " independent reals," of Montague who derided consciousness as a diaphanous substance, of Pitkin who led the biological attack on the old realists.

But with all these affinities there are marked divergences. James's last labors were quite different from his first, and yet both have been improperly lumped together under the name pragmatism. An initial impulse was the pragmaticism of Peirce, that cold formula by which one might be enabled to obtain a detached view of things. James began in an unemotional fashion, but ended in a burst of emotion. His Gifford lectures presented lines of religious interest tangential to the instrumental form of pragmatism. Now of all the new realistic writers only two have shown any like tendency, Perry referring in a perfunctory way to the pragmatic attitude towards religion and Spaulding making religious problems mere subsistent entities, as artificial as extracting the square root of minus two. No, pragmatism as developed by James is at the opposite pole from current neo-realism. James and the younger writers are indeed alike in being iconoclasts of idealism, but while he erects a modern pantheon filled with all the gods of his fancy, they are more akin to Nietzsche's superman who goes on his way destroying temples and churches. To the independent realists, especially, James's departure from the straight path of instrumentalism is a cause of irritation. Yet even this departure can be explained. James was early obsessed by the idea of the absolute. He hated it. He wished to smash it. Yet he always kept coming back to it in one way or another. That dark body may have been disintegrated by his logic, yet like an exploded meteor its fragments periodically cut across the orbit of his thought.

With this interpretation we may compare the views of one of the continental critics of new realism. That movement, declares Chiappelli, arose by a sort of opposition to William James's doctrine of pluralism, and has led step by step to the foundations of the ancient doctrines of immobility. There are signs, he explains, in modern scientific culture, of a gradual return to a static conception of the world which leads to an elimination of the idea of creative evolution. Pragmatism as evolutionary was the last word of the nineteenth century; in its place has sprung up a doctrine of anti-evolutionism which testifies to the inexhaustibility of reality, or what is fundamentally the same thing, the fecundity of the human spirit. Now this very spirit denies the excesses of the late idealism, especially the doctrine that consciousness was the dominating and central force of the universe. New realism brings consciousness down to the level of things, and considers it no longer necessary for the existence of reality, reality which can well be an entity independent of being known. The analytic conceptions of science, which the intuitionalists and pragmatists and critics of science, like Mach and Poincaré, considered an economical system, a method of easy conventions, of useful hypotheses for work, are now held to be empty categories, motionless abstractions, unfit to approach the flowing and living reality. These are no longer thought by the realists to be mere mental instruments, but objective entities. As the very substance of the world independent of our personal interest, they are but so many possible forms of exterior relations. The subject, absolute or individual, is no longer the measure to which all things are referred, as idealism has always maintained, for reality, if not irrational, is almost independent of rationality. But this opposition to subjectivism does not mean a return to the principles of mechanical materialism. The moderate Anglo-Saxon spirit, and especially the American, repudiates that form of pseudo-scientific thought. The new realists, far from reducing reality to measure and number, grant not only size, weight, and figure, but consider color, light, and sound as real properties of the object, and leave to mind the sole function of determining as pleasurable or painful the subjective effects of the aforesaid properties. In short, the so-called secondary qualities, as well as the primary, are considered real properties of body, and metaphysics is rendered independent of any theory of consciousness. Hence this doctrine of objective reality renders null and void the so-called Copernican revolution of Kant, for the center of gravity is again transferred to the world of the object. Pragmatism started the movement in its revolt against subjective idealism, since the old idealism was incapable of imagining such astonishing discoveries as wireless messages, X-rays, and aeronautics. But as the age of Edison and Marconi discovered these things and did not create them, just as America was discovered and not created by the fifteenth and sixteenth centuries, so the logical laws back of them neither came into being, nor were created, but existed in the human mind,—objective, independent, preëxistent. So these elements of thought, common and constant from individual to individual, existing prior to the objective acts, assume a character of universality in which the ideal and real are combined. The new realism has thus paradoxically returned to an ancient way of thinking: the world is formed of conceptual entities, which constitute the independent and immutable conditions of existence. In other words, the pluralistic conception of the universe, the last form of James's pragmatism, leads spontaneously to a logical-mathematical view akin to the Platonic theory of eternal ideas which, while forming a world of intelligible entities, do not go so far as dissolving into a unity of universal consciousness as happens in Christian theism and Hegelian idealism.

A similar criticism is offered by Aliotta of Naples. Given a certain number of entities and of simple relations, each one of which is independent of the others, and which we can combine in various ways, then these, in the last analysis, are the elements from which result reality and consciousness. Such is the simple solution offered. But what, inquires the critic, is the means by which these fragments can be united? In the Platonic philosophy it was only the Demiurge who could accomplish the miracle of union. But now we ask of the transatlantic realists how they can obtain any system—outside of the individual consciousness—in this chaos of elements. By their neutral monism they attempt to cancel all distinctions between psychic and physical facts and are forced to refer to the nervous system to define that group of objective entities which constitute the mind. In all this there are three mysteries: how consciousness arises from the simple delimitation of a group of objective entities; how from their plurality arises the unity of the subject; and how, finally, it is possible to speak either of action, or even of the nervous system, which in no way alters objective reality. In this criticism of the functional theory of consciousness one must not forget, continues Aliotta, that one fundamental postulate of the new realism is the immediate presence of the object of consciousness. But to respond physiologically to the stimulus and to be conscious of that stimulus are two diverse facts which may or may not coincide. For example, the stomach of an animal reacts chemically and mechanically without there being any knowledge of the chemical and mechanical facts. The new realists insist upon the absolute independence of object and thought, and yet they hold that consciousness arises from the relation of the nervous system to objective entities, from its motor reactions which they define as a particular group. But we have already pointed out that the organic response to an object, or to a system of external objects, is not always symptomatic of consciousness, since the external relation between organic movements and objective things is not sufficient to constitute consciousness.

2. CRITICAL REALISM

The " Six Little Realists " are now replaced by the seven critical realists and the latter, like the Seven before Thebes, have various methods to reduce the city. Drake furnishes the approach; Lovejoy attacks pragmatism; Pratt the problem of knowledge and Rogers the problem of error. But the plans for storming the very citadel of consciousness had already been laid by Sellars. This was in his *Critical Realism* of 1916, published in the same year in which the coöperative volume of his colleagues was projected. To Sellars consciousness is a variant within those logically developed parts of the world we call organisms. Here the most novel idea is that consciousness is actually extended. Critics would call this materialism. The author prefers to call it naturalism. At any rate it is opposed to pan-psychism which assumes that the mental cannot contain knowledge of the non-mental. It is also opposed to the assumption that scientific knowledge is an intuition of the stuff of the physical world, that science can picture the physical world. It agrees with natural realism in holding that things are there where we judge them to be, but it is against it in holding that we do not perceive the objects, but only the percepts causally connected with them. At first, like Narcissus, we see our own reflections and are not aware that they are our own. In short, the percept hovers between the individual and the thing, and can be identified with neither. It seems to be in a world of its own which has other laws than those which physical things obey.

On a cursory glance this triad of the critical realists appears like the scheme of the old-fashioned realists: subject, object, and subject-object, and this view of percepts like the medieval sensible species floating half-way between the object perceived and the mind perceiving. But it is neither, for, after the separation of the primary from the secondary qualities, perception is gradually displaced by conception, much as in petrifaction the wood fiber is displaced by minerals. This is so because we no longer perceive the elements of nature—such as atoms and molecules—but instead think them. In a word the skeleton of natural realism remains, while the content has undergone a fundamental alteration. So in the more abstract sciences nature is now regarded as a series of processes rather than a collection of things. For nature is now seen in the context of relations, which common sense failed to note. But though the scientific distinctions are like glimpses of a mountainous country seen through a wind-broken mist, science should not fall an easy prey to idealism. The advance of the personal tends that way, but because appearances are personal and intervene between the individual percipient and the physical thing, it does not follow that we have any less reason to believe in the existence of the physical things, nor that any two minds can share the same experience.

Idealism eventuating in mental pluralism is inadequate; meanings are not to be considered homeless, mere wandering adjectives which have no abiding place; nor are universals supposed to be changeless entities which subsist out of space and time, else they would correspond to the objects of living thought in individual minds much as museum specimens do to the free-living animal. However, we may accept mental pluralism, but not in the idealistic sense of an all-enfolding consciousness, the locus of all thoughts. Because my conceptions are un-thinkable apart from my relations to my fellow men, it surely does not follow that they are social possessions in the sense that a municipal lighting plant is. Individuals and society are not aspects of the same thing. The worlds of individuals are microcosms which evolve side by side, yet never mingle, in a literal sense. Furthermore, we suspect that the unity of experience depends as much on the objects as on the self. The old monarchical simplicity has given way before the realization of the democratic organization of that which is actually given.

So to maintain, as does the American type of the new realism, that the cognitive relation does not affect the reality known is to offer a foundation even more unstable than the idealistic principle. But our own assimilation of the mental field to the physical is unjustified, unless there are strong analogies to maintain it. But where are the analogies? Many arguments for the cognitive relation are based on a comparison of knowledge to a physical act, cognition as an act of the mind being directed upon an object outside the mind. Idealism is right in assert-ing that the object is connected with the mind by a relation; rational realism is right in asserting that this cognitive relation is not experienced, but is a creation of reflection, a contrast in which the object is experienced as independent. But here a difficulty arises. As a result of the advance of the personal the external world seems to lose the independence which it possesses for common sense, and to shrink into a temporal continuum of one's own percepts and concepts. For other people the same metamorphosis has to be postulated; the one common world transforms itself into as many worlds as there are individuals, a pluralism of minds with partially similar but altogether unsharable contents. Now how may this Chinese wall of exclusion be broken down? The answer is obviously by making consciousness extended, and thus allowing for an overlapping of the circles of personality. This, then, is the insufficiency of mental pluralism, that self-centered fields of experience make each system a universe of finite dimensions beyond which there is nothingness. Yet the advance of the personal does not necessitate solipsism and hypothetical nihilism. Unflinchingly followed to its conquest of other selves, our knowledge of these selves is seen to be content just as is our knowledge of physical things. This does not mean that such knowledge is based on a kind of intermonadic telepathy, a species of mysterious intuition between isolated individuals. This sympathetic " rapport " existing between individuals would be an inexhaustible wonder, or rather a counsel of despair whose supposed thinkableness rests more in feeling than in thought. But the real problem to-day is not whether monads have windows, but what kind of windows they have. There is only one serious answer to this inquiry. Connection is by means of the body, and is therefore indirect; cognition at a distance without a medium is even less indicated by our experience than action at a distance.

Critical Realism was published in 1916. Four years later appeared the coöperative *Essays in Critical Realism*. This volume propounds a doctrine claimed to be distinctly different from the " new " realism of the American group. It is said to be not a physically monistic realism nor a merely logical realism, but one which escapes the many difficulties of each. Let us attempt to summarize the critical attacks of this, the most recent school. Two general theories have been advanced to bridge the gap between subject and object, between mind and matter. The new realists did this in various ways, such as by extending consciousness or considering consciousness to be a cross-section of a neutral mosaic. On review many have considered this fanciful and inadequate. It might be compared to the " ectoplasm " of the latest species of spiritualists. This ectoplasm is the means by which the " soul " projects itself in a weird manifestation of " spiritual " matter, an inchoate kind of " psychic " protoplasm which gradually takes definite form and in turn may be withdrawn back into the person. But the projective theory in both cases seems too fanciful to be workable, a kind of metaphysical magic uncalled for in this scientific age. So the critical realists would fain resort to a different hypothesis. Instead of projecting the self into the not-self, instead of making the ego elastic, they assume a *tertium quid,* the so-called " essence." This is briefly defined as the *what* divorced from its *that,* as a purely logical entity which is not an existent, and not in space and time. It partakes in a measure of the neo-realistic subsistent, that is, it is any character or " fact " capable of being held before the mind. It is further defined as a universal, of any degree of complexity and definition, which may be given immediately, whether to sense or to thought; an object of pure sense or pure thought, with no belief superadded, an object inwardly complete and individual, but without external relations or physical status.

At first sight this " essence " is a cryptic quiddity; if it is equivalent to " meaning," it also has a hidden meaning. How can a third somewhat, which has no external relations, enable the mind to pass over from itself to an external object? The answer is it can do so by a belief in the essence itself or in that meaning or intellectual content which we transfer to an object; when we know an object we are assigning a certain essence—a character, or group of characters,—to some reality existing independent of the knowledge-process. But this process of " assigning " an essence does not mean a mere transference of our thoughts to things. That would be the pathetic fallacy in extreme form. Knowledge is transitive in the sense that self-existing things may become the chosen objects of a mind that identifies or indicates them. In other words, the essences or characters of things are not supplied by the mind out of its own bosom (that would be a fatuous idealism) ; nor are they brought to the mind by objects (that would be a simple sensationalism). Rather, essences are those entities which are taken out of a third realm and applied by the mind to objects. Or, as Santayana puts it, knowledge is not only transitive but relative, so that the things indicated may have at least some of the qualities that the mind attributes to them.

But what is this third realm of which they talk? The being proper to essence is not existence; when the datum is said to exist something is added to it which it does not and cannot contain; in other words, the datum cannot appear under the form of existence, but only as a pure essence. The great characteristic of what exists is to be in flux; it is a creature of circumstance, compacted and surrounded by external relations; and while the essence as the datum may have acquired one external, contingent and unstable relation—that it was given then, there, and to that person,—it did not change its nature when that person abandoned it for another nor did it acquire existence because he thought of it.

Such is Santayana's subtle description of the critical realistic " essence." At first blush it has certain advantages. It disposes of certain monopolistic ways of thinking, ranging from the middle ages to the present age. It is better than the medieval realism where all is in the body, including substantial forms. It is better than the modern idealism where all is in mind; where the world is an eject of the ego, like a caterpillar tractor which rolls forward on itself. It is better than the neo-realistic monism, that neutral mosaic which like the head of Janus is both this and that, both mind and matter. It is better than all these because it avoids confusing coalescences and allows for finer distinctions. As Strong says: here lies the immense advantage of the term essence; for the first time we get the datum characterized with absolute logical sharpness; with the replacing of the term " datum " by " essence," the thing designated is recognized not to be psychological, not physical, but logical, an entity of the peculiar type belonging to logic. Or, as Santayana puts it: the essence is not a state of mind, nor an existing thing, but an ideal essence. As ideal, then, the sort of being that essences have is indefeasible; they cannot lose it or change it as things do and must if their being is existence, since what exists continually lapses and moves forward and thus abandons some part of its essence. Again, as ideal, this being is also independent, not in the physical sense, but in the sense of its being perused. Finally, its logical character (which is all the reality it has) is inalienable; for that reason, perhaps, it was called by Plato being which is intrinsic, essential, and contingent on nothing else, least of all, of course, on knowledge. So that when our roving thought lights upon one of these intrinsic possibilities, it discovers an object ontologically far more necessary and fundamental than are physical things or pulses of feeling. It follows that acquaintance with essences or ideal terms is preëminently realistic knowledge. The circle of essences which human faculty can bring before us is limited, not by the absence of other possible themes, but by the bias of our endowment and the circumstances of our life. Pure intelligence within us—if we have such a thing—is by no means hostile to what, so far, has remained outside. Those yet unintuited essences can be brought into our experience, of course, only by an enlargement or shift in human nature. But human nature is elastic, and the realm of essence is infinite; and if we grew more imaginative and less egotistical we might be more ready to pour out our spirit, in sacrifice or in playfulness, on what is not relevant to our own fortunes. What we have not intuited has as much ideal reality, and for other possible souls as much possible charm as what we call beautiful. In hugging our humanity, as we very properly do, we need not grudge a speculative respect for what remains non-human. For it surrounds us on every side, ideally as well as materially, and we know that it surrounds us.

In this eloquent passage we seem to be listening to the voice of the ancient charmer with his call to philosophy as the disinterested pursuit of knowledge. It is therefore somewhat vain to have the concept of essence described as a " discovery "; it is rather a rediscovery, an old name applied to new complications of thought. Here Strong, like a master in intellectual chess, presents the various openings in the game, from the fool's gambit of naïve realism to advancing the knight of logical objectivism. As to the nature of the datum, he explains, there are six different views that have succeeded each other in the course of modern philosophy. To these must be added a seventh, distinct from any of the foregoing, namely, that the datum is the logical essence of the real thing. As to how Strong reached this " precious conception " he gives some interesting notes: I had long been convinced, he explains, that cognition requires *three* categories for its adequate interpretation; the intermediate one—between subject and object—corresponding to the Kantian " phenomenon " or " appearance." At one time I used to designate this category as " content," since it agrees with the current conception of a " content of consciousness "; but, in my efforts to conceive it clearly, I was continually falling off either into the category of " object " or into that of " psychic state." What was my relief when at last I heard Mr. Santayana explain his conception of " essence," and it dawned upon me that here was the absolutely correct description of the looked-for category. As he informs us elsewhere, Strong acknowledges that he owed this invaluable conception to his friend; its application to the problem of sense perception—the recognition that what is given in sense perception is only an essence—he considers his own. Several statements, then, may be made regarding data as essences: they are not the real things themselves; they are not psychological in their nature; they are not existences. As to the first point, data are not real things themselves, because reality is something attributed to the data; they are not objects themselves because they are merely presentments of objects from the point of view of the organism. For example, when the straight stick thrust into the water looks bent the datum in this case contradicts the object. Again, data are not psychological in their nature, because the givenness is not given along with the thing. For example, a mental image, as of some one's face, is supposed to exist, but the trouble is that, when we see faces, we do not see our seeing of them,—we see only the faces.

Before going on with Strong's third point we confess that his line of reasoning carries little conviction to us. In order to prove that data belonged to a kind of no man's land he seems to argue in this fashion: that data are not objective because they are subjective; they are not subjective because they are objective; in other words, they are not Tweedledum because they are Tweedledee, and not Tweedledee because they are Tweedledum. Under either alternative the datum seeks to prove an alibi and in both cases remains so evasive that it verges on the disappearing act. Such at least is our impression, more or less verified by Strong's labored explanation of his third point. This is that data are not existences, since we are capable of having things, given to us, which are not existences, for example, centaurs, perfect squares, ideas of virtue. Now the question will be whether a datum can be so concrete as even to have sensible vividness, and yet not be an existence, but only an entirely concrete universal, a universal of the lowest order. This would mean that the same datum exactly might be given to another person, or to the same person at a different time and place; in such wise that the datum as such would not be in time and space. That the data of perception are in fact universals of this description is the thesis of Strong's paper, and is what has been meant by calling them essences. The proof that these essences are not existences is the proof of parsimony. For example, when I touch ice I feel in the particular way called feeling cold; but at any moment I could turn my attention from the object felt to the new state of my sensibility; now this state is indeed an existence, for if it did not exist, it would be impossible for the external object, the ice, to appear before us as a datum. But because the vehicle of the givenness of this essence is an existence it does not follow that the essence was an existence also. If it were, we should have three existences concerned in sense perception—the physical thing, the state of our sensibilities, and the essence—which even the most determined multipliers of metaphysical entities would think too many.

All this strikes us as a verbal quibble. As Strong has already said, he had long been convinced that cognition requires three categories; beside the category of " object " and that of " psychic state " there was needed that of " essence." But we ask whether is it not just as much a multiplication of mental entities to add the conception of essence, as to call it an existence. The real saving of effort would come by getting entirely rid of this *tertium quid,* for to those who are not of the medieval realistic type essences which are not entities, hovering between subject and object, outside of space and time, require an insuperable effort to grasp. To the " dull Lockist " of a dualistic turn, objects and those psychic states called ideas seem sufficient to account for cognition. Given these two existences essences appear to be squeezed not only into non-existence but into non-entities in the usual sense of the word. Read this final admission of Strong and judge for yourself: " I admit that an unfelt sensation, in the sense in which the word sensation is ordinarily used, is absurd; but I persist in thinking that *that which* we feel, when we feel, i.e., distinctly attend to, a sensation, is capable of existing when it is not felt, and does so exist in all vision, hearing, and touching of external objects. This is a realistic view of introspection which is not popular.''

Since the doctrine of essence is put forward as their chief contribution we leave the other critical realists to their particular views. *Essays in Critical Realism* contains highly ingenious and interesting chapters on the approach to critical realism, its relation to pragmatism, its attitude towards the possibility of knowledge and the problem of error, and its opinion of knowledge and its categories. The essays of Santayana and Strong appear to offer the crux of the controversy. There we leave them in a brighter Hellas of their own making, a twentieth century empyrean, a realm of essences which are little but archetypes brought up to date.

In conclusion, we judge that the neo-realistic movement in America in this its last issue appears to end in a cul-de-sac, an unscalable blind wall. It therefore seems about time for American philosophers to retrace their steps, shake off the dust of an artificial epistemology, awake from a dream within a dream, and apply their energies to the world of philosophic ideas latent in modern art, modern literature, modern politics, and modern science. For ten years they have been encamped before the walls of Ilium and the topless towers have not yet fallen.

CHAPTER XI

SOME FRENCH INFLUENCES

1. Eclecticism: Victor Cousin

With the decay of the old Franco-American materialism there came a transitional era, a veritable prologue to
New England transcendentalism. This is well portrayed
by Frothingham in a brilliant but little known chapter
on transcendentalism in France. He shows how from
the principles of sensationalism atheism naturally proceeded, atheism not of opinion merely, but of sentiment
and feeling; for at that time the " potencies " of matter
impressed no such awe on the mind as they have done
since; " the mystery of matter " was unfelt; physiology
was an unexplored region; the materialist simply denied
spirit, putting a blank where believers in religion had
been used to find a soul; and had no alternative but to
run sensationalism into sensualism and to give the senses
the flavor of the ground. From such an impasse Maine
de Biran rescued his compatriots by making will the seat
of activity, the core of personality, the soul of causation,
in a word the corner-stone for a new structure to re-
place the old one of the encyclopædists. Important deductions followed from such a first principle: the dignity
of the moral being, freedom of the moral will, the no-
bility of existence, the persistency of the individual as a
ground for continuous effort and far-reaching hope, the
spirituality of man and his destiny. To recover the will
from the mass of sensations that had buried it out of

sight was the achievement of this philosopher. It was an achievement by which philosophy was disengaged from physics, and sent forth on a more cheerful way.

The guide upon this better way meets us in the person of Victor Cousin. As early as 1829 President Marsh, the first American editor of Coleridge's *Aids to Reflection*, refers to Paris as the place where the doctrines of a rational and spiritual system of philosophy are taught to listening and admiring thousands by one of the most learned and elegant philosophers of the age.

Now eclecticism first reached this country in a filtered form. Contrary to the common opinion, the foreign impulses to the New England transcendentalism did not come directly from Germany, but in a roundabout way through England and France. Coleridge's *Aids to Reflection* was the first guide book through the palpable obscure of Teutonic thought. Within three years it was followed by Ripley's *Specimens of Foreign Literature* of which the first volume was a translation of Cousin's *Fragments*. And as early as 1832 a native critic made Cousin and not Kant the protagonist in the new movement. This judgment is valid, for it can be measured by three things: by the welcome afforded to it by the new generation; by the criticism evoked from the old school; by the sober expositions of the system among scholars. Yet to the period during which eclecticism penetrated into our country an unfortunate name has been given. It has been called the negative period. It should rather be called the neglected period. Possibly, as Sanborn said, for the years between 1820 and 1850 no single sufficient representative has been found. Yet this period he acknowledges was like the age immediately following adolescence in men—a vigorous, ungoverned, risky time. This acknowledgment is significant. Adolescence may be ungoverned, but from it may arise such an abiding enthusiasm as was engendered by Cousin himself among his young compatriots. Now similar conditions were to be met with in America as in France, for it was a time when denunciations of materialism in philosophy, formalism in religion, and utilitarianism in personal and social ethics rang through the land.

At this point we must insert the oft-quoted opinion of Emerson upon Cousin, but preface it with a word of caution. It is wrong to put the leader of transcendentalism among the conservatives, for his criticism of eclecticism is not that of conventionality, but of unconventionality. Emerson's point of view is the opposite of that of the orthodox. When they held that eclecticism was too vague, he held it was not vague enough. They rejected it because it did not fit their system; Emerson criticized it because it was too systematic. As his college could not pin him down to its rules, nor his church to its standards, so now before the new philosophy he was as elusive as Ariel. With this word of explanation one can perhaps better understand the position of the Sage of Concord. He writes on the subject of French eclecticism which Cousin esteems so conclusive: "I would say there is an optical illusion in it. It avows great pretensions. It looks as if it had all truth, in taking all the systems, and had nothing to do but to sift and wash and strain, and the gold and diamonds would remain in the last colander. But Truth is such a fly-away, such a sly-boots, so untransportable, unbarrelable a commodity, that it is as hard to catch as light."

The rôle of advocate against the various charges brought against Cousin is now undertaken by the professor of philosophy in the University of the City of New York. Having written a history of French philosophy in the first half of the nineteenth century Caleb Henry was well qualified to portray the real connection between Cousin and his Scotch and German predecessors. Moreover, his translation of the *Elements of Psychology* and his extracts from the *Fragments* enabled him to meet the various counts of the conservative reviewers who charged the eclectic with misinterpreting Locke as fatalist, materialist, and almost pantheist, and at the same time inconsistently burdening Cousin with these same opprobrious epithets. In a word, eclectism needed the defense of a scholar, one familiar with the historical antecedents. Such was Caleb Henry, who devoted twenty years to the exposition of French philosophy in New York City. As a sign of the popularity of that philosophy Henry published four editions of his translation of Cousin's *Elements*. And as a proof that he was able to vindicate Cousin against the charge of being a misinterpreter of Locke and of the Scottish system, he recommends that his work be used as a textbook in connection with the *Essay Concerning Human Understanding* and Reid's writings. He is now prepared to defend Cousin against all comers. The strongest attack came from the ablest of the denominational journals, the *Princeton Review*. This summarily represents the great eclectic as a pantheist, denying the personality of God; as denying also the essential difference of right and wrong; and as maintaining a scheme of fatalism.

To meet these strictures is easy, but the general charge of Cousin's being shallow and superficial, because he is an eclectic, is harder to meet. The word itself was at this time in ill repute in the land. In education the eclectic textbook betokened a polite form of literary piracy; in medicine the eclectic school fell between the two schools of allopathy and homeopathy. In politics, to be an eclectic was to be a mugwump, a word borrowed from the aboriginal savages because there was nothing in English that could so well express the contempt of the stalwart veterans for those who were not loyal party men. But against this charge eclecticism might count upon three favoring factors: clarity of style due to the age of reason; a dependence on instinctive impulses due to the philosophy of common sense, and that new characteristic, at this time in the process of formation, the belief, as Emerson had just put it, "that there is one mind and every man is a porch leading into it." As a further illustration of the congeniality of the Gallic and American mind, what Ripley said of eclecticism might be said of New England transcendentalism—that it marks the period of transition from the skeptical and sensual theories of the eighteenth century to more elevated and spiritual views as to the nature of man. This, then, is the vindication of French philosophy, that it should no longer be identified with naturalism and atheism, but that it restores philosophy to the eminence which it held in the golden days of English literature, and that it revives the lofty spirit of Hooker, Cudworth, and Milton in the midst of modern unbelief and selfishness.

Now what are the grounds of success in America for such a system, an eclecticism in the best sense of the word? It may be said to possess a fourfold root, namely, that it is non-partisan; that it is clear and distinct; that it is democratic; that it is religious. From this root Ripley expects a sturdy growth in American soil. How far that expectation was to be justified is a problem. The spirit of the times was not so admirable as the editor of the *Miscellanies* would have us believe. Most Americans were party men, in philosophy as well as in politics. In later criticisms of these *Miscellanies* we shall find them attacked by partisans of the English, or Scotch, or German schools,—by the followers of Locke, or Stewart, or Hegel. As to the clear expression of distinct thoughts this might attract both cultivated lovers of French literature and those rationalists who held to the demands for distinctness. Yet the very romanticism of which eclecticism was an expression required more than Cartesian clarity. It might be averse to mystery and miracle in the sense in which Thomas Paine reprehended them; it was not averse to occasional excursions into the clouds. The younger generation which revolted against the precision and formality of tradition were enraptured by the empyrean. Emerson himself, in his *Natural History of Intellect*, follows his chapter on "The Powers and Laws of Thought" by one on "Instinct and Inspiration." As for the democratic spirit of eclecticism, it in no way reached the proletariat as did the succeeding positivism. "Respect for the spontaneous beliefs of humanity" sounds a little condescending. It was not half so good a catchword as the "common sense" of the Scotch school. Finally, as to the religious appeal of eclecticism, critics agree that the object of Cousin, like that of Coleridge, was to furnish aids to reflection. Nevertheless they balked at the results of that reflection. Especially when Ripley compared Cousin to the most famous of New England divines—Jonathan Edwards— the defenders of the old faith were up in arms. Edwards' advocacy of spiritual intuition was generally interpreted as being confined to the "saints" among the Puritans. Edwards' adumbration of the eclectic doctrine of impersonal reason, that is, of reason independent of personality and involving a divine principle, as Ripley acknowledges, was likewise a doctrine limited to Edwards' own persuasion.

Despite these strictures it has been rightly said that
the tendency of Cousin's philosophy was to produce
thinkers rather than mere disciples. One may judge
how numerous these were from the Parisian eclectic's
voluminous American correspondence. To that correspondence we now turn as furnishing a review of the
field and a forecast of the future. Cousin had already
entered into a network of personal relations with many
of the best minds in America. As early as 1834 he had
expressed his gratification for the use of his educational
treatises by the states of Massachusetts and New Jersey;
he had been highly pleased by the founding of Girard
College by a Franco-American; he had publicly thanked
Linberg for the first American translation of his course
of philosophy. He now enters into an extended correspondence with Henry of New York for his translation
of the *Essay* on Locke's *Essay;* with Brownson of Boston
for energetically upholding the principles of French
spiritualism, and with George Ripley for putting first,
in his *Specimens of Foreign Literature,* the works of
himself and of his colleagues Constant and Jouffroy.

How far westward did the star of eclecticism take its
way? One American who had listened to the lectures
of Cousin was inspired with the Parisian's scheme to
plant philosophy in the west. Another in his " winding
journey around the world " settled in Wisconsin and
described himself to Cousin as a member of his philosophic family. But the western focus of eclecticism was
Ohio. William H. Channing, a nephew of the preacher,
gives what is perhaps the best combined defense and exposition of the movement. Channing does this in examining the system of Cousin's pupil, the " clear and
candid " Jouffroy. Such gross misconceptions, he says,
as to the character of modern French philosophy still

prevail among us, notwithstanding the full expositions which have been laid before the public, that it seems unjust to let any opportunity pass unused of making known the true position which the writers of this school occupy.

Briefly, then, the eclectics did three things: they acknowledged the value of Reid's first truths, but cleared away the Scotch mist of common sense as based on observations "hasty, partial and confused." Next, they recognized the profound reflective powers of Kant, but decried that skepticism which confessed itself unable to probe the existence of objective realities. Finally, the French school imbibing, in some degree, the principles of both the Scottish and German, blended them in a method of its own. Their leading principles are, in turn, three: psychology is the basis of philosophy; the highest proofs of ontology may be solved by inductions from the facts which psychology ascertains; psychology and the history of philosophy reciprocally explain each other. In fine, while the Scotch make introspection the foundation of metaphysical science, the French have applied it more strictly than their teachers; and while the Germans begin with the absolute, and descend to man, the French begin with man and ascend to the absolute. All this, then, concludes Channing, renders the writers of the French school safe guides in philosophical investigation, for eclecticism means exactly the contrary of a commingling of heterogeneous systems, being intended to designate a discriminating selection of the elements of truth which may be found in each system.

Here we leave the subject of eclecticism in America. The abundance of translations made, the variety of views expressed, the number of readers gained, all attest the length and breadth of its influence. As its earliest reviewer suggested, there was in it an appeal to Americanism, for it was " vast, optimistic, and unitary." And as one of its latest critics, Dean Mansel, inadvertently implied, it met the necessary conditions for the progress of philosophy in the west, the position of America in many respects qualifying it admirably for the task of sifting the wheat from the chaff in the various conflicting philosophies of Europe, and producing from the materials of the older literature, aided by the independent spirit of her own thinkers, a system adapted to the character and marks of the age.

2. POSITIVISM: AUGUSTE COMTE

Positivism in America is a forgotten chapter in our intellectual history. It shone for a day, then suffered an eclipse. It remains for us, then, to study the long coronal rays. Auguste Comte declared in 1851 that he could not feel himself an utter stranger to the Western World, where in 1816 he intended to transplant his incipient philosophical career, under the distinguished patronage of the good General Bernard and also, indirectly, the noble President Monroe.

The master did not come, but his thoughts did, and it is with the influence of positivism that there arises the third phase of French philosophic thought on this side of the water. The first was the negativism of the Revolution, Voltaire being the gadfly of the state; the second eclecticism, when Victor Cousin found a host of sympathetic critics, especially in the colleges. The third was positivism, when Comte, as author of the *Cours*, provided the silken thread in the labyrinth of speculation, and, as author of the *Systéme*, stimulated the local longings for a religion of humanity. A Theseus of thought, the classifier of Paris performed a signal service as a guide in the mazes of metaphysics left by the trans-scendentalists.

That this service as a guide in the intricacies of knowledge met a genuine need was evident from two facts: the early scarcity of systems of classification, and the later abundance, due directly to the stimulus of Comte. Thus in 1851 appeared a translation of Comte's *Philosophy of Mathematics* in which the American editor declared that the want of a comprehensive map of the wide region of mathematical science—a bird's-eye view of its leading features, and of the true bearing of the relations of all its parts—is felt by every thoughtful student. A panoramic view of the whole district, presenting at a glance all the parts in due coördination, with the darkest nooks clearly shown, is invaluable to either traveler or student. Comte views his subject from an elevation which gives to each part of the complex whole its true position and value, while his telescopic glance loses none of the details.

So far the earliest readers of Comte agree in their sentiments. That agreement is due to a common cause. During the first half of the century New England transcendentalism had greatly flourished, and the trans-cendentalists, it is needless to say, had the defects of their qualities. In a subjective, intuitional way of thinking there was naturally a lack of system; as Emerson intimated, in his Paris journal, an *a priori* metaphysics cannot be fashioned after the plan of the Jardin des Plantes. Besides a distaste for system, the transcendentalists had a penchant for the obscure style, as shown in the dark utterances of Margaret Fuller and the " Orphic Sayings " of Bronson Alcott. It was here that New England ran off into the obverse side of neo-Platonism,

and that the theory of lapse, and man's fall into an
inferior state of being, found curious expression in such
baffling pieces of literature as the *Marble Faun.*

It was, then, in this lower world, this shadowy realm
of abstract entities, that a Vergil was needed, and it was
Comte who led many to see that there was a way of
escape from—shall we say?—the sorrowful city of Boston, the eternal grief of Puritanism. Those of New England stock were not only spiritually overwrought as to
the soul's fate, but they were also mentally confused in
the din of systems about them. All the philosophers
were crying up their wares, the realists in the colleges,
the transcendentalists in their clubs, the materialists in
the market places. In the midst of this noise and confusion appeared Comte, and as a guide, philosopher, and
friend, performed a welcome office. His was the scheme
which authoritatively presented a metaphysical map
showing the metes and bounds of the various rival
schools. So young and ardent spirits, even at the risk of
disillusionment, desired to gain an objective, a dispas-
sionate point of view. And nothing could be more cool-
ing to the brain than this exercise in speculative car-
tography, this triangulation of rival systems. Here, for
the first time, they learned that philosophy is not a
static thing, that the realists with their " fundamental
truths," the transcendentalists with their " eternal
archetypes," the materialists with their " ultimate elements " are, if not all wrong, at least only partially
right. Thus Comte came to adjudicate the conflicting
claims. As yet, there was hardly a notion of the development of speculation, hardly an idea that there might
be a history of ideas. But as, with three given points,
a line can be projected, and with the drawing of the line
a feeling of motion and of change emerges,—so was it

with the three current points of view in philosophy. It happened, at this time, that the old realists inclined towards the theological, the transcendentalists towards the metaphysical, and the materialists—at least in their observation of concrete objects—towards the positive. Hence with three given systems, arranged in a series, a certain progress might be observed. As Jefferson had seen Condorcet's *Progress of the Human Spirit* exemplified in the hunting, the agricultural, and the industrial regions of his native Virginia, so in the North it seemed possible to gain a perspective glimpse of Comte's three stages.

But there were two deterrent factors: a certain state of mind, and a certain state of confusion. As yet there could be no wide acceptance of the notion of the history of ideas, because the genetic point of view was considered heretical. The acceptance of the notion of such a history was the counterpart of the notion of evolutionism, but at this juncture truths were declared eternal, just as species were declared fixed. This was a state of mind which disappeared only after the combined efforts of the Lamarckians and Darwinians. In addition there was a confusion of mind, a false identification of positivism with materialism. This error was perpetuated not only by the theological magazines—the first to notice Comte— but even by the historians of metaphysics who put Comte in the succession of Condillac and La Mettrie.

In looking upon America as the land of promise for positivism, Comte had evidently modified his reputed opinion that, if Lagrange were to come to the United States, he could only earn his livelihood by turning land surveyor. As to the favorable reception to be accorded the religion of humanity, its high priest was evidently at fault. This is clear from comparing his hopes with the opinion of a native critic who discloses the conflicting rôles played by Comte's earlier and later writings, a conflict which Comte himself recognized in referring to his religious system as his " second career." So it was that the writings of Comte have tended to become separated into two distinct groups, upheld by two equally distinct classes of followers. The author of the *Cours* was hailed as a new star of the first magnitude, surpassing in brilliancy such lesser lights as Descartes, Leibniz, and Bacon. The publication of the *Systéme* lost Comte the greater part of his former followers, and those who did not forget his previous work have quietly ignored the whole body of his later writings, or dismissed them as the product of a great mind gone wrong. Another class of followers have stood steadfast, discovering in the author of the *Systéme* a new apostle, the teacher of a new rule of life, and the founder of a new religion. A few hardy disciples have tried to harmonize this with the *Cours*. Their success has not been flattering. The Comtist philosophy and Comtist religion have remained, and must remain, contradictory in nature and purpose.

Along with two classes of followers Comte had three classes of critics in this country: the theological being more or less contemptuous, the metaphysical rather hypercritical, but the scientific were both critical and sympathetic. Thus Lester F. Ward, the author of *Dynamic Sociology*, declares that the supreme excellence of Comte is his insistence upon the ultimate unity of all the processes of nature. It is not enough to say that others have held the same truth. No one before Comte had made it the basis of a system of philosophy. Judged by any other standard, all claims to originality in anything would be invalidated. To do this would be like awarding to the American savage the merit of discovering the New World. But Comte is perhaps too rigorous in his monistic consistency. Think of the severity of his logic which led him to reject psychology as distinct from biology, the brain from the nervous system, the man from the animal. Yet that same severity should have led him to accept the advanced speculations of Lamarck. But it was probably owing to a certain timidity, as not being himself a master in any department of biological science, that he thought best to discountenance these speculations and plant himself safely down upon the doctrine of discontinuity in the biological sciences and upon the fixity of existing forms. This failure to accept the developmental theory in biology,—the theory of a slow progress by small increments—is also explained by Comte's extravagant attachment to the celebrated theory of the destiny of the human race regarded as a perpetually progressive individual.

Ward closes his elaborate study with a summary estimate of Comte, both as to his excellences and defects. He is the founder of the science of sociology, the first to establish the true principle of the natural dependence of all the sciences, the first to classify the history of human thought according to the fundamental conditions of the human mind,—the world is surely under heavy and lasting obligations to this somewhat erratic philosopher,—erratic because the iron consistency of his general logic is in marked contrast with the flimsy fallacies that stare at the astonished reader from every page. He is a great general in the army of thinkers, but, when he descends, as he continually does, to meddle with the brigades, regiments, and platoons, he throws them into confusion by the undue severity and amazing stupidity of his commands.

With Ward we leave the academic critics. His final

remarks afford a point of transition to the final group, the proletaires. But the simile of Comte as the commander of an army does not apply locally. As a matter of fact he had but few adherents in carrying out his scheme,—scarcely a corporal's guard in Philadelphia; hardly a company in New York. The reason was obvious,—the lack of a proper milieu for the spread of positivism. Ward, writing in the 'eighties, speaks of the overworked millions in the great cities, but in the 'fifties, when Comte directed his first letter to American Conservateurs, the social conditions in the New World were not particularly oppressive. This is to be gathered from the third circular, dated January, 1852. Comparing this circular with the letter to the *Methodist Review,* four months later, Frederic Harrison makes two deductions: that Comte greatly exaggerated the number and importance of Americans who took a great interest in his affairs and were prepared to accept him as their chief, and yet that at this time there was a great receptivity in the United States to new ideas, which was extremely favorable to the diffusion of positivist thought, despite the predominance of biblical orthodoxy. The immigration of Germans and other skeptics, of Russian Jews and sectaries, the strange confusion between immigrants as to races and religions, tended to prepare the soil for intellectual development, yet the mobility and flux of all things American has prevented the existence of permanent positivist groups.

These general considerations may now be analyzed in detail. There was, indeed, at the beginning, a spirit of receptivity among the leaders of thought in America. In 1852 Harriet Martineau declared that Emerson's Phi Beta Kappa Address on " The Duties of Educated Men in a Republic " breathed a philosophical reverence for humanity. The following year William Ellery Channing announced that the end towards which all the highest spiritual energy of Christendom is now resistlessly tending is the organic Unity of Societies, confederated in larger societies where religion and politics are made one as spirit and body. . . . This is confirmed by Auguste Comte. In 1856, Frothingham wrote to Theodore Parker: If the world is not an audacious '' quiz of nature,'' as Emerson holds, I think all creeds must ultimately be merged into this positive, or, as you would say, absolute religion.

As to the significance of immigration the matter is not so clear. By the 'seventies the newcomers to the country had prospered enough to form clubs and publish pamphlets. But in the 'eighties, as the author of *Religion in America* declared, many of the most turbulent and restless people of the Continent—socialists, radicals, infidels —the very sweepings of Europe were coming to the New World, while some of the most dangerous newspapers in the United States were edited by foreigners. Finally, as to the mobility and flux of all things American which prevented the permanent existence of permanent positivist groups,—the problem is not so easily disposed of. There was a complex of causes which militated against these groups. The New England leaders were intellectually radical, but socially conservative; they represented the college caste as against the common people. The religious leaders, also college bred, were not only socially, but also intellectually conservative. The predominance of biblical orthodoxy was not a minor but a major cause opposed to the founding of radical clubs. The history of early free thinking societies in America is proof of this. The Franco-American Jacobin clubs, affiliated with the Grand Orient of Paris, were finally overwhelmed by the

" war-whoop of the pulpit." The Anglo-American clubs, such as the Deistical Society of New York, were also denounced as atheistical, anarchical, and a menace to orderly government. Lastly, the communities like New Harmony, patterned after the plans of Robert Owen, the English socialist, were pronounced odious to polite society.

Such was the complex of religious, political, and social prejudices which met the earlier attempts at radicalism. Despite Halls of Science, Free Press Associations, and Declarations of Mental Independence, a projected General Association of Liberals never succeeded. The socialistic schemes of Owen, of course, had some success, especially as they were reënforced by Fourierism, but Owen had wealth and social prestige and had been invited to explain his grandiose plans before the President and Congress. What chance, then, had the humble followers of Comte, who were found chiefly among poor emigrants, the humble proletaires on the East Side of New York?

If the " precious foyer " of Philadelphia resolved itself into one man, so did that of New York, at least in its beginnings. At the time when Comte expressed his great expectations there had been published in the metropolis but a single positivist tract, a reprint of the Positive Calendar. With the second imprint of this calendar there appears on the scene the naturalized Englishman, Henry Edger. This interesting character was described in 1870 as the actual hierarch of positivism, one of the ten apostles *de propaganda fide* appointed by Comte, a resident of the village of Modern Times, Long Island.

It was a strange company in which the first official positivist found himself,—disgruntled coöperative reformers, individual " sovereigns " whose views on free love were a rich morsel for the newspapers; the disciples of the " Grand Pantarch " who indulged in " scientific classification " as if it were a game of logomachy. It is no wonder that Henry Edger made but slight advances as a propagandist of positivism in this curious mental menagerie. And possibly the notoriety gained by this suburban experiment reflected upon the genuine groups of proletaires in the city. These were at least three. By 1871 there came into existence the New York Positive Society, and, shortly after, a Society of Humanity, and a Society of Humanists. From these positivist centers there emanated various positivist primers, epitomes, and prayers. A sample of one of these will do for all. The best of the positive primers is that by a member of the earliest society, David's " Familiar Conversations on the Religion of Humanity." This religion, it is claimed, involves a ritual but no belief in a personal immortality; it involves a heaven, but only one that can be realized upon earth; its golden age is not in the past but in the future, its gardens of the Hesperides are in the west, toward which we are always marching. David next essays to form a Calendar for worship, a scheme doomed to failure in this country. The Theophilanthropists tried it and were ridiculed even when their roster included General Washington. Comte's own calendar had two local reprintings, but that was all. A similar fate faced the proposed priesthood of philosophers, scientists, and artists. Here the propagandist is forced to be vague. He knew that the native philosophers of the day were mostly of a conservative stripe, and that the local followers of Hæckel, Darwin, Wallace, and Herbert Spencer were as yet few and far between. As for the artists the less said the better,—this was the period, in our architecture, for example, variously known as the Reign of Terror, the Early Pullman, and the North German Lloyd. For his spiritual power, then, David is forced to descend from the " thinkers " to the lower class of practical men who had actual control of business affairs. These are the men with the real social mission. No one would think of making Longfellow or Bryant or Whittier president or senator. But much could be accomplished for the improvement of the proletariat by the great capitalist class, provided they should consider their wealth social, not personal. The Stewarts and Vanderbilts are doing this unconsciously through consolidating retail trade and railroad traffic, and Peter Cooper consciously in both his preaching on the duties of wealth, and in that practical center of propaganda, the Cooper Union.

This is as far as the cult of humanity reached among local proletaires. It hardly bears out the statement of Comte, a quarter of a century before, that the principal conservateurs of the United States have nobly invoked the positive religion as their sole systematic shelter against the subversive tendencies of the most anarchic of the western peoples. Against this too optimistic statement should be put the estimate of Moncure Conway, a taster of systems, a wandering Ulysses among the religions of the world. To this American free lance, who visited the festival of Humanity in London at this very time, the ceremony was all pathetically picturesque, but no more. To him also the positivist deity was but another " Incomprehensible " like the triune. He found no such entity as Humanity conceivable. In the effort his imagination was lost in a vast cloud with many nuclei,—here of man-faced bipeds devouring or slaying one another, there, of men helping each other. Nowhere could he find any clear definition of divine humanity. So he gradually reached a belief that positive religion is a refined variety of the general democratization of Christianity.

What chance, we may ask in conclusion, is there for a popular revival of positivism? Very little. There are two possible channels of interest, but both of doubtful value. The proletariat, a generation ago, published a few pamphlets, but the present beliefs of the American workman, as an English positivist has recently assured us, are too vague to be put in books. The professoriate is left, but the professional philosopher in America, to speak by the mark, is sophisticated to a degree. Since our country was drenched with Hegelianism, any form of absolutism is looked upon as so much poison gas. But will the younger generation be interested in Comte? Possibly. There is one essential discipline we lack, and that is a knowledge of the history of science. Some consider this discipline a substitute for the study of the history of metaphysical systems. At any rate the old conception of philosophy as a guide of life has disappeared in academic circles. No longer do teachers attempt to give their pupils doses of " fundamental " truths, to offer first aid packages for religious difficulties. In place of these they would offer a knowledge of the history of ideas, from the beliefs of prehistoric man, to the latest conceptions of science. Here, as an inspirer of the consciousness of continuity may Auguste Comte take his rightful place.

3. CREATIVE EVOLUTION: HENRI BERGSON

The author of *Creative Evolution* has visited us, and our opinions of him and of his system are as varied as the persons who propound them. How diverse these are may be seen from certain summary statements of our critics:—Bergson is a pragmatist because of his utilitarian view of the universe; he is an anti-pragmatist because pragmatism leaves too much to the accidents of volition. He is a rationalist because of his apprenticeship to the sciences; he is an anti-rationalist because of his rebuke to the haughtiness of the scientists. He is an idealist because to him duration means the creation not only of spirit but also of body; he is not an idealist because he points out the inadequacy of conceptual knowledge. He is a personalist because life and the vital impetus are synonyms for consciousness; he is not a personalist because creative evolution takes little account of individuality. He is a religious leader because he gives us God through his vital impetus, freedom through the laws of contingency, immortality through the doctrines of duration; he has no religious message because, as a mystic, his intuition is ineffable and his goal indefinable. He is a conservatist because his appeal to instinct is a return to the old romanticism; he is " the most dangerous man in the world " because his radicalism is opposed to stand-pat capitalism.

To this table of antitheses, where particular affirmatives are cancelled by particular denials, may be added general opinions which connect Bergson positively with our two foremost thinkers. Like Emerson, Bergson may be called a prophet of the soul, a friend and aider of those who would see with the spirit and enter into the mystery of creation through intellectual sympathy or intuition, instead of making the vain attempt to do so through the logical and scientific understanding. Like William James, Bergson is a poet rather than a philosopher. With him, philosophy once more becomes a part of literature. Bergson himself is convinced that metaphysics is a dramatic pursuit of a living object, reality being a flux and not a system. With such a medley of impressions, can we say that our critics have understood Bergson; that following our national motto they perceive the unity despite the plurality? The answer is in the affirmative only if Bergsonism, creative evolution, the philosophy of change be looked upon as was the city of Leibniz, in itself one, in its perspectives many.

Some twenty-five years ago Bergson was "discovered" by an American. Over two decades before the appearance of *Creative Evolution,* with its immense vogue, William James was wont to urge his students to read "*Essai sur les données immédiates de la conscience.*" But unfortunately this appeal had little effect and it was not until after the appearance of James's more popular works that the public was prepared to accept what the scholar of Cambridge recommended. The chapter concerning Bergson in the *Pluralistic Universe* constituted the formal announcement that a new and great philosopher had arisen in France. This announcement was made abroad but James's wide audience at home was ready to welcome it. Whatever the famous pragmatist said was of interest to the generality and whatever the psychologist said to academic circles. Our first concern will be with the latter, for the burning rays of criticism were immediately brought to a focus by the experts, whereas the average reader took a more general and a more generous interest in the larger aspects of Bergsonism. Accepting without too close a scrutiny the doctrines of *Creative Evolution,* its duration, contingency, intuition, they sought to apply these to the practical matters of ethics and religion, of politics and art. So with the coming of Bergson himself to these shores in

1912 the tide of popular favor reached its height. It was more than a nine days' wonder when the master appeared on the scene. The reception took on the aspect not only of an academic event of the first importance but to a certain degree of a religious acclamation, for the lectures at Columbia University dealt with the persistent problems of spirituality and liberty.

The after effects of all this upon the public imagination we shall describe later, for besides a decided success, there was a certain reaction of distortion and disfavor, an inevitable accumulation of débris consequent upon the ebbing of the tide. But the first intimation of a rising of a new tide, as has been said, was given by William James. In his sixth Hibbert Lecture he went so far as to say that Bergson's philosophy was what had led him personally to renounce the intellectualistic method and the current notion that logic is an adequate measure of what can or cannot be. The reason for this concession was a sort of double repercussion on James's part. He rebelled against the ruling tradition in philosophy, namely, the Platonic and Aristotelian belief that fixity is a nobler and worthier thing than change; he also rebelled against the Kantian tradition that the relief from the supposed contradictions of our world of sense is to be found by looking forward to an absolute, conceived as its integration or logical completion. In other words, the intellect, speaking through Hume, Kant and Company, finds itself obliged to deny that activities have any intelligible existence.

In writing these appreciations James was well aware that criticism would arise. He therefore issues a series of caveats. He declares that, following our sensational life, continuity is not a return to ultra crude empiricism, but merely accepting the immediate point of view in regard to our smooth-running finite experience; that the criticism of concepts is not a surrender to anti-intellectualism, because direct acquaintance and conceptual knowledge are complementary of each other, each remedying the other's defects; and that to fall back on raw unverbalized life as more of a revealer of reality than conceptual knowledge, is not a recourse to mysticism, for the mystics always have an absolute and the inventing of such a supernumerary conceptual object is an oddity.

James's three caveats in regard to Bergson's real immediaticism, his alleged anti-intellectualism, and his so-called mysticism furnish the main lines on which the interpreters and critics were to range themselves. Here James's younger colleagues are in point. Perry's account is significant as an early attempt to systematize Bergson; that of his colleague Hocking as an early attempt to Bergsonize a system. But if James had read Bergsonism with enthusiasm, Perry with sympathy, Hocking with a genuine liking, to Santayana enthusiasm is bad form, sympathy out of place and the philosophy of change not to his liking. For him, as a taster of systems, the first taste decides—if the hors d'œuvres are bad, so is the rest of the feast. A critic of the immediacy of Bergson, he yet displays an instantaneous repugnance to the new French philosophy. But to connect this esthetic egotist with the previous critic. To Hocking Bergson is half an idealist, an intuitionist of the intellectual type; to Santayana he is wholly an idealist, and an intuitionist of the mystic type. Put among the hereditary idealists Bergson, because of his insistence on immediacy, is declared to fall in the line of Plotinus and Spinoza. But though the most representative and remarkable of living philosophers, he is pronounced "persuasive without argument, and mystical without conventionality."

Does the reviewer mean by these phrases that Bergson is an unconventional Plotinus, and an illogical Spinoza? So it seems. He assumes Bergson to be an instinctive mystic but never takes the pains to point out in what respects the Frenchman fulfills the precise and rigid conditions of a thoroughgoing quietist.

An equally severe but more thorough critic is Arthur Lovejoy of Johns Hopkins. His thesis is briefly that Bergsonism was made in Germany. Creative evolution is merely romantic evolutionism revived. The creation of new forms is due to the *élan vital*, but this, Teutonized, is little but Schopenhauer's will to live. And just as the renowned pessimist presented a dualism of good and evil principles, so does he who is popularly counted an optimist. The critic here gives a clever description of the life force as tending to fatigue and breakdown, a strain of cosmic neurasthenia. This description would perfectly fit the arch pessimist whose personal neurasthenia was transferred to his philosophy; but this is not the way that we read *Creative Evolution,* for the chapter on the "Ideal Generation of Matter" presents what might be called in the language of our New Thoughters a fight against fatigue poison. Between matter and spirit there is not necessarily a fatal friction; the universe may be retarded, but to use an Americanism, "it will get there just the same."

If Bergsonism is not a derivative of Schopenhauer, much less is it from Schelling. It is not necessary to go round Robin Hood's barn to reach the spring. It may be true that it is in the nature-philosophy that one finds the first typical and influential expression of an activistic or voluntaristic theory of the universe and that Bergson's teacher, Ravaisson, admired Schelling. But as Lovejoy himself points out, Schelling tended toward the eternal changelessness of neo-Platonism, whereas Ravaisson tended toward the self-subsistent god of Aristotelianism. It is, therefore, quite impossible to interpolate the philosophy of change into this kind of an apostolic succession which preserves the faith once delivered to the ancients. Lovejoy may claim that half the body of Bergsonism doctrine was first made in Germany and then finished in France, but his own arguments tend to disprove it. Just as the old voluntarism across the Rhine was the product of a reaction against the older French mechanism—of man as a machine, man an animated statue, and all that— so Bergson's doctrine of creative evolution was a declaration of independence against that alliance of evolution and mechanism which was formed about the middle of the nineteenth century. Spencer was largely responsible for what might be called the law of the descending scale—that the quantity of matter and energy in the world being constant, the laws of psychology were reducible to the laws of biology, these to the laws of chemistry and so on down. But just as in a religious hierarchy a pope cannot be reduced to a cardinal, a cardinal to a bishop and so on down to the acolyte, so is it in the system of *Creative Evolution*. Bergson, as Lovejoy has elsewhere pointed out, belongs to the school of Boutroux, and Boutroux reverses the formula of Spencer and contends that contingency, the possibility of novelty, is renewed in every higher stage of the hierarchy.

It is a mistake, then, to go back to the eighteenth century instead of utilizing the immediate data of the nineteenth; to consider Bergsonism an antiquated syncretism instead of a fresh personal repercussion against current views. Lovejoy acknowledges as much in his generous conclusion to this whole matter of sources in saying that, at the present juncture in the history of thought, the eternal absolute of the post-Kantian idealist is being found by many logically impossible, and that there is need of a final reversal of the medieval view, in favor of a creative evolutionism which finds no place for the primacy of the perfect, for an eternal entity, but only for the upward reaching activity of the imperfect, in fine for " a god in the making."

Lovejoy has not proved his case against Bergson. The original charge was one of mystification, the final charge that of mysticism. The first may be true as a matter of feeling, the latter is not true as a matter of fact. If one implies that a certain complex constitutes a disease, he must be able to diagnose it. To bring a charge of mysticism in metaphysics is as easy as to bring, for example, a charge of Bolshevism in politics, and equally hard to prove. And there is another point in which the critic betrays a certain inconsistency. He declares that the fact that a philosophy gratifies the craving for a sense of initiation proves nothing either for or against it. But he proceeds to show the evil results of the katharsis required of the candidates for initiation into Bergsonism. Such initiation, it is explained, is only to be had through intuition and this requires three things: that we must turn away from logical thought, from action, and from the conditions of social life.

Such, according to Lovejoy, are the negative pre-requisites to an attainment of the Bergsonian intuition. The turning away from logical thought, from action and from the conditions of social life are indeed the minor marks of mysticism as shown in the various manuals directing to higher thought, to quietism, to aloneness. But these marks are fastened to Bergson's doctrine only by affirming his lack of logic. The same procedure is adopted in a final attempt to make the object or end of that intuition the same as that of the genuine mystics. By making Bergson give several irreconcilable accounts of his ultimate reality, one can prove that he is a mystic of the absolutist type, a modern Heraclitus who would have our souls return to the universal flux, or even a revolutionary syndicalist.

The analyst is on safe ground in calling the syndicalist theory an original and paradoxical synthesis of Marxian and Bergsonian ideas. And he performs a service in pointing out further permutations and combinations of Bergsonism with other current doctrines, theories and movements. But because Bergson has affinities with these movements is no valid reason for holding him responsible for them, any more than the manufacturer of dynamite for the ends for which an explosive is employed. It may be granted that it is hard to find any possible view which is not Bergsonian, but that merely signifies the richness of the source of supply, not the various uses to which the materials are put. There has been many a poet's poet who has had a sorry host of imitators, but if Bergson be considered a philosopher's philosopher, he is scarcely to blame for those who use these "convenient weapons" in defense of mysticism and syndicalism, of modernism and ultramontanism in France, and in America of idealism and pragmatism, of orthodox Protestantism and "New Thought." It reminds one of the perplexing problem of the munition makers and their rôle—one can either suppress them, or restrict their sales, or allow an open market. Thus, if the ultra-montanists have tried sup-

pression in the Index Expurgatorius, and certain Protestants have tried restriction in the way of interpretation, it may be best to let philosophers enjoy free discussion.

Of the two types here mentioned we will take the
Protestant first. Thus, Miller of Princeton finds in
Bergson a defender of the faith and that faith an
orthodox Protestantism! What Voltaire said of Ha-
bakkuk, might be said of Miller: he is capable of proving
anything. This is his argument: Some of the greatest
changes in human history have begun with protests.
Bergson has crossed swords with absolutistic rationalism, with scientific determinism and finally with materialism. Therefore, he is a Protestant. Yet Bergson does
not impeach intellect, but only those who have misused
it; nor determinism, but only those who have pushed it
beyond limits; nor materialism, but only those who suppose that mechanism can give a complete translation of
what happens in the world. Now the upshot of such a
protest is heartening to religionists. Bergson is on the
side of Christianity and he frowns upon pessimism,
pessimism that deadly nightshade in the garden of man,
one of whose roots is agnosticism, an agnosticism such
as that of the Spencerian scheme of evolution which
ends in the doctrine of the unknowable.

All this has a familiar ring. It is the genuine old-
fashioned Princeton polemic such as president McCosh
once directed against positivism. And the method is the
same: as long as you can attack an ism, it does not make
much difference what you say against it. And further,
if you can qualify any movement, you can utilize it for
your own purposes. As McCosh transmogrified mechanical evolution into what he called a Christian
evolution, so Miller turns the Creative Evolution into

a Protestant evolution, despite his admission that evolution has become a synonym for Anti-Christ in the minds of so many sincere religious people.

Miller's directions as to how to create a Christian creed out of Bergsonian elements, reminds us of the directions of the prestidigitator on how to cook an omelet in a silk hat. It may be done, but, after it is done, we would not care either to eat the omelet or wear the hat. But the *reductio ad absurdum* of this method of turning creative evolutionism into an orthodox Christianity of the "warm-hearted evangelical type" is found in this passage: "Perhaps the best test would be to hold in mind, as vividly as possible, a conception of God which conforms to the Bergsonian position. Then repeat slowly the petitions of the Lord's Prayer, and note whether there arises any feeling of incongruity between the petitions of the prayer and the character of God so conceived."

The argument, for the author at least, is conclusive. No devils of unorthodoxy can be found lurking in Bergsonism, since the Pater Noster will not exorcise them. Such is the Protestant test; the Catholic is different. By the time that Bergsonism reached the scholars of Rome *in partibus infidelium*, videlicet North America, the Encyclical and Syllabus of Pius X had banned that movement. On this side of the water, then, modernism in ecclesiastical metaphysics had as little chance for full development as did "the American Idea" in ecclesiastical politics. So in the very year in which Bergson's works were placed upon the Index, Father Dubray writes from Washington that when some Catholic philosophers and apologists hoped that Bergson's philosophy might be auxiliary to the Catholic religion, that hope had to be abandoned. Like Aristotle,

Bergson starts from the obvious fact of movement, but when Aristotle distinguishes between the reality that changes and the change itself, that is between being and becoming, it leads Bergson to the negation of being and to the assertion that becoming is the reality itself. Now while Bergson is not a monist like Spinoza, creation is understood by him as literally not creation as understood by the church, but some kind of an emanation of all things from the divine reality. This is clear, but it is not all. Besides Aristotle there is Aquinas. Is Bergsonism true or false? The test is simply one of Thomism. At this point one of our Paulist theologians continues the argument as to Bergson's alleged confusion between being and becoming. If there is a vital push we may ask who started it pushing; who pressed the button for such a wonderful system of change? Grant that there is a pure becoming, it could never be a first cause; the following axiom is self evident: that actuality is always prior to potentiality. So we are driven back from the god of change to a god of a full and active eternity as described by St. Thomas.

We pass from this author, with his metaphors from the age of electricity and his metaphysics from the age of cathedrals, to the last of the Catholic critics. It is a Chicago Jesuit who begins with a valuable comparison between Plato and Bergson and ends in the usual fashion of putting the modernists to torture on the rack of Thomism. At first glance, declares Father Dunne, the two leaders seem far apart, Plato beginning with a colorless, formless, impalpable existence, Bergson with a perpetual flux. Yet there are certain agreements between the two, for both hold to the essential inadequacy of mechanistic theories of life and the universe, the ideal genesis of matter, the natural incommensurability of philosophy and science, the value of supra-intellectual vision or intuition, and the antagonistic cosmic currents of ascent and descent as explanatory of consciousness and matter, freedom and necessity, good and evil. Nevertheless, along with these agreements there are important differences. Plato having posited immutability as belonging to the world of ideas, the world of reality, change must be regarded as a diminution of perfection, an attribute of the unreal. This awful chasm between existence and apparent existence has yawned dark and wide for twenty-four centuries. It is there, open, unexplained, if we accept Plato; it never existed, except in the imagination of the philosophers who advocate it, if we follow Bergson. This is the main crossroads corner of the two philosophers; let the wayfarer choose. Bergson is for becoming, for that ceaseless movement nowhither or somewhither which he calls creative evolution. All things change; Alps are leveled into valleys; empires fashioned by a Napoleon melt into democracies conceived in the phlegmatic minds of his slow-witted followers; the sun itself, as Pater observes, goes out only a little more slowly than the human eye. . . . Worked out to its ultimate absurdity, this position requires the assumption that the first cause is non-being. But as the system is alogical, this need not worry us. . . . It is not easy to understand why Bergson, and indeed the whole school of modernist philosophers, should prefer a variable God to an unchanging, all perfect one. It is perhaps because of a confusion in the use of undefined terms. A study of St. Thomas and his differentiation of actuality might help to clear matters up. Modernists develop the whirl of fitful fever we call life into a concept of an evolutionary cosmic flux which is to take the place of God. Their mistake is in not seeing the inadequacy of human forms, when the object of the description is unspeakable reality. They confuse the unchangeable with the inactive.

Bergsonism in America has not succeeded as a form of fideism. No more has it as a form of syndicalism. We go from one extreme to the other, from ecclesiastic orthodoxy to political anarchy, in order to show how strange are the uses made of creative evolutionism. There have evidently been a number of LeRoys among us, the foregoing criticism being implicitly directed against modernist neo-Catholics. Yet there have been no Sorels among us; no scholars proclaiming to the proletariat that the philosophy of change is the philosophy of direct action. There have been symbolists and futurists of the Greenwich Village type, who have looked upon Bergson as their prophet, but our parlor socialists of lower Fifth Avenue are not to be identified with the syndicalists. A radical socialist has recently called the latter a '' bunch of anarchists.'' In other words they care for culture as little as they do for collars. Thus, André Tridon, writing from New York, has declared that not only have the American unions nothing to do with the various philosophers whom the press is wont to characterize as '' the prophets of syndicalism,'' but, in the majority of cases, the workers are totally unfamiliar with the names of these intellectual worthies. For the direction followed by an economic movement does not depend upon the mental attitude of passive observers but on the activities of the militants within the movement. To search the works of a contemporary philosopher, however recondite, to find a few sentences in accord with the principles of a current movement and establish a relation of cause and effect between them (a theory being the cause and syndicalism the effect) is utterly futile.

This opinion that Bergsonism and syndicalism are not causally related is borne out by another of our authorities. John Graham Brooks declares that the bitterness of economic disappointment had wide expression before any philosopher had appeared, and that though the new warfare has its metaphysics, the succor of Bergson was only suppositious. This conclusion is echoed by our well-known socialist writer, John Spargo, who asserts that, Sorel to the contrary notwithstanding, anti-intellectualism has no philosophical basis and that our I. W. W. editors undoubtedly derive their conception of the class war from the class struggle theory of Karl Marx. Finally a California critic has said the same thing by indirection. Lewis declares that Bergson is held in less honor in France than in the United States, due, in part, to his being taken up by the French syndicalists because they wish to make their ethics as they go along.

Bergsonism is hard to classify. If it be granted the name of a new philosophy like one of the new nations, we can at least allow it the right of self-determination. But the desire to classify, to delimit, to define is unquenchable. So, in conclusion, we refer to the most elaborate of all the attempts to bound the land of Bergsonia. Perry, now a neo-realist, essays this in his latest book whose very title suggests the difficulties confronting the metaphysical map-maker. To the author of *The Present Conflict of Ideals, or a Study of the Philosophical Background of the World War,* the four main boundaries are irrationalism, immaterialism, quietism and pluralism. And these four suggest the reasons why the new land has so many visitors. First, a philosophy which disparages the intellect will please those who find it impossible or disagreeable to think; not that Bergson does not think and that his philosophy is not hard, but only that by the fundamental thesis of his philosophy he encourages us to take the pictures and let the thinking go. Next, the vogue of Bergsonism is due not only to an elusiveness in its fundamental conceptions but also to the fact that, like idealism in the last century, it has gained miscellaneous adherents who have been driven into its camp by the common fear of materialism. Again, Bergson appeals not only to the moral ideal but the religious emotions as well, in his emphasis on quietism. In practical action we may invoke the intellect to guide us, but to be aware of life itself as the deeper reality we must not look forward and outward, but backward and inward as in mystical insight. Finally, as to pluralism, the philosophy of change holds that we must not build our hopes on any monistic principle that would explain the world as the systematic realization of spiritual ideals. In the widest view that one can take, the world remains a vast chaotic manifold in whose very lack of system and completeness there is a certain consolation in the fact that it prevents science from drawing any final conclusions.

SELECT BIBLIOGRAPHY

(Chief authorities are starred)

INTRODUCTORY

BECELAERE, J. L. VAN. *La Philosophie en Amérique, depuis les origines jusqu'à nos jours.* 1904.

CURTIS, M. M. In the *Western Reserve University Bulletin.* 1896.

JONES, ADAM L. *Early American Philosophers.* 1898.

RILEY, WOODBRIDGE. *American Philosophy: The Early Schools.* 1907.

SANTAYANA, GEORGE. *Winds of Doctrine.* 1913.

TYLER, M. C. *A History of American Literature.* 1878.

WENDELL, BARRETT. *A Literary History of America.* 1905.

I. PURITANISM

1. PHILOSOPHY AND POLITICS

BORGEAUD, CHARLES. *The Rise of Modern Democracy.* 1894.

FRIEDENWALD, H. *The Declaration of Independence.* 1904.

* MERRIAM, C. E. *American Political Theories.* 1903.

WILLOUGHBY, W. W. *The Nature of the State.* 1896.

2. THE NEW ENGLAND FATHERS

ELLIS, G. E. *The Puritan Age.* 1888.

FOSTER, F. H. *A Genetic History of the New England Theology.* 1907.

UHDEN, F. H. *The New England Theocracy.* 1858.

WALKER, WILLISTON. *Ten New England Leaders.* 1901.

3. THE REVOLT AGAINST PURITANISM

* ALLEN, ETHAN. *Reason the only Oracle of Man, or A Compenduous System of Natural Religion.* 1784.

II. EARLY IDEALISM

1. SAMUEL JOHNSON

BEARDSLEY, E. E. *Life and Correspondence of Rev. Samuel Johnson, D.D.* 1874.

COLDEN, CADWALLADER. *The Principles of Action in Matter.* 1751.

* JOHNSON, SAMUEL. *Elementa Philosophica.* 1753.

PORTER, NOAH. *Bishop Berkeley.* 1885.

2. JONATHAN EDWARDS

ALLEN, ALEXANDER V. G. *Jonathan Edwards.* 1890.

* GARDINER, H. N. *Jonathan Edwards: a Retrospect.* 1901.

3. MYSTICISM. FROM QUAKERISM TO CHRISTIAN SCIENCE

FRIENDS' LIBRARY. (*Ed. Evans.*) 1837-1850.

PENN, WILLIAM. *No Cross, No Crown.* 1668.

* RILEY, WOODBRIDGE. *The Personal Sources of Christian Science. Psychological Review.* 1903.

WOOLMAN, JOHN. *Journal.* (*Ed. Whittier.*) 1871.

III. DEISM

1. THE ENGLISH INFLUENCES

COBB, S. H. *Pioneers of Religious Liberty in America.* 1903.

SCHERGER, G. L. *The Evolution of Modern Liberty.* 1904.

2. THE COLONIAL COLLEGES

* CHAUNCY, CHARLES. *Benevolence of the Deity.* 1784.

DEXTER, F. B. *The Literary Diary of Ezra Stiles.* 1901.

MATHER, COTTON. *Essay for the Recording of Illustrious Providences.* 1684.

* MATHER, COTTON. *Reasonable Religion.* 1713.
* MATHER, COTTON. *The Christian Philosopher.* 1721.

3. PHILADELPHIA AND FRANKLIN

FORD, P. L. *Franklin Bibliography.* 1889.
* FRANKLIN, BENJAMIN. *Works.* (*Eds. Bigelow, Ford, Smyth.*)

4. VIRGINIA AND JEFFERSON

FOLEY, J. P. *The Jeffersonian Cyclopedia.* 1900.
* JEFFERSON, THOMAS. *Works.* (*Eds. Ford, Lipscomb, Bergh.*)
TOMPKINS, H. B. *Bibliotheca Jeffersoniana.* 1887.

5. THOMAS PAINE

* PAINE, THOMAS. *Works.* (*Ed. Conway.*)

IV. MATERIALISM

1. THE FRENCH INFLUENCES

BOUTMY, ÉMILE. *Éléments d'une Psychologie politique du Peuple américain.* 1902.
DABNEY, ROBERT L. *The Sensualistic Philosophy of the Nineteenth Century.* 1875.
TOCQUEVILLE, ALEXIS DE. *Democracy in America.* 1898.

2. JOSEPH PRIESTLEY

BROUGHAM, HENRY. *Lives of Men of Letters and Science.* 1845.
MARTINEAU, JAMES. *Miscellanies.* 1852.

3. BENJAMIN RUSH

* RUSH, BENJAMIN. *Diseases of the Mind.* 1812.

4. THE MINOR MATERIALISTS

* BUCHANAN, JOSEPH. *Philosophy of Human Nature.* 1812.

V. REALISM

1. THE SCOTTISH INFLUENCES

* McCOSH, JAMES. *The Scottish Philosophy.* 1874.

2. THE PRINCETON SCHOOL

* MILLER, SAMUEL. *Retrospect of the Eighteenth Century.* 1803.

WITHERSPOON, JOHN. *Lectures on Moral Philosophy.* 1810. (American Philosophical Association reprint.)

3. THE LESSER REALISTS

* BEASLEY, FREDERICK. *A Search of Truth in the Science of the Human Mind.* 1822.

McCOSH, JAMES. *Realistic Philosophy.* 1887.

VI. TRANSCENDENTALISM

1. THE NEW ENGLAND MOVEMENT

FROTHINGHAM, O. B. *Transcendentalism in New England.* 1903.

* GODDARD, H. C. *Studies in New England Transcendentalism.* 1908.

2. EMERSON

* EMERSON, R. W. *Works.* (*Riverside Ed.*)

SANBORN, FRANK B., and HARRIS, W. T. *The Genius and Character of Emerson.* 1885.

VII. EVOLUTIONISM

1. THE FORERUNNERS OF EVOLUTIONISM

HITCHCOCK, EDWARD. *The Religion of Geology.* 1851.

* SMITH, SAMUEL STANHOPE. *Essay on the Causes of the Variety of Complexion and Figure in the Human Species.* 1810.

2. The Antagonism of Agassiz

* Agassiz, Louis. *An Essay on Classification.* 1857.

Agassiz, Mrs. E. C. *Louis Agassiz, His Life and Correspondence.* 1885.

Le Conte, Joseph. *Evolution, Its Evidences and Its Relation to Religious Thought.* 1891.

3. The Reception of Darwinism

Cope, E. D. *The Origin of the Fittest.* 1887.

Dana, James Dwight. *Manual of Geology.* 1891.

Gilman, D. C. *Life of James Dwight Dana.* 1899.

* Gray, Asa. *Darwininana.* 1878.

McCosh, James. *The Development Hypothesis: Is It Sufficent?* 1876.

McCosh, James. *Development; What It Can Do and What It Cannot Do.* 1883.

* McCosh, James. *The Religious Aspect of Evolution.* 1890.

Rankin, H. W. *The Philosophy of Charles Woodruff Shields.* 1905.

* Shields, Charles W. *Philosophiæ Ultima.* 1905.

4. John Fiske

Fiske, John. *Darwinism, and Other Essays.* 1885.

* Fiske, John. *Outlines of Cosmic Philosophy.* 1902.

5. J. Mark Baldwin

Baldwin, James Mark. *Mental Development in the Child and the Race.* 1895.

* Baldwin, James Mark. *Development and Evolution.* 1902.

Baldwin, James Mark. *Fragments in Philosophy and Science.* 1902.

* Baldwin, James Mark. *Darwin and the Humanities.* 1909.

VIII. MODERN IDEALISM

1. The German Influences

* Murdock, James. *Sketches of Modern Philosophy, Especially Among the Germans.* 1842.

2. William T. Harris

Harris, W. T. *Journal of Speculative Philosophy.* 1867-1893.

* Harris, W. T. *Introduction to the Study of Philosophy.* 1889.

Harris, W. T. *Exposition of Hegel's Logic.* 1895.

* Snider, Denton J. *A Writer of Books.* 1910.

3. Josiah Royce

* Royce, Josiah. *The Spirit of Modern Philosophy.* 1892.

Royce, Josiah. *The World and the Individual.* 1901. *The Problem of Christianity.* 1913.

4. George Trumbull Ladd

Ladd, George T. *A Theory of Reality.* 1899.

* Ladd, George T. *Knowledge, Life and Reality.* 1909.

IX. PRAGMATISM

1. The Philosophy of Practicality

Bawden, H. H. *The Principles of Pragmatism.*

* Pratt, J. B. *What is Pragmatism?* 1909.

Schiller, F. C. S. *Studies in Humanism.* 1907.

2. Charles Peirce

* Peirce, Charles. *Illustrations of the Logic of Science.* (*Popular Science Monthly*, 1878.)

3. John Dewey

Dewey, John. *School and Society.* 1899.

* Dewey, John. *Studies in Logical Theory.* 1903.

* DEWEY, JOHN. *The Influence of Darwin on Philosophy.*
1910.

4. WILLIAM JAMES

* JAMES, WILLIAM. *Pragmatism.* 1907.
JAMES, WILLIAM. *A Pluralistic Universe.* 1909.
JAMES, WILLIAM. *The Meaning of Truth.* 1910.

5. THE SOURCES OF PRAGMATISM

See articles in the *Journal of Philosophy, Monist, Philosophical Review* by
FULLERTON, GEORGE.
HUME, J. G.
LOVEJOY, ARTHUR O.
MILLER, DICKINSON S.
MONTAGUE, W. P.
RILEY, WOODBRIDGE.
WOODBRIDGE, F. J. E.

6. THE CRITICS OF PRAGMATISM

ALIOTTA, A. *Il pragmatismo anglo-americano.* 1909.
* BOURDEAU, J. *Pragmatisme et Modernisme.* 1909.
FLOURNOY, H. *La Philosophie de William James.* 1911.
* HÉBERT, MARCEL. *La Pragmatisme.* 1909.
JACOBY, GUENTHER. *Der Pragmatismus.* 1907.
RILEY, WOODBRIDGE. *Continental Critics of Pragmatism.*
(*Journal of Philosophy*, 1911.)
ROYCE, JOSIAH. *William James and Other Essays.* 1911.
SCHINZ, A. *Anti-Pragmatisme.* 1909.

X. MODERN REALISM

1. NEW REALISM

THE NEW REALISM. *Coöperative Studies in Philosophy.*
1912. (See also current philosophical journals.)
ALIOTTA, A. *Il Nuovo Realismo.* 1920.

Brown, H. C. *Civilization in the United States,* pp. 168-170. 1922.

Chiappelli, A. *La Crisi del Pensiero Moderno.* 1920.

Holt, E. B. *The Concept of Consciousness.* 1914.

Kremer, René. *Le Néo-Réalisme Américain.* 1920.

Marvin, W. T. *The History of European Philosophy.* 1917.

* *The New Realism. Coöperative Studies in Philosophy.* 1912.

Mouvement général de la neusée américaine. Revue de metaphysique et de la morale. Oct.-Dec., 1922.

Spaulding, E. G. *The New Rationalism.* 1918.

2. Critical Realism

* *Essays in Critical Realism.* 1920.

Cohen, Morris R. *Cambridge History of American Literature* (Vol. III, Chap. XVII). 1921.

Riley, Woodbridge. *New Realism and Its Critics.* Logos, 1921-22.

Sellars, R. W. *Critical Realism.* 1916.

Strong, C. A. *The Origin of Consciousness.* 1918.

XI. SOME FRENCH INFLUENCES
1. Eclecticism

Henry, C. S. Cousin's *Elements of Psychology.* 1856.

* Ripley, George. *Specimens of Foreign Standard Literature.* 1838.

2. Positivism

* Fiske, John. *Outlines of Cosmic Philosophy.* 1874.

Mahan, Asa. *A Critical History of Philosophy.* 1883.

Noyes, J. H. *History of Modern Socialism.* 1870.

3. Creative Evolution

Dubray, C. A. *Catholic University Bulletin.* 1914.

* Lovejoy, Arthur O. *California Chronicle.* Vol. XV.

Riley, Woodbridge. *La Philosophie Française en Amérique.* 1917, 1919, 1921.

Santayana, George. *Winds of Doctrine.* 1913.

INDEX

433

Poyen, Charles, 115
Pratt, J. B., 377, 430
Prichard, 181
Priestley, Joseph, 73, 78, 97, 98, 100-108, 113, 122, 123
Protagoras, 304, 321, 331
Prout, 92

Quarles, 160
Quesnay, 98
Quimby, 44, 48

Rankin, H. W., 429
Rauch, 234
Ravaisson, 414
Ray, 70
Reid, Thomas, 118, 119, 121, 127, 129, 137, 169, 358, 392, 396
Renan, 248, 326
Rey, Abel, 325, 333, 335
Riley, Woodbridge, 425, 426, 431, 432
Ripley, Ezra, 93
Ripley, George, 237, 393, 394, 395, 432
Rochefoucauld, 98
Rogers, 377
Romaine, 64
Royce, Josiah, 211, 247, 253-265, 270, 276, 277, 304, 356, 430, 431
Rush, Benjamin, 82, 104-117, 122, 127, 135, 427

Sacheverel, 5
Sanborn, F. B., 390, 428
Santayana, George, 382, 383, 412, 432
Schelling, 159, 171, 185, 186, 231, 237, 239, 246, 259, 333, 413, 414
Scherger, G. L., 426
Schiller, 229
Schiller, F. C. S., 321, 331, 430
Schinz, A., 431
Schmucker, 234
Schopenhauer, 413
Sellars, 377, 432
Shaftesbury, Lord, 63

Shields, Charles W., 206-207, 429
Smith, Samuel Stanhope, 130-133, 178, 180, 428
Smith, William, 26, 77
Snider, D. J., 240, 243, 430
Socrates, 73, 146, 248
Solon, 76
Sophocles, 76
Sorel, 421
Spargo, 422
Sparks, Jared, 12, 17
Spaulding, 359, 362, 363, 364, 371, 373, 432
Spencer, Herbert, 365, 414
Spinoza, 62, 146, 412, 413, 419
Sterrett, J. M., 245
Stewart, Dugald, 92, 119, 121, 394
St. Hilaire, 202
Stiles, Ezra, 62-65, 73, 126, 129
Strong, 383, 385, 386, 432
Swedenborg, 166, 329, 336, 338

Taine, 326, 333
Taylor, Thomas, 166
Tenneman, 170
Thoreau, 149, 240
Ticknor, George, 159, 162, 231
Tindal, 88
Tocqueville, 98, 427
Tompkins, H. B., 427
Tridon, 421
Turgot, 98
Tyler, M. C., 361

Uhden, F. H., 425
Upham, 43

Valdés, Juan de, 41
Vandyke, Joseph, 207
Vaughan, 166, 167
Vico, 190
Volney, 89, 98
Voltaire, 76, 77, 89-91, 119, 397, 417

Walker, Williston, 425
Ward, L. F., 401

COSIMO CLASSICS

COSIMO is an innovative publisher of books and publications that inspire, inform and engage readers worldwide. Our titles are drawn from a range of subjects including health, business, philosophy, history, science and sacred texts. We specialize in using print-on-demand technology (POD), making it possible to publish books for both general and specialized audiences and to keep books in print indefinitely. With POD technology new titles can reach their audiences faster and more efficiently than with traditional publishing.

> **Permanent Availability:** Our books & publications never go out-of-print.

> **Global Availability:** Our books are always available online at popular retailers and can be ordered from your favorite local bookstore.

COSIMO CLASSICS brings to life unique, rare, out-of-print classics representing subjects as diverse as *Alternative Health, Business and Economics, Eastern Philosophy, Personal Growth, Mythology, Philosophy, Sacred Texts, Science, Spirituality* and much more!

COSIMO-on-DEMAND publishes your books, publications and reports. If you are an Author, part of an Organization, or a Benefactor with a publishing project and would like to bring books back into print, publish new books fast and effectively, would like your publications, books, training guides, and conference reports to be made available to your members and wider audiences around the world, we can assist you with your publishing needs.

Visit our website at www.cosimobooks.com to learn more about Cosimo, browse our catalog, take part in surveys or campaigns, and sign-up for our newsletter.

And if you wish please drop us a line at info@cosimobooks.com. We look forward to hearing from you.

Printed in the USA
CPSIA information can be obtained
at www.ICGtesting.com
LVHW091917020624
782067LV00001B/9

9 781596 053052